Enhydra XMLC Java Presentation Development

David H. Young

SAMS

201 West 103rd St., Indianapolis, Indiana, 46290 USA

Copyright ©2002 by Sams Publishing

FIRST EDITION

International Standard Book Number: 0-672-32211-0

Library of Congress Catalog Card Number: 2001090937

04   03   02   01   4   3   2   1

Interpretation of the printing code: the rightmost double-digit number is the year of the book's printing; the rightmost single-digit, the number of the book's printing. For example, a printing code of 98-1 shows that the first printing of the book occurred in 1998.

Composed in Function Condensed, AGaramond and MCPdigital by Macmillan Computer Publishing

Printed in the United States of America

Trademarks

Warning and Disclaimer

EXECUTIVE EDITOR
Michael Stephens

DEVELOPMENT EDITOR
Tiffany Taylor

MANAGING EDITOR
Matt Purcell

PROJECT EDITOR
Andy Beaster

PRODUCTION EDITOR
Seth Kerney

PROOFREADER
Harvey Stanbrough

INDEXER
Tina Trettin

MEDIA DEVELOPER
Dan Scherf

TECHNICAL EDITOR
Chad Fowler

TEAM COORDINATOR
Pamalee Nelson

INTERIOR DESIGNER
Anne Jones

COVER DESIGNER
Aren Howell

PAGE LAYOUT
Julie Swenson

Overview

Contents

About the Author

David H. Young is Chief Evangelist for Lutris Technologies in Santa Cruz, California, for whom he writes technical papers, gives speeches on wireless and Web development, and serves as editor of the Lutris Enhydra Journal. David has penned magazine articles for publications including *ComputerWorld*, *WebTechniques*, and *Network Telephony*.

As the father of three daughters, he believes in going overboard with all his efforts whenever possible. So, in late 1995, he left his engineering career at The Santa Cruz Operation at the behest of colleagues Paul Morgan and Michael Browder, the original founders of Lutris Technologies. There he started by serving as president for 2 1/2 years, leading some of the consulting projects that spawned Paul's vision of a consultant's portable toolbox, later dubbed "Enhydra" by Lutris' Yancy Lind. David was instrumental in the proposal to turn this Lutris technology into a full-blown open source project.

After collecting his Bachelor of Science degree in Earth Sciences from the University of California at Santa Cruz, David eventually landed a job at Amdahl Corporation in 1983 where he learned PL/I. After he wrote a program that shaved days off the process of re-routing circuit boards, Amdahl incorporated it into their production software and had no choice but to promote David to the role of full engineer. From there, David joined SCO in 1987 where he not only met Paul, Michael, and John Marco, but was also taken under the wing of Tcl guru Mark Diekhans, who eventually joined Lutris and developed Enhydra XMLC.

Working for SCO gave David the opportunity to see the world as an X/Open Systems Management Working Group representative and establish his own niche as Product Manager for Future Technologies. Earlier, as an SCO Development manager for SCO's Motif scripting tool, Visual Tcl, David was inspired by its champions Mark and Paul to write *The Visual Tcl Handbook* (Prentice Hall). Unfortunately, this great technology was never open sourced, limiting its access and evolution. Enhydra and Lutris have given him the opportunity to make amends.

David lives in Aptos, California with his wife Kathy, daughters Amanda, Nicole, and Claire, and cat Autumn.

Dedication

To the true loves of my life: Kathy, Amanda, Nicole, Claire, and Carolyn.
Dorothy, Leland, and Al are very proud indeed.

Acknowledgments

Before Apple Computers introduced Silicon Valley to the world, Cupertino was a community of apricot farmers and blue collar workers. My Dad, Leland Young, took delight as president of the Peninsula Machinists and Aerospace Workers Union, fighting for asbestos-free working conditions after a long day of buffing brake pads and cleaning re-built carburetors with solvents. I've always wondered why people I work with take computers so seriously. They don't crack the skin of your hands or make you wear long-johns to brave a long day with the garage doors open to let the exhaust out. But I have come to stand in awe of the people I'm about to acknowledge. Their hard work, imagination, creativity, and drive to contribute great technology to the world makes me proud to be associated with them and a great open source effort. With their help, this book represents something that I want to give back to my Dad for buffing all those brake shoes.

The names listed here represent people who have in some way made this book possible or have affected its quality. These folks either sat down with me to explain concepts, or contributed content for the book through the Enhydra.org mailing list. Others were simply inspirational and supportive beyond the call of duty.

First, my early Lutris brothers Paul Morgan, Michael Browder, Mark Diekhans, John Marco, Andy John, Kyle Clark, and Shawn McMurdo all made this possible with their vision and early implementation of Enhydra and Enhydra XMLC.

Christian Cryder, Matt Schwartz, Bill Karwin, Eric Friedman, Xavier Stonestreet, Rand McKinney, Joseph Shoop, Jeff Bean, Glen Carl, Bob Bourbonnais, Lisa Reese, Aidan Hosler, Russ Duckworth, Mark Beaulieu, Christopher Reed, Mike Gardner, Michael Maceri, and Peter Darrah are the highly motivated and equally clever people who helped me conceptually and motivationally.

Lutris management gave me all the space I needed to feel good about getting this book completed. And my colleagues were always supportive. Yancy Lind, Keith Bigelow, and Mr. EAS, Klaus Krull. Gillian Webster originally inspired me to go for it.

Moral support came from Dennis Chatham, Daryl Tempesta, Lynda Hall, Nanette Henneuse (!), Jay Felkins, Scott Kleinberg, Lisa Welch, Linda Ritchie, and Lupe Adame.

And thanks to my colleagues in the Enhydra.org community: David Li, Chad Fowler, Nick Xidis, Dave Peckham, David Wood, Richard Kunze, Kevin Austin, William G. "Enhydra Rocks" Thompson, Jr., Mark Stang, Paul Gresham, Ian Purton, and David McCann.

It's no wonder Sams Publishing's Michael Stephens is so prolific. He's a genuinely curious and nice human being, and his team of editors reflects his good nature. Thanks to Seth Kerney, Andrew Beaster, Chad Fowler, and a special thanks to the gentle "voice in the dark," Tiffany Taylor.

Special thanks to Lutris' Robert Sese for losing a weekend to give me a hand with the Zeus stuff. And, of course, Brett McLaughlin as my co-Enhydra evangelist for delivering Zeus and motivating me to come anywhere close to his wonderful Java books.

There are many people about whom I can say, we would have never gotten Enhydra out the door without their involvement. Russell "Rusty" Berg is one of them. It was his early contributions of wisdom and encouragement in the early Lutris team that gave us the ability to transition from the hairy edge of subcontracting to a prime contractor. Looking back, I don't know how we would have made that critical transition without his faith and commitment.

My daughter Amanda is the hero in my life. For the past 16 years, she has supported the wanderlust and hyperactive antics of a hopelessly romantic father. She's paid the price, and I thank her for loving me through all of the balloons I've ridden.

My beautiful wife Kathy has supported me throughout, reflecting the love and passion that I always knew could be a part of daily life. And Nicole has become my best friend. I am looking forward to the years to come.

Development took place on a Windows 2000 laptop so I could write at the Red Room, Capitola Book Cafe, Seascape Resort (thanks for the great service from Assita, Rory, and Leigh-Ann), London, and the Aptos Library.

Lutris Technologies

This book is about open source Enhydra. But Enhydra wouldn't have been here without a core group of Lutris engineers and executives, so let me acknowledge Lutris for a few paragraphs before I enter a fairly agnostic discussion about Enhydra from here on out. About six years ago, November 1995, I came to Lutris, then "The Information Refinery," to lead training and marketing, later to become President, and after replacing myself with a real President, Yancy Lind, have served as Chief Evangelist for the past three years.

One of the keys to establishing and perpetuating a successful open source project is to seed that project with a great technology.

One way to approach a new product is to sit in a room and think of great architectures, talking to a few customers, then toss a coin. Another is to simply hire great developers, who happen to be great people, and trust their experience and sense of commitment. Then do major consulting work, and find out "the truth" from those who will eventually reflect your customer.

It started with a hard-nosed and very, very creative architect, Lutris CTO Paul Morgan, acknowledging the need for a pure, highly adaptive architecture to support our consulting business. We did something very good—hiring solid software engineers. People who appreciated testing, version control systems, and elegant designs. We lucked out.

Under the umbrella of an evolving consulting business, Paul Morgan, Mark Diekhans, John Marco, Andy John, Kyle Clark, and Shawn McMurdo applied their UNIX server and networking backgrounds together to lay the foundation for a highly extensible, pragmatic architecture that started with a simple but elegant way to lay out source code.

Tell Us What You Think!

As the reader of this book, *you* are our most important critic and commentator. We value your opinion and want to know what we're doing right, what we could do better, what areas you'd like to see us publish in, and any other words of wisdom you're willing to pass our way.

As an Executive Editor for Sams Publishing, I welcome your comments. You can fax, e-mail, or write me directly to let me know what you did or didn't like about this book—as well as what we can do to make our books stronger.

Please note that I cannot help you with technical problems related to the topic of this book, and that due to the high volume of mail I receive, I might not be able to reply to every message.

When you write, please be sure to include this book's title and author as well as your name and phone or fax number. I will carefully review your comments and share them with the author and editors who worked on the book.

Fax: 317-581-4770
E-mail: feedback@samspublishing.com
Mail: Michael Stephens, Executive Editor
          Sams Publishing
          201 West 103rd Street
          Indianapolis, IN 46290 USA

Introduction

It was almost eight years ago on a balmy Southern California January at the beautiful La Jolla Shores Hotel. And there we were. Indoors. Arguing the merits of assorted remote procedures called APIs: Sun Microsystems' ONC RPC versus everyone elses'. The occasion was an X/Open Systems Management Working Group meeting. The task before us was to select a standard RPC API. With it, we could establish a base platform upon which we could further accept implementations that would form the basis for a standard management platform. But a resolution never came. The "RPC Wars" were too fraught with N.I.H. (Not Invented Here) and things political. By week's end, there was no resolution or progress. The folks from the east coast would have to head back and dig their way out of the airport parking spots that they had to dig into just to park a few days before. The Northridge Earthquake that had thrown me out of my bed the night before the meeting began failed to assert itself as a good omen that things were about to get shaken up. Instead, it was the same old standards process, guided by large companies, politics, and feature creep. (That is, should we boil the oceans or solve a more narrow issue?)

Then, to paraphrase the prophetic bumper sticker, "a miracle happened." A cool little desktop client called a browser led the world to vote Internet. Suddenly, all the wannabe distributed computing standards—OSI, Novell, Microsoft, and DCE—were looking suspect. What's more, the desktop standard Microsoft was suddenly vulnerable.

I am a refugee of the old-style standards process and I couldn't be happier that the Internet is here to stay. Today, there is a new standards mechanism, powered by a 25-year old Internet mechanism, dubbed only a few years ago by Eric Raymond as *open source*. Thanks in part to the open source process, the standards process is now more empowered. W3C.org is a great example. Wisely, they use the open source community to refine and process standards specifications through worldwide implementations. We all benefit when standards-defining activities are forged on the anvil of world application.

Enhydra

Since its introduction as an open-source technology on January 15, 1999, Enhydra has steadily expanded its reach as a favorite set of technologies in the application server market.

The first audience to appreciate its value were the consultants of the world, represented by companies like Tivano in Germany, I-exposure of the US, Plugged In Software of Australia and Digitalsesame of Taiwan. Drawn by Enhydra's elegant and pragmatic architecture, simple development philosophy, and well-organized source code, these consultants, and eventually, developers of corporate IT, have taken Enhydra from its simple application server roots to a broad set of open source technologies for areas Lutris never anticipated, namely voice and wireless development.

This book is about perhaps the most popular of the Enhydra projects—Enhydra XMLC for the development of wired and wireless Web presentations. Enhydra XMLC is powering Web sites powered by open source Enhydra as well as commercial application servers, including BEA WebLogic. As you'll soon read, Enhydra XMLC appeals as much to project managers and presentation architects as it does to presentation developers.

Who Should Read This Book

This book is written for computer professionals, with a special focus on application architects, Java Web application developers, and those who are just ramping up on Java and are excited about immersing themselves into Web application development.

Taking a task view wherever possible, this book is written to support those seeking a more elegant, maintainable, and flexible mechanism for building Web application presentations. While we spend some time introducing the Enhydra application server for those who are new to the topic of application server development, this book is focused primarily on the topic of Enhydra XMLC and how to use it to improve the lifecycle requirements of your Web application.

A modest knowledge of the Java language is assumed, but key supporting topics, such as XML and DOM development, are introduced for those who are new to them. There is even a chapter dedicated to thinking out the requirements of an application based on an application service-provided (ASP) model. For those who are already well-versed in presentation frameworks, a technical overview of XMLC with other presentation technologies is provided.

For those who are curious about Enhydra XMLC and Enhydra in general, we've presented sufficient information to appreciate its value and unique approach to building dynamic, Web-based presentations for browsers, mobile devices, and even good old telephones when taking advantage of freely available voice portal services from TellMe or Voxeo. More importantly, it is also written to demonstrate how to build Web applications and some of the strategies you could employ.

We've also used this opportunity to explain and compare supporting concepts such as XML and HTML, explaining their historical differences as well as their basic reasons for being. The use of a pronounced demonstration application modeled after a conference showfloor that you'd encounter at any major computer show is targeted at the reader who is just embarking on the topic of building Web applications. It's used as a means for exploring the process of how you might integrate different display devices into the overall application.

Enhydra definitely carries a Unix flavor, although the Enhydra Kelp project has done a lot to integrate Enhydra with popular Windows Interactive Design Environments, such as JBuilder and Forte. In order to focus more on the xmlc command itself, we have chosen to use RedHat's Cygwin tools to emulate a Unix command line environment for the Windows environment.

Finally, I love new innovations. So, at the end of the book, I leave you with an introduction to Barracuda, which was a lot of fun to discover and write about. The promise of this new technology is incredible.

Lutris Technologies, Steward of Enhydra.org

Enhydra.org, one of the world's most popular and well-known open source efforts, is the result of the efforts of the Java developers at Lutris Technologies. After a great deal of preparation, Lutris introduced Enhydra.org on January 15, 1999. The bootstrapping technology of Enhydra.org was Enhydra, a Java application server, developed by Lutris' consulting organization and used for engagements with many dot coms as well as large IT organizations, including the Kinko's Corporation.

The emergence of the popular Internet has been a blur to most of us. Few are aware that it wasn't until the move by Netscape to define the Mozilla license for the Netscape browser when the term *open source* was coined by Eric Raymond.

Lutris was no stranger to open source. Most of Enhydra's early development was conducted on FreeBSD. Mark Diekhans, the creator of Enhydra XMLC, was well-known in John Ousterhout's Tcl community, having co-authored the TclX extensions, influencing the core Tcl APIs. He and his Lutris colleagues knew what open source was about, what its value was, long before IDC and others started trying to explain this emerging concept to the business community.

Lutris also gives Enhydra its business flavor. Noted earlier, Enhydra was developed in support of professional consulting engagements. One of the business considerations that drove Enhydra's design was to make it easily adaptable to the favorite tools of Java developers.

Today, despite the fact that Lutris is still very much a leading force behind this unique open source effort, Enhydra has a life of its own. Much of the scope of Enhydra.org will be covered in Chapter 1, "Enhydra and XMLC."

Servlet Programming

Enhydra 3 features two types of servlet development. The first type, Enhydra Application Framework (EAF; more commonly referred to as the *superservlet*), was developed by Lutris in advance of the introduction of the standard servlet programming. The other type, of course, is Sun Microsystems' standard servlet development based on servlet 2.2. As we'll explain in Chapter 10, "Servlet Web Applications," you can use Enhydra 3 to develop and generate a WAR file, then deploy it with a few clicks of the mouse in a BEA WebLogic and Lutris EAS 4 enterprise-class application server. Or you can simply download the XMLC-only package from xmlc.enhydra.org and use XMLC as a part of your native WebLogic development environment. With some exceptions, we will be using Enhydra EAF-style servlet programming, characterized by presentation objects. As you'll quickly see, EAF looks very much like standard servlet development. The two styles of programming are so similar that servlet programmers won't be put off.

Organization

This book was written to give you a gut feeling of what Enhydra XMLC is all about. To support this goal, there are numerous notes that explain the background on what motivated certain features of XMLC. If you are new to Web development, then we encourage you to focus on Chapters 1–9, which explain the basics of XMLC, its supporting technologies, and how they relate to other technologies that address presentation development. Any experienced Web developer can pick and choose chapters depending on, for example, her level of experience with DOM programming. The latter third of the book should be interesting for those exploring wireless, voice, and Flash development, as it is driven by data shipped from a back-end application server. We encourage everybody to read the last chapter on Barracuda, a very promising next step in the evolution of XMLC to a full presentation framework.

Chapter 1, "Enhydra and XMLC"—High-level introduction to Enhydra XMLC and the Enhydra.org family of technologies.

Chapter 2, "XMLC Development"—A first introduction to the experience of XMLC development, with a walkthrough of development examples. The concept of DOM development is introduced.

Chapter 3, "Presentation Technologies"—A survey of presentation technologies, including XSLT, JavaServer Pages, Servlet Development, and Cocoon. A comprehensive set of observations on the comparative strengths of XMLC concludes this chapter.

Chapter 4, "The ShowFloor ASP Application"—An application reflecting an application server provider business model is introduced. The concept of UML design is introduced. The rest of the chapter speculates on the potential uses of wireless technology for enhancing the features and attractiveness of this fictitious application.

Chapter 5, "Enhydra, Java/XML Application Server"—A presentation technology is useless without an application server behind it. This chapter introduces Enhydra and its architecture for the development of both superservlets, as well as standard Web application servlets. Enhydra DODS for creating Java object-to-RDBMS mappings is also introduced.

Chapter 6, "XMLC Basics"—The basic elements of XMLC development are introduced, with a focus on comparing and contrasting the XML and HTML markup technologies and how they feed into DOM development. The remainder of the chapter focuses on the value that XMLC brings to DOM development.

Chapter 7, "The `xmlc` Command"—All of the aspects of the `xmlc` command for generating DOM templates and the features of runtime XMLC programming are addressed here.

Chapter 8, "HTML Presentations"—An introduction to the unique nature of HTML development with XMLC. Template cloning, table construction, and DOM operations are covered. A questionnaire application, VendQuest, is introduced to illustrate template-driven forms and HTML control development.

Chapter 9, "Presentation Strategies"—More complex XMLC development situations are addressed. Strategies for designing and implementing composite views introduce the ability to import nodes and leverage the XMLC `-ssi` option. The VendQuest example is enhanced with the introduction of Zeus XML data binding, another Enhydra.org open source technology.

Chapter 10, "Servlet Web Applications"—A focus on Enhydra XMLC's ability to address standard servlet programming. A WAR built with Enhydra is migrated to both the Lutris EAS and BEA WebLogic J2EE application servers.

Chapter 11, "Wireless Markup Presentations"—Introduces the concepts and strategies behind XMLC's support for WAP's WML language. This chapter also introduces VoiceXML and how XMLC can drive voice presentations through voice portals.

Chapter 12, "Client-Server Development with J2ME and Flash"—Introduces the concepts and capabilities of these smart client presentations, as driven by XML and generated and consumed by Enhydra XMLC. An introduction to using XMLC with the new Scalar Vector Graphics (SVG), the XML standard, is presented.

Chapter 13, "Barracuda Presentation Framework"—An introduction to an impressive new open source presentation framework constructed on top of Enhydra XMLC. Barracuda introduces a Swing-like component view of DOM development.

About OtterPod Productions

OtterPod Productions is this book's model ASP company. The Web site `http://www.otterpod.com` is real. It is operated by the author.

You can find the following at `www.otterpod.com`:

- A working version of the ShowFloor application, source code and all.
- Notes and updates relevant to the book.
- Announcements about Enhydra XMLC, as learned by the author.

- Hints/Tips as acquired by the author.

- A page for registering your comments, feedback, and suggestions for the book.

The entire site is a combination of static HTML and dynamic pages powered by open source Enhydra XMLC and the Enhydra Java/XML Application Server.

The www.otterpod.com site is wireless friendly! That's because the index page, index.po, is an Enhydra presentation object whose chore it is to detect the device type that is accessing the site. Why access this site with your i-mode phone? That will be a surprise, but a well-formatted surprise delivered in the appropriate markup language for your mobile device.

Conventions and Tools

Unless indicated otherwise, all of the commands illustrated in this book are given in standard Linux/Unix form. What good does this do for those using Windows environments? I recommend downloading the Cygnus tools, a UNIX shell emulation environment.

Cygnus can be downloaded from http://sources.redhat.com/cygwin/.

If you are looking for a Java IDE environment to simplify Enhydra servlet and Enhydra XMLC development, be sure to check out http://kelp.enhydra.org. This open source project provides the tools needed for the integration of Enhydra technology into JBuilder 4 and 5, as well as Sun Microsystems' Forte.

Enhydra 3 Versus Lutris EAS 4

Enhydra XMLC development is enhanced by the inclusion of sub-DOM class implementations that address both HTML and WML. To put their value simply, they support a set of methods that help insulate the developer from raw DOM API programming. Having said that, there's nothing about XMLC programming that requires the use of per-XML language DOMs. If the XMLC compiler can coerce your targeted markup file into a DOM, you're in business. You just need to be comfortable with DOM API development.

If you want to take advantage of the sub-DOMs available for cHTML (the i-mode standard), XHTML (the new W3C.org standard), or VoiceXML 1.0 (also from W3C.org), then you have a choice of either purchasing Lutris Enhydra 3.5 from Lutris Technologies, or using the 45-day evaluation copy of the Lutris EAS 4 J2EE Application Server that's included with this book. This is not a requirement to enjoy the chapters that focus on wireless and voice topics.

Downloads

If, like me, you want to assure yourself of working with the latest and the greatest, everything on the book's CD can be downloaded from a number of locations.

- `http://enhydra.enhydra.org`—The open source home for the Enhydra 3 Java/XML Application Server.
- `http://xmlc.enhydra.org`—The open source home for the Enhydra XMLC.
- `http://barracuda.enhydra.org`—The open source home for Barracuda, a presentation framework built on top of the XMLC layer.
- `http://kxml.enhydra.org`—The open source home for Stefan Haustein's micro XML parser, key to bringing J2ME and Enhydra XMLC together for a client/server relationship.
- `http://zeus.enhydra.org`—The open source home for Zeus, a data binding facility for marshalling and unmarshalling XML into and from Java logic.

The Book's CD

A CD is included with this book to simplify the chore of putting all the elements together that you'll need. All of the examples presented in this book are available on the accompanying CD.

- Open Source Enhydra 3 Application Server
- Open Source XMLC.zip (Standalone portable XMLC environment)
- BEA WebLogic 6.1
- RedHat Cygwin Tools
- Open Source Enhydra Barracuda 1.0
- Lutris EAS 4.1

Be sure to read the `index.html` file for instructions on how to install each component.

Enhydra and XMLC

IN THIS CHAPTER

The Enhydra eXtensible Markup Language Compiler, or XMLC, is a highly portable XML/HTML software application. Sometimes referred to as an XML/HTML processor, XMLC makes it possible for Java applications to negotiate with a wide range of devices, from cell phones to browsers or other applications that speak languages based in XML or HTML. It can be used with any Java application server, including open source Enhydra or BEA WebLogic. We will use the Enhydra application server as the backdrop for our XMLC journey, with a later discussion on how to use XMLC with other Java application server platforms.

XMLC is now widely used to enable modern Java/XML application servers to serve many flavors of devices, both established and emerging. Browsers, cell phones, auto navigational units, home appliances, and rotary phones can be driven by XML languages. Those languages and protocols, XML, HTML, XHTML, WML, J2ME, and VoiceXML, are all native to the XMLC environment.

By the end of this book, you will know how to build wired and wireless applications with Enhydra and Enhydra XMLC. You will also know how to incorporate Enhydra XMLC in other application servers.

By the end of this chapter, you will have a solid picture of where Enhydra XMLC came from, what problems it was built to solve, and, at a simple level, how it works. You'll also understand why it's a unique strategy for supporting disparate display devices and applications with minimal changes to existing code.

A Taste of Enhydra XMLC

Enhydra XMLC is a technology that was designed to enable Java logic to generate a markup language in a dynamic, loosely-coupled manner. From the point of view of the designer and developer, there is never an overlap of XML or HTML markup with Java logic.

Most presentation technologies permit the markup language syntax to "bleed" through to the programming logic. In fact, in most cases, the presentation technologies or strategies permit the structure of the markup page to dictate the flow of the application.

XMLC puts Java in full control of markup language manipulation. By leveraging the Document Object Model, or DOM, as defined by the World Wide Web Consortium (W3C) at w3c.org, XMLC presents a page composed of HTML, WML, or VoiceXML *as an object* to the Java application. By doing this, Java is 100% in control of the flow of the presentation. The markup language is now simply *a resource* that has been abstracted from Java logic. XMLC presents the markup page and its content as an object. As an object, the page is manipulated by Java logic.

For Enhydra XMLC, the markup language only needs to reflect one common ancestor: XML. HTML, developed before the emergence of XML, is treated as a special case. The comparison with JavaServer Pages (JSP) design and development is inevitable and appropriate. After all, XMLC was designed as an alternative to the strategy used by JSP and Active Server Pages (ASP) of embedding programming logic, directly or indirectly, inside a markup language. The reasons for this are varied, many of which we'll explore in Chapter 3, "Presentation Technologies." Before we review the reasons, let's take a first look at how XMLC works.

> **NOTE**
>
> HTML is anything but XML-compliant. Netscape and Explorer browsers cannot use generic XML parsers to process HTML because it breaks some key XML language rules. Some of those violations include the inclusion of presentation information (for example, <bold> and ill-formed elements, such as <BR>). We'll visit some of these rules in Chapter 6, "XMLC Basics."

With XMLC, the convenient way to access markup content from Java logic begins with the use of id attributes, as shown in the following series of figures. XML id attributes are used to uniquely identify a particular element within a markup page. Figure 1.1 shows how XMLC leverages an id attribute in an HTML table cell to identify a targeted area of content for replacement by dynamically generated content during runtime. Note the complete absence of Java scriptlets or the use of custom tags or elements in this example (or anywhere else in this book).

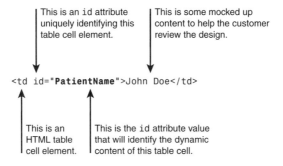

FIGURE 1.1

Using the id attribute to identify markup content for dynamic update.

Figure 1.2 shows how XMLC compiles the mocked-up HTML page into a DOM object. This is one of two products generated during this process. The DOM becomes a malleable data structure or *template* that is loaded, manipulated, and converted back to HTML during runtime execution. As with XML and HTML, the DOM is defined by a W3C specification at w3c.org.

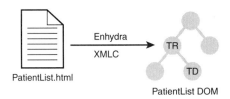

FIGURE 1.2

Converting an HTML page to a DOM source tree.

The first two figures represented the "development phase" of the sample Web presentation. In Figure 1.3, a method call is made during runtime using the other XMLC compilation output, one of the automatically constructed Java methods. It doesn't take long to figure out how the id value, PatientName, was used to construct the method. This convenience method makes it a straightforward process to update the DOM result tree with the new, dynamically generated content. The call to writeDOM() completes the runtime process by streaming the reworked contents of the updated DOM tree back to the client as HTML.

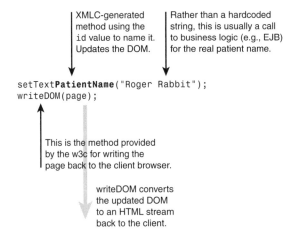

FIGURE 1.3

Using the XMLC-generated convenience method to create a dynamically transformed DOM result tree.

If you're a JSP or Cocoon programmer, I'm sure this highly simplified flow of XMLC processing illuminates a different approach to generating dynamic content. Hopefully, this modest exercise has illustrated how XMLC converts markup pages to potentially device-specific DOM templates that are loaded into memory, where they can be manipulated at runtime to generate dynamic presentations. If you've had some experience with DOM programming, you might be wondering if XMLC is just another presentation strategy that exposes a lot of DOM programming. The answer is no. XMLC has been designed to alleviate the more tedious aspects of

DOM development without shutting out the ability for experienced DOM developers to access low-level DOM methods when desired.

XMLC has inspired the Enhydra open source project Barracuda with the goal of delivering a higher-level presentation framework. Barracuda models itself after the Java Foundation Class Swing library, specifying an event model and UI components.

Chapter 3 will compare XMLC with other popular presentation technologies in some detail. Much of the remainder of this chapter will focus on the "why" behind that difference.

Modern Three-Tier Application Design

I've made a fairly aggressive attempt to explain the role of Enhydra XMLC in Web presentation development. I assume that you have performed some flavor of CGI-style development, or even JavaServer Pages programming. Let's raise the discussion a bit higher in order to describe XMLC's value to the role of presentation logic.

Presentation logic is one aspect of Web application architecture design and development. The terminology and lines of division might be a bit inconsistent at times, but there are generally accepted models of application architectures that take advantage of "layer cake" strategies. Typical three-tier application architectures isolate functionality based on role. Illustrated in Figure 1.4, areas of common functionality are represented as collections of common services and programming logic. The three typical divisions are presentation logic, business rules or logic, and data logic.

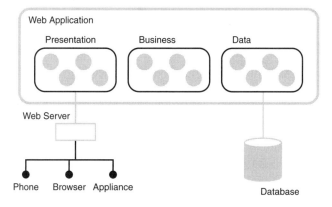

FIGURE 1.4

High-level view of a three-tier Web application architecture.

Dividing an application into multiple functionally-discrete tiers helps to reduce the impact of change to an application over its lifetime. A data layer will insulate the rest of the application when one brand of database is swapped out for another. When a pricing algorithm needs an update to reflect a new marketing promotion, only the business logic requires modification.

Functionally-discrete tiers make it easier to divide up responsibilities according to programming talents and core competencies in medium-to-large scale development projects. And, as new client technologies are supported, changes to the presentation logic pose no threat to the stability of previously tested business and data logic.

Sun takes another view of application architecture in the J2EE world. XMLC and JSP are components of "*Web-centric applications*," represented by collections of servlets, HTML pages, templates, classes, and related resources, such as images. In the J2EE view, these applications become EJB-centric when they start leveraging EJB in a Model-View-Controller (MVC) architecture, where enterprise beans maintain data. Sun maintains that this architecture also supports a clean separation of presentation, business, and data logic, enabling developers to focus on what they do best. We will address how Enhydra XMLC can fit into the MVC picture later in the book.

Although we will exercise every tier of a modern Web application design as we proceed through this book, our focus is primarily through the eyes of Enhydra XMLC, and how it addresses the needs of presentation layer development in a world deluged by new client product introductions on a weekly basis.

A Fortuitous Decision: Going with XML (Eventually)

As an open source technology, Enhydra XMLC has been steered by the subtle yet powerful forces of the open source process. Key contributions and support from the worldwide Enhydra open source community have transformed XMLC into its current role as an elegant, practical template-based mechanism for enabling single applications to negotiate with clients through multiple XML client languages and protocols.

The decision to view markup documents through the eyes of the W3C's Document Object Model proved to be fortuitous for XMLC. When XMLC was first defined by Mark Diekhans of Lutris Technologies in the fall of 1998, XML was anything but the "sure thing" that it is today. In fact, the first version of XMLC was based on an HTML DOM package. But the DOM interface was extended by the W3C to support XML, and it wasn't long until XMLC was enhanced to support standard XML.

As sharp as Mark is, he'd be the first to tell you that he never could have foreseen that XML might become the basis for the markup languages of the world's mobile devices. HTML, XHTML, WML, compact HTML, and XML are the international languages of today's mobile phones. Smart devices, with their own enhanced computing capability, such as J2ME devices or PDAs with embedded Flash support, rely on XML to stream data and convey results back to remote application servers.

Mark might also tell you that the irony is that XMLC was not originally developed for device-independent development. In fact, the top requirements could be characterized as reflecting the needs of conservative project management and software engineering practices. Some of the top requirements that drove XMLC's original design center were the following:

- Support truly maintainable Web application HTML presentations.
- Support the true separation of markup language and Java logic. Implement this strategy so as to simultaneously enable role-based separation of HTML designers and Java developers for large scale Web building/consulting engagements.
- Use nothing but standards.
- Avoid the use of custom tags. Give designers the capability to use their favorite best-of-breed HTML design tool or editor.

The move to using markup as modifiable templates gave designers the ability to leave mocked-up content, such as rows in a table, in the HTML, later to be removed at XMLC compile-time. By leveraging the id attribute instead of HTML/XML elements (often referred to as *tags*), XMLC enabled designers to pick their own design tools without fear of unrecognized tags wreaking havoc.

Placing Value on XMLC From Your Unique Perspective

Depending on who you are and what your role is in building Web applications, there are interesting advantages to using XMLC. From designers and information architects to developers, project managers, and, oh yes, customers, there are a lot of perceived upsides to using Enhydra XMLC, as outlined in Table 1.1.

TABLE 1.1 Perspectives

Role	Perceived Value
Designer	Because no embedded logic is used, you need only create one HTML file, rather than two.
	You might leave mocked up "dummy" data, such as dummy table rows, in the page for customers to review.

TABLE 1.1 Continued

Role	Perceived Value
	There are no custom tags to confuse your favorite HTML design tools.
	You can change the ordering of columns in a table by simply switching id attributes.
	You can do your job without depending on the Java developer down the hall. That's particularly convenient if you're working as a contractor to a consulting agency on the other end of town (or the other side of the world, for that matter).
Developer	You can design your Java application in full control of flow. There is no "introduction" of Java between lines of HTML.
	Your logic can be mostly written independent of device specifics. It's only when you "bind" your data to a page template that you must consider real estate issues, such as number of lines in a cell phone display device.
	You don't have to hover around the designers to answer questions about changing the logic to change the ordering of columns in a table.
	Fewer mistakes are made in the handshake between markup page and Java logic because the code and XMLC-generated template is validated at compile-time, not runtime.
Project manager	It's much easier to work with third party designers.
	It's easier to divvy up tasks between designers and developers.
	You are able to accommodate inevitable last minute changes in your project plan because you don't need to go find a developer (who has since left for another project).
Application Service Provider (ASP) customer	You can change the look of a generic credit check application to match the logo and colors of a local credit union bank without modifications to the application logic.
Independent Software Vendor (ISV) customer	You can update your Web-based product to support new devices with only modest changes to presentation layer, and no re-coding of business layer.
	You can leverage XMLC as a portable technology, no matter what Java application server is used.
	You can localize your presentation in German by simply creating a German language based-page template.

Some of the descriptions of perceived value might be a little unclear at this point, but we'll address them as the book moves on. It should, however, be obvious by now that XMLC was defined as a response to hands-on, real-world needs. How XMLC came to extend its reach to any device that can be driven by an XML language is a great open source story told later in this chapter.

Enhydra Java/XML Application Server

In preparation for explaining XMLC and driving home some points with sample code, let's elevate the discussion a bit and visit the Enhydra family of technologies, of which Enhydra XMLC is a member.

The Enhydra Java/XML application server is a partial J2EE platform. For the purpose of this book, we will need only to address the *Web container* portion of Enhydra, as defined in J2EE lexicon. Our experience at Lutris has generally been that the Web container as implemented by Enhydra is sufficient for the majority of IT projects where the training and performance overhead of EJB programming is not required.

Introduced as an open source technology in January 1999, Enhydra has become one of the more popular Java/XML application servers worldwide. The Web container portion of Enhydra can be leveraged as a lightweight but powerful server fully capable of supporting modern three-tier architectures. Many choose to forgo the EJB server to avoid the training and development overhead that EJB strategies bring to projects. Because of its integration with a full J2EE platform, Enhydra Web applications are easy to migrate to an EJB-centric application.

We'll be using Enhydra as the development environment for the purpose of developing the ShowFloor Web application. The ShowFloor application will take us through a series of coding exercises, explaining XMLC development along the way. After explaining the requirements for the ShowFloor application in Chapter 4, "The ShowFloor ASP Application," we'll learn about the Enhydra Web container and its supporting development tools in Chapter 5, "Enhydra, Java/XML Application Server."

The Enhydra Story

There is little doubt that XMLC is the most popular component of the Enhydra open source Java/XML application server. It addresses real-world technical and project challenges that make it a worthy alternative to JavaServer Pages. XMLC is supported and evolved under its own open source project hosted at xmlc.enhydra.org. One of the reasons for creating this site was to make Enhydra XMLC available as a highly portable technology for addressing the presentation layer needs of any Java application server.

The XMLC story shares common roots with the parent open source project, Enhydra. The XMLC project is a major sub-project under Enhydra.org. It is impossible to explain XMLC without talking about the same factors that drove the design and development of the rest of the Enhydra environment.

Some Essential Enhydra Points

- Enhydra is the name of the open source Java/XML application server.
- Enhydra.org is the name of the open source project that supports Enhydra and XMLC.
- Enhydra XMLC is a tool for creating dynamic Web presentations, as well as delivering content in any XML language from any application tier.
- Tomcat is the Apache implementation of the Sun servlet Web container that is also incorporated in Enhydra.
- The Enhydra Application Framework (EAF) is an alternative to the Web container for building complete three-tier applications.
- Enhydra XMLC works with either the EAF or standard servlet API.

A Genesis in Consulting, Not System Vendor Engineering

Enhydra's genesis is unique compared to most popular open or closed source application servers. First of all, Enhydra was defined and implemented in the process of rubbing elbows with enterprise IT and dot-com start-up customers. In the early days (1996-97) of intranet and dot-com development, the definition of a standard Web application had yet to be settled. The hot technologies were Java applets and ActiveX controls. They were technologies in search of a real-world application.

But most IT managers were not intrigued. They were still focused on the resource-depleting issue of re-booting Windows boxes on a daily basis. HTML was still a powerful yet simple concept. Pure HTML applications avoided the firewall topic of downloading Java applets and ActiveX controls. The possibility of HTML browsers reducing the standard worry of Windows compatibility was intriguing, to say the least. But, IT managers being IT managers, they wanted to take one conservative step at a time.

It was clear that the availability of shrink-wrapped Web applications was years in the future. Why? Because early adopters of these applications weren't sure what to ask for. And no standards existed, other than the new servlet API, defined for the purpose of extending the functionality of Web servers with Java logic. The definition of the servlet API gave rise to the emergence of "servlet runners," which set the stage for an entirely new industry.

The folks behind Enhydra had the advantage of leveraging their hands-on consulting experience to define Enhydra from what appeared to be the most common requirements that different consulting customers were asking for. It is no accident that Enhydra's features, functions, and architecture address the needs of a consulting business and its customers, from start-up dot-coms to enterprise IT. For example, rather than incorporate its own sophisticated Interactive Development Environment (IDE), Enhydra defines the Kelp tools (`kelp.enhydra.org`) for integrating Enhydra into best-of-breed IDE environments, such as Borland JBuilder and Sun Forte. Consultants are picky, preferring to use their own tools, and Lutris consultants were no different.

The only graphical, IDE-like component is Enhydra Data Object Design Studio (DODS). It was developed to relieve developers from repeatedly hand-coding the same painstaking data logic for accessing and manipulating SQL tables as viewed through the emerging standard, JDBC. DODS uses a graphical drag-and-drop environment to display table and attribute relationships, resulting in auto-generated data layer logic.

> **CAUTION**
>
> *ASP* can stand for Active Server Pages *or* Application Service Provider. From here on out, we'll use ASP to refer to Application Service Provider.

Who specifically influenced Enhydra's evolution in the early days? Originally, it was Kinko's Corporation, Federal Express, and a great many dot-com start-up companies like WizShop, the application service provider behind the Earthlink and Intranets.com shopping malls. Later, after Enhydra had become an open source project, support came from a great many consulting companies worldwide, such as Digitalsesame of Taiwan and Tivano of Germany, both of whom pioneered key Enhydra features through enthusiastic source code contributions and daily involvement.

> **What's an Enhydra?**
>
> *"Enhydra Lutris"* is the scientific name of the California sea otter. The name and mascot were selected by virtue of this kelp-dwelling sea creature's proximity to Santa Cruz, California, home of Lutris Technologies, creator of Enhydra.

That was the beginning of the first phase of what Enhydra is today. The second phase was the introduction of Enhydra XMLC, in response to the need for making Enhydra applications more maintainable for the long haul. The third phase was when the open source effect first took place, delivering Enhydra as a wireless platform.

The Practical Enhydra Application Framework Model

The architectural backdrop for these features again reflected requirements that were heavily influenced by project management and business requirements to get the job done with a minimum of training or deployment complexities. The *Enhydra Application Framework (EAF)*, formerly referred to as a "superservlet" architecture, was designed to support a balance of leanness, flexibility, and adaptability with large scale project capability and deployment potential. Its characteristics include the following:

- A simpler programming model for developers
- A smaller footprint for performance and memory issues
- An easy-to-learn programming model

The Enhydra Web Container is a complete development and runtime environment. We'll explore this in greater detail in Chapter 5, "Enhydra, Java/XML Application Server"; but for now, here is a partial list of Enhydra's attributes:

- Enhydra Application Framework (EAF) with session, presentation, and database manager services.
- Enhydra XMLC, of course!
- Enhydra Director for cluster support and server-level failover.
- Web administration console with a graphical servlet debugger.
- Enhydra Multiserver servlet runner for both Tomcat (servlet 2.2/JSP 1.1) and Enhydra EAF applications.
- Enhydra DODS for generating data objects.
- AppWizard for initializing and deploying WAR and EAF applications. AppWizard initializes the application source tree in a presentation-business-data organization.

Enhydra.org, the Open Source Project

If you come from the Linux or Unix world, you're probably highly familiar with the topic of open source and the open source mechanism. Seed a community of highly motivated developers with source code of significant value and a software license that basically lets them run wild, and the result can be magic. That's open source. There's no doubt about it. Open source has a way of generating superior code, thanks to an environment that makes constant worldwide code reviews possible.

The open source process also has a way of reflecting cutting edge trends. At first, this might appear threatening to the more conservative IT manager. But the meaningful trends survive the filter of worldwide scrutiny. This makes the open source process the "canary in the mine," alerting us to worldwide application development trends that should be monitored with great interest.

The Fortune 1000 has gotten heavily involved in the open source phenomenon as well. At first glance, you might see a lot of e-mail postings to open source list servers from someone like `dhy01@hotmail.com`. But the fact is that `dhy01` is likely to be an employee of Merck Pharmaceuticals or General Electric. We're not saying that these folks are better programmers. Instead, we're suggesting that these folks help drive practical, real-world requirements for the direction of open source software features and capabilities. These mailing lists are composed of a worldwide audience as well. The presence and involvement of an international community gives open source the ability to rapidly incorporate support for new, legitimate technology trends. As we'll see at the end of this chapter, the impact of wireless trends outside the United States is an excellent example of the value of an open source organization composed of a worldwide community.

Because all these communications are on public view via the Internet, there are never any feature surprises with new versions of open source software. Compare that experience to what you might have experienced with new versions of Microsoft Word, a sore point with this author.

Lutris released the Enhydra Java/XML application server as Enhydra 2.0 to the open source world on January 15, 1999. The announcement was made with a few e-mails to well-known Java discussion groups that encouraged the curious to join the Enhydra mailing list.

FIGURE 1.5

Open source lineage of the Enhydra universe.

As a member of the overall open source community, there should be little surprise that Enhydra has evolved with the contributions of other excellent open source projects to construct a complete application server development and runtime environment. One look at the list of contributing open source projects shown in Figure 1.5 establishes Enhydra's heavy open source composition.

The Magic Ingredients of Open Source Mechanism

If you think of open source mechanism as generating magic, then the ingredients are simple:

- Easy access to source code
- Developers tied together by e-mail/newsgroups
- Great technology that shows real value

Other Enhydra.org projects

Enhydra.org is the central site and organization behind Enhydra and its family of related technologies. Table 1.2 lists some of Enhydra's projects.

TABLE 1.2   Selected Enhydra.org Projects

Project	Description
zeus.enhydra.org	Zeus addresses the topic of data binding, where XML documents are turned into Java code and back again. The chair of the Zeus project is Brett McLaughlin, author of *Java and XML* (O'Reilly).
xmlc.enhydra.org	The XMLC project is dedicated to spreading the goodness of XMLC well beyond the boundaries of the Enhydra project. Mark Diekhans, of Lutris Technologies and inventor of XMLC, chairs this project.
barracuda.enhydra.org	Barracuda is trying to raise the level of abstraction above the XMLC layer. The chair of the Barracuda project is Christian Cryder.
instantdb.Enhydra.org	InstantDB is a 100% Java relational database. Peter Hearty, the creator of InstantDB, oversees this project. InstantDB is used in our ShowFloor App demo application.
kxml.enhydra.org	Initiated by Stefan Haustein, the kXML project focuses on small footprint XML parser technology for small devices, such as handheld J2ME phones.

TABLE 1.2 Continued

Project	Description
dods.enhydra.org	The project that supports the DODS tool for mapping data logic to relational database tables.
kelp.enhydra.org	Kelp focuses on tools for integrating Enhydra into popular development design environments, such as Forte and JBuilder.

The Enhydra Public License

Every open source technology comes with a source code license. From FreeBSD to GNU Public License, there are plenty to go around. The Enhydra Public License (EPL) is based on the Netscape Mozilla license.

The EPL states the following:

- There is no restriction on re-shipping the source code with your product, other than to do so under the EPL.
- You're given a license to use any patent concepts within Enhydra as long as you use those concepts by incorporating the Enhydra application server. In other words, you couldn't use a patented concept for an implementation not involving the Enhydra application server.
- You're required to return any code changes made to the core Enhydra technology, including tools such as Enhydra XMLC and Enhydra DODS, as well as the runtime Enhydra application server.
- All the code you develop outside the Enhydra technology, that is, your application and its intellectual property, is yours. It's only when you get inside Enhydra source code that you must return code changes to Enhydra.org as candidates for possible inclusion.

Open Source Delivers Wireless

There's no way I can end this chapter without explaining how XMLC technology eventually embraced wireless devices. How did it inherit this capability, even though Lutris developers, at the time, had no wireless experience whatsoever? This is the first major example of how the open source side of Enhydra's world determined a new destiny for this evolving bit of Internet infrastructure technology.

A funny thing happened to Enhydra along the open source route. It's generally well known that wireless communication has grown faster outside the United States. Given Enhydra's worldwide accessibility, it was only natural that the forces of wireless, represented by consultants in Germany, Taiwan, and Sweden, would apply their customers' needs to Enhydra. As participants in the wireless wave that had yet to hit the shores of North America, it was the international representatives of the Enhydra.org community that saw the potential for wireless device support in XMLC.

The moral of the XMLC story? Who needs product managers when a worldwide open source community is there to identify a need, define the solution, and deliver it?

Summary

This chapter has given you the first taste of Enhydra XMLC development. I've explained how XMLC turns a markup page of HTML into an object representation in the form of a DOM template. XMLC simultaneously uses designer- or developer-inserted id attributes to identify those portions of the DOM that will most likely be manipulated for dynamic content. The result is a set of convenient accessor methods that bypass the need for low-level DOM API development. We asserted that the use of the DOM tree as a "middleman" for representing the markup document removes the inter-mixing of markup and Java logic. The result is a clean, consistent division of markup and programming logic. The implications are many, as we've identified from the different hypothetical perspectives of members of typical Web application development projects.

We also covered the following:

- Modern three-tier Web application architectures.
- Value perspectives on Enhydra XMLC.
- A brief introduction to the Enhydra Java/XML application server.
- A brief introduction to the open source process.
- How Enhydra XMLC gained its wireless capabilities through the open source process.
- An introduction to Enhydra.org, the open source project that is the umbrella effort for other related projects, including Zeus for data binding, Kelp for integrating Enhydra in third-party Interactive Design Environments and DODS for the data object to relational database mapping tool.

XMLC Development

IN THIS CHAPTER

Let's transition the discussion of why XMLC was created and for what purpose to how XMLC works, and how it can influence the working relationship of HTML designers and Java developers in a Web application development project. In this chapter, we'll explore enough of the underpinnings of XMLC to set the stage for explaining the impact of XMLC on the design of a Web application and the development process of Web presentations.

We will also walk through the example of the development of a login screen for our upcoming discussion of the ShowFloor demonstration application. During this exercise, we will begin the first of many discussions of key XMLC topics. One of these topics will address the conceptual necessity of understanding the role of the DOM in XMLC programming.

This discussion will also provide the backdrop for some comparisons with other presentation technologies in Chapter 3, "Presentation Technologies."

Taking Control from HTML

Beginning with CGI programming, dynamic Web presentations were created by Perl scripts that were welded to the HTML markup language. Print statements with hard-coded HTML elements enabled rapid development at the price of creating presentations that were next to impossible to rework. This style of development led to a large market of valuable hybrid HMTL/Perl designers/developers. Often, the developer's value lay in the prospect of the chaos that would result if they were to leave the company.

The requirement for first generation enterprise-quality Web applications, typically built by consultants, drove the emergence of server-side Java. The proliferation of server-side Java resulted, in part, from the consultants who used it for the "platform independent" story they needed to use in an attempt to address the largest range of possible customers. From IBM AS/400s to HP e3000s, as long as there was a ported Java Virtual Machine, a Java application could be proposed.

The steady trend of server-side Java Web applications built by a rapidly growing community of new age Internet consultants yielded significantly more scalable and maintainable Web applications. But the baggage of old style CGI/Perl presentation strategies, featuring hybrid coding of HTML and programming logic, was carried over into the Java realm. Servlet programming and the introduction of JavaServer Pages and Active Server Pages represented the first claims to taking more maintainable template approaches to presentation development. The music was different, but it was the same dancing around HTML that led even an object-oriented language like Java to be used in ways that broke its own rules.

The irony is that HTML, as founding king of the Internet presentation languages, drove legions of application architecture designs that undermine true object-oriented design at the interface of markup language and programming logic. This book is about XMLC and how it turned the tables on HTML.

This chapter brings out the true object-oriented nature of XMLC development. XMLC supports loose coupling between presentation objects and XML/HTML documents. As a direct result, it also supports loose coupling between those who build these application components, namely designer and developer. In Chapter 1, we established the creation of XMLC as a response to project management needs in large consulting engagements. In keeping with the project emphasis, we'll approach the topic of XMLC development from a process view in order to bring out some of the how's and why's of XMLC development. While we're doing this, we'll also take a first pass at understanding the concepts behind the document object model (DOM) and DOM development, and how it interweaves with XMLC development.

Development Flow with XMLC

Enhydra XMLC was introduced into the open source mechanism in the spring of 1999. It was the first presentation technology to put Java in command of HTML. XMLC gave Java application logic the capability to view HTML as one of any number of presentation resources, including WML, VoiceXML, and XML, that can be read, updated, and transmitted. We've already discussed how XMLC was an engineering response to project management needs. In particular, XMLC development represents

- A strategy to support parallel development by presentation designers and Java developers.
- A strategy for large scale development projects, particularly where third party designer and developer companies were involved.

As we hinted in Chapter 1, only later was the role of XMLC expanded to support

- A strategy for device independence.
- A strategy for delivering XML data to other devices.

A Sample Project Scenario

The demonstration application we will introduce in Chapter 4 is called the ShowFloor application. It will serve as our platform for introducing the XMLC development language and environment. We'll focus on HTML to begin with, but later we will expand the demo to support Flash, WML, and VoiceXML presentation languages and technologies as well.

The ShowFloor application will be the platform for a fictitious *application service provider*, or *ASP*. It will support the capability to take on the look and feel of the company that has rented it to host a large event. This is often referred to as *re-branding*. The event attendee thinks they're dealing with a Web site custom built for the event host, when in reality, it's a kind of rent-a-Web application that is possibly hosted by the same company that rents it to others. Again, we'll get into specifics in Chapter 4, "The ShowFloor ASP Application."

Among its many features, this demo application will support an administrative interface for event hosts and vendors to add or update information for a particular conference. But for our immediate needs, let's speculate on the development process of the HTML-based login screen. This Web page will be used by the event administrator to log into the system.

NOTE

Storyboarding is the practice of creating mock-up presentation screens that can be used to convey the look and feel and general features of each screen, as well as the navigational flow from one screen to the next. Often this storyboard takes the form of one large Photoshop image that can be transferred onto a large board, or a series of on-line images linked together by some level of mocked-up active button behavior.

Storyboarding is an ideal way to begin *scrubbing* the customer's requirements and get an immediate response from the customer (as in, "Is this what you're asking for, and are you sure it's what you want?") The goal of XMLC is to minimize the number of steps required for a project to transition from storyboard to functional presentation. Lutris consultants coined the term "*visual contract*" to acknowledge how important storyboarding is to defining Web applications.

Let's assume that the requirements, architecture and storyboarding phases have been concluded, and it's time to start development. Our login screen looks something like Figure 2.1.

FIGURE 2.1
Mocked-up SFAdmin Login screenshot.

Designer and Developer Assign `ids`

With an approved sketch or mockup of the login screen in hand, the designer and Java developer (that is, software engineer) discuss the dynamic nature of the presentation. They identify three areas that will be the target of dynamic content:

1. the event logo,
2. the error message STOP graphic, and
3. the error message string.

The event logo must reflect the name of the company hosting the event. It might be a large original equipment manufacturer (OEM) like Intel or Sun, or a large vertical industry player like Boeing or J.P. Morgan. The event could be a Solaris development conference, or a financial industry vendor show. Depending on the URL used to access the login page, such as `http://www.showfloorApp.com?eventHost=Intel`, the logo associated with the event host must be displayed.

The error message string will be updated dynamically if the administrator makes an error during login. Simultaneously, the STOP sign graphic must also appear. Both the string and the graphic are in table cells inside a table row. The table acts as a "geometry manager" to control the layout of your screen. In the event that you need to remove the error message and STOP sign graphic, you can simply remove the entire row.

Within the scope of addressing the login presentation, the designer and developer have one task to perform. They must choose and agree on an `id` to uniquely identify each target for dynamic content. `id` attributes are a special type of attribute that uniquely distinguishes a specific instance of an XML or HTML element from other like-named elements. In other words, no two elements of the same name, such as `td`, may have the same `id` attribute value in an HTML/XML document.

Figure 2.2 illustrates how the XMLC compiler will map the `id`'s value into the generated associated accessor method. In this case, the `id` value `EventLoginLogo` will influence the name of the method that the developer will eventually use to modify the contents of the `src` attribute associated with the `image` element.

These `ids` are what the XMLC compiler will use to simplify the following tasks:

1. Dynamically loading the appropriate logo image
2. Removing the STOP graphic
3. Removing or updating the error string

2

XMLC DEVELOPMENT

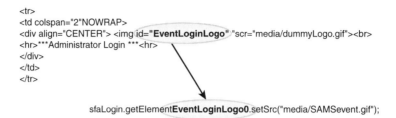

```
<tr>
<td colspan="2"NOWRAP>
<div align="CENTER"> <img id="EventLoginLogo" "scr="media/dummyLogo.gif"><br>
<hr>***Administrator Login ***<hr>
</div>
</td>
</tr>
```

sfaLogin.getElement**EventLoginLogo0**.setSrc("media/SAMSevent.gif");

FIGURE 2.2

How id *attributes map to Java/DOM methods.*

> **NOTE**
>
> Using cascading style sheets (CSS) for HTML design has become a standard approach to simplifying the tasks of both the designer and the developer. The CSS gives the designer full control over look and feel. Simultaneously, the use of CSS frees up the developer to focus on solid coding, as opposed to remembering to insert <FONT> directives here and there during the development process. We'll assume the use of CSS in page examples through this book.

Tasks 2 and 3 appear a bit odd. What's the idea of "removing" content? The answer is that there are many strategies for designing screens for processing by XMLC. This is the one we have chosen. Rather than define a collection of login screens reflecting different scenarios, such as failed login or successful login, we've created one mocked-up screen that contains all the possible elements. Later we'll see how we handle this programmatically.

The following sample of three HTML fragments speculate on how the placement of the ids for all three dynamic components might appear:

```
<img id="EventLoginLogo" src="media/dummyLogo.gif">
<tr id="ErrowMsgRow">
<td id="LoginErrorMsg">** Error message goes here..</td>
```

With the assumption that this process for assigning ids was repeated for all the other screens of our ShowFloor application, the designer and developer can now part ways and perform concurrent, independent development, without having to talk again, in theory. All that was required was to identify and name the ids that will be used to name all targeted areas for dynamically-generated content. The assignments are illustrated in Figure 2.3.

This scenario of the working relationship between designer and developer is a distinguishing attribute of XMLC. This is what XMLC means by a clean separation between the two roles of a Web application building project. There are many more interesting benefits and implications of this process that will be itemized later in this chapter.

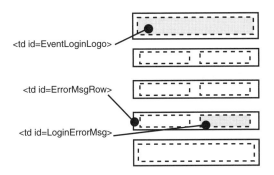

FIGURE 2.3
Assigning selected id *attributes.*

> **NOTE**
>
> Read our lips: "No new tags."
>
> Did you notice that not one new HTML tag was introduced in this process? That is one of the key features of XMLC development. No new tags, or, more importantly, no illegal tags are required by XMLC programming. One of the benefits of this feature is that XMLC can be used with any HTML design tool on the market.

The Developer's Path with XMLC

The developer walks away from her meeting with the designer knowing the general complexion of the login page and the ids that identify the areas of dynamic content. But what does this do for the developer in terms of getting her job done on the Java side of the application equation? Specifically, how is the designer going to use those ids to leverage Java logic to generate the required content? How will this accelerate the development process, and do so in a manner that makes the application easy to maintain for a long time?

Working with HTML and ids

The raw HTML page in Listing 2.1 is an example of the mocked-up login screen. By "mocked-up," we mean that it might contain content that will be replaced with real content when the application is deployed. In conventional JSP development, this would be impossible to do without creating separate files, one for the mockup and the other for the HTML/JSP scriptlets.

LISTING 2.1   SFAdminLogin.html

```
<html>
<head>
<title>ShowFloor Administration Login</title>
<meta http-equiv="Content-Type" content="text/html; charset=iso-8859-1">
</head>
<body bgcolor="#FFFFFF" text="#000000">
<form name="SFAdminForm" method="post" action="SFAdminLoginProcess.po" >
 <table width="80" border="0" cellspacing="0" cellpadding="5">
   <tr>
     <td colspan="2" NOWRAP>
         <img id="EventLoginLogo" src="media/dummyLogo.gif" ><br>
         <hr>*** Administrator Login ***<hr>
     </td>
   </tr>
   <tr>
     <td width="22%">
       <div align="RIGHT">User:</div>
     </td>
     <td width="78%">
       <input type="text" name="usernameTF">
     </td>
   </tr>
   <tr>
     <td width="22%">
       <div align="RIGHT">Password:</div>
     </td>
     <td width="78%">
       <input type="PASSWORD" name="passwordTF">
     </td>
   </tr>
   <tr id="ErrorMsgRow">
     <td height="49">
       <div align="CENTER"><img src="media/stopSign.gif" width="60"
height="62"></div>
     </td>
     <td id="LoginErrorMsg">** Error message goes here..</td>
   </tr>
   <tr>
     <td colspan="2">
       <div align="RIGHT">
         <input type="image" border=0 src=media/loginButton.gif" width="75"
height="31">
       </div>
     </td>
```

LISTING 2.1   Continued

```
   </tr>
  </table>
 </form>
 </body>
 </html>
```

Whether we are looking at a target HTML page that was constructed by the designer or the developer doesn't really matter. XMLC supports a placement-independent view of dynamic content. Therefore, all that matters right now is that the developer has a page in which to insert the ids that she and the designer agreed to use. In the HTML page, you can see the IMG element and the id value EventLoginLogo. The src attribute points to a placeholder GIF image that the Java presentation logic will deal with later.

> **NOTE**
>
> From here on out, we will be discussing the use of the xmlc command from the command line. For the Windows NT/2000 audience, please note that a bash shell is provided with Enhydra for you to follow along.
>
> Enhydra also comes with the Kelp library, which gives it the capability to integrate into popular graphical *Interactive Development Environments (IDEs)* such as Oracle's JDeveloper, Sun's Forte and Borland's JBuilder. In the IDE environment, many of the command line options we'll discuss can be found as radio buttons or check boxes in the graphical world.
>
> The recent addition of Apache's Ant technology has also simplified and made more portable the Enhydra build environment. We'll address this popular new Java technology in Chapter 10, "Servlet Web Applications."

The xmlc Command

With ids inserted into the mocked-up page, it's now time to use the xmlc command to turn the page into an object representation in the form of a Java class that can be manipulated by Java logic. There are a great many runtime options provided by the xmlc command. In this discussion, we'll use only the options that reveal what happens "under the hood" as XMLC transforms the page into a Java object.

The xmlc command that we use for the development of our login presentation might be executed as follows:

```
xmlc -class FSAdminLoginHTML options.xmlc FSAdminLogin.html
```

Terminated with a required `.xmlc` extension, `options.xmlc` is the name of a file that might contain one or more `xmlc` command line options. This feature helps conserve the length of the command line. We'll explore the many `xmlc` options in Chapter 7, "The `xmlc` Command."

The `-class` option instructs `xmlc` to create a Java class named `FSAdminLoginHTML.class`. This class will contain the fields and methods to generate a DOM representation of the login page and convenient accessor methods auto-generated by XMLC using the `id` attributes the designer and developer chose. These methods provide the shortcuts that make it very easy to directly access the specific DOM element from the developer's Java logic. Without these methods, the developer would have to perform a great deal of work to traverse the tree and make the changes necessary to create dynamic content.

We have just entered a very large topic area known as the DOM. Let's talk about the role of the DOM, what it is, how it works, and how it makes it possible for XMLC to address its real-world requirements. We'll then resume our development phase discussion of the `xmlc` command.

The Document Object Model

The DOM is an object model for representing markup documents of XML or HTML. The model uses the concept of *nodes*, which can represent every aspect of markup components, such as elements and attributes, enabling the document to be completely recreated, after possible additions of dynamic content, from the model.

The DOM is defined by the W3C as a set of interfaces and objects that are implemented by different language bindings, such as C or Java. How it is represented by the Java language bindings is the responsibility of the implementation. Enhydra uses the Apache Xerces XML parser, as contributed by IBM Corporation, and the HTML Tidy parser from the W3C, for HTML documents. The `xmlc` command examines the first line content type at the top of the targeted document in order to select which parser to use.

The DOM is the key to XMLC's capability to let a Web application view the presentation as a resource. By turning the presentation into a resource, often called a *template*, different templates can be selected, loaded, and manipulated by the application. These resources may represent documents of HTML, or any legal XML language such as WML, VoiceXML, or custom XML for communicating with a Flash 5 or J2ME client.

The DOM describes a standard API for building, traversing, and manipulating the hierarchical representation of an XML document. Node types are defined that provide object representations of markup components. Figure 2.4 illustrates most of the DOM node types.

The DOM was originally specified by the W3C to specifically address HTML. It was later amended to incorporate support for XML. This was part of the natural course of things, because the W3C also defined the XML specification. The specs can be found at `www.w3.org/TR/DOM-Level-2-Core/`. If you look under the hood of Enhydra, you'll find that it supports the specification for DOM Core Levels I and II.

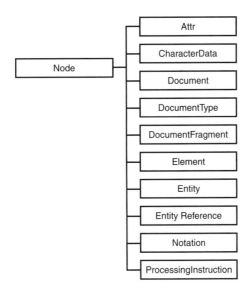

FIGURE 2.4
DOM node types.

But, other than demonstrating Enhydra's use of a standard specification, the fact is that the XMLC developer doesn't need to have full knowledge of the DOM classes, methods and all. For 95% of XMLC programming, the only nodes of interest are the following three:

- `Document` Node
- `Element` Node
- `Attr` Node

Integrated DOM support means an XMLC strategy can be used with any XML-compliant language. VoiceXML, WML, compact HTML (cHTML), and XHTML are just a few examples.

DOM Nodes Represent HTML/XML Objects

Defined by the DOM `Node` interface, each node has a type, a name, a value, and an associated set of methods. A node can represent any HTML/XML object, such as an `ELEMENT_NODE`, `TEXT_NODE`, or a `_NODE`. Table 2.1 lists the recognized node types and their predefined short values that are used by `getNodeType()`. We will talk about most of these node types in Chapter 6, "XMLC Basics."

TABLE 2.1 Node Types

DOM static variables	Short Integer
ELEMENT_NODE	1
ATTRIBUTE_NODE	2
TEXT_NODE	3
CDATA_SECTION_NODE	4
ENTITY_REFERENCES_NODE	5
ENTITY_NODE	6
PROCESSING_INSTRUCTION_NODE	7
COMMENT_NODE	8
DOCUMENT_NODE	9
DOCUMENT_TYPE_NODE	10
DOCUMENT_FRAGMENT_NODE	11
NOTATION_NODE	12

WML, the wireless markup language, is an XML language and therefore conforms to the standard definition of an XML document. Figure 2.5 illustrates how the markup in a WML page is identified as XML objects that will be parsed and eventually represented in a DOM tree. (Note that this example doesn't work for an HTML document because entity declarations are not permitted in HTML.) Figure 2.6 shows a portion of DOM tree created by a DOM parser such as Apache Xerces. This tree demonstrates how the parser uses nodes to organize XML objects into a hierarchy of relationships.

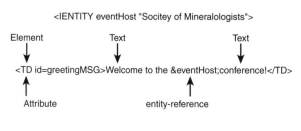

FIGURE 2.5

Labeling objects in a WML document.

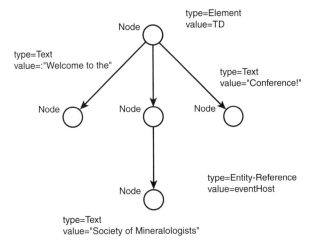

FIGURE 2.6
WML objects as nodes represented in a DOM tree.

DOM Navigation and Manipulation

The Node interface defines the methods necessary to navigate, inspect, and modify any node. The methods listed in Table 2.2 are a representative subset of methods identified by the org3.dom.node interface. The ones that have been chosen for this list are the ones most commonly used in XMLC programming. For example, you might use appendChild() to add another radio button to a form, or a new row to a table. getFirstChild() is used, for example, to retrieve the first option item in a menu form. For our SFAdminLogin screen, we'll use removeChild() to remove the STOP GIF and the error message string when the administrator successfully logs in to the system.

TABLE 2.2 Commonly Used Node Methods in XMLC Development

Method	Return value
appendChild(Node newChild)	Node
cloneNode(Boolean deep)	Node
removeChild(Node oldChild)	Node
replaceChild(Node newChild, Node oldChild)	Node
getFirstChild()	Node

cloneNode() provides a telling insight into how XMLC programming leverages the Node interface. cloneNode() reflects XMLC's role as a templating tool because you can take the source tree and clone selected portions of it to act as a template for adding new XML objects. For instance, you can take a row in a table and treat it as a sub-tree template to add new rows of dynamic content. Using cloneNode() you simply make a copy of the existing row to stamp out new rows, appending them to the cloned copy. Your work is done after you delete the portion of the document you cloned, then attach the updated cloned portion back to the tree with appendChild(). Chapter 8, "HTML Presentations," will explain template cloning in detail.

Figure 2.7 illustrates how different methods apply depending on the contextual position of one node relative to another. The black node in the middle represents the current context.

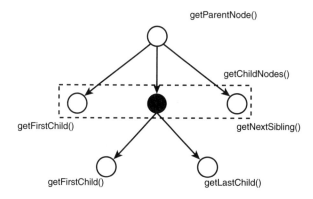

FIGURE 2.7
Examples of methods associated with the contextual position of the current node.

Some methods of the Node interface are not always applicable to the node in question. For instance, text nodes never have children. A Java exception would result if you were to attempt to delete a child from a text node using deleteChild(). The motto for DOM programming: "Have your JavaDoc ready."

XMLC-Supported DOM Packages

The DOM tree represents the hierarchical relationship of markup elements and their attributes and content as described in the original document. Enhydra supports the packages that are implementations of the DOM Node sub-interfaces specific to the particular XML language such as HTML, VoiceXML, or other DTD-defined XML languages. A partial example of one of these packages is listed in Table 2.3.

TABLE 2.3   HTML Table-specific Sub-interfaces of the `Node` Interface

HTML Element	Description
`HTMLOListElement`	Ordered list element. Includes `setStart()` for starting sequence number.
`HTMLBodyElement`	Body element. Includes `setBgColor()` for setting background color.
`HTMLInputElement`	Form element. Includes `setChecked()` when check boxes or radio boxes are present.
`HTMLTableCellElement`	Cell element object used to represent the TH and TD elements.

These packages give you the capability to perform type-safe programming within the context of each XML language. But no requirement prevents you from performing generic DOM programming. The DOM sub-class interfaces for XHTML, WML and VoiceXML are as follows:

```
org.enhydra.xml.xhtml.dom
org.enhydra.xml.wml.dom
org.enhydra.xml.voicexml.dom
```

How the DOM interface is used to extend an HTML or a VoiceXML implementation can be examined in the class file generated by executing the `xmlc` command with the `-keep` option. In our example, the generated XMLC document class `SFAdminLoginHTML` implements the interfaces as defined by the generic `XMLObject`, as well as the HTML package, `HTMLObject`. `HTMLObjectImpl` is the implementation of the `HTMLObject` interface.

```
public class SFAdminLoginHTML extends org.enhydra.xml.xmlc.html.HTMLObjectImpl
implements org.enhydra.xml.xmlc.XMLObject, org.enhydra.xml.xmlc.html.HTMLObject
```

`xmlc` Value to DOM Programming

With XMLC programming, the good news is that you won't have to worry a lot about creating traversal logic for moving around the DOM tree looking for `id` attributes. That's because the convenience functions automatically created by XMLC during compile-time provide direct access to the node in question.

DOM programming is actually quite simple. The challenge is to clearly conceptualize the boundary between the generic DOM model and the objects of the document-specific HTML/XML page. Until you are comfortable with this model, you might want to work with XMLC programming on small projects. Hopefully, this chapter and the more detailed discussion in Chapter 6 will help you clear that hurdle.

Examining the DOM Tree Representation of `SFAdminLogin`

Let's return to the `xmlc` command. Using the `-dump` option, we can take a look at our DOM tree in Listing 2.2 in human-readable language.

LISTING 2.2   Output from `xmlc -dump -dom xerces SFAdminLogin.html`

```
SFAdminLogin.html:8: Warning: <table> lacks "summary" attribute
SFAdminLogin.html:11: Warning: <img> lacks "alt" attribute
SFAdminLogin.html:34: Warning: <img> lacks "alt" attribute
DOM hierarchy:
 HTMLDocumentImpl:
   HTMLHtmlElementImpl: HTML
     HTMLHeadElementImpl: HEAD
       HTMLTitleElementImpl: TITLE
         TextImpl: ShowFloor Administration Login
       HTMLMetaElementImpl: META: content="text/html; charset=iso-8859-1" http-
➥equiv="Content-Type"
     HTMLBodyElementImpl: BODY: bgcolor="#FFFFFF" text="#000000"
       HTMLFormElementImpl: FORM: action="SFAdminLoginProcess.po" method="post"
➥name="SFAdminForm"
         HTMLTableElementImpl: TABLE: border="0" width="80"
           HTMLTableRowElementImpl: TR
             HTMLTableCellElementImpl: TD: colspan="2" nowrap=""
               HTMLDivElementImpl: DIV: align="CENTER"
                 HTMLImageElementImpl: IMG: id="EventLoginLogo"
➥src="media/dummyLogo.gif"
               HTMLBRElementImpl: BR
               TextImpl:
               HTMLHRElementImpl: HR
               TextImpl: *** Administrator Login ***
               HTMLHRElementImpl: HR
           HTMLTableRowElementImpl: TR
             HTMLTableCellElementImpl: TD: width="22%"
               HTMLDivElementImpl: DIV: align="RIGHT"
                 TextImpl: User:
             HTMLTableCellElementImpl: TD: width="78%"
               HTMLInputElementImpl: INPUT: name="usernameTF" type="text"
               TextImpl:
           HTMLTableRowElementImpl: TR
             HTMLTableCellElementImpl: TD: width="22%"
               HTMLDivElementImpl: DIV: align="RIGHT"
                 TextImpl: Password:
             HTMLTableCellElementImpl: TD: width="78%"
               HTMLInputElementImpl: INPUT: name="passwordTF" type="PASSWORD"
               TextImpl:
```

LISTING 2.2   Continued

```
            HTMLTableRowElementImpl: TR: id="ErrorMsgRow"
              HTMLTableCellElementImpl: TD: height="49"
                HTMLDivElementImpl: DIV: align="CENTER"
                  HTMLImageElementImpl: IMG: src="media/stopSign.gif" width="60"
              HTMLTableCellElementImpl: TD: id="LoginErrorMsg"
                TextImpl: ** Error message goes here..
            HTMLTableRowElementImpl: TR
              HTMLTableCellElementImpl: TD: colspan="2"
                HTMLDivElementImpl: DIV: align="RIGHT"
                  HTMLInputElementImpl: INPUT: border="0"
⇒src="media/loginButton.gif" type="image" width="75"
```

Note that we've intercepted a few warnings from the results of the XMLC compile. This brings out a huge advantage of XMLC, namely the capability to perform validation during compile-time that our page is a well-formed HTML or XML document.

> **NOTE**
>
> *Well-formed* and *valid* are not synonymous terms. *Well-formed* applies to a properly declared physical structure that is in sync with XML rules. A *valid* document is one that is in line with an associated Data Type Declaration (DTD) file. In practice, DTDs are essential for defining standard XML languages as well as enforcing data integrity.

The dump reveals that markup elements are recognized by the DOM package and that attributes are associated with each element. These attributes are not technically nodes themselves.

You also see reference to "*LazyText*." This ironic term is a side effect of the LazyDOM, which is a special extension of the Xerces parser. It greatly improves standard DOM performance (and reduces a potentially large memory footprint) by instantiating only those nodes that are targeted for manipulation by the Java application. There are cases where you may choose to use the Xerces parser instead. An XMLC command-line option for analyzing how to evaluate which parser to use will be called out in Chapter 6. The command

```
xmlc -dom xerces
```

can be used to override the LazyDOM default parser.

The rest of the output in Listing 2.2 illustrates the DOM organization of our login page. As you follow the familiar HTML elements—HTML, HEAD, TITLE, and so on—you'll note the HTML element type associated with each node.

> **NOTE**
>
> The -dump XMLC option has a counterpart on the runtime side. Leveraging the Java class DOMInfo under the hierarchy org.enhydra.xml.dom, you can dump the tree at any stage of its modification during runtime to the console or to a file:
>
> ```
> DOMInfo.printTree("SFAdminLogin DOM:", SFAdminLogin);
> ```

The form attribute action="SFAdminLoginProcess.po" is a reference to a Java class referred to as an *Enhydra Presentation Object (PO)*. This PO is responsible for processing the login screen after it is submitted by the user. This mechanism is covered in detail in Chapter 5, "Enhydra, Java/XML Application Server.."

> **NOTE**
>
> The .po in Enhydra presentation files stands for presentation object. Odds are that if you find a URL terminated with .po (just before the parameter list) you are looking at a reference to an Enhydra "super-servlet." Because Enhydra also supports standard servlet 2.2 development, you can't always be sure if you're looking at an Enhydra application.

The event host's image is identified by the id that we inserted in the HTML. It labels the HTML image element that currently points to a dummyLogo.gif acting as a placeholder.

Examining the Generated DOM Java Code

An xmlc compiler translates an HTML or XML file into a DOM-based Java class. To generate the class, xmlc must construct an intermediate Java source file. By default, this file is removed during compile-time. But xmlc can be told to leave this file intact with the –keep option. This is an excellent option to use while learning how xmlc leverages the id attributes to create accessor methods.

> **NOTE**
>
> There's no reason to wait until you've written your Java code to see how xmlc works. xmlc generates the Java class that your application will eventually import and manipulate. As soon as you've got your HTML or XML file created, insert some ids and run xmlc -keep to see what it does with them.

Resuming `xmlc` and the Development Phase

We now want to take the source tree, represented as a DOM class, instantiate it as an object and massage it with dynamic content created by Java logic. When completed, we then turn it into a result tree that can be returned as an updated presentation screen.

The XMLC compilation provides us with direct access methods for getting to the areas of the DOM that we are most interested in. Keying off the `id` attributes that we assigned early, XMLC generates the following set of convenience methods for our working example:

```
public org.w3c.dom.html.HTMLImageElement getElementEventLoginLogo()
public org.w3c.dom.html.HTMLTableCellElement getElementLoginErrorMsg()
public org.w3c.dom.html.HTMLImageElement getElementLoginErrorStopSign()
public void setTextLoginErrorMsg(String text)
```

The developer now has these convenience functions at her disposal to get the job done with a minimum amount of DOM-specific traversals.

Linking the DOM class with the SFAdmin Application

You'll recall that earlier we specified an output class name of `SFAdminLoginHTML` to inherit the document template class generated by the `xmlc` command. In our presentation object, we instantiate the class using the `xmlcFactory.create()` method, illustrated in the code:

```
SFAdminLoginHTML sfaLogin;
sfaLogin =(SFAdminLoginHTML)comms.xmlcFactory.create(SFAdminLoginHTML.class);
```

We could have used Java `new`, but would have lost some of the special features of `xmlcFactory`, discussed in Chapter 7. The generated object is stored in the variable `sfaLogin`. All subsequent operations will be applied to the tree represented by the `sfaLogin` object.

EventLoginLogo

Let's leverage the first `id`, `EventLoginLogo`, to set the stage for replacing the dummy logo with the event sponsor's logo at runtime. Recall that this application is being written to represent a leaseable service from an application service provider. Therefore, the application will support many event hosts. Our application supports a dynamic approach to displaying event-specific content. The HTML `id` attribute `EventLoginLogo` will be used to identify the location of the dummy image in the tree, then swap in the appropriate logo.

With our template object loaded, the following code retrieves the image that represents the event host's logo, dimensions and all:

```
// A bit of pseudo-code to fetch an image from a fictitious
```

```
// eventHost object from the business layer.
eventImage image = fetchEventHostLogo(eventHost);
sfaLogin.getElementEventLoginLogo().setSrc(image.getName());
sfaLogin.getElementEventLoginLogo().setWidth(image.width);
sfaLogin.getElementEventLoginLogo().setHeight(image.height);
sfaLogin.getElementEventLoginLogo().setAlt("Sponsored by the wonderful folks
from ACME");
```

getElementEventLoginLogo() is the XMLC-generated method that points us to the logo node in the DOM tree represented by the sfaLogin object. setSrc(),from the standard HTMLImageElement sub-DOM package, updates the node reference containing the dummy logo with the correct logo image. For completeness, we add an ALT value with another HTMLImageElement method, setAlt(),which will be displayed if the administrator places his or her cursor over the image.

LoginErrorMsg and ErrorMsgRow

Updating the EventLoginLogo probably seemed pretty intuitive. Locate the node (element) and update its associated content. For the error message scenario, we're going to do something different. As we mentioned earlier, our strategy in using these ids is to make it so that the designer and developer can decide on one login screen that would account for successful and unsuccessful logins. There are two points to this strategy.

1. Before displaying the page to the administrator for logging in, remove the row containing the StopSign GIF and error message string. Reference ErrorMsgRow to do this.

2. If an error is encountered, reload the original template and simply update the error message string with a message specific to the error that occurred. Reference LoginErrorMsg to do this.

The following code fragment uses the id attribute ErrorMsgRow to remove the entire row containing both the error message and the stop sign image:

```
sfaLogin.getElementErrorMsgRow().removeChild();
```

If an error is detected during login, the following code fragment updates the original template with an error message specific to the error condition:

```
sfaLogin.setTextLoginErrorMsg("Wrong password. Try again");
```

This approach to how we handled the login screen might appear to be a bit confusing at first, but the fact is that there are many other ways this could have been approached. We chose this strategy to bring out the flexibility around XMLC implementation options.

Mapping the DOM to a Client Response

Lest we forget, there's still the issue of how to take the updated DOM tree and stream back an HTML document to the administrator sitting at their browser console. `writeDOM()` automatically figures out the MIME type based on the document type (`sfaLogin`):

```
comms.response.writeDOM(sfaLogin);
```

> **NOTE**
>
> JavaDoc is a life saver in the beginner's DOM programming experience. As noted earlier, Node interface methods don't always make sense to the node type that you want to apply an operation on. The Enhydra application server environment includes the entire DOM documentation via online JavaDoc and should be bookmarked for quick reference to maximize your productivity and reduce your frustration level.

Loosely Coupled Development

In object-oriented design, defining object classes that are *loosely coupled* is a good thing. It means that a class can do its job without having to know much about the implementation details of neighboring or remote classes and the way they perform their tasks. All the class needs to know is the signature (that is, methods and properties) of the class it requires the services of. In the material world, this means that changes can be made to one class very easily without creating a ripple effect of required changes elsewhere in the application environment.

XMLC supports a loosely coupled model in more ways than one. We've established that the DOM view of the markup page and the ability to dynamically load DOM templates establishes a loose coupling between the page and the Java logic that manipulates it. And, as we'll see in Chapter 7, XMLC's DOM class factory has the capability to compile and load new versions of reworked markup documents, without requiring compilation of the application's presentation logic.

The use of the DOM approach with XMLC's generation of accessor methods supports the loosely coupled relationship between the roles of designer and developer. The use of ids removes the designer from "the need to know" about how the Java logic affects his or her design. And the developer only needs to focus on manipulating the template through the DOM interface, not on having to directly touch any of the markup.

The Designer's Path with XMLC

The designer's job is both the easiest and the hardest at the same time. The designer, with storyboard in hand, needs only to apply her creative skills to produce the Web presentation screens. That sounds great, but it's also the designer's role to take the flack from the customer. And, let's face it, it's always the "look" of the application that generates the greatest amount of comment and criticism. XMLC is an unusual Java tool. It was actually designed with the designer as well as the developer in mind.

Making the Inevitable Changes

If the storyboarding of pages turns out to be relatively solid, then it is possible that the designer and developer need only meet once, at the beginning of the project just following storyboard approval, to move on with their respective development roles.

However, anyone who builds custom products for customers knows that change is inevitable. XMLC was designed to support this reality. The use of id attributes achieves a certain level of independence between the evolving environment of the interface and the underlying, server-side Java code. Again, the designer must use the ids that the designer and developer agreed to with respect to a particular markup page. If this rule is violated, the designer and developer must revise both the page and the XMLC presentation object.

To maximize the independent relationship of designer and developer, our designer's goal is to develop the mockup while requiring as little change as possible to the dynamic "topics" in the page. In other words, the designer should make changes only to the layout, and not to the content topics. This model is relatively fair in the real-world, given that customers often just want to see changes to the look and feel or placement of existing components.

XMLC's auto-compilation capability further supports designer independence. *Auto-compilation* means that a designer can make changes to a page, then by simply placing the reworked page in an agreed upon "resource" director, automatically update the application with no intervention required by the developer (except for a friendly "heads up"). Of course, this can be very dangerous if handled without testing or an agreed-upon methodology.

At this point, we will defer the discussion of the impact of loose coupling on the application's architecture itself. In Chapter 3, we'll visit this topic after we have had a chance to review other presentation technologies, particularly JavaServer Pages.

TIP

A simple trick used by Java developers is to just get a list of the ids and their associated elements in order to begin work right away. Because ids are position-independent, it doesn't matter where the designer decides to place the ids within the page.

XMLC for Servlet Programming

XMLC was originally developed for the Enhydra Application Framework (EAF) also known as the "superservlet." EAF differs from standard servlet development by viewing the entire three-tier application as one single (super)servlet. This approach makes Enhydra an excellent platform for rapid development and deployment for projects where a lightweight server is more than sufficient. We'll learn more about this in Chapter 5, "Enhydra, Java/XML Application Server," during our review of the Enhydra environment.

At the same time, XMLC is also available for the standard servlet environment, following the servlet 2.2 specification that is part of J2EE. In fact, Enhydra supports both EAF and standard servlet development and deployment. Listing 2.3 shows how the XMLC SFAdminLogin object can be served up by a standard servlet object.

LISTING 2.3   Standard Servlet Using XMLC

```
public class SFAdminLoginPresentation extends HttpServlet {
    public void doGet(HttpServletRequest request, HttpServletResponse response)
        throws ServletException, IOException
    {
        XMLCContext xmlc;
        WelcomeHTML sfaLogin;
        xmlc = XMLCContext.getContext(this);
        sfaLogin = (SFAdminLoginPresentationHTML)
        xmlc.getXMLCFactory().create(SFAdminLoginPresentationHTML.class);
        eventImage image = fetchEventHostLogo(eventHost);
        sfaLogin.getElementEventLoginLogo().setSrc(image.getName());
        sfaLogin.getElementEventLoginLogo().setWidth(image.width);
        sfaLogin.getElementEventLoginLogo().setHeight(image.height);
        sfaLogin.getElementEventLoginLogo().setAlt("Sponsored by the wonderful
➡folks from ACME");
        xmlc.writeDOM(request, response, sfaLogin);
    }
}
```

This topic will be covered at length in Chapter 10, "Servlet Web Applications."

Internationalization

As you might expect of a technology that has been nurtured and evolved by a worldwide open source project, support for internationalization is a key feature of XMLC. One of the other advantages of viewing HTML/XML pages as templates that can be loaded into your Java program is that you can localize each template as well.

The template approach is good for more than device independence. In Figure 2.8, you can see that a per-language/per-template approach gives your application the capability to load the appropriate page object depending on the requested language.

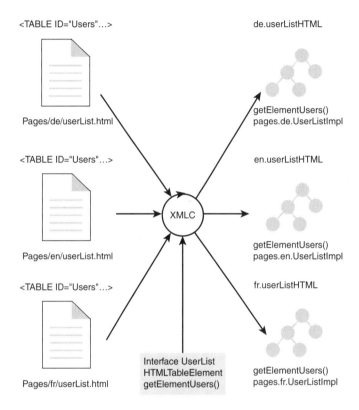

FIGURE 2.8
Using XMLC templates to achieve localizations.

Device Independence in an XML World

The discussion on internationalization maps well to the topic of device independence. Figure 2.8 could easily represent each page as a device specific page, say a browser or a mobile phone. In today's Web world, the variation in characteristics of device types is incredible. Devices including Web browsers, phones, car navigational units, and even kitchen appliances support different

- footprints
- markup languages
- levels of intelligence on the client side; for example, a J2ME phone versus a WAP WML phone

Device support can be viewed as "template" support, where your program loads the appropriate template depending on which device type was detected on the client side. This book will address different strategies for implementing this mechanism in servlet development.

XMLC also provides subclasses of the DOM interface that are specific to supported markup languages. These sub-interfaces make it possible to create type-safe template implementations. If you are addressing a new device that might not be supported by the list of XMLC sub-interfaces, you can then simply treat the markup language as a generic template. You can still use XMLC. You can still use `id` attributes to identify XML objects for easy access to specific areas of the DOM tree.

The following list provides a few examples of the subclasses of `org.w3c.dom`, and some example methods that are supported in the XMLC environment:

- `org.w3c.dom.voicexml`:

  `VoiceXMLAssignElement, VoiceXMLAudioElement, VoiceXMLBlockElement,`
  `VoiceXMLBreakElement, VoiceXMLCatchElement, VoiceXMLChoiceElement,`
  `VoiceXMLClearElement, VoiceXMLDisconnectElement, VoiceXMLDivElement,`
  `VoiceXMLDocument, VoiceXMLDtmfElement`

- `org.w3c.dom.wml` (WAP Devices):

  `WMLAccessElement, WMLAElement, WMLAnchorElement, WMLBElement, WMLBigElement,`
  `WMLBrElement, WMLCardElement, WMLDocument, WMLDoElement, WMLElement,`
  `WMLEmElement, WMLFieldsetElement, WMLGoElement, WMLHeadElement, WMLIElement,`
  `WMLImgElement, WMLInputElement, WMLMetaElement, WMLNoopElement,`
  `WMLOneventElement`

- `org.w3c.dom.xhtml`:

  `XHTMLAbbrElement, XHTMLAcronymElement, XHTMLAddressElement,`
  `XHTMLAnchorElement, XHTMLAppletElement, XHTMLAreaElement, XHTMLBaseElement,`
  `XHTMLBaseFontElement, XHTMLBdoElement, XHTMLBElement, XHTMLBigElement,`
  `XHTMLBodyElement, XHTMLBRElement, XHTMLButtonElement, XHTMLCenterElement,`
  `XHTMLCiteElement, XHTMLCodeElement, XHTMLDdElement`

XMLC Benefits

Now that we have presented our first pass at the flavor of XMLC programming leveraging the DOM specification, let's bring out some new and reviewed points about XMLC development:

- XMLC is built upon standards. In particular, XML and DOM are specifications of the World Wide Web Consortium.
- XML/HTML templates are stored as Java objects. DOM and XMLC methods are then applied to the template object.

- Flow of control is clearly separated from the page markup language and its content. In other words, WML, HTML, and XML are manipulated as resources by Java logic.

- XMLC introduces no non-standard modifications, such as new tags or magic comments where Java scriptlets are inserted in a markup page.

- XMLC leverages preprocessing of HTML/XML pages to add typed access methods to the template object

- XMLC implements compile-time checking to ensure that pages are well-formed and valid before they are executed at runtime.

- XMLC supports the capability to leave mocked-up code inside of page templates so that there is one page involved in the product lifecycle. There is no need to maintain two parallel documents: one with mocked-up data for the customer to review, and another with the embedded Java code. There is no embedded Java code with XMLC.

Summary

XMLC turns markup pages of HTML and XML into DOM templates that can then be loaded at runtime depending on the required language, type of device (for example, Nokia WAP phone versus Motorola J2ME phone), or any other criteria that is relevant to your application and the audience you support. Once loaded, your application can then manipulate the contents of the DOM tree, taking advantage of the XMLC-generated direct access convenience methods created using `id` attributes.

We have introduced the notion of what it means for a designer and Java developer to leverage XMLC to work together in a professional application development scenario. Clearly, there are guidelines for the designer to follow in order to maximize the benefit of XMLC development; however, they are very simple and do not bog down the process if significant changes are required. The inherently loose coupling made possible by the reliance of XMLC on the standard HTML/XML `id` attribute beneficially impacts both architectures and project roles. Furthermore, the flexibility of XMLC development enables many custom strategies. There is no one right path for projects to take.

For some, DOM programming can be a real challenge. Luckily, 95% of XMLC is about elements and attributes, reducing the amount of DOM knowledge required. Although new GUI libraries are emerging, such as Barracuda, understanding DOM-level XMLC programming will assure your programs of the highest adaptability in a world of significantly different client-side devices.

Presentation Technologies

IN THIS CHAPTER

In the world of Web development, there are many, many ways to skin a cat. Or, in our case, skin a Web application. Perl, Tcl, Java, Python, ASP, and many other languages and tools bring different strategies for building Web applications to the table. In the case of Java alone, there are many frameworks that leverage some level and combination of Java, XML, and/or XSLT.

Each strategy represents strengths and pitfalls that will vary depending on your background, training, development style, prejudices, preferences, and long-term goals. No one technology represents a "boil the oceans" solution. The only way to select the right tool is to survey the field and make an informed decision. This chapter will attempt to introduce the models and strategies of some of the nearest competitive technologies to Enhydra XMLC.

The presentation-building strategies we'll introduce include simple servlet programming, JavaServer Pages, XSLT, and Cocoon. In this non-exhaustive survey, the goal will be to flesh out some of the unique value in each technology for generating Web presentations. Where the opportunity presents itself, I'll throw in some comparison comments with XMLC to capitalize on a particular aspect of presentation development. In doing so, I hope to give you a better backdrop for understanding XMLC's world through reasonable comparison and contrast.

NOTE

All the technologies reviewed in this chapter are also supported in Enhydra 3 and 4, including XSLT. The lone exception is Cocoon, which can easily be integrated into the Enhydra environment.

Publishing Frameworks for Adapting to the Future

The dynamic beginnings of the Web started with Perl CGI scripting. Perl scripts heavily leveraged print statements to spit out hardcoded HTML. Servlet programming and JavaServer Pages do much the same. It wasn't until later that developers started to see the limitation to this approach. When it was time to make changes to the presentation, what was fun to build was not as fun to maintain.

Perhaps this style of generating markup language is coming to an end, as the development world moves to adopt device-independent strategies in preparation for the black box of a device-crazy world. Is your application prepared to adopt yet another set of clients enabled by yet another W3C specification? After all, HTML is no longer the only game in town.

The good news is that there are plenty of technologies and publishing frameworks (explained in detail later in this chapter) from which to select. From simple Web page presentations to generating PDF files on the fly, there's a framework for you. Even JavaServer Pages has addressed many of its criticisms with the introduction of Taglibs. And, if you are prepared to add an entirely new dimension of programming to your projects, Apache's Cocoon is a promising new technology to watch as well.

All these approaches can be categorized into one of three camps. Of course, *simple servlet* development is the least structured style of presentation development, where the developer acts as HTML designer and developer, interweaving hard-coded HTML print statements side-by-side with other Java logic.

Template engines, on the other hand, permit the document to drive. At least they appear to be a step in a document-oriented direction. JSP, WebMacro (www.webmacro.org), and Apache's Velocity are examples of template strategies that insert markup-generating logic between the lines of static markup language. Taken from Velocity's Mud Store example, the following example of Velocity Template Language (VTL) reflects the nature of template engines to insert an intermediate, embedded language directly in the markup document:

```
<HTML>
<BODY>
Hello $customer.Name!
<table>
#foreach( $mud in $mudsOnSpecial )
    #if ( $customer.hasPurchased($mud) )
        <tr>
            <td>
                $flogger.getPromo( $mud )
            </td>
        </tr>
    #end
#end
</table>
```

Finally, there's *DOM manipulation*. This is also a templating mechanism, but it introduces an object-oriented way of representing the template as a document tree that can be manipulated "from afar" by Java logic, thus avoiding the error-prone embedded logic approach, in addition to other limitations. Cocoon, XSLT, and XMLC are implementations of the DOM approach.

Presentation Versus Publishing Frameworks

Cocoon and others refer to their technology platforms as publishing frameworks. Cocoon, for example, can generate XML, XHTML, and PDF documents from source XML files. XMLC can do the same, including the generation of XML-based SVG (W3C's Scalar Vector Graphics). There is another class of technology beginning to emerge that focuses on interactive user interfaces. These *presentation frameworks* resurrect the environment of Swing and Motif, repositioning the topic as one of interacting with the user through user interface components, as opposed to altering and presenting documents.

3

PRESENTATION
TECHNOLOGIES

Jakarta's Struts and Apache's Turbine are examples of a new category of frameworks that are more presentation-oriented. Enhydra's Barracuda is an exciting new project that addresses the presentation framework category for XMLC. For the XMLC community, Barracuda is the one to watch for those seeking a componentized, event-driven GUI library strategy for generating Web presentations.

Our perspective will ask the questions, "What do all these technologies mean to real-world development by professional design and development organizations? What do they mean in terms of product lifecycle, time to market, and life in general? And, of course, how do they compare with Enhydra XMLC?" Keep the following points in mind:

- Cutting edge Web presentations require high-end designers, commonly working with a third party, highly talented "backend" Java development team. What will the chosen technologies require in terms of training, and how will these technologies impact cooperative development, particularly if the teams are separated by a significant distance?

- The customers of these presentations are more savvy now. They know there are technologies for separating logic and markup language. Add to that corporate IT's insistence that the technology you use comply with "standards."

- The framework you choose will affect your ability to react quickly to changing requirements. Cocoon is very cool, but how long will it take a newbie to ramp up? Is it good enough to know Java, or will they need to learn two languages?

Let's now spend the rest of this chapter taking a look at some pretty interesting strategies for generating Web presentations. Again, we're going to do this for the purpose of finding ways to better explain XMLC development and how it differs from other strategies. By the end of the chapter, when all the smoke has cleared, we'll be ready to spend the rest of this book in XMLC development.

Model-View-Controller

You can't pick up a book on modern Web presentation development without having to wade through a discussion about Xerox Parc's Model-View-Controller (MVC) design pattern. MVC is a useful interpretation of a strategy for presentation architectures and their place within the larger application architecture.

MVC was originally defined to reduce the programming effort required by applications that had to render the same information in more than one presentation format. MVC is also a good model for discussing the isolation of functional roles within any object-oriented application.

The impact of an MVC architecture addresses some of the more interesting real-world project and product issues:

- Long-term application maintenance
- Insulating business data generation from the display
- Defining a presentation architecture that can support a variety of client types, from browsers to phones, with minimum impact to the application's overall implementation
- Isolating functional roles

Figure 3.1 illustrates a generic MVC and the relationship of the model, view, and controller.

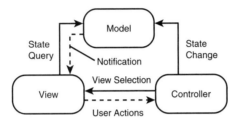

FIGURE 3.1

J2EE Blueprints' interpretation of Model-View-Control.

The *view* is responsible for interacting directly or indirectly with the client. In the case of browsers, the view is delivered as-is to the client. For J2ME, Flash 5, and other "smart clients," the view is delivered as raw data subject to display by the client display engine. The view conveys one or more events reflecting the user's intent (for example, edit, browse, delete), and any data associated with it, such as a login user name and the password, is conveyed via HTTP request. Other data that the controller will be interested in will tell you about the nature of the client—for example, whether the client is a simple Netscape browser or a small J2ME phone.

The *model* is responsible for tracking and maintaining the application's state. It generates an asynchronous event when something interesting has happened, such as a change in the state of information. The model couldn't care less about what is done with the information that it provides.

The *controller* is the traffic cop logic that enables the view to interact with the model. The controller handles the events that put the model into edit mode, browse mode, and so on.

Applying MVC to Presentation/Publishing Technologies

Sun did a great job implementing MVC with the Java Swing API and its component-style implementation. Swing is being used as a great example of an MVC implementation for the Barracuda project, which is part of the Enhydra suite of open source projects.

But this discussion is not going to shove XMLC onto the MVC model. In fact, we're going to tell you why XMLC doesn't reflect the MVC model and why that's a good thing.

The great irony is that same company that brought us Swing is touting JSP as what is really an "MVC-ish" technology. Sun has watered down the definition and intent of MVC, moving it from a component model to a more granular discussion of moving grosser objects, such as pages, around in a largely server-side application.

This makes a lot of sense as you become familiar with JSP. As we cover JSP in this chapter, it will become clear that this is a presentation strategy that was defined with the "server-side view," where Web application programmers abound. If you've been in the industry awhile, you've probably observed that there is a large difference in orientation between server-side, operating system developers, and client-side desktop application developers. Somewhere in between, there are true client-server developers.

JSP was really defined to address the large market of server-side developers who have never really been client-server developers and therefore have little client-side experience. Embedding Java in markup language is really something that speaks to the server-side developer. It's to Sun's credit that they've been able to map a client-server-like model, MVC, onto a very server-side technology, JSP.

Servlet Presentation Programming

The servlet environment is responsible for integrating all Java application servers with the outside world. It was, after all, the publishing of the servlet API that gave Web servers the capability to be extended with object-oriented Java functionality. Although many developers are just now entering the world of servlet development, a significant portion of the Java community has expanded its attention to consider what it means to support modern application servers that give the developer the capability to create multi-tier application architectures. Even the application servers themselves are moving past proprietary APIs to well-defined standards reflected in specifications, such as J2EE.

Basic servlet programming, with the introduction of standard Java print statements, can be quite effective for building CGI scripting-like presentations. Let's face it. Sometimes you just want to get a simple job done, and the point of your task is to create something quick and dirty without requiring the services of an HTML designer. Embedding HTML strings directly into a servlet is one way to quickly generate a markup presentation, especially if your goal is to build a one-off application in a hurry.

Servlet programming for creating presentations is very reminiscent of Perl CGI programming. HTML is delivered by `out.print()` and `out.println()` methods. Logic is clearly intermingled with markup language and content. In scenarios like this, there's usually no requirement for a compelling Web presentation or a long product lifecycle.

In an example of extremely tight coupling that might be cynically referred to as strangulation by the integration of markup and programming logic, Listing 3.1 shows markup language as explicitly printed from Java logic.

LISTING 3.1   Simple HTML Presentation Development with Servlet Programming

```java
// Servlet imports
import javax.servlet.ServletException;
import javax.servlet.http.HttpServlet;
import javax.servlet.http.HttpServletRequest;
import javax.servlet.http.HttpServletResponse;
// Standard imports
import java.io.*;
public class WelcomeServlet extends HttpServlet {
    public void doGet(HttpServletRequest request, HttpServletResponse response)
        throws ServletException, IOException
    {
        response.setBufferSize(8*1024);
        response.setContentType("text/html");
        PrintWriter out = response.getWriter();

        out.println("<HTML>");
        out.println("<HEAD><TITLE>Enhydra XMLC Programming</TITLE></HEAD>");
        out.println("<BODY>");
        out.println("<P>"Welcome to today's class"</P>");
        out.println("</BODY>");
        out.println("</HTML>");

        if (scheduleDay.equals("Saturday") {
                response.reset();
                out.println("<HTML>");
                out.println("<HEAD><TITLE>Servlet Programming</TITLE></HEAD>");
                out.println("<BODY>");
                out.println("<P>"No class on Saturday"</P>");
                out.println("</BODY>");
                out.println("</HTML>");
        }
    }
}
```

3

PRESENTATION TECHNOLOGIES

Servlet Web application development was greatly improved with the introduction of the servlet 2.2 specification, which introduced the notion of *response buffering*, giving the program the capability to flush the resultant markup page only when the processing of the page has been smoothly concluded.

If an error is encountered, the servlet has the option of taking a different path, such as creating a friendly HTML page indicating the nature of the error encountered. In either event, the servlet now has the capability to pre-build the page before deciding to flush it back to the client or not. Listing 3.1 also shows how the method reset() can be used to reset the output buffer.

The presentation strategy that pure servlet programming implements is relatively simple, and should be familiar to long-time Web developers who have used Perl sometime in the past.

> **NOTE**
>
> Yes, you can use Enhydra for standard servlet development. Enhydra supports servlet 2.2 (as well as JSP 1.1 development). All the examples in this chapter were tested using Enhydra.

The implications of this style of presentation development are obvious. Servlets do not benefit from the presentation-specific features of JSP and XMLC. Usually, the page is designed by the trial and error method of directly typing HTML tags, or by the manual process of transposing the output from an HTML design tool into the source file.

There really is no notion of a template mechanism in this style of presentation development. For instance, there's no dynamic loading of a template depending on what type of presentation device is detected.

This kind of presentation development should be reserved for only the simplest of dynamic Web applications. If the application starts to take on a life of its own, switch to JSP or XMLC immediately. These presentation technologies are so easy to use and are so well supported by design tools, there's little reason left for presentation development by pure servlet programming.

JavaServer Pages

JavaServer Pages (JSP) is an interesting, and sometimes controversial, strategy for developing Web presentations. Whether or not you are a fan of JSP, it is a de facto standard by virtue of its incorporation into the Java 2 Enterprise Edition (J2EE) specification, not to mention the very large audience of JSP developers that exist today. Over time, it has been extended from the simple embedding of Java statements within an HTML page to the latest version, which now includes support for custom tags, or *taglibs*.

The distinguishing attribute of JSP is flexibility. A developer has the option of inserting Java directly into HTML or leveraging taglibs to achieve better separation of markup and Java logic. For our purposes, we'll start with the standard examples of JSP, later evolving them to introduce the topic of custom tags.

The name "JavaServer Page" somewhat implies its role. Java is inserted into a markup page for the purpose of generating dynamic content. The result is a hybrid of HTML or another markup language such as XML or WML intermixed with JSP tags and/or markup comments incorporating contiguous and non-contiguous calls to the Java language.

JavaServer Pages are not processed until the first invocation of the Web application. The algorithm for serving a page from a JSP environment is thus:

1. The request for a JSP, as generated from a client, comes from the Web server.
2. If the request has been seen before, skip to Step 4. If the JSP has never been requested since the application server was booted, the JSP is translated into a Java servlet source file. This translation is also carried out by a reloading mechanism if the JSP has been re-introduced by the developer.
3. The class is compiled into a Java class.
4. The servlet class is then loaded into the Web/servlet container for execution.
5. The servlet streams HTML back to the Web server and onto the client.

All the embedded Java code is turned into one big method in the generated servlet. The URL request from a client might look something like

```
http://localhost:9000/myDemoApp/showChildren.jsp?value="Claire"
```

The servlet runner has been configured to associate the URL with the specific JSP, handing the request over to the Web container. Assuming the requested JSP page has been used before, the JSP engine then locates and loads the Java class that matches the name showChildren.class. If it's the first time the page has been requested, the JSP engine generates the class from the runtime compilation of the JSP file.

Inside the Web container, an application servlet is loaded into execution. A call is made to the init() method in order to perform last-minute setup and housekeeping chores, such as loading configuration information, before the servlet begins to accept requests. Eventually, calls to jspInit() launch the JSP-generated servlets. And for each HTTP request thereafter, the servlet creates a new thread to run service(). For JSP servlets, jspService(), a direct product of JSP page compilation, is called by service().

JSP Expressions, Declarations and Scriptlets

JSP is most well known for its capability to embed Java code directly in the markup page. For example, the following code fragment demonstrates the use of the JSP <%= and %> tags to insert a JSP expression. The first statement is actually a JSP directive, explained later. A JSP expression returns a string value to a response stream:

```
<%@ page import="java.util.Date, java.text.DateFormat" %>
<html>
<body>
<P>Welcome to JSP development
where the time is: <%= DateFormat.getTimeInstance().format((new Date()) %>
</body>
</html>
```

In expressions, you'll note the absence of the statement-ending semicolon. This is a JSP-ism that is required only of expressions, not of declarations or scriptlets. The golden rule of JSP programming is that every JSP expression must return a string or a primitive. If any part of an expression returns an object, the `toString()` method is invoked.

Listing 3.2 illustrates the use of expressions, declarations, and scriptlets. A declaration is used to define an array of daughters and their ages. A scriptlet is then used to traverse the array of daughters, generating rows of cells with each daughter's name and age. The actual name and age is embedded in the cell with two JSP expressions.

LISTING 3.2   Expression, Declaration, and Scriptlet Usage in a JSP Page

```
<%@ page contentType="text/html;charset=WINDOWS-1252"%>
<HTML>
<HEAD>
<META HTTP-EQUIV="Content-Type" CONTENT="text/html; charset=WINDOWS-1252">
<META NAME="ENHYDRA" CONTENT="ToolBox">
<TITLE>
Server side redirect
</TITLE>
</HEAD>
<BODY>
<%! String daughters[][] = {{"Amanda","16"}, { "Claire","1"},
➡{"Nicole","11"}}; %>
<h1>Dynamic demo using static data</h1>
<TABLE BORDER=1>
<%
for (int i=0; i<daughters.length;i++){
%>
        <TR><TD><%= daughters[i][0] %></TD>
        <TD><%= daughters[i][1] %></TD></TR>
<%
}
%>
</TABLE>
</BODY>
</HTML>
```

NOTE

Although modern HTML design tools can now work comfortably with hybrid pages of JSP and HTML, the issue of mocking up meaningful prototypes still requires the designer to build a parallel document for customer review. The designer must then ensure that the two documents are kept in sync. As discussed earlier, support for included mocked-up content is a distinguishing feature of XMLC.

JSP Directives

JSP directives, identified by their surrounding <%@ and %> tags, are instructions and information passed to the JSP engine during page translation and compilation. This is how JSP pages influence control over how the servlet is built. JSP directives take effect at the time that the JSP page is translated into a servlet. Therefore, once the servlet exists, the directive can no longer be changed without forcing the servlet to be rebuilt.

The page directive deals with such topics as error page re-direction, importing of Java classes, the setting of content type and the setting of the output stream buffering and the associated autoFlush flag. The following page directive indicates that the JSP will generate output for an SVG (Scalar Vector Graphic) viewer:

```
<%@ page contentType="text/svg-xml" %>
```

The include directive notifies the servlet container to perform an inline inclusion of another JSP page. This approach can be used to minimize the obvious Java presence in a page, thus reducing the potential for errors created by HTML designers:

```
<%@ include file="menuBar.jsp" %>
```

File inclusion happens only when the JSP is translated into a servlet. In the example, if any changes are made afterwards to menuBar.jsp, no effect will be seen.

The taglib directive is best known to XMLC programmers, because they tend to hear the phrase "JSP taglibs are just like XMLC." This topic deserves the attention we give it later in the chapter.

JSP, Servlets, and JSP Implicit Objects

The topic of JSP implicit objects is an interesting one. These are Servlet API methods that are made available for use by scriptlets via wrappers. Each object is listed with its associated implementation class (in parentheses):

- request (HTTPServletRequest)
- response (HTTPServletResponse)

- application (`ServletContext`)
- config (`ServletConfig`)
- page (`Object`)
- out (`JspWriter`)
- exception (`Throwable`)
- pageContext (`PageContext`)
- session (`HttpSession`)

These are described as JSP features, but all they really are access points to the underlying servlet container. There is nothing unique about JSP that makes the information they contain available only to the JSP environment.

JSP Taglibs

To say the least, standard JSP programming is a clear example of tight coupling between two very different languages and two very different development practices, namely HTML and Java. The good news is that over time, modern HTML design tools such as Macromedia's Dreamweaver and Adobe's GoLive, have learned to handle non-standard HTML tags. The result is that the design community can now interact more directly with Java developers.

Supporters of JSP maintain that JSP helps to maintain the healthy separation of HTML designer and Java roles. To make this claim, they are really relying on "best practices" to suggest a heavy reliance on encapsulating functionality inside Java Beans. Some would consider that claim to be a bit of "marketecture," but let's take a look at custom tags, the next great hope for true separation of content from logic.

Better encapsulation and separation of markup from programming logic is the goal of JSP's Custom Tag Libraries, referred to as *taglibs*. This capability has spawned many organized efforts including Apache Struts and, for better or worse, product-specific library definitions. Before we talk about the implications of this newest wrinkle in JSP development, let's review how it works.

Taglibs enable the indirect embedding of Java logic via the use of developer-defined HTML/XML tags. A custom tag may have a body or no body. Examples here leverage a possible tag library called "`showFloor`:"

```
<showFloor:displayBoothInfo customer="ACME"/>
```

or

```
<showFloor:displayBoothDescription>
This is a rectangular booth in the middle of the floor.
</showFloor:displayBoothDescription>
```

It's even permissible to use JSP expressions to complement custom tags:

```
<showFloor:login date="<%= today %>" />
```

Table 3.1 lists the types of tags and the methods as defined by the tag library interface that the developer must implement in order to process the tags. For example, if you are writing a tag that is going to process the content within the body of the tag, such as the preceding `showFloor:displayBoothDescription` tag, then you must implement `doInitBody()` and `doAfterBody()`.

TABLE 3.1 Tag Handler Types and Their Required Methods

Tag Handler Type	Methods
Simple	doStartTag, doEndTag, release
Attributes	doStartTag, doEndTag, set/getAttribute1...N
Body, No Interaction	doStartTag, doEndTag, release
Body, Interaction	doStartTag, doEndTag, release, doInitBody, doAfterBody

Creating a Custom Tag

Creating a custom tag requires the creation of a Java-based *tag handler* that implements the tag. With a tag handler in hand, you must then associate the JSP with a tag library descriptor file, cross-referencing the tag library with the custom tag. Creating custom tags requires two significant steps:

1. Create the tag handler.

   The tag handler is the actual core of your tag library. A tag handler will reference other entities, such as JavaBeans. It has full access to all the information from your page using the `pageContext` object. It is handed all the information associated with the custom tag, including attributes and body content. As processing completes, the tag handler sends the output back to your JSP page to process.

2. Create the Tag Library Descriptor (TLD).

   This is a simple XML file that references the tag handler. The servlet container is told everything it needs to associate the custom tag with the tag handler file. The markup fragment that follows shows how the JSP indicates the location of the TLD file using a tag library declaration:

   ```
   <% taglib uri="WEB-INF/showfloor.tld" prefix="showfloor">
   ```

   This defines the namespace, `showfloor`, that is associated with the tag lib dictionary, `showfloor.tld`.

Keeping true to the JSP attribute of flexibility, custom tags can be used in any manner of organization. For example, they can implement control flow behavior, such as the `jLib:for` custom tag in the example in Listing 3.3. This listing is taken from the Apache Jakarta taglibs project.

LISTING 3.3   Using Jakarta's Taglib for Iterating an Array

```
<html>
<body>
<%@taglib uri="http://jakarta.apache.org/taglibs/utility" prefix="jLib" %>
<%! String [] color = new String[5]; %>
<%! String [] values = { "yellow", "red", "green", "blue", "pink"}; %>
<jLib:for varName="i" iterations="5">
  <% color[i.intValue()] = values[i.intValue()]; %>
</jLib:for>
<ul>
<jLib:for varName="j" iterations="<%= color.length %>" begin="2" >
  <jLib:If predicate="<%= j.intValue()==3 %>">
    <li>  <%= color[j.intValue()] %>
  </jLib:If>
</jLib:for>
</ul>
</body>
</html>
```

You might ask, "Why not just write a Javabean that accomplishes similar results?" The answer is that taglibs are a mapping of Java functionality to the HTML/XML markup language format. It supports the "bindings" necessary for Java to participate in the XML structure. This becomes necessary in the absence of a leveraged DOM model.

The apparent value of taglibs is its capability to support standard, reusable functionality, as long as the industry is able to identify those standards. Sun's Java Community Process is attempting to address that goal with a committee of leading application server vendor representatives participating in JSR #52, "Standard Tag Library for JavaServer Pages."

Back-Filling in the Evolution of the Web

The Web is littered with a great many examples of back-filling to compensate for the fact that the Web infrastructure was really best-suited for "newspaper-style" publishing abilities, not highly dynamic, multiple-tier application development, deployment, and management. For example, browsers are inherently stateless. That drove the introduction of cookies as between-URL tokens that could help the CGI script "remember" what occurred before.

> JSP taglibs are a similar notion. JSP was reverse engineered with taglibs in order to support better separation of presentation and business logic. HTML as an XML language is another one. Instead of fixing the widely deployed HTML, XHTML is the safer road taken.

Cascading Stylesheets

Cascading stylesheets (CSS) are not exactly a full blown publishing framework. Instead, they are used in conjunction with XML documents to associate stylistic behavior with elements of the document. Instead of hard-coding a font element in an HTML or XHTML document, you can instead reference a stylesheet component via a style attribute that contains the font information. The following XML fragment demonstrates how you can point your XML document to a CSS:

```
<?xml version="1.0"?>
<?xml-stylesheet type="text/css" href="wml.css">
```

So, if this is all you can do with stylesheets, why am I even discussing them here? The answer is that stylesheets are an essential component in supporting even more loose coupling of content and presentation. For example, if you reserve the style issues to a CSS, the Java developer doesn't have to worry about whether a font is to be red or green. Instead, the developer focuses on, for example, setting the style reference, a *selector*, that references style information in the stylesheet.

In CSS, a selector represents one or more style declarations. For example,

```
title { font-family: "Garamond"; font-size: 18; font-color: red }
```

Without going into great detail here, CSS selectors have the capability to reach far into the hierarchical organization of an XML document to apply specific style rules, such as "second level paragraphs inside a Level 2 heading."

Let's leverage the anticipated ShowFloor application and come up with an administrative table that tracks which booths are occupied and which are not. Listing 3.4 is an HTML file that is ready for compilation by the XMLC compiler. I've used font color to indicate if the booth has been assigned or not. Red represents the fact that the booth is still available. Black represents that it has been assigned.

LISTING 3.4   Using Cascading Stylesheets to Remove Presentation Information from HTML

```
<html>
<head>
<title>Untitled Document</title>
```

Listing 3.4 Continued

```
<meta http-equiv="Content-Type" content="text/html; charset=iso-8859-1">
<style type="text/css">
<!--
.unassigned {  font-family: Arial, Helvetica, sans-serif;
➡ font-size: 12px; color: red}
.assigned {  font-family: Arial, Helvetica, sans-serif;
➡ font-size: 12px; color: black}
-->
</style>
</head>
<body bgcolor="#FFFFFF" text="#000000">
<table width="50%" border="0" cellspacing="0" cellpadding="0">
 <tr><th>Booth Status</th></tr>
 <tr>
   <td id=boothNumber class="boothStatus">123</td>
 </tr>
</table>
</body>
</html>
```

In this listing, two stylesheet directives are embedded in the HTML document, though they easily could be removed and stored in an associated file and referred to by a link, as illustrated earlier. Deeper in the HTML, I've identified the targeted table cell in which to insert dynamic content reflecting the actual booth number and its status. boothStatus will be overwritten during runtime with the stylesheet selector name assigned or unassigned.

Listing 3.5 Java Presentation Logic for Updating the HTML Page with Current Data

```
public void run(HttpPresentationComms comms)
      throws HttpPresentationException, IOException {
      BoothStatusHTML boothStatus;
      // A couple of hardcoded values to be replaced later during development.
      String boothNumber = "437";
      boolean boothOccupied = true;
      boothStatusPage =
➡(boothStatusPageHTML)comms.xmlcFactory.create(BoothStatusHTML.class);
      // Use xmlc generated method to update the cell's
➡text node with correct booth #.
      boothStatusPage.setTextBoothNumber(boothNumber);
      // Use another xmlc generated method to fetch the child node
      // inside the current element.
      HTMLTableCellElement address = boothStatusPage.getElementBoothNumber();
      if (boothOccupied == true) {
```

LISTING 3.5   Continued

```
        cell.getAttributeNode("class").setValue("assigned");
    } else {
        cell.getAttributeNode("class").setValue("unassigned");
    }
    comms.response.writeDOM(boothStatusPage);
}
```

Listing 3.5 shows a partial, hard-coded example of possible presentation logic manipulating of the HTML page. The HTML page is represented as a template object, BoothStatusHTML, as generated by the XMLC compilation. It represents the DOM class and convenience methods that might be used to manipulate the DOM. First, the example updates the cell's content with the "real" booth number, hard-coded for this example. Second, the status of the booth is determined and the class attribute is set to point to the correct CSS selector. The generated HTML will include the fragment

```
<td id=boothNumber class="assigned">437</td>
```

When leveraged with any number of presentation technologies, including XMLC and JSP, the use of CSS grants more control to the designer and removes more "decisions" and hard-coding of stylistic information, such as fonts, from the server-side code.

XSLT

It's only natural to transition from CSS to XSLT (Extensible Stylesheet Language for Transformation) programming. Although CSS helps us assign styles to style-free XML content in a passive, rule-based manner, XSLT actually rolls up its sleeves and restructures an XML document. There are three ways to render an XML/HTML document:

- Associate CSS declaratives with the markup document, and rely on the browser to process the style instructions.
- Use XSLT to transform the document using XSL, giving even greater control over how the document is to be rendered spatially and stylistically. This can occur on either the client or server.
- Focus on server-side processing, using XSLT (or Java programming) to transform the document completely to HTML, XHTML, or WML.

XSLT has gained popularity as a nifty, lightweight programming language for transforming XML into a variety of presentations. It also plays a significant role in the back end, where "data integration" is a hot topic in B2B and old-style EAI applications. XSLT transforms or *re-purposes* industry-defined XML documents generated by a remote application into a format that is familiar to the local host application.

XSLT is the most successful aspect, so far, of the XSL standard from the W3C.org folks. Much of the fanfare around XSL was the FO (Format Object), which has yet to find a large audience other than with the Cocoon community, discussed later. Instead, it's the XSLT mechanism that is ruling the day. People want what is useful and compelling. XSLT is that kind of technology. FOs in many ways are redundant with the functionality of CSS, having, in fact, incorporated some of the CSS functionality, as illustrated in Figure 3.2.

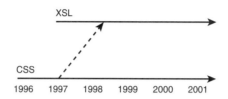

FIGURE 3.2

The somewhat redundant relationship of CSS to XSL, both products of W3C.org.

Illustrated in Figure 3.3, XSLT can be used to transform a single XML document into multiple documents that are specific to the manufacturers, for example, that use its contents to build products. For example, each shoe manufacturer might have its own way of defining a shoe-string. Adidas might deal with shoestrings described as

```
<?xml version="1.0" encoding="UTF-8"?>
<Shoestrings>
<shoestring color="white" length="12" units="inches"/>
<shoestring color="blue" length="16" units="inches"/>
<shoestring color="blue" length="12" units="inches"/>
<shoestring color="green" length="10" units="inches"/>
</Showstrings>
```

whereas Nike might recognize the shoestrings in their own format of

```
<shoe>
<string>
<color>white</color>
<length>12</length>
<units>inches</units>
</string>
</shoe>
```

XSLT can easily make the transition from one format, perhaps based on a shoe industry con-sortium's official XML standard, to one that they prefer for their legacy applications.

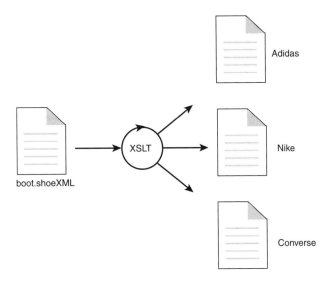

FIGURE 3.3
XSLT re-purposes a single document to suit multiple client applications.

NOTE

Speaking of shoes, Customatix.com is one of Enhydra XMLC's first and most successful commercial deployments. Built as an Enhydra-powered site for former executives from Adidas, this site uses XMLC and a single Java Applet to give the visitor the capability to select a basic shoe or boot model, then completely alter it, colors, materials, graphics and all. XMLC is also used to deliver build instructions in XML format for the manufacturing of the customer's shoes.

How XSLT Works

Representing the form of an *instruction tree*, an XSLT document drives an XSLT processor to turn an XML document (*source tree*) into another XML document (*result tree*). Collectively, XSLT instructions represent a special type of XML document as indicated by the following lines of an empty XSLT document:

```
<?xml version='1.0'?>
<xsl:stylesheet version='1.0'
  xmlns:xsl='http://www.w3.org/1999/XSL/Transform'>
...
</xsl:stylesheet>
```

Template expressions guide the transformation process using Xpath naming to identify one or more nodes in the source tree for treatment. A template rule is represented by the XML element `<template>`. The template element's attribute represents the selection process by which the template rule identifies the level of the source tree.

There are 34 elements supported by one or more attributes. Some of them are clearly program logic-like commands such as `for-each`, `if`, `otherwise`, `sort`, `when`, and `variable`. But even restricting your uses of XSLT elements to only a few, particularly `apply-templates` and `value-of`, impressive transformations are possible.

XSLT uses Xpath to reference a relative position in the source tree based on your current position. In the following example, the `template` element, using the `match` attribute, identifies all the Xpaths to every occurrence of the element `units` in our earlier shoe string example:

```
<xsl:template match="shoestring/units">
<units>cm</units>
</xsl:template>
```

In this example, the purpose of matching every `units` element is to generate a new result tree that uses centimeters instead of inches to determine the shoestring length. But of course, this is only a partial conversion, because we haven't addressed the conversion of the length itself.

Listing 3.6 simply constructs an HTML table of shoestring colors, lengths and length units. Listing 3.7 is another version of the same transformation, with the exception of the introduction of shoestring lengths as calculated in centimeters.

LISTING 3.6   Creating an HTML Table Shoestring Attribute

```
<?xml version="1.0"?>
<xsl:stylesheet xmlns:xsl="http://www.w3.org/1999/XSL/Transform" version="1.0">
<xsl:output method="html" indent="yes" />
<xsl:template match="Shoestrings">
    <table>
    <tr><th>Color</th><th>Length</th><th>Units</th></tr>
    <xsl:apply-templates />
    </table>
</xsl:template>
<xsl:template match="shoestring">
    <tr>
        <td>
        <xsl:value-of select='@color'/>
        </td>
        <td>
        <xsl:value-of select='@length'/>
        </td>
```

LISTING 3.6   Continued

```
        <td>
        <xsl:value-of select='@units'/>
        </td>
    </tr>
</xsl:template>
</xsl:stylesheet>
```

LISTING 3.7   Updating the Length Value to Reflect the Units Change

```
<xsl:template match="shoestring">
    <tr>
        <td>
        <xsl:value-of select='@color'/>
        </td>
        <td>
        <xsl:value-of select={'@length' / 2.54} />
        </td>
        <td>cm</td>
    </tr>
</xsl:template>
</xsl:stylesheet>
```

NOTE

XSLT support is incorporated into Enhydra by virtue of Apache's Xalan XSLT processor. The examples given here were tested using Lutris Enhydra 3.5.

Do the roles of XSLT and XMLC overlap? You bet. But there are differences that might drive you one way or the other. For one, XSLT performance can be a problem, particularly as you come up with more complex transformations. Secondly, if you're in a Java environment running XSLT transformations, error handling can be a bit tricky. To avoid this situation, upfront testing of anticipated transformations is a must.

XSLT Summary

On its own merits, XSLT is clear, at times elegant, and like Perl, appears cryptic enough to fascinate the nerd in all of us. XSLT processing has emerged as a serious candidate enabling XML-based presentations to adapt on-the-fly to all those mobile phones and other yet-to-be-defined devices that will eventually chat with application servers. There is little that XSLT

3

PRESENTATION
TECHNOLOGIES

cannot do to modify an XML document. XSLT contains all the capability to make conditional tests, sort data, and leverage built-in functions for conducting serious transformations.

XSLT can be used in a number of roles, including processing XML for presentations. For example, different XSLT instructions can be used, depending on the device that is being displayed to. The Enhydra application server incorporates the Apache Xalan XSLT parser, making it possible to combine Java development, XMLC programming, and XSLT transformations.

An XSLT strategy appears to be a good one if you don't mind supporting multiple languages for your application, namely Java and XSLT. If that's not an issue, be sure to consider performance characteristics of XSLT processing, because it does not benefit from fast Java compilers.

I thought that Erik Ray, author of O'Reilly's *Learning XML* said it best: "To do anything sophisticated with XSLT, we have to move around the document as nimbly as a monkey in the tree."

Cocoon

Cocoon is a very interesting project that has both a great deal of promise and a huge challenge to make itself relevant to a large audience. Unlike JSP and much like XMLC, the Apache Cocoon project views the world through the eyes of XML. But rather than rely on Java for DOM manipulation as XMLC does, Cocoon goes the route of emergent technologies XSLT and formatting objects. At the same time, XSP does indeed take on JSP-like features when embedded Java manipulation is an option.

How wedded to XML is Cocoon? So much so that the Cocoon project page points out that Cocoon is not appropriate for generating standard HTML output, because HTML is inherently not well-formed XML. Obviously, XHTML support in future browsers will be important for the successful adoption of Cocoon.

The Cocoon framework supports three steps of content and presentation delivery:

1. *XML creation* addresses the role of the content owners. These are the experts in their field; for example, fly fishermen writing about fly fishing.
2. *XML processing* takes place. This is where programming logic is applied to the content, such as fetching descriptions and prices for very expensive fishing lures.
3. *XSL rendering* delivers the end result to the client, using an XSL stylesheet to transform the presentation into HTML, WML, or other popular formats.

XSP for Dynamic Content Creation

At first glance, XSP (eXtensible Server Pages) appears similar to JSP. Its role is to complement the static content contained in XML documents with dynamic content as fetched, for example, from a database or a live news feed. However, as you'll soon see, XSP is a more flexible, Java-independent language that melds more gently with its host markup language.

If you think XSP markup looks suspiciously like a custom tag from a JSP tag library, you'd be right. Cocoon has its own implementation of tag libraries. This is how the Cocoon project can maintain that it separates logic for the creation of dynamic content from markup, thus respecting the needs for the roles of designers and developers. Tag libraries remove the complete reliance on procedure-based XSP code, shown in this example:

```
<table>
<xsp:logic>
for (int i=0; i &lt; items.length; i++) {
<tr>
<td>
<xsp:content>
<xsp:expr>items[i].getName()</xsp:expr>
</xsp:content>
</td>
</tr>
}
</xsp:logic>
</table>
```

In this example, XSP cannot escape the fact that XML parsers treat < and & characters uniquely, therefore leading to the requirement of using &lt in the for loop. Also, expressions cannot be imbedded directly inside areas of XSP Java logic without being encapsulated with <xsl:content> tags. XSP makes coding a bit simpler than JSP, such as automatically casting all Java types to strings.

Even with XSP, you can see how heavily Cocoon relies on XSL. XSP uses XSLT stylesheets for source code generation. Each tag maps to an XSLT template. The template generates the supporting program logic to implement the tag's stated purpose. It is this underlying mechanism that makes just about any scripting language besides Java a candidate for supporting Cocoon XSP development.

Cocoon Trade-Offs

Cocoon is an excellent option for a publishing house, such as a journal or newspaper Web site, where the functionality of the site is defined in a structured, consistent way. Users expect these presentations to be consistently displayed from issue to issue.

The flipside is that Cocoon is a rather large, complex system. As the Apache Cocoon site acknowledges, its processing complexity is not well-suited for real-time operation on the server. In order to overcome performance challenges, a great deal of effort is going into compiler strategies and caching techniques.

The issue for Cocoon is that, like XMLC, it is butting heads with JSP. XSP versus JSP development is probably perceived as more contentious an issue as compared to these technologies and XMLC, which avoids the embedding of Java in HTML or XML. Cocoon must also help XSL's formatting objects emerge as a standard. To date, whereas XSLT is enjoying a great deal of popularity, FOs have only seen acceptance within the Cocoon project.

If the presentation results require a lot of on-the-fly processing, XMLC is the better option, always showing the users the same view from their requests.

> **NOTE**
>
> So how was it that Lutris Consulting gained firsthand experience with JSP even before it came up with XMLC? Well, it wasn't JSP, it was JDDI, an invention of Lutris' before JSP hit the market. It did some things very similar to JSP, including embedding Java inside HTML pages and supporting a macro language for conditional selection of Java code. What became of JDDI? Well, it's still in Enhydra 3.

Final Comparative Discussion

Short of the use of simple `id` attributes and span tags for substring manipulation, XMLC is a presentation technology that is completely transparent to anybody viewing a markup page about to be processed in the XMLC environment. It achieves this by turning the page into a DOM structure, then manipulating the structure. It is, however, more than direct DOM manipulation. As a compiler, XMLC offers significant capabilities and conveniences that greatly simplify the tasks of the designer, the Java developer, and the application architect. A couple of features have been reviewed in our previous two chapters, with many more to be discussed in Chapter 6, "XMLC Basics."

Clearly, standard servlet programming, JavaServer Pages programming, XSLT programming, and Cocoon/XSP programming have something for just about everybody. We now have sufficient context with respect to these technologies to makes some observations about XMLC. In this section we're going to use the context of this chapter to make some assertions about XMLC programming, and bring to light advantages of XMLC that are made more clear when described relative to JSP and XSLT.

XMLC Views Markup Pages as Template Object Representations

By accessing markup through the DOM API, XMLC views all markup as object-oriented resources that can be manipulated with a minimum of markup idiosyncrasies. The DOM library insulates the Java logic from the need to understand markup language conversion issues, such as how to replace ampersand characters with the appropriate entity references. Letting the DOM represent the page, there's no JSP or XSP embedded logic that looks like

```
if (( request!= null &amp;&amp; (e.hasMoreElements())))...
```

Finally, DOM development guarantees that well-formed XML documents are generated from the object representation.

XMLC Sticks with One Programming Language: Java

Cocoon and XSLT incorporate yet another language (or two) for project and product managers, and sometimes their customers, to consider. Debugging becomes complex and integration issues more difficult. With XMLC, you are operating with only one language, Java. Yes, there are the inevitable JavaScript issues for supporting client-side browser programming, but that's the case for all the presentation technologies discussed in this chapter. With XMLC, there is no new category of "page programmer," an intermediate between Java developer and the page designer.

Figure 3.4 attempts to show by relative position on a triangulation of Java, DOM, and XSL programming where the presentation technologies we've discussed might lie. Clearly, JSP is the most Java-centric. But, without DOM support, JSP programming has had to engineer an alternative, non-standard strategy for generating HTML/XML content.

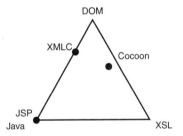

FIGURE 3.4
Relative use of Java and Scripting/XSLT templating.

XMLC Enables Type-Safe DOM Programming

Markup language-specific DOM sub-interfaces are incorporated with the XMLC environment. These include HTML, WML, VoiceXML, and cHTML. Unlike JSP, which relies entirely on the developer to construct the resultant markup page, markup language-specific libraries increase type-safe programming. XMLC has an escape hatch for those who aren't interested in leveraging markup-specific libraries. You always have the option to do standard DOM programming and still take advantage of the use of id attributes. This means that you can use XMLC for any type of markup language as long as it is based in XML.

XMLC Is a True Template Presentation Technology

With thoughtful designs on how to detect client types or preferred languages, XMLC supports the capability for Java servlets to load the appropriate DOM representation of a markup page. This template encapsulates the markup page, reducing the amount of Java logic required to generate the presentation page. Unlike JSPs, these templates never contain Java code.

As a template resource and lacking any embedded logic, the page has no impact on the flow of logic. It also eliminates the need for special tag elements representing the namespace for Java or XSLT code.

XMLC Greatly Simplifies DOM Programming

The use of developer/designer-chosen id attributes greatly simplifies the manipulation of DOM elements. XMLC uses the id values to auto-generate Java methods that the developer has the option of using. These methods bypass much of the DOM intrigue of traversing, removing, appending, and updating tree nodes and text elements.

XMLC Is Designer-Friendly

With JSP, a designer must maintain two documents: One with scriptlets embedded that will, eventually, populate a table with dynamically-gathered row data; and another that is the mock-up page, which shows what the page might look like when the application is operational.

With XMLC, the document used by the application and as the mocked-up page are one in the same. The XMLC compiler incorporates options that make it easy to remove mocked-up data during compilation.

And, of course, the designer never sees a lick of code. Other than accidentally changing an id attribute value, there's no chance to accidentally break the application. Even in the case of missing id attributes or renamed id values, the XMLC compiler includes options for validating ids.

XMLC Eliminates the Need to Introduce New Tags (Elements)

Again, XMLC keys off of id attributes. There is no need for taglibs. There is no need for scriptlets. The implication is that XMLC will work with any standard HTML or XML browser without having any required update to the list of supported elements.

XMLC Is a True Loosely Coupled, Object-Oriented Presentation Strategy

XMLC was designed to keep Web applications truly object-oriented. This was in reaction to the observation that JSP really let HTML do the steering, as it were. The absence of Java logic embedded in a markup page makes XMLC as loosely coupled as you can get when gluing two very differently purposed languages together: markup and Java. XMLC's avoidance of embedding logic in the markup makes XMLC programming more polymorphic. Any action can connect any page. There is no pre-knowledge of page and action, which is typically the case with JSP pages. Instead of the page calling code, the code calls the pages into memory.

With XMLC, you can string actions together to form a business process. Because XMLC doesn't depend on a series of visual clues, you can string them together differently on, for example, a per-user basis. An example might be the behavior defined for an average user as opposed to an administrator. Recognizing an administrator, the logic determines that another page requiring another type of login is to be loaded and displayed.

The XMLC Mechanism Is the Same for Everybody

Unlike JSP taglibs and XSP taglibs, XMLC introduces a standard relationship between the markup page and how it references Java logic "underneath." Attributes, not elements/tags, are defined by the programmer. There is no option for inserting Java logic directly in the markup page. Until there is a unified standard JSP or XSP custom tag library, the approaches taken by different parties to define custom tag interfaces will vary from organization to organization and product to product.

XMLC Detects Errors Early

XMLC identifies page creation errors during compile-time. Unlike JSP, XMLC detects malformed markup pages during the development phase. It is impossible to generate a malformed markup page when leveraging the DOM standard. XMLC development is much less error prone than JSP development. There is less opportunity for making errors as compared to JSP development, where the developer performs a specialized form of Java development—connecting JSP declarations, scriptlets, and expressions. And there is a much higher likelihood of understanding the error, because it is expressed in the context of standard Java, not JSP scriptlet-isms.

XMLC Is Built Heavily on Standards

Finally, although it is not a defined technology under J2EE, in many ways XMLC is actually more "standard" than JSP. XMLC leverages the XML and DOM standards, both defined by the World Wide Web Consortium. XMLC is also an open source technology, which for many, offsets its definition outside the J2EE specification.

Taglibs Do Not Make JSP Like XMLC

The most common response an XMLC developer hears in a discussion about JSP versus XMLC is "JSP can do that with taglibs." The reality lies somewhere between an answer of

"Somewhat yes, and mostly no." For example, a designer-friendly JSP developer could create a custom tag that enables mocked-up data to be included in the body of the element, like XMLC does natively. But even this feature will be non-standard, as different implementers of different tag libraries do it differently.

The leveraging of HTML/XML elements to identify and install a new custom tag again forces a tight coupling between markup and logic. Not even XSLT defines new elements. Its elements are standard, thus guaranteeing a common language from implementation to implementation.

My observation is simply this: If you want extreme flexibility of strategies that you use to link markup presentation and logic, JSP is absolutely your choice. If you want to standardize on one strategy for achieving separation of presentation and logic, and you want it to be the same approach used by anybody else using that same technology, then XMLC is the route to take.

Templates, MVC, and XMLC

Let's be clear about one thing. XMLC was designed to deliver a pure templating strategy for Web presentations, not an interpretation of the MVC model. Heavily leveraging the Document Object Model standard and the intelligent use of a compiler-based strategy to simplify DOM programming, XMLC achieves complete isolation of Java logic from the markup language. That is what XMLC brings to the table.

This separation makes XMLC a true template mechanism. Illustrated in Figure 3.5, there is no logic in the template, and therefore the template becomes highly portable and can be manipulated by any number of Java objects that load it into memory. In XMLC, development the "controller" is the servlet that identifies the nature and requirements of the client device:

- A Flash client that requires an XML stream
- An HTML browser user that indicates she expects a page in German
- An i-mode phone user with some graphics capability

Often in Enhydra programming methodology, presentation objects, sometimes sub-classed from an abstract "Base Presentation Object," process a request and load, manipulate, and return the DOM template that best suits the client and the nature of the request (for example, edit or browse).

XMLC has become an excellent strategy in a multi-device world. An application might support taxi drivers in the field as well as dispatchers back in the office. The taxi drivers use WAP phones, the dispatchers do not. Both, however, are required to log in.

Both users, the taxi drivers and dispatchers, access the application using the same URL. Checking the header information of the HTTP request, the servlet determines if the device is specific to WML or HTML. Depending on which is detected, the appropriate login screen is displayed. For the taxi driver, the screen is very simple in order to fit onto the small handset. For the dispatcher, it is larger, taking advantage of a standard browser's real estate to, perhaps, list the date and company banner.

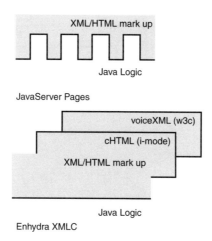

FIGURE 3.5

Relationship of markup language and XMLC/JSP from the perspective of the HTML/XML designer.

MVC for XMLC?

XMLC will eventually provide support for the MVC model. But it will do so by supporting a new architecture, most likely in the form of colleague project Barracuda, which is being designed from the ground up to support XMLC, and potentially JSP, with a true component-based MVC model.

Summary

We've had some fun categorizing and performing high-level overviews of interesting light-weight and heavyweight publishing frameworks, attempting to draw out some observations that might give us some perspective on how presentation strategies can differ. Clearly, there is a distinction between the DOM-oriented technologies and the rest.

When looking at Cocoon and XMLC, they appear to be more closely related than XMLC and JSP. JSP Taglibs certainly represent a lot of promise (and industry activity) for delivering components of template engine functionality, but it appears likely to become an API library that is growing out of control. Cocoon is clearly the most comprehensive framework, addressing everything from publishing just about anything written in XML, to setting the stage for supporting languages other than JSP. But it is huge in its scope and capabilities, representing a daunting learning curve for most average-sized Web application projects.

I've provided many of the reasons why XMLC is different and wonderful. Perhaps another way of looking at it is that XMLC falls somewhere in the middle of a pure Java method to spit out content and a pure XML/XSLT strategy that strives to keep everything neutral with regard to system programming language, like Cocoon. XMLC is, perhaps, the best of both worlds, and definitely suited for a sizeable audience reflecting its current popularity.

CHAPTER

4

In the interest of getting you started with real-world Enhydra development as quickly and effectively as possible, we're going to spend the major portion of this book defining and constructing a real-world Web application. I will define and refine a modest description of a ShowFloor application that can be used by a company hosting an event to assign vendors to booths, schedule in-booth presentations, and provide kiosk displays to visitors seeking the booth location of a specific vendor.

The development of ShowFloor will be used to illustrate the use of the Enhydra XML Compiler (XMLC) for solving different presentation challenges, including supporting HTML form elements and a wide variety of modern client devices. We will attempt to break out of the mold of straightforward HTML programming and look at what it means to design an application that leverages the best of new display devices and the technologies behind them.

This chapter is focused largely on those of you who are new to Java and perhaps object-oriented development. If you're already a Java and UML expert, you might want to focus on those sections addressing the requirements of the ShowFloor application.

To structure this discussion a bit, I'm going to use a little UML in this chapter, focusing on use cases to draw out requirements. My hope is to inspire those of you who are new to Java development to take a deeper look into UML and see if it can help you become a more organized, effective programmer. I want to stress "a little UML" to make it clear that this chapter isn't intended to present a comprehensive discussion of all UML modeling strategies and terminology. The idea is to raise your curiosity to take advantage of the extensive catalog of UML books that are dominating the bookshelves of your local bookstore.

> **NOTE**
>
> *Universal Modeling Language (UML)* is a specification from the *Object Management Group (OMG)*, home of the CORBA architecture. If you are familiar with CORBA, much of its value lies in its language-independent design. It should then be of no surprise that UML is likewise language independent and will serve you no matter what your preferred language.

Traditionally, modeling languages have reflected something that only university professors might take seriously. That's not the case with UML modeling today. UML can define a software system and scope a project in a manner that just makes practical, real-world sense.

As you read this chapter, you might start wondering whether this is a book on programming. I'll discuss off-programming topics such as branding, the ASP model, business paradigms, and long lifecycle application platforms. The reason for stretching the discussion a bit is to acknowledge the new-world developer, brought on largely by the Web. The most successful programmers are often the ones who have internalized business issues. The Internet, open source, and start-up fever have altered the way developers used to operate, often coding applications with limited awareness of what becomes of their software. Modern developers are now more aware of the issues, business and otherwise, that drive application discovery, design, deployment, and adaptation.

This is where UML and leveraging the UML use case meta-model comes into place. In this chapter, you'll play the role of developer, customer, architect, and domain expert. UML will give us the structure to systematically flesh out what we're about to build.

You might also be asking yourself why I would devote an entire chapter to defining a demonstration application when all you want to learn about is how to use XMLC to add rows to an HTML table template. First of all, I didn't set out to write a plain vanilla how-to book. Second, thanks to its DOM-based approach for expressing dynamic content in a markup language, XMLC supports a generic foundation for supporting devices of all types. The goal of this chapter is to bring out a discussion of what it means to support different devices from the same application. Finally, XMLC is a low-level form of presentation development. It offers a degree of flexibility that can sometimes get you in trouble. It probably isn't a bad idea to start bringing out some best practices when it comes to explaining and demonstrating XMLC programming.

Building a Device-Independent Application

Let's drill down into some of the options our ShowFloor application can take advantage of in today's world of mobile phones, PDAs, voice activated devices, and, of course, computers with Web browsers. Having concluded the device survey, we will next attack the requirements of the ShowFloor application.

The goal with this application is to achieve the following:

1. Demonstrate how to build device-aware presentation elements of Web-based forms with XMLC.
2. Show how to craft different tasks for appropriate devices, such as cell phones or Flash-enabled HTML browsers.
3. Illustrate the use of Enhydra for building a three-tier Web application.
4. Convey why this application can easily be reworked for future capabilities, including supporting new devices.

To complement your focus on the Enhydra environment for implementing the application, I will spend some time in the remainder of the book illustrating how to accomplish these same implementation tasks using standard servlet 2.2 programming.

> **NOTE**
>
> Enhydra supports two styles of servlet application development. First, there is Enhydra's EAF environment for superservlet development, representing applications as a single servlet. Then there is the standard J2SE servlet Web container, implemented from Apache's Tomcat project. Which route you ultimately choose won't affect the path you take with XMLC presentation development.

I've chosen to implement an application that is relevant to many who attend trade shows, such as JavaOne or LinuxWorld. In fact, my goal is to generalize this application so that it will even be useful for the Automated Loom Manufacturers Trade Show.

I picked this application because it is a natural for bringing out a multi-device strategy that can be addressed by XMLC's capability to support a wide range of devices, such as those shown in Figure 4.1, and the markup languages that support them. Before I describe the application, let's review some fundamental topics that require discussion to set the stage.

Figure 4.1
The possibilities of devices.

Consider the Possibilities

Let's examine some of the more intriguing features of client side devices that our application design may take into consideration. Each device or device technology offers something that might be perceived as enhanced value to the ShowFloor customer. Here is a quick overview of the features you can look forward to tackling with Enhydra and Enhydra XMLC:

- A Flash 5 client for rendering the layout of a ShowFloor map view of vendor booths and aisles to see the path to get to a specific booth
- A cell phone user interface for looking up a vendor's booth number

- A non-Web phone that rings 10 minutes before vendor presentation is about to start, using a soothing voice to tell you to get on your way

- Detecting which device is accessing the application and displaying only those capabilities that make sense to the particular device

- An `Admin` interface that adapts its look and feel to reflect the event's host

As client-side devices of all types join the Web, our options for delivering specialized services and functionality increase on almost a monthly, per device basis. By coming up with a plausible strategy for building a service, give some thought to how the ShowFloor application might take advantage of the unique attributes of traditional and emerging devices.

Compelling, Meaningful Roles for the Right Device

Today's phones are characterized by their mobility, screen size, voice orientation, and small bandwidth for processing a modest amount of data. With the accent on reasonable expectations, phones give the user the ability to indicate simple things such as yes or no, enter a few numbers, or acknowledge what's displayed on the screen. You wouldn't use your Nokia 7110 for intensive data entry. But perhaps you want the ShowFloor application to inform a show attendee when a booth presentation is about to begin. Or do a quick look up of a vendor's booth location. And because VoiceXML is so easy to access these days with the emergence of Voice portals, such as Voxeo and BeVocal, why not autogenerate calls announcing that a booth show is about to start?

Voice Portals

How do you get from a phone to your application when "voice" is the application presentation? And how do you do it without buying expensive voice recognition hardware? Voice portals such as Voxeo (`www.voxeo.com`) don't care if you're calling from a high-end Nokia cell phone, a phone booth, or a low tech rotary phone at Aunt Carolyn's house. They provide the connection technology that links voice recognition with a URL that is assigned to your application.

Unless you want to build the entire infrastructure yourself, voice portal services provide the link between John Doe on the phone and an application using the VoiceXML standard. Popularized by the TellMe service (`www.tellme.com`), voice portals are an excellent example of how to get a lot out of existing, old world technology.

Smart Devices

J2ME and Flash turn mobile devices such as phones and PDAs into smart clients that go beyond browser-based mobile computing. They are able to keep persistent information between intermittent connections with backend application servers. They also make it easier for designers to define a user interface that can adapt to its local client display. It's still early in their development and introduction; however, smart devices appear to be gaining a foothold in the market for enhanced gaming as well as the enterprise market, where employees in the field access and download back-office data such as customer information or part numbers.

Phone Browser Devices

Browsers are still key to connecting PC, Mac ,and Linux users to the Internet. Their role has also been extended to WAP and i-mode phones that, depending on the underlying carrier service, support the XML languages of WML, XHTML, and compact HTML. Browsers on phones apply to people on the move who don't have a lot of time to do typing, such as bike messengers or taxi drivers. The use of browsers simply relates to the size of the screen and the size of the keyboard.

Although support for XHTML, a true XML language, is on the way, HTML is still the dominant browser language. PC style browsers are still ideal when it comes to forms-based data entry such as an administrator might use.

XML, the Common Device Language

A common thread runs through all the languages supported by these devices: It's XML. Traditionally, in a rapidly developing market, we're saddled with lots of incompatible protocols and languages, waiting to see which one becomes the de facto standard, reminiscent of the 1980's "VHS versus Beta" battle to be the standard format for the emerging VCR market.

Perhaps by riding the coat tails of the success of the Internet as the new backbone of network computing, XML has defined a new baseline for expressing and carrying information. With HTML as a special case, it would be suicide for any vendor to propose or leverage a language based on anything else.

Even Flash Speaks XML

Just when you thought Flash had settled into its very successful niche as a compelling client technology for animations and graphics, Macromedia came up with one leap better. In 2000, Macromedia rolled out Flash 5 with an embedded XML parser for handling asynchronous XML communications. The simple, but powerful result is that Flash 5 has emerged a powerful client-side device that might give WAP and i-mode devices a run for their money.

This is where the relevancy of the XMLC architecture enters. By viewing the world as speaking the common language of XML, XMLC is prepared for just about any new language that leverages XML.

The ShowFloor Application

My fictitious ASP, Otter Productions, is in the business of providing convention show services for large events. One of the many services Otter offers is called ShowFloor. The ShowFloor service is targeted at corporations that want to host a show or conference. The ShowFloor services give these customers the ability to administer the creation, assignment, and presentation of the vendor booths that occupy the show floor without having to build their own infrastructure for doing so.

The ShowFloor service will provide many features for the perspectives of

- The event host
- The vendor participating in the event
- The visitor attending the event

Some of the features will include

- Creating a layout of show-floor booths
- Assigning a vendor to one or more booths
- Displaying the show-floor layout in a kiosk
- Notifying visitors of a pending in-booth presentation

From the perspective of Otter Productions, the paying customer is an Intel, an Apple, or a Martha Stewart Enterprise. The customer will want to *brand* the ShowFloor application and all of its interfaces. In other words, the ShowFloor service will make it appear as though the application was created solely for Intel, Apple, or Martha Stewart. Giving the ASP the capability to support rebranding of the ShowFloor application without requiring massive rework will be one of the challenges to our application design.

Brand

A brand is typically a visual clue that tells you you're approaching a Coke bottle long before you can actually read the words. If somebody mentions the word *Coke*, you know it's a soft drink. That's a very important thing to keep, preserve, and perpetuate for any business. The notion of *brand* is somewhere in the same category of *goodwill*. It's almost a gut-level experience that a company is looking to establish with the public. That's *brand recognition*. Companies put a lot of money into advertising campaigns such as "Intel Inside," in order to create brand and brand awareness. After awhile, the idea is that, in the view of the consumer, the brand will precede what the company actually does. This is why supporting the capability to incorporate the customer's brand will be important to the ShowFloor application.

Finally, Otter Productions can also make interesting marketing information available to subscribing vendors and event hosts by tracking some of the activities of the visitors. Statistics can include which vendor's booth was sought out the most, or information about the visitors themselves. Otter can even generate information about which devices were the most commonly used by show participants.

> **NOTE**
>
> The idea behind ShowFloor business mode is nothing new. Internet Exposure (www.iexposure.com) has implemented a similar application using Enhydra for its customer Cygnus Expositions. It clearly goes well beyond what we're building in this book, hosting sites such as Strictly eBusiness (www.strictlyebusiness) and homeandgarden.com.

As with any thoroughly written product requirements document, I'll make it clear what we won't address with ShowFloor. We're not going to address the conference sessions portion of the show, such as scheduling talks or BOF sessions. We're also not going to find visitors a hotel. All of this is left as an exercise for you.

Supporting an ASP Business Model

Even those of us who reside in open source land still have to find a way to collect a paycheck to pay for DSL or that Linux server hosting my family Web site in the garage. That paycheck comes from somebody turning a business model into a steady flow of revenue that keeps the lights turned on. If you think Apache runs on goodwill, well, in a way it does. But that goodwill comes largely from IBM, which has a vested interest in the success of Apache, and therefore justifies the donation of person power to help lead the Apache.org effort. IBM and other large corporations' interest in Apache benefits us all.

A fundamental consideration when beginning the design of a business application is to take into full account the business model behind the application. Its design and functionality must set a path for a lifetime of evolution through extensions, maintenance, and redesign. Its lifecycle must require a quantifiable and justifiable investment of time and money in order to serve as a foundation for an evolving business model. In most cases, the goal is to set the stage for an application that can evolve in functionality without major rework.

The business model behind the ShowFloor application incorporates an ASP strategy whereby we lease our application to typically large customers, such as Intel, Sun, Martha Stewart, and the Society of Herpetology. *Application Server Provider* (ASP) is a relatively new business notion that has been made popular by the emergence of the Web. It makes sense to lease remotely hosted applications that address the intermittent needs of companies that have no desire to support a full-time infrastructure with dedicated staff.

There are many examples of other types of ASP business models. For instance, a large bank might support an ASP line-of-business by making a suite of online financial services available for lease by smaller member institutions. A feature of the application might be that it can be *re-branded* by the company subscribing to the ASP service. To the end user, it appears to us that we're using, for example, the Santa Cruz Credit Union Financial Planner Web service, even though it's actually hosted by an ASP back in Omaha, Nebraska.

Essential UML

As they say in UML land, let's keep the ceremony to a minimum, and get to the problem at hand. In the world of OO design and development, it's all about up front thinking and setting the stage for iteration, prototyping, and refinement. Object-oriented programming existed a long time before it finally took hold in the business world. Its adoption was slowed by the reluctance of many software project managers who were reticent to embrace a process that delayed actual coding for so long. But the payoff for a well thought-out object-oriented architecture has finally begun to sell itself. For many, Java and its strong ties to the Internet finally delivered OOP to the enterprise.

UML is a modeling language. It defines meta-models, such as use cases, class diagrams, and sequence diagrams to describe larger model elements that represent your software application, the components it contains, and how they interact internally and externally with the actors of the system (for example, administrators, vendors).

Although UML is technically a modeling language that can be applied to any development process, there is a general description of the process influenced by UML as you read the many UML books from Fowler and friends.

The typical UML-leveraged project describes the development cycle as an iterative process of continuous refinement, leading the eventual creation of a software product.

The Cycle Begins

Inception, elaboration, construction, and transition are the phases of the development process. *Inception* deals with bootstrapping the project by focusing on the user's requirements, bank roll, and goals. What is the big picture and the end game? Who's the customer's customer? Is this a one off, feasibility application, or one that sets the stage for the long haul?

Elaboration focuses on organizing the observations and early requirements into meta-models of charts and diagrams of how, for instance, classes send messages to other classes and the sequence they observe. During elaboration, the goal is to identify all the potential use cases that exist. Apply class and sequence diagrams. Then rework use cases as needed. Start proto-typing as soon as you can, and start to fill out the description of the model.

After you've done that, you're on your way to quantifying the scope of the project. You now have enough detail to analyze risk and present tradeoffs to the customer. And, of course, go back to your customer, Otter Productions, to validate that the scope and subsequent project management appraisal of implementing to the scope are acceptable.

During *construction*, you're generating code and discovering that—through application and the unit testing of individual components— for example, more thought needs to be put into the use cases. Construction involves iteration, constantly refining your working model through proto-typing and component development leading to full integration and system test.

Finally, *transition* addresses beta testing and performance tuning because your application has thickened into a feature-complete status.

Getting Started with Use Cases

We're out to define the *domain model* that describes all meaningful aspects of the ShowFloor application. The domain model accounts for

- the world of the convention show floor;
- the ASP model, including billing and branding, as applied to the show-floor industry;
- the participants in the show floor world, namely visitors, vendors in booths;
- and the Otter Productions customers who host these events.

These are the elements of the ShowFloor domain model that we can begin to flesh out with an initial list scrawled on a white board. The *use case diagram* is a UML meta-model that helps us work with the domain expert, namely, Otter Productions, as well as our design and develop-ment team members, to capture elements of the domain model (see Figure 4.2). And don't for-get the folks who will eventually have to deploy the application, especially one that is supposed to simultaneously support multiple event hosts without fail.

Use cases capture the identified roles (*actors*) and how they interact with the system. A use case consists of one or more scenarios to bring out the most useful workflow, including the branches that occur when, for example, pilot error occurs. Use cases are a collection of scenar-ios that address a particular task, such as add a vendor to the event. Honesty is the best policy when describing your software in the real world. I love starting a project with use cases exer-cises. It immediately raises more questions with intriguing implications for the customer to consider.

UML defines actors as parties (that is, organizations and individuals), places, or things that carry out use cases. Actors can be other systems, such as an accounting system (for billing our event hosts, or reservation systems for setting up event visitors in hotels). Also, think about external events that trigger interactions between actors and the system. For example, what should happen the week before an event? The day before an event? Identifying actors helps to start our task of fleshing out a first pass at some use cases.

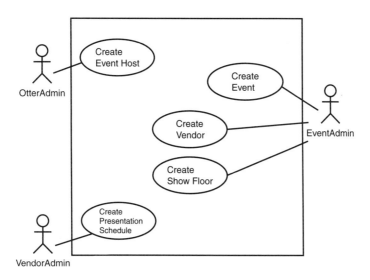

FIGURE 4.2
Actors of the administration system.

> **NOTE**
>
> Sitting in a room with key participants (that is, stakeholders and domain experts) to build use cases with multiple scenarios can be a lot of fun. It's kind of like charades. But, if you're itchy to type like I am, moving quickly to prototyping can help flesh out some scenarios that didn't appear on the white board. It's the prototyping that sets the iterative process into motion.

All this activity is what Fowler describes as the elaboration phase. It's kind of like growing something from a few seeds, making sure that they reflect the business model.

Modeling the ShowFloor Application

Let's transition from talking about everything we could do to what we want to do. Picture a bunch of folks in a room, simply walking through elements of the proposed ShowFloor application. We'll organize our thoughts, identifying likely candidates for the domain's actors, their activities and attributes. From this collection of notes, we can begin the definition of use cases. I've italicized actors and objects where they are first identified:

Event—The event has a date or range of dates, a city location, a venue (for example, San Francisco's Moscone Center or New York's Jacob Javitts Convention Center) and an *EventHost*. The Event has categories of *Vendors*, such as consultants, hardware, groomers, and dog walker services. The event is initialized by *OtterAdmin*.

EventHost—The EventHost is the Otter Production's primary customer. As a satisfied customer, the EventHost might host more than one event, such as JavaKennel in New York and JavaKennel in London, using the same ShowFloor application. Otter Productions supports an OtterAdmin to provide the highest level of administration over Event, EventHost and *EventHostAdmin*, such as creating the new account and associated event or events. The EventHostAdmin adds details about the Event, including travel directions, vendors and booth assignments.

Vendor—A Vendor is a company that has secured one or more booths at an event. Each Vendor has one or more products or services to sell. A Vendor might optionally schedule in-booth presentations throughout the day or days of the event. A Vendor can fall into different *categories* that are defined by the EventHost. Categories will vary from show to show, depending on the industry. Categories will give the show *Visitor* the ability to say, "Show me all the application server vendors here." Vendors are administered by the EventHostAdmin.

Sponsor—Just about every event features something like a gold, silver, or bronze Sponsor. These are Vendors who have paid an EventHost-determined sum of money in order to help sponsor the event and get preferred treatment as a result—perhaps in terms of booth real estate, prominent positioning, or prominent banners hung from the ceiling. Sponsors and Sponsor categories are created by EventHostAdmin.

Visitor—You and I are the Visitors who go to the event and want to look up booth information using our browser from work, or from the Flash-powered kiosk while we're at the show. A Visitor might already be in the ShowFloor visitor database, having registered for another show that was also hosted by a customer of Otter Productions. This provides an excellent addition to our ASP's business model where marketing metrics can be sold to potential customers (that is, event hosts). But, for this demo, we'll treat the Visitor as volatile data that goes away when the event is over.

Booth—A Booth is a geometric area of the ShowFloor that can be an occupied booth, an unoccupied booth, or an area of walking aisle. It will have a number and a dimension. As an occupied booth, it is associated with a vendor and, possibly, a *BoothShow*. A Booth can be reduced to a grid element, where it represents a booth, an area of floor space, a restroom, an entrance, an emergency exit, or an obstacle, such as a column holding up the show floor's ceiling. Booths are assigned by the EventHostAdmin, and they are organized according to the *ShowFloorMap*.

BoothShow—Each vendor has the option of providing regular or irregularly scheduled in-booth presentations. Presentations have a start time and a title. Individual visitors can register for a presentation. Presentations are managed in the system by the *VendorAdmin*.

We have probably made a reasonable first pass of identifying the ShowFloor actors and some of the potential entity classes, described next, of the ShowFloor model. Table 4.1 attempts to summarize them by category.

Note that there are some likely candidates representing features that will never see the light of day, such as tracking every visitor who has ever enrolled through the ShowFloor application. We'll treat it as volatile data so that issues around backing up data and reconciling duplicate entries don't raise the overhead of maintenance costs.

TABLE 4.1 ShowFloor Actors and Nouns

Party/People	*Thing/Place [Nouns]*
EventHost	EventHostAccount
EventHostAdmin	SponsorType
Person	VendorAccount
Sponsor	Event
Vendor	Booth
VendorAdmin	BoothShow
Visitor	ShowFloorMap

A Use Case

UML tells us that use cases can be used to identify actors. Actors are anybody or thing outside the system that uses the system. Let's apply a use case template to the activity we'll call Create EventHost:

> *Description*—Create EventHost. This initializes the EventHost (that is, the customer) and the EventHostAdmin. The EventHostAdmin now has the ability to create the event.
>
> *Preconditions*—The Otter sales person must have closed the deal (that is, signed the contract) with the EventHost. The EventHost's account must have been created in the account system.
>
> *Deployment constraints*—We need access to the accounting system in order to validate the EventHost's account.
>
> *Normal flow of events*—The Otter Administrator, OtterAdmin, gets a call from the sales person that he has just sold an event to a company. The OtterAdmin initializes the EventHost into the Event system. Secondary chores include creating the EventHostAdmin and adding contact information.
>
> *Alternate flow of events*—None identified at this time.
>
> *Exception flow of events*—If OtterAdmin cannot find that EventHost is already in the system, refer back to the Otter sales person.

Activity diagram—TBD.

Open issues—None so far.

Note that we could have done a number of things differently. For example, we could have required that Otter Productions create the Event itself. Instead, we chose to let the EventHost do that.

Summarizing Interactions

With the first set of actors identified, I will write a paragraph about each interaction between the actor and the system, which UML calls a *specification*:

Create EventHost—The Otter Production's OtterAdmin creates a new EventHost.

Create event—The EventHostAdmin initializes a show or Event. The Event at this point is just a placeholder for meaningful information to be added.

Edit Event—The EventHostAdmin takes the newly-created Event and adds key content, including the Event's name, location, directions, and floor layout. The EventHostAdmin also sets the beginning visitor badge number and creates categories for vendors and sponsorships.

Create Vendor—The EventHostAdmin initializes a Vendor. Vendor information includes name, address, list of categories (for example, ISV, VAR, OEM), Booth assignment, contact person and his information.

Add Vendor—EventHostAdmin enters info representing the deal made with the vendor. The Vendor name and address are added. Account information is added. One or more booth assignments are made in response to the terms of the vendor's request for booth footage. Will the Vendor need an Internet drop? Will he require one or more of the show-supplied flat screen displays? Vendor will be categorized. This is probably two tasks: create a Vendor account, then add the Vendor to the Event.

Edit Vendor—Vendor adds info beyond general account info. This might include the general Booth description, company information including address, products and services. The Vendor might also add his in-booth presentation topic(s) and times.

Create Booth—The EventHostAdmin initializes a Booth from one or more objects on a ShowFloorMap. A Booth can be a booth, aisle, pillar, men's room, women's room, dining area, and so on.

Create Visitor—Initialization establishes the Event's name, location, directions, and floor layout. The visitor adds himself to the system. Visitor enters name, address, title, and any promotional codes. Visitor might also fill out an online survey.

View ShowFloor—Anybody can view the ShowFloorMap whether they're at a kiosk or at their desk. It's available to anybody. The viewer can identify booth locations by selecting vendors from a drop-down list. Clicking on the booth will bring up vendor information including products and in-booth presentation times. Individuals can register to be notified regarding specific presentation times.

Create Presentation—The VendorAdmin initializes a series of BoothShows, including titles and times.

Given this white board list of data points from discussions with the customer, Figure 4.3 expands the ShowFloor Administration System from Figure 4.2.

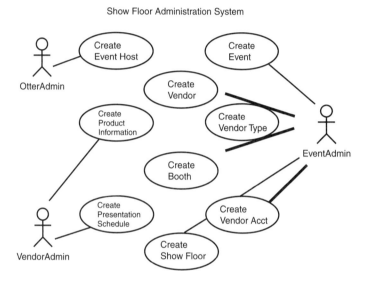

FIGURE 4.3
Expanded version of actors of the Showfloor administration system.

Identifying Objects: Entity, Boundary, Control, Lifecycle

Let's assume that we have developed a relatively comprehensive set of use cases from which to continue building the model. It's time to discover the objects that we can use to begin building UML sequence diagrams. Sequence diagrams will help us illustrate the interactions between the objects of a use case.

Boundary objects represent the interface between the actor and the system. A specific example is the user interface. Well designed boundary objects know nothing about the business rules and data. Their role is to get input from the actor and present results. This is the fingerprint of the beginning of a well-designed three-tier application.

Entity objects, on the other hand, contain the business data and business logic of the system. Entity objects are identified by extracting important sounding nouns and behaviors from the use case. For example, "log in the administrator" is a significant behavior. A *Booth* is a significant noun. The Vendor's *account* represents significant data.

Control objects are the traffic cops within the use case. They address workflow and provide services to other objects. Control objects are key to minimizing the complexity of both boundary and entity objects. The ideal entity object can serve many boundary objects. The control object handles the complexity of interacting with one or more entity objects that might otherwise make the boundary object more complex than it needs to be.

NOTE

In day-to-day life, we deal with control objects all the time. The guy behind the counter who takes our order for an espresso relieves us of having to figure out the financial transaction, the technique (and learned experience) of making the espresso, and, most importantly, the coordination of the washing of the used cup. Our life, at the boundary, is made much simpler.

Finally, *object lifecycle classes* are things that keep track of all the entity objects. For example, the individual booth entities must be tracked, sorted, added, and removed. The term object lifecycle classes is a reference coined by CT Arrington in his book *Enterprise Java with UML* (Wiley/OMG Press).

From Use Case Scenario to Sequence Diagram

Let's take another use case and postulate the model through a UML *sequence diagram*. The end result will be a more detailed use case scenario that gives us the ability to flesh out the interactions between the actor and identified objects (see Figure 4.4):

Description—Assign Vendor Booth. The EventHostAdmin has logged into the system to allocate one or more booths for a Vendor. Selecting from a list of authorized Vendors, the EventHostAdmin reads notations and the Vendor's sponsorship level in order to determine a booth assignment.

Preconditions—The EventHostAdmin has successfully logged in and has been authorized to perform this task. The Vendor has been previously added at the request of the EventHost's sales organization to the Otter accounting system.

Deployment constraints—TBD.

Normal flow of events—The EventHost successfully assigns one or more Booths.

Alternate flow of events—TBD.

Exception flow of events—If the Vendor does not appear in the system, the EventHostAdmin must manually address the situation.

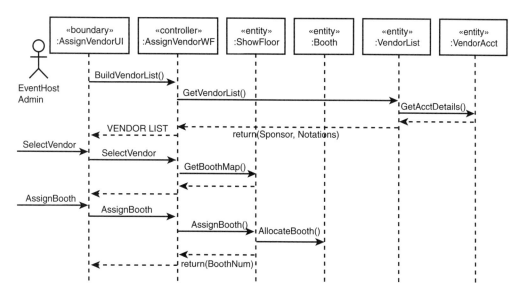

FIGURE 4.4

The sequence diagram for an Assign Vendor Booth use case.

One of the implications of this use case is that the Vendor is sold floor space, but not a specific Booth assignment.

Let's follow the sequence diagram. The EventHostAdmin, our actor, uses the user interface to select from a Vendor list. This ensures that only Vendors who have been sold floor space can be selected from. The controller is responsible for satisfying all the user interface interactions. A map of the ShowFloor is retrieved to display the available Booth space. Once assigned, a new Booth object is allocated for deferred processing by, perhaps, the Vendor. Finally, the system displays the confirmation that the booth number has indeed been assigned.

Device-Driven Tasks

We've leveraged enough UML to start thinking about the requirements and scope of this application. It's time to throw something new into the mix, which is determining our *views* based on who is accessing the application using what sort of device. These notions apply directly to the boundary objects, representing a two-way street of user presentation tempered by the limitations of the selected device. Table 4.3 suggests possible per-device tasks to be supported by the ShowFloor application.

4

THE SHOWFLOOR
ASP APPLICATION

TABLE 4.3 Matching Roles and Tasks with Devices

Role	Task	Device
Admin	Create an instance of a Vendor company.	Browser
Visitor	Locate a Booth #.	WAP Phone
Visitor	Call me when the presentation is five minutes from start.	J2ME Phone
Visitor	Participate in a Vendor-rating promotion for best in-booth presentation and most obnoxious BoothShow.	WAP Phone
Visitor	Select a company to identify Booth.	Flash
Visitor	Click on a Booth for details.	Flash
Admin	On-the-floor EventHostAdmin uses J2ME phone for immediate access to critical information for last minute changes, such as fixing the IP associated with a vendor.	J2ME Phone
Admin	Create a ShowFloor.	Browser
Vendor	Schedule BoothShows.	Browser

Note that WAP phone could easily be replaced by i-mode phone, depending on which area of the world we're talking about.

The task that uses the J2ME phone is particularly interesting. The admin can access the same EventHostAdmin page that they would normally access from their PC browser. The application will see that the device is a J2ME phone and put the EventHostAdmin into on-floor mode, presenting only the info that makes sense for being on-the-move with a smart phone.

Summary

We have performed a reasonable first pass within the elaboration phase of fleshing out a few of the requirements for the ShowFloor application for our fictitious ASP, Otter Productions.

We used a sub-set of UML features to introduce some of the useful tools of UML modeling for developing customer requirements, including the actors and operations that our application will require. We've also included our own speculation about how the customer could take advantage of the growing availability of mobile devices to create attractive new features, such as vendor rating systems and in-booth presentation notifications, to make the event more enjoyable for visitors.

Enhydra, Java/XML Application Server

IN THIS CHAPTER

This is the grand tour of the technology platform that originally inspired Enhydra XMLC. XMLC addresses the presentation tier of a Web application. We'll leverage the Enhydra application server to address not only the business and data tiers, but other deployment and development issues as well. We'll introduce the topics of database and session managers, as well as how you connect an application server to the outside world.

After briefly introducing key Enhydra components, we'll take a few pages to walk through the exercise of creating an Enhydra "stub application." This experience will bring out key discussion and conceptual topics that we'll expand upon in the remainder of the chapter. We'll wrap up our discussion with how to use the Enhydra DODS to create a mapping of data logic to a SQL database table, and how to deploy the ShowFloor application with the Enhydra Administration Console.

NOTE

All the examples within this chapter and the rest of the book were created using open source Enhydra 3.1b1, running inside a Cygwin UNIX emulation environment on a Windows 2000 desktop.

This chapter is just the first wave of explaining Enhydra application development. We'll continue to expand the discussion as we use XMLC and other Enhydra technologies to fill out the ShowFloor application.

If you are new to Java, perhaps coming from the worlds of CGI/Perl or Visual Basic programming, the rest of this book will leverage Enhydra 3.1 to introduce you to servlet development in a step-by-step fashion as we systematically roll out Enhydra and the ShowFloor application.

NOTE

Just getting started with Java? Enhydra is a great way to get going. Why? Because it builds a working *stub application* that you can incrementally add logic to as you discover the capabilities of Java. Enhydra also encourages a good three-tier application design philosophy.

Enhydra and J2EE

The name of the game in the Java world today is "standards." The concern for most of us is "Am I learning about something that is proprietary- or standards-based?" In a short four years, we've come from a roll-your-own approach to application server design to the highly structured and standardized Sun J2EE blueprints for Enterprise Java Beans computing. Judging by the success of J2EE platforms such as BEA's WebLogic, JBoss, and Lutris' EAS, the development community is happy to embrace implementations built on the J2EE standard.

With standards in mind, there are two application servers included on the CD with this book: the lightweight open source Java servlet application server Enhydra 3.1, and Lutris EAS 4. Lutris EAS 4 is a full implementation of a J2EE application server. You can develop XMLC applications on the lightweight Enhydra, then easily migrate them to Lutris EAS with a few simple file transfers. Thanks to the standard servlet API, you can migrate the applications you develop with Enhydra to any J2EE or servlet-compliant Java application server, including IBM's WebSphere or BEA's WebLogic. If you are comfortable with the J2EE environment, you can implement everything directly on Lutris EAS 4. The choice is yours. Even if you just want to use Lutris EAS 4 as a deployment platform, you can create the ShowFloor application as an Enhydra 3 application, then install the generated `enhydra.jar` file in the CLASSPATH of a J2EE environment and run the application from there.

> **NOTE**
>
> Enhydra 3.1b1 is the version of Enhydra that you can download from `enhydra.enhydra.org`. We'll refer to it in this book as "Enhydra 3." Enhydra 4 references refer to the open source elements of Lutris EAS 4.

Enhydra XMLC and J2EE

Enhydra XMLC has been designed for the Java Servlet environment. Anyone can download XMLC from its open source home at `xmlc.enhydra.org` and build application presentations for any standard Java servlet environment, from Apache Tomcat to BEA WebLogic.

Enhydra XMLC is not a part of the J2EE specification. But nor is Cocoon, XSP, or XSLT. Enhydra XMLC is, however, an open source technology. Most of the J2EE services are not.

Standards compliance is clearly a key attribute to any technology discussion. But there is something equally compelling to say about de facto standards, as powered by open source licensing. In addition to helping to promote API specifications, open source has also delivered many de facto standards in lieu of official specifications. As we mentioned in Chapter 3, "Presentation Technologies," XMLC is also based on more standards than JSP by virtue of support of the w3C's XML and DOM specifications, as well as Java itself.

Enhydra Application Framework Genesis

Prior to becoming an open source project, the Enhydra development and runtime environment was developed by Internet development consultants as a platform for achieving rapid development of Web applications for a wide variety of customer requirements.

As a 100% servlet implementation, Enhydra's architecture and feature set anticipated the eventual introduction of Sun's servlet 2.2 APIs. The original developers of Enhydra were UNIX networking experts who were happy performing application development with Unix text editors vi and Emacs. Starting from the flexibility of the UNIX command line and a well-organized source tree and Make file system, they evolved Enhydra functionality as they identified common requirements from a growing cross-section of customers.

Early versions of Enhydra introduced the underpinnings of a well-thought out three-tier source hierarchy and a system of Make files for building and deploying an Enhydra application. Starting with session services for abstracting the use of cookies and eventually URL re-writing, Lutris added additional services, including the management of the connection with the database using early third party JDBC drivers.

Configuration files were added to help running applications minimize the impact of changing environmental requirements, ranging from swapping SQL databases to setting the timeout for login sessions.

Over time, as more customer experience was gained in the early days of Internet consulting, Enhydra evolved into a highly integrated set of framework and common services for supporting a wide swatch of Web application requirements. Most importantly, it made possible Web application architectures that were easy to maintain and evolve over time.

Despite the integrated nature of Enhydra, it became an extremely flexible environment, enabling developers to replace one service implementation with another. Use of interface definitions at the service levels makes this possible.

> **NOTE**
>
> As you'll discover, the Enhydra application is one big servlet. The result of this is that you can execute Enhydra applications in any servlet running environment, such as Allaire's Jrun or New Atlanta's ServletExec.

In keeping with the desire to simplify Web application development as much as possible, the Enhydra architecture introduced the notion of a *superservlet* model. This model implements Web applications as a single servlet; the organization of three-tier architectures is achieved at the class and source code level within the servlet. The end result was that Enhydra applications were much easier to implement, as opposed to those built through traditional servlet chaining.

The sum total of these manager services and the superservlet model is the Enhydra Application Framework, or EAF. Additional tools including the management console and the data object generation tool, Enhydra DODS, were added around the time that Enhydra was introduced as an open source project on January 15, 1999.

It was not long afterwards that Enhydra XMLC and support for the standard J2EE "Web Container" via incorporation of servlet 2.2/JSP 1.1 were added.

Using EAF for the ShowFloor Demo

The Enhydra Application Framework (EAF) will be the platform for the development of our ShowFloor application. EAF is a specialized form of Java servlet programming that precludes the need for chaining servlets together to develop a fully functioning three-tier application.

Because we're focusing on presentation development with Enhydra XMLC, it matters little which application server platform we use "underneath," as long as it supports servlet programming. EAF is ideal for our needs because it greatly simplifies the construction of a Web application from presentation layer through to the database. EAF is an ideal environment for rapid prototyping of applications that can easily be migrated to lightweight standard servlet environments, or with a little more work, J2EE platforms.

For a pure servlet 2.2 implementation of ShowFloor, we will revisit some of the implementation details in Chapter 7, "The xmlc Command," and elsewhere in the book. As you will see, there is very little impact to overall implementation details of ShowFloor in either EAF or servlet 2.2 environments.

The Package Tour

One of Java's improvements over C and C++ programming is its natively enforced hierarchical naming convention for referencing other Java class libraries. The result is that you can interpret a lot about an application by simply examining the names of imported packages and classes. This is particularly true when many of the incorporated packages represent well-known open source efforts. Before we dive into Enhydra 3 development and deployment, let's take a look at a few collections of these packages.

Tables 5.1 and 5.2 represent the core personality that distinguishes much of Enhydra from other application servers. The com.lutris package addresses Enhydra's support for login, HTTP processing, presentation manager, SQL database connectivity, and data object to relational database mapping, as well as a number of utilities for updating log files and applying filters to HTTP requests. The classloader package serves Enhydra's unique EAF implementation for launching and partitioning Web applications. We'll talk about the `class-loader` later in this chapter.

TABLE 5.1 The `com.lutris` Package

```
com.lutris.applet
com.lutris.appserver.server
com.lutris.appserver.server.httpPresentation
com.lutris.appserver.server.jolt.joltpo
com.lutris.appserver.server.session
com.lutris.appserver.server.sql
com.lutris.appserver.server.sql.informix
com.lutris.appserver.server.sql.msql
com.lutris.appserver.server.sql.oracle
com.lutris.appserver.server.sql.standard
com.lutris.appserver.server.sql.sybase
com.lutris.appserver.server.user
com.lutris.classloader
com.lutris.dods.builder.generator.dataobject
com.lutris.dods.builder.generator.query
com.lutris.html
com.lutris.http
com.lutris.logging
com.lutris.mime
com.lutris.util
```

Too much should not be read into the naming conventions `com.lutris` and `org.enhydra`. There is no "pure" division of what is "owned" by Lutris and what is "owned" by Enhydra.org. Most of the naming conventions can be attributed to "historical reasons." Both sets of packages and classes fall under the Enhydra Public License, with some exceptions, such as the VoiceXML, Compact HTML, and the XHTML DOM package.

TABLE 5.2 The `org.enhydra` Package

```
org.enhydra.wireless.chtml
org.enhydra.wireless.chtml.dom
org.enhydra.wireless.voicexml
```

TABLE 5.2 Continued

```
org.enhydra.wireless.voicexml.dom

org.enhydra.wireless.wml

org.enhydra.wireless.wml.dom

org.enhydra.xml.dom

org.enhydra.xml.io

org.enhydra.xml.lazydom

org.enhydra.xml.xhtml

org.enhydra.xml.xhtml.dom

org.enhydra.xml.xmlc

org.enhydra.xml.xmlc.dom

org.enhydra.xml.xmlc.html

org.enhydra.xml.xmlc.reloading

org.enhydra.xml.xmlc.servlet
```

Enhydra 3 also supports standard "Web Container" servlet 2.2/JSP 1.1 programming. This is captured in the Apache Tomcat project's `javax` package, an implementation of the servlet 2.2 API illustrated in Table 5.3. As you can see from the table, Enhydra supports JSP and its taglib capabilities for those who choose to port their existing Web applications to Enhydra or simply prefer JSP over XMLC development.

TABLE 5.3 The `javax` Package

```
Javax.servlet

Javax.servlet.http

Javax.servlet.jsp

Javax.servlet.jsp.tagext

Javax.xml.parsers
```

Enhydra leverages Xpath and the Apache project's Xerces for the XMLC compiler. Xerces is used to parse all markup pages that are non-HTML, such as WML and VoiceXML. From the list in Table 5.4, you also see that Enhydra supports XSLT development with regard to the Apache `Xalan` package.

TABLE 5.4   The `org.apache` Package

```
org.apache.xalan.xpath
org.apache.xalan.xpath.dtm
org.apache.xalan.xpath.res
org.apache.xalan.xpath.xdom
org.apache.xalan.xpath.xml
org.apache.xalan.xslt
org.apache.xalan.xslt.client
org.apache.xalan.xslt.extensions
org.apache.xalan.xslt.res
org.apache.xalan.xslt.trace
org.apache.xerces.framework
org.apache.xerces.parsers
org.apache.xml.serialize
```

Full DOM support is included in Enhydra. Table 5.5 reflects XMLC's basis in W3C standards, listing the packages required for DOM Level I and Level II support. The W3C's Java implementation of HTML Tidy is used by the `xmlc` command for processing HTML, bad form and all, to construct the output HTML DOM class. Enhydra supports SAX development when an alternative to the DOM's tree view of XML data is required.

TABLE 5.5   The `org.w3c` Package

```
org.w3c.tidy
org.w3c.dom
org.w3c.dom.events
org.w3c.dom.html
org.w3c.dom.range
org.w3c.dom.traversal
org.xml.sax
org.xml.sax.ext
org.xml.sax.helpers
```

One last package not listed is `gnu.regexp`, which is also supported by Enhydra 3. This regular expressions package is used by XMLC's command line parser, but can be very useful when strong pattern matching is needed.

The online JavaDoc-generated documentation that accompanies Enhydra 3 has been adjusted to list only those packages and their classes that are user documentation only. This is reflected in the package listing discussed in this section. The Enhydra documentation philosophy is to show only those APIs that would be used by a developer to develop Enhydra and Enhydra XMLC applications. If you want to see the JavaDoc for underlying APIs of the Enhydra development and runtime environment, you can run the _javadoc_ command to build new HTML Web pages.

Enhydra Documentation and Source Code

Good documentation can make a great piece of software even greater. The JavaDoc that comes with the open source distribution, shown in Figure 5.1, is a great way to become familiar with all the methods available from the session manager class or the XMLC OutputOptions class, for example.

The JavaDoc browser provides multiple ways to search for the method you're looking for. You can search by package, class, or sometimes most conveniently, an alphabetized list of all known Enhydra methods. This includes all the methods belonging to the packages we toured in the previous section.

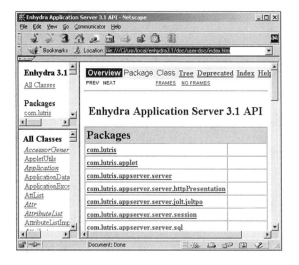

FIGURE 5.1
Enhydra 3 JavaDoc.

If you've installed Enhydra 3 under /usr/local, you'll find the JavaDoc at

/usr/local/lutris-enhydra3.1b1/doc/user-doc/index.html

Don't forget, you also have access to the entire Enhydra 3.1 source code, downloadable from enhydra.enhydra.org. If you're not sure how things work, such as the Enhydra Multiserver classloader mechanism, odds are you can figure it out just by examining the source code.

Development, Runtime, and Deployment

Modern application servers address the topics of both development and deployment. For a commercial situation, both are equally important, especially if you are building an application that is to be supported, maintained, updated and re-deployed over time. Enhydra was designed to work with your favorite development and development tools to build and deploy Enhydra applications. On the other hand, armed with just your favorite text editor, open source Enhydra comes self-contained with the tools necessary to support a full Web application lifecycle.

Figure 5.2 illustrates the major components of the Enhydra 3 runtime and deployment environment. Administration, Web server connectivity, standard servlet support, and EAF are all introduced in this section. Not shown in the figure are the development tools: Enhydra XMLC, Enhydra DODS, and Enhydra Kelp.

Runtime and Deployment

The deployment features of Enhydra, including Enhydra Multiserver, Enhydra Director, and the Enhydra Administration Console, address the real-world topics faced by a system administrator: How do you connect with the Web server? How do you scale Enhydra as traffic demands increase? How do you monitor deployed applications? The runtime components of EAF deal with the Presentation, Session, and Database Managers and how they address the immediate needs of the Enhydra application.

Enhydra Director

Enhydra Director gives Enhydra applications the capability to scale. Director uses load balancing and cluster support to address the average scalability requirements of typical Web applications.

As a plug-in module for major Web servers, Director mimics the capabilities of Cisco Local Director. Like this popular hardware router, Enhydra Director uses a simple round-robin algorithm to route requests to two or more servers, each running a single instance of Enhydra. Support for a cluster of multiple Enhydra servers is what gives Enhydra the capability to support server-level fail-over. The session manager offers configuration hooks that make session-level fail-over possible through custom development.

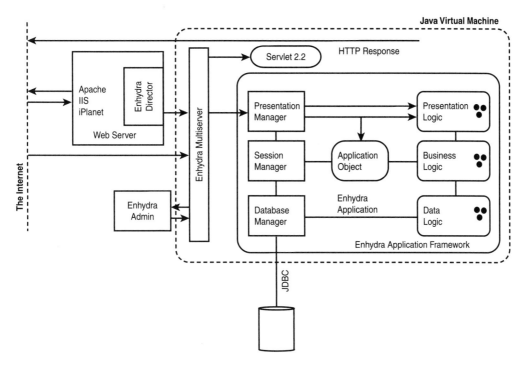

FIGURE 5.2

High-level view of the Enhydra 3 environment.

NOTE

The term *lightweight framework* is often applied to Enhydra, even though it has been used to build many high-traffic sites requiring extensive processing. In fact, the majority of Web applications built on top of J2EE platforms are done so without the use of EJBs. If you do not require the use of EJBs, Enhydra is most likely sufficient for most of your application building and deployment requirements. In particular, the ramp-up and development times are particularly reduced by its simple application development model.

Enhydra Multiserver

Enhydra Multiserver is the Enhydra servlet runner. It accepts HTTP/HTTPS requests directly from the client or in-directly from Enhydra Director when routed from a Web server. The Multiserver is designed to launch both EAF applications as well as standard Web Container (servlet 2.2) applications. It works hand-in-hand with the Enhydra Presentation Manager to locate and launch Enhydra applications.

Enhydra Administration Console

The Enhydra Administration Console is a Web application for managing the lifecycle of Enhydra applications. Implemented as an Enhydra application, it can be run over the Internet for remote administration as well as HTTP request/response and servlet API debugging. It addresses per-application lifecycle (Start, Stop, Pause) as well as offering choices for connection types, such as direct-to-Multiserver or through Enhydra Director. As a graphical tool, it makes it very easy to visually debug HTTP requests and responses. Servlet API-level debugging is observable through small applet that gives administrators and developers the capability to view servlet API requests on a per-URL request basis. The Admin Console is capable of managing EAF servlets as well as standard Web Container servlets.

Configuration Files

Configuration files, called *conf files*, are ASCII text files that conform to `java.util.Properties` file definitions. Different conf files are responsible for different functions within the Enhydra environment. Their contents affect the behavior of Enhydra applications as well as the Multiserver itself. Name-value pairs are used to instruct the Multiserver and Enhydra applications where files are, where the database is, timeout parameters and so on. For example,

```
Application.defaultURL=ShowApp.po
```

defines the default URL for the application. Conf files can also be used by individual applications to access their own name-value pairs for persistence needs during runtime.

> **NOTE**
>
> It is highly likely that open source Enhydra make files and conf files will eventually be replaced by ant, a popular new Java utility from the Apache Ant project that uses XML configuration files and Java logic to give unlimited build control to the developer. ant has replaced the use of make files in Lutris EAS 4, the J2EE version of Enhydra included in the book's CD.

Development Overview

More than any other aspect of Enhydra, the development environment reflects Enhydra's consulting heritage. The Enhydra development environment was developed by consulting engineers. In 1996, they were very happy using the Unix command line, the GNU Make file system, and standard Unix editors vi and Emacs.

As it turned out, this was a serendipitous beginning to the flexibility of the Enhydra development environment. By beginning with the "lowest common denominator" of a command line environment, Enhydra was designed with minimal "policy" in terms of its features' assumptions about the development environment.

This set the stage for the emergence of the Enhydra Kelp tools, which are plug-ins that give Enhydra the capability to incorporate itself into popular IDE environments. Kelp is a growing library of plug-ins designed for specific IDE tools, such as Sun's Forte, Oracle's JDeveloper and Borland's JBuilder.

Figure 5.3 illustrates one perspective of Enhydra 3's integration with Forte. The dialog box is a Kelp extension to Forte that presents the developer with compile-time options for compiling a markup document with Enhydra XMLC. Compile-time errors are captured within the Forte environment.

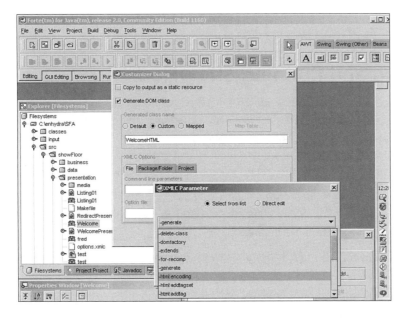

FIGURE 5.3

XMLC dialog inside the Forte Development environment.

As a Java Foundation Class (*Swing*) implementation, Enhydra Data Object Design Studio (DODS), is Enhydra's only native fully graphical development tool. Lutris chose to build this application in order to simplify the often redundant, time-consuming task of generating Java logic that maps Java data objects to counterpart SQL database tables. DODS is not without its idiosyncrasies. It has, however, become one of the more popular components of Enhydra development.

And, of course, there's Enhydra XMLC; you should have a pretty good feeling for its value by now.

> **NOTE**
>
> What is the difference between Lutris Enhydra 3.5 versus Open Source Enhydra 3.1b1?
>
> The good news is, very little. Lutris Enhydra 3.5 is Lutris' commercial version of Enhydra 3.1. In order to expand the feature set of 3.5, Lutris added support for the W3C's extended DOM interfaces of the cHTML, VoiceXML, and XHTML XML languages. Other than the expanded documentation and standard product support features, there is little difference. Even in the absence of these extended DOM interfaces, you can still build any type of presentation based on standard XML with Enhydra XMLC. However, without the specific extended DOMs, you lose the benefits of comprehensive data typing. The result can be less readable, error-prone code. All the examples in this book were built with Enhydra 3.1b1 except where noted.

Building and Running ShowFloor

Before we take a more in-depth, semi-systematic walk through the Enhydra environment, let's slice our way through an Enhydra development experience. In doing so, you'll use the Enhydra AppWizard to instantiate your ShowFloor application. In the process of creating this minimalist but runnable stub application, we will identify and explore some key files, how they're organized internally, and how they relate to each other. Finally, we'll wrap up with how you can launch this first incarnation of the Enhydra ShowFloor application.

To present the path we are about to take, we've outlined a typical sequence of events that characterize Enhydra application development:

1. Install Enhydra. This task is trivial and well-documented at `enhydra.org` as well as on the book's CD.

2. Create your application source tree and build system with AppWizard.

3. Type `make` to build the tree.

4. Type `./output/start` to launch the stub application.

5. Enter the development cycle. In no particular order, you might

   a. Update your application configuration file with database connection values and other information.

   b. Use Enhydra DODS to design and build your database.

   c. Continue with code development, creating business objects, and so on.

   d. Test, test, test, launching with `./output/start`.

Then there's the deployment phase that you begin when you're ready to test your application in a staged environment. By *staged*, I mean that you want to mimic the production deployment environment as much as possible on a staging server:

1. Migrate configuration and jar files to the Enhydra runtime environment.
2. Install the application through the Admin Console.
3. Launch the application from the Admin Console.

This, of course, is just a suggested outline. Let's explore the details of bootstrapping Enhydra application development.

> **NOTE**
>
> There's that *stub application* reference again. What is it? A stub application is the application that is automatically constructed by the AppWizard, pre-configured to reflect the desire to build a standard Enhydra EAF application or a servlet 2.2 Web application. The result is a simple "hello world" style application that you can run before you add a single line of Java code.

Application Bootstrapping with AppWizard

Enhydra application development is performed inside a well-thought out source hierarchy that encourages the organization of application design as three-tier architectures. The compilation process is managed by a hierarchy of make files, located in virtually every sub-directory. When the developer wants to add new source files or resource files, such as image media, the local make file must be updated as well.

The Enhydra Application Wizard (AppWizard) is the preferred method for bootstrapping the application development tree. It is a JFC application that leads the developer through a series of questions before creating the source tree. AppWizard is launched at the command prompt:

```
appwizard
```

AppWizard also supports command line options that make it possible to bypass the graphical presentation altogether.

Let's initialize the ShowFloor application with AppWizard. Figure 5.4 presents the first two AppWizard screens. They will lead you through the process of bootstrapping the application development environment, initially asking you to choose the preferred servlet programming model:

- Enhydra Super-Servlet (EAF)
- Web Application (servlet 2.2)

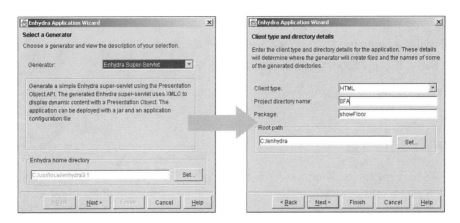

FIGURE 5.4
The first two AppWizard screens.

Super-Servlet is another name for the single servlet Enhydra Application Framework. Web Application represents standard servlet 2.2 Web Container applications. Figure 5.5 shows the Web Application option. For this book, we will focus on EAF-style applications, although we spend some time on how to perform XMLC development with standard Web Container applications.

Enhydra Home Directory identifies the location of your installed Enhydra application server. Root Path refers to the root of the source hierarchy. If you call the Project SFA for ShowFloor Application, the root of the application source tree will automatically become

```
/enhydra/SFA
```

Finally, you can initiate the client type as HTML or WML. If you are using Lutris Enhydra, version 3.5 or later, you'll have more options. We'll stick with HTML for now, adding other client types by hand.

NOTE

No matter which style of servlet programming you choose, the AppWizard will assume you are using Enhydra XMLC for the stub application presentation. To use JSP with the Web Application model, you will have to perform a simple conversion.

FIGURE 5.5

Configuring AppWizard to generate a Web Container application.

The final two AppWizard screens are relatively trivial. The third AppWizard screen provides the opportunity to generate copyright headings for the generated source files. In Figure 5.6, we've added a simple SAMS Publishing copyright. The final screen shows the typical selection of check boxes that you'll want to make. (The reference to Enhydra 4 addresses the Lutris EAS application server and should be left unchecked at all times.) The shell scripts make it possible to easily launch the generated application without having to install it under the Multiserver.

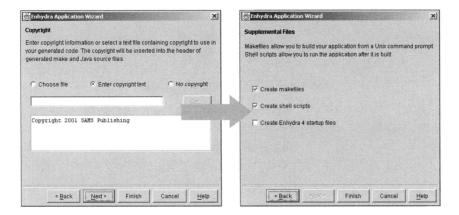

FIGURE 5.6

The last two AppWizard screens.

Click Finish and you're on your way to a fully populated ShowFloor source tree for beginning the development process. Before you take the next step of building the SFA stub application, let's take a look at the composition of the source tree.

Enhydra Application Source Tree

The AppWizard has created the following types of files for ShowFloor:

- Configuration files
- Skeleton application Java files
- Skeleton application HTML file
- make files
- Startup script

These files are organized under two SFA sub-directories: input and src. Two more sub-directories, output and classes, will be generated as a result of the make process. Table 5.6 explains their roles, as well as some additional sub-directories.

TABLE 5.6   Enhydra Application Directories

Directory	Role
SFA/	Root of the ShowFloor application source tree. Contains the parent make file used to build the entire application.
src/	Location for all source code.
src/showFloor/	Directory named after the package created by the AppWizard for our Show Floor Application.
src/showFloor/presentation/	Locations for the application's presentation objects, markup files and associated media.
src/showFloor/business/	Location for the application's business objects.
src/showFloor/data/	Location for the application's data objects.
classes/	Directory for all generated application classes and media files. These files are added to the jar file under output/. As a collection of classes, this directory can become very useful during the debugging process. [Generated by make]
input/	Directory created by AppWizard for skeletal configuration files and startup script.
input/SFA.conf.in	File containing application-specific information, such as default URL name, session parameters, for example, timeout.

TABLE 5.6   Continued

Directory	Role
input/servlet.conf.in	File containing information for Multiserver servlet runner, such as port number, channel, and filter parameters.
output/	The generated jar file as well as the corresponding configuration files and startup script from the input directory are stored here. Unless configured to point elsewhere, the Multiserver generates a log file here as well. [Generated by make]

As you might have guessed, there is a direct relationship between the contents of the input and output directories. The input directory contains configuration files and the startup script for launching the Multiserver and the application. These files can be modified as needed by the developer in the input directory from which they are copied during the make process into the output directory. Note that the contents of the output directory are overwritten. So, be sure to make your changes to the input configuration files only!

NOTE

Enhydra relies on the file layout of this single servlet environment to encourage a three-tier application design. However, it's only a suggested organization, because there is nothing to prevent the developer from building the entire application in, for example, the presentation directory.

The ShowFloor Application Object

Every Enhydra application is represented by an application object. This object persists during the lifetime of the executing application. The object is derived from the abstract class StandardApplication. When the Multiserver launches an Enhydra application, the application object is instantiated. It is at this time that the ShowFloor application can read the initial parameters of operation as stored in its configuration file. After the application object has been instantiated, the application is ready to receive HTTP requests.

Table 5.7 lists some of the fields that are inherited by the application as a subclass of StandardApplication. The meaning of these fields will become more significant later in the chapter.

TABLE 5.7   Selected Fields From the Enhydra `StandardApplication` Class

Field	Description
appName	The name of the application, otherwise defaults to the unqualified class name.
config	`Config` object for this application. Contains all keys and values found in the application's configuration file.
databaseManager	Database manager instance for application.
defaultUrl	Default URL used for this application as defined in the application configuration file.
logChannel	The log channel for this application to write messages to.
presentationManager	Presentation manager instance of this application.
sessionManager	Session manager for all application sessions.
xmlcFactory	XMLC Factory for dynamically loading XMLC-generated DOM templates.

Listing 5.1 shows the skeletal SFA application object represented by `SFA.java`, as created by AppWizard. The method `startup` is invoked by the Multiserver when the application is booted. `RequestPreprocessor()` is the only Enhydra method that examines all URL requests that are associated with the application. It is therefore an ideal place to perform any preprocessing of client requests. Upon examination of the request's content, you might want to generate a page re-direct at this point. You can also perform extra security checks here as well. The Enhydra standard debugger makes use of this facility in order to provide per-request debug information to the Admin Console.

LISTING 5.1   `./src/showFloor/SFA.java`

```
package showFloor;

import com.lutris.appserver.server.*;
import com.lutris.appserver.server.httpPresentation.*;
import com.lutris.appserver.server.session.*;
import com.lutris.util.*;

public class SFA extends StandardApplication {

    public void startup(Config appConfig) throws ApplicationException {
        super.startup(appConfig);
        //  Here is where you would read application-specific settings from
        //  your config file.
    }
```

LISTING 5.1   Continued

```
public boolean requestPreprocessor(HttpPresentationComms comms)
            throws Exception {
    return super.requestPreprocessor(comms);
}
}
```

Later in our discussion about configuration files, we'll revisit the application object and how you can use it to access configuration data as well as capture URL/HTTP information before it arrives at the presentation object.

Building the SFA Stub Application

You are now just a couple of steps away from running the stub application from which you will construct the ShowFloor application. Pretty impressive, considering that you have yet to create a single line of hand-crafted Java code.

Let's go to the head of the SFA source tree, /enhydra/SFA, and type

make

What follows is the cascading of make processes that will

1. expand the source tree to include (and populate) the classes and output directories, and

2. invoke xmlc and javac to compile the AppWizard-generated source files.

You now have the following ShowFloor tree, which has been expanded with a fully constructed Enhydra application and the files and scripts needed for a simple, "in-tree" deployment. The only missing components are the business and data source files that must be created from scratch by the developer:

```
./SFA
        readme.html
        Makefile
        config.mk

./SFA/classes
        /showFloor/presentation
        /showFloor/presentation/media
        /showFloor/presentation/media/Enhydra.gif
        /showFloor/presentation/media/Makefile
        /showFloor/presentation/RedirectPresentation.class
        /showFloor/presentation/WelcomeHTML.class
        /showFloor/presentation/WelcomePresentation.class
        /showFloor/SFA.class
```

```
./SFA/input
        /conf/servlet/servlet.conf.in
        /conf/SFA.conf.in
        /conf/start.in

./SFA/output
        /start
        /archive/SFA.jar
        /conf/servlet/servlet.conf
        /conf/SFA.conf

./SFA/src
        /showFloor/Makefile
        /showFloor/SFA.java
        /showFloor/business/Makefile
        /showFloor/data/Makefile
        /showFloor/presentation/Makefile
        /showFloor/presentation/options.xmlc
        /showFloor/presentation/Welcome.html
        /showFloor/presentation/RedirectPresentation.java
        /showFloor/presentation/WelcomePresentation.java
        /showFloor/presentation/media/Enhydra.gif
        /showFloor/presentation/media/Makefile
```

Launching the ShowFloor Stub Application

You can use the start script generated by the AppWizard tool, and migrated to output during the make session, to launch the Multiserver and your Web application. If you look inside the start script, you'll see that it invokes the Multiserver, passing the name and location of the SFA application's configuration file.

Listing 5.2 shows what the startup script is doing to invoke the Enhydra Multiserver to launch the SFA stub application. After ensuring that the Enhydra application server jar is on the Java classpath, as well as accounting for the Windows versus Unix file system naming conventions, the startup script invokes the Multiserver by passing it the SFA configuration file.

LISTING 5.2   SFA/startup

```
JAVA="C:/jdk1.3/bin/java"
ENHYDRA_LIB="C:/usr/local/enhydra3.1.1b1/lib/enhydra.jar"

if [ "X${OSTYPE}" = "Xcygwin32" ] ; then
    PS=\;
else
    PS=:
fi
```

LISTING 5.2 Continued

```
APPCP="${ENHYDRA_LIB}${PS}../classes"

if [ ! "X${CLASSPATH}" = "X" ] ; then
    APPCP="${APPCP}${PS}${CLASSPATH}"
fi

exec ${JAVA} \
        -cp "${APPCP}" \
        com.lutris.multiServer.MultiServer \
        "./conf/servlet/servlet.conf"
```

So, what does the SFA configuration file have that would be interesting to the Multiserver? Listing 5.3 brings out some of the answers. For instance, you can probably figure out that the port number for the invoking URL will be at port 9000. There's also a log file that's pointed to in the output directory. multiserver.log is the log file that the Multiserver will write all messages to that are at the message levels listed in Listing 5.2, namely EMERGENCY, ALERT, CRITICAL, ERROR, WARNING, INFO. As the developer, you might want to add the recognized value of DEBUG as you beef up the SFA application with real functionality.

LISTING 5.3 SFA/output/conf/servlet/servlet.conf

```
Server.ConfDir = "C:/enhydra/SFA/output/conf"
Server.LogFile = "C:/enhydra/SFA/output/multiserver.log"
Server.LogToFile[] = EMERGENCY, ALERT, CRITICAL, ERROR, WARNING, INFO
Server.LogToStderr[] = EMERGENCY, ALERT, CRITICAL, ERROR, WARNING, INFO

Application.SFA.ConfFile = SFA.conf
Application.SFA.Description = "SFA"
Application.SFA.Running = yes
Application.SFA.defaultSessionTimeOut = 30

Connection.http.Type = http
Connection.http.Port = 9000

Channel.http.channel.Servlet = SFA
Channel.http.channel.Url = /
Channel.http.channel.Enabled = yes

Filter.StandardLogger.ClassName =
➥org.enhydra.servlet.filter.StandardLoggingFilter
Filter.StandardLogger.Description = "Standard Enhydra Logging."
Filter.StandardLogger.InitArgs.logFile = "C:/enhydra/SFA/output/access.log"
```

5

ENHYDRA,
JAVA/XML
APPLICATION
SERVER

Launching and accessing your ShowFloor stub application requires two steps. The first one is to execute the startup script. Change directories to the output directory and type

```
./start
```

After you see that the Multiserver has displayed its copyright message, you'll know that the Multiserver has SFA ready to receive its first HTTP request.

To generate that first request, invoke your favorite browser and supply the URL

```
http://localhost:9000
```

The result is shown in Figure 5.7.

FIGURE 5.7
The SFA stub application presentation.

Pardon the Slight Delay...

As with most application servers, there is a detectable pause before the first application presentation is displayed when the server receives an application's first URL request since being started. In the case of Enhydra, there is a moderate delay when you first launch Enhydra, followed by the first application. Some of the delay can be attributed to a randomizer function that takes place only when an application is first launched. The randomizer is used as part of generating a unique session key. All subsequent URL requests will be noticeably faster.

Enhydra Multiserver

Now that you have some insight into the workings of the Enhydra development and runtime environment, let's begin our expanded discussion of key Enhydra components.

The Enhydra Multiserver is the broker of the Enhydra runtime environment. It is responsible for

- supporting connection methods for linking clients to Enhydra applications, including accepting HTTP or HTTPS requests directly;
- using classloaders to launch individual Enhydra applications; and
- serving the servlet 2.2 Web Container.

Connection Methods

How do you route an HTTP request from a client browser or client smart device to the launching of a Java application? The delegation of this chore is traditionally made by the Web server to a *servlet runner*. A servlet runner is often the Java extension of a Web server that handles the off-loaded HTTP/URL request, invoking the servlet that is responsible for servicing the URL in question.

The Enhydra Multiserver is an enhanced servlet runner that was designed to take URL requests directly or indirectly from a Web server. It is also a standalone Web server that alleviates the need for a nearby Web server during development-time configuration.

> **NOTE**
>
> Over time, the Multiserver has become quite capable in a production deployment. However, when it comes to serving static content, the Multiserver is no match for the well-tuned caching features of standard Web servers.

Illustrated in Figure 5.8, the Multiserver can be configured to accept HTTP or HTTPS (secure socket) requests directly (1) or indirectly through the Web server plug-in Enhydra Director (2, 3). The protocol used between Director and Multiserver is a private protocol designed to support Director's load balancing and fail-over capabilities.

Multiserver's ability to accept HTTP requests directly was originally intended to simplify the installation and configuration of a Web application development environment for developers, making it especially easy for consultants to perform development on long plane rides between Santa Cruz and Memphis.

Although it is still best to leverage a true Web server for serving static pages, it has become popular to set up Enhydra deployments that distribute dynamic requests directly to the Enhydra Multiserver. This was made particularly pragmatic by the addition of SSL support to enable the Multiserver to process HTTPS-secure connections.

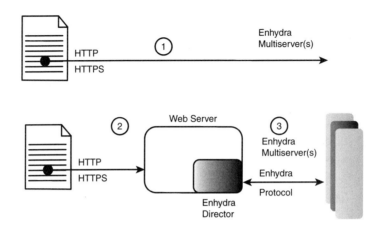

FIGURE 5.8
Multiple scenarios for sending an HTTP request to Enhydra.

Classloaders for Application Partitioning

Enhydra Multiserver has all the features of competitive servlet runners. It also has unique capabilities that address the improved lifecycle management of Java applications. This includes its approach to loading applications as well as its support for the graphical Admin Console.

Enhydra applications represent a collection of classes, usually contained in a single jar file. Each application, using either EAF or Web Container, is assigned its own classloader by the Multiserver for the entire running lifetime of that application.

The advantage of this unique classloader architecture is that applications are inherently partitioned. This makes it possible to start and stop applications without bringing down the entire Enhydra application server environment. This hot-swap feature is particularly important to ASP environments when an upgrade of only one of a suite of applications is required.

Configuration Files

Enhydra configuration files tell the Multiserver everything it needs to know about its execution environment and the applications that it must serve. Configuration files are also used by individual Enhydra applications, including both EAF and standard Web applications, for their own startup configuration needs. One of these Enhydra applications is the Enhydra Admin Console:

- `./conf/servlet/servlet.conf` (when used with the `start` script)
- `multiserver.conf` (when the Multiserver is invoked generically)
- `./content/WEB-INF/web.xml` (Web Container)

- `SFA.conf` (Enhydra EAF Application)
- `multiserverAdmin.conf` (Admin Console)

`multiserver.conf`

`multiserver.conf` is located at the root of the Enhydra application server distribution tree. `servlet.conf` is located in the SFA application's output sub-directory. What is the difference between these two files that are both read by the Multiserver? `servlet.conf` is needed only when running the Multiserver locally while developing and debugging the application. After you decide to deploy the SFA application, typically using the Admin Console, you no longer require the `servlet.conf` file.

> **NOTE**
>
> We're introducing a lot of Enhydra in one big chapter. By covering the big picture, big ticket items here, I can then introduce the second level points in subsequent chapters. We'll cover them as we deploy pieces of ShowFloor.

The expected objects to be found in `multiserver.conf` are listed in Table 5.8.

TABLE 5.8 Expected Name-Value Pairs in `multiserver.conf`

Conf Entry	Description
Application	Application-specific information that instructs the Multiserver on location, status, and configuration options.
Server	Options and values that address the behavior and knowledge of the Multiserver, such as where the jar file or classes for a specific application are located.
Servlet	Information for the Multiserver to know about running standard servlets. Servlets can be added individually or as collections in WAR files. Examples of servlets include the servlet "CGIRunner" used for executing CGI scripts.
Connection	Connection information used by the Multiserver to assign connection types, such as HTTP, HTTPS, or Director to individual ports.
Channel	A description of the entry point between a connection and a servlet.
Filter	Filters that can subsequently be associated with a particular channel. The StandardLogger filter is the default logger assigned to application channels.

The `multiserver.conf` contents that follow indicate where the applications are installed and where log messages should be delivered:

```
Server.ConfDir = "/usr/local/enhydra3.1/apps"
Server.LogFile = "/usr/local/enhydra3.1/logs/multiserver.log"
```

[your application].conf

Every Enhydra application gets a conf file. It originates as the file `/SFA/conf/SFA.conf.in` where SFA is the project name you are using for your ShowFloor application. It's automatically generated by the AppWizard when you instantiate your application source tree. By default, your application conf file contains the hierarchical name-value pairs shown in Listing 5.4. `@JAVA_DEPLOY_PATH@` is an Enhydra-specific directive used by the Enhydra ToolBox during the `make` process. It points the Toolbox to the late binding information it needs to make sure the migrated configuration file incorporates the correct directory path.

LISTING 5.4   `input/conf/SFA.conf`

```
# Comma separated CLASSPATH directories and files used by this application.
# Assumes run from the output directory for debugging.
# If you run from the jar you must rebuild after every change to the app.
Server.ClassPath[] = "@JAVA_DEPLOY_PATH@/../classes"
#Server.ClassPath[] = "@JAVA_DEPLOY_PATH@/archive/SFA.jar"
#
# The fully qualified name of the application class.
Server.AppClass = showFloor.SFA
#
# Prefix used to derive presentation object class
# names and paths from URLs.
# Assumes run from the output directory for debugging.
Server.PresentationPrefix = "showFloor/presentation"
#
# Flag to indicate that application classes and resources should be reloaded
# automatically if ANY file in the CLASSPATH changes.
Server.AutoReload = false
#
# Maximum number of minutes a user session can list.
SessionManager.Lifetime = 60
#
# Maximum number of minutes a user may be idle before being logged off.
SessionManager.MaxIdleTime = 2
#
# If the URL "/" for this application is accessed, the user will be
# redirected to this URL. This should be a relative URL.
Application.DefaultUrl = "WelcomePresentation.po"
```

From the listing, we can see that the default application conf file provides default information to the Multiserver, the Session Manager, and the Database Manager. Of course, if the application forgoes the use of a database, the information is ignored and should be stripped out by the developer.

The `Config` Object

The contents of the configuration files are made available to applications by the `Config` object. `Config` is subclassed from the Enhydra `KeywordValueTable` class.

When the application object method `startup` is called, it receives the `Config` object for the application to examine. The next four code fragments demonstrate how the application, including the Multiserver Admin Console, use the `Config` class methods to access data from the keyword-value table:

```
username = appConfig.getString("Admin.Username");
password = appConfig.getString("Admin.Password");
debugQueueSize = appConfig.getInt("Admin.DebugQueueSize");
saveResponseData = appConfig.getBoolean("Admin.SaveResponseData");
```

Other methods supported by `Config` support the capability to recover values that are listed as an array, or to test for the presence of a particular key.

multiserverAdmin.conf

Just as Enhydra applications require a conf file, so does the Admin Console. As an Enhydra application, the Admin Console can be used just as any Web application, particularly from remote locations when remote administration is necessary.

As you can see in Listing 5.5, this conf file looks like any other Enhydra application configuration file, with the exception of the application-specific name-value pairs at the bottom of the list. This is where `Username` and `Password` are established, with admin and enhydra as the default values. `DebugQueueSize` and `SaveResponseData` are specific to the debug and data capture tools built into the Admin Console.

LISTING 5.5   multiserverAdmin.conf

```
Server.ClassPath[] = /usr/local/enhydra3.1.1b1/lib/admin.jar
Server.AppClass = com.lutris.appserver.admin.Admin
Server.PresentationPrefix = "com/lutris/appserver/admin/presentation"
Server.AutoReload = false
Server.XMLC.AutoRecompilation = false
Server.XMLC.AutoReload = false
SessionManager.Lifetime = 60
SessionManager.MaxIdleTime = 20
SessionManager.MaxNoUserIdleTime = 4
```

LISTING 5.5 Continued

```
SessionManager.IdleScanInterval = 30
SessionManager.RandomizerIntervals[] = 301, 1001, 5003
PresentationManager.CacheClasses = true
PresentationManager.CacheFiles = true
Application.DefaultUrl = "Admin.po"
Admin.Username = "admin"
Admin.Password = "enhydra"
Admin.DebugQueueSize = 64
Admin.SaveResponseData = true
```

Logs, Filters, Channels, and Connections

The Multiserver provides the capability to monitor and track the interaction between the client and an Enhydra or standard servlet application. Taking things one step further, the Multiserver supports different connection methods for a single application. This feature makes it possible, for instance, to debug an application over Multiserver's HTTP connection, bypassing the application's Enhydra Director connection in a clustered deployment.

Channels are the data structure used by Enhydra to sort out the fact that one application can be serviced through multiple connection methods. Each channel represents the association of three entities:

- A URL
- An application
- A connection method (for example, HTTP, HTTPS, Director)

Enhydra Multiserver also supports the capability to apply software filters to each HTTP request, independent of the particular connection type.

A typical configuration is shown here. First, the configuration file dictates that a connection method of type http will be associated with port 9002. Recall that method http means that the Multiserver will act as a Web server. The Channel key then associates that port configuration with the StandardLogger filter, the application (servlet), and the URL:

```
Connection.HttpConn9002.Type = http
Connection.HttpConn9002.Port = 9002

Channel.HttpConn9002.WelcomeChannel.Servlet = SFA
Channel.HttpConn9002.WelcomeChannel.Url = /showfloor
Channel.HttpConn9002.WelcomeChannel.Filters[] = StandardLogger
Channel.HttpConn9002.WelcomeChannel.Enabled = yes
```

A StandardLogger is packaged with Enhydra, supporting standard levels that can be used by the application developer to send messages that can be controlled and delegated by the administrator using the `multiserver.conf` file. `StandardLogger` is a sub-class of the abstract class `Logger`. If you were to write your own custom logger, you'd want to sub-class it from `Logger` as well.

`StandardLogger` writes to the `LogChannel` object. Be sure not to confuse `LogChannel` with the channels we just discussed. This object is the equivalent of a file descriptor that can be adjusted via configuration file by the administrator:

```
Server.LogToFile[] = EMERGENCY, ALERT, CRITICAL, ERROR,
Server.LogToStderr[] = EMERGENCY, ALERT, CRITICAL, ERROR, WARNING, INFO
```

The administrator can reset the list of logger levels depending on the situation they are in with debugging an application, or simply maintaining a record of the state of the application over time.

Table 5.9 lists all the possible logger levels, some of which are used in the preceding sample conf record. UNIX folks will recognize the heavy resemblance to syslog conventions.

TABLE 5.9 Supported Enhydra Logging Levels

Level Keyword	Description
EMERGENCY	Indicates a panic condition.
ALERT	A condition that should be corrected immediately, such as database corruption.
CRITICAL	Critical conditions such as bad device errors.
ERROR	General errors that are not usually fatal, but must be resolved.
WARNING	Warning condition that might need attention, although the need is not immediate.
NOTICE	Conditions that are not error conditions, but might require special handling, such as infrequent conditions.
INFO	General informational conditions, knowledge of which will help to keep the server in good order.
DEBUG	Messages that contain information normally of use only when debugging an application.
CLASSLOAD	Information about the loading of application classes. Very useful for debugging class path problems.
REQUEST	The `StandardLoggingFilter` logs hits to this facility if this is specified (normally it writes to its own file).
XMLC	Information about auto-compiling XMLC pages.
XMLC_DEBUG	Debug information about auto-compiling XMLC pages.

Administration Console

The Enhydra Administration Console (Admin Console) is served by the Multiserver. In truth, the Admin Console is implemented as an Enhydra application that is launched by the Multiserver like any other Enhydra application. This implementation strategy enables the console to be run from remote locations for administering other Enhydra applications served by the same Multiserver.

The Admin Console supports many tasks to manage the lifecycle of both Enhydra applications and Web (servlet 2.2/WAR applications). These tasks include the following:

- Starting and stopping Enhydra and Web applications.
- Monitoring and capturing HTTP requests and responses.
- Monitoring the state of the database manager, session managers, and session objects.
- Establishing one or more connection methods between a single application and a URL/port.

To access the Admin Console, the Multiserver must be running. You can start it up by executing the following command:

```
/usr/local/enhydra3.1/bin/multiserver
```

To bring up the console, point your browser to

```
http://<your machine name>:8001
```

The Admin Console HTTP client requests and responds to the client. Requests are followed on their path to the presentation object straight to the servlet API.

Later in this chapter, we'll show how to conduct a debugging trace at the servlet API level using the console, as well as present the steps to an early deployment of the ShowFloor stub application.

Enhydra Director

Enhydra 3 is often characterized as a lightweight server. That label is really motivated by the absence of an EJB container. But the fact is that Enhydra powers very impressive Web sites and applications, including Hewlett Packard's anywhereyougo.com, a site for wireless developers, and Earthlink's Shopping Mall.

One of the keys to a high performance profile is the load balancing provided by Director. Director has the distinction of being the only Enhydra logic written in a language other than Java. As a C language implementation, Director was designed to install directly in the hosting Web server. Director uses the native Web Server API to integrate with the Web Server. In the case of Netscape, this is NSAPI. For Microsoft's IIS Web Server, it's ISAPI. And for Apache, it's the Apache Module interface. For other Web Servers, Director defaults to using the standard CGI interface.

Session Affinity for Simple Fail-Over Protection

Director routes client requests to one or more Enhydra servers, illustrated in Figure 5.9. A "cluster" of Enhydra instances, typically one per server system, give the enterprise administrator greater options for increasing Web application scalability and fault tolerance. Director was designed to be simple as well. It uses *session affinity*, or "sticky sessions" to ensure that a client, represented by a particular "session ID," is always served by the same Enhydra application instance.

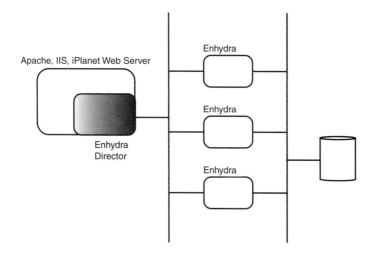

FIGURE 5.9

Director for server-level load balancing and fail-over.

This approach to fail-over greatly reduces the complexity of the fail-over algorithm. Performance is kept high because there's no need for session state to be saved to disk. The downside is that if there's a crash, the current client is out of luck. The next client, however, is assured access to a healthy server.

When more ambitious fail-over characteristics are required, the session manager can be configured to save state to disk or database, in which case, with the addition of additional logic, the client's session can be inherited by other Enhydra servers.

NOTE

Your requirements for server-level fail-over, session-level fail-over, redundancy, and so on should reflect the natural goals of your application. Is your Web application designed for a massive audience to browse and perhaps conduct e-commerce? If so, you'll probably want to take advantage of Director's cluster support. The investment in designing your application for session-level fail-over, on the other hand, might be a waste of time. If, on the other hand, your application focuses on high-end corporate customers who cannot tolerate having their application login "disappear" on them, then session-level fail-over might be a necessity. The following section on Session Manager explains how Enhydra supports session-level fail-over.

Load-Balancing Algorithms

Director supports load balancing that selects from one of two algorithms according to traffic load. A simple round-robin strategy for selecting which Enhydra server to route a client to is used when traffic is low.

When traffic gets heavy, Director adopts a scoreboard load balancing scheme to measure the current load of each Enhydra server candidate before determining which to route the request to. The server with the highest score is assigned the next request. If traffic saturates the cluster and the scoreboarding system, then Director returns to the round-robin algorithm.

The Enhydra Application Framework

We've journeyed from the deployment capabilities of Enhydra to the application environment itself. Let's review how the structure, organization, and collection of common services affect the design of Enhydra applications implemented with the Enhydra Application Framework.

The first perspective is the simple but powerful impact of a well organized source tree. The first question one might ask is, "If EAF is the implementation of a single servlet, then how do you consider Enhydra to support three-tier application architectures?" The answer is illustrated in Figure 5.10.

Yes, the fact is that you can write a two or monolithic one-tier application with Enhydra. But, again, Enhydra was built for flexibility that would support solid three-tier application architectures when desired. The term *tier* refers to a layer of coupling between different roles within the application. Enhydra's default package structure gently encourages application designs that are composed of a loosely coupled application architecture.

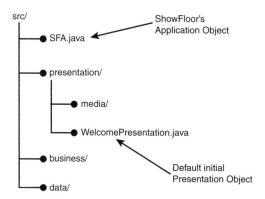

FIGURE 5.10
Source organization of presentation, business, and data tiers.

Presentation Object (`./src/presentation`)

It is the responsibility of the presentation object (PO) to add the presentation language, such as HTML, XHTML, VoiceXML, or XML, to the results of queries made to business objects.

In standard servlet programming, there is normally a mapping of one servlet per page. In Enhydra development, the mapping is one PO per page. Collectively, the POs represent the presentation tier.

The PO is the controller piece of the Enhydra application. HTTP requests are mapped to a PO. Every PO must contain a `run()` method in order to be launched when a URL request is matched to that PO. We'll discuss this in detail in the next section. It is up to the PO to synthesize a response and send it back to the client in the form of a response object.

Business Object (`./src/business`)

Business objects (BO) are the middle-tier portion of the Enhydra application that gives it its distinguishing personality, such as "I am a financial application for hospitals," or "I calculate the cost of making X numbers of copies at a Kinko's store." For the most part, the presentation and data tiers are told what to do. The value is computed and delivered by the business layer.

Business objects are the Java files that contain no presentation information or SQL methods. Instead, they represent the intermediary layer of logic that applies business rules to requested data, then presents the results to the presentation logic for display. The BO has no knowledge whether the client is accessing the application from a phone or browser. It also has no idea whether the data it requests is coming from a SQL database or another application. With the exception of a single Make file, stub applications generated by AppWizard contain an empty source tree's business sub-directory.

Data Object (`./src/data`)

The data object (DO) is responsible for satisfying the requests of the business objects by making queries, typically of a SQL database, using the JDBC interface. Much of the hand coding work of creating the data layer is alleviated by the use of the Enhydra DODS application, which we will explore in greater detail at the end of this chapter.

NOTE

POBODO, Superservlet, Enhydra Application Framework. These are three labels, all of which apply to the same implementation of a framework for building Web applications. On the Enhydra.org mailing list, you'll find that Enhydra developers use them interchangeably. POBODO, by the way, is usually pronounced "poh-boh-doh."

As with the business sub-directory, the source tree's data sub-directory is left empty by the AppWizard.

The Pre-Request Application Object

The Enhydra application server's entry point for any Enhydra application is the application object. The application object is created once when the application is started by the `./output/start` script, or by the Admin Console when it is fully deployed.

When invoked by the Multiserver, the application object can perform a number of optional tasks:

1. Examine the `Config` object from inside the application object's `startup` method. `Config` contains all the key-value pairs from the application's conf file. An example of this task was presented in the earlier section on application configuration files.

2. Use the calling of the `requestPreprocessor()` method to define how each HTTP request is to be examined and tested for every request that is routed to the application. `RequestPreprocessor()` is called by the Multiserver every time an HTTP request is made to the application. By default, the calling of the `requestPreprocessor()` establishes the session manager. This is a good place to determine whether the user is properly logged in. If not, they can be re-directed to another page requiring them to log in.

How a Session Begins

Just the simple invocation of `requestPreprocessor()` sets up a session data structure if one doesn't exist (meaning if this is the first request for a new session of the application by a specific client). A login is not a prerequisite for a session to exist; therefore, you can use the session object to save state information during the session whether or not a login has taken place.

> **NOTE**
>
> If the URL request references something other than a presentation object (that is, a file that ends with something other than ".po"), then no session object will be created. Why, for instance, would you want a session for the request of a GIF image?

In Chapter 8, "HTML Presentations," we will demonstrate how to enforce a login for the ShowFloor Admin interface.

Enhydra Services and the EAF Runtime

Let's introduce the Enhydra Services, or Managers, from the point of view of how a client's URL request flows through an Enhydra application, as shown in Figure 5.11.

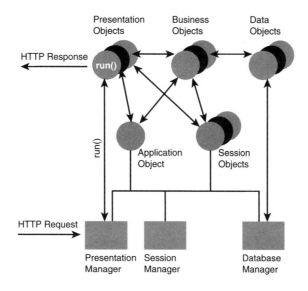

FIGURE 5.11

How a request flows through the Enhydra Application Framework for a single application.

The three managers of the EAF are Session Manager, Presentation Manager, and Database Manager. All these services are referenced in the packages found under `com.lutris.appserver.server.*`. We will delay the discussion of the Database Manager until the end of this section because it is an optional ingredient in the application's architecture.

The client HTTP request is processed by the Multiserver and interrogated from the application object by the call to `requestPreprocessor()`. Recall that it is during the processing of the `requestPreprocessor` that a session key is allocated and linked to the current application and user session.

The Presentation Manager decomposes the request in order to match the request for an Enhydra PO object to the PO's class. Once located, the Presentation Manager invokes the PO's `run()` method.

The PO, or any of the application's other objects, then has the option of querying the session object associated with the user's current session. From the session object, the PO or BO may store new state information or request information from prior session requests, including an answer to the question "Is this person logged in?"

The generated markup that results from having processed the HTTP request is then streamed, perhaps having invoked the `writeDOM()` call, from the PO through the Multiserver back to the originating client. Attached to the URL is a session key that will be returned by the next client request. It will be stored in the form of a cookie or an encoded portion of the URL (using the technique of *URL encoding*). This key acts as a baton that the application uses to identify which user session each request is associated with.

This is a high-level view of the possible flow of activity within a single Enhydra application. The next sections deal with a more detailed view of the roles of key players and entities that make these interactions possible.

Presentation Manager

If the Multiserver is the broker of Enhydra applications, the Presentation Manager is the broker of Enhydra application pages. It processes the HTTP request in two simple steps:

1. Identifies the correct presentation object by matching the URL name (for example, `showfloor.po`) to the presentation object (for example, `showfloor.class`).
2. Loads the selected PO by invoking the PO's `run()` method. Included in the call is the `comms` object, which includes details about the session key, the request, and the response.

How the Presentation Manager handles the steps of processing first the login, then the request for processing an Admin request is illustrated in Figure 5.12. This brings out the Enhydra organization of one PO per user interface (that is, markup document). The session key that was fetched from a cookie or an encoded URL is passed to both presentation objects in order to access the correct user session.

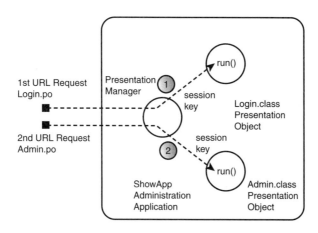

FIGURE 5.12

How Presentation Manager fires off presentation objects.

Listing 5.6 shows the SFA stub application presentation object source file as generated by AppWizard. `Welcome.class` is the XMLC-generated DOM for that page. `WelcomeHTML` stores the default "Hello World" presentation page template of the stub application.

LISTING 5.6   ./showFloor/src/presentation/WelcomePresentation.java

```
package showFloor.presentation;

// Enhydra SuperServlet imports
import com.lutris.appserver.server.httpPresentation.HttpPresentation;
import com.lutris.appserver.server.httpPresentation.HttpPresentationComms;
import com.lutris.appserver.server.httpPresentation.HttpPresentationException;
// Standard imports
import java.io.IOException;
import java.util.Date;
import java.text.DateFormat;

public class WelcomePresentation implements HttpPresentation {

    public void run(HttpPresentationComms comms)
        throws HttpPresentationException, IOException {

        WelcomeHTML welcome;
        String now;

        welcome = (WelcomeHTML)comms.xmlcFactory.create(WelcomeHTML.class);
        now = DateFormat.getTimeInstance(DateFormat.MEDIUM).format(new Date());
```

LISTING 5.6   Continued

```
        welcome.setTextTime(now);
        comms.response.writeDOM(welcome);
    }
}
```

NOTE

In servlet 2.2 development, there is only one instance of any servlet. You must therefore take multithreading into consideration in order to satisfy multiple requests from multiple clients. Member variables are global to all threads of the servlet instance. With EAF development, each request creates a new instance of a single threaded presentation object. Therefore the developer is freed of threading issues during development.

The comms object is an instance of the class

```
com.lutris.appserver.server.httpPresentation.HttpPresentationComms
```

It holds all the information the presentation object will need to know about the request. Some of the fields associated with this instance are listed in Table 5.10. All parameter-value pairs, for instance, passed along the URI are retrievable using the code. For example, the following URL

```
http://showFloor/register.po?mode=browse
```

will generate a single parameter called mode. The following line will retrieve the value browse:

```
String mode = comms.request.getParameter("mode");
```

TABLE 5.10   Selected Fields of the Comms Object

Field	Description
application	References the application object that this presentation is associated with.
request	References the request object used to access HTTP request data.
response	References the response object used to generate the HTTP response.
session	References the session object that this presentation is associated with.
sessionData	References the object of key-value pairs associated with the session.

The response that is generated by the presentation object, usually containing a string of HTML or other markup formatted result, is delivered by writing out the manipulated XMLC DOM using the writeDOM() method.

```
comms.response.writeDOM(welcome);
```

Session Manager

Because HTTP is a stateless protocol and therefore HTTP requests are inherently stateless, session must be addressed by the application or its hosting framework. As should be expected, the EAF provides a Session Manager for applications to store session state on a per-user basis.

There is one Session Manager assigned to each application. Upon request, the Session Manager instantiates a single session object for each application's client session. The session object is then used during the lifetime of the session to track the progress of the user session for which it is responsible. How the application defines *session* is up to the application's architect. It is the application's responsibility to either close the session or allow it to timeout.

The Session Manager uses cookies or the technique of URL re-writing to pass the session ID back and forth between client requests. The session ID, as the name implies, is used to identify a client request as belonging to a current session.

URL re-writing automatically appends the encrypted session key to the end of the URL. For developers who want to avoid the cookie approach, the following key-value line in the application configuration file will ensure that URL re-writing is used:

```
SessionManager.EncodeUrlState = Always
```

Tracking and Controlling Session Duration

There are number of features built into the Session Manager in order to address common concerns about maintaining session state. Some of these features are required by real-world business concerns, such as making it so that applications can be configured to timeout if a user leaves for the day.

Using the application's configuration file, it's possible to dictate certain timing behaviors, such as requiring a user to log in again after a certain period of time. Maximum session existence time and maximum session idle time are some of the parameters that can be configured in the application's configuration file:

```
SessionManager.Lifetime = 60
SessionManager.MaxIdleTime = 2
```

Implementing Session Level Fail-Over

It is possible to create robust fail-over hooks for Enhydra applications. By default, the session manager saves state in memory, clearly the wisest thing to do for maximizing performance.

The Session Manager can be configured to save state information to memory (default mode), to disk, or to a database:

```
SessionHome.Mode: {BASIC | PAGE_TO_DISK | PAGE_TO_DB | CUSTOM}
```

In BASIC mode, the standard Session Manager manages sessions in memory. In PAGE_TO_DISK the Session Manager saves session state to disk, and PAGE_TO_DB saves it to an indicated database. CUSTOM is provided for those who want to implement their own session-level fail-over scheme.

Database Manager

One of the many reasons that Enhydra is so flexible is its reliance on the JDBC SQL driver. The JDBC specification is part of the J2EE specification and has been adopted by virtually every database vendor of significance. JDBC supports everything from successful commercial databases including Oracle and Informix, to well-known open source databases mySQL and PostgreSQL. Even Enhydra.org has its own freeware SQL database, InstantDB, as sponsored by the instantdb.enhydra.org project (and used in this book for the ShowFloor application).

As with the Session and Presentation Managers, there is one Database Manager per application. Upon instantiation, the application's Database Manager reads the configuration file associated with the application. The configuration file includes

- The URL (location) of the database.
- The login information required by the database.
- The mapping of the database's types to the logic database types.

The Database Manager deals with issues that no application wants to. It manages runtime connection to the logical database, as presented through the eyes of JDBC. Enhydra relies completely on JDBC for its database independence.

ShowFloor Database

Let's examine what the configuration file might look like for the ShowFloor application and its use of the InstantDB database. Here is where you create a virtual name for the database, "ShowFloorDB":

```
DatabaseManager.Databases[] = "ShowFloorDB"
DatabaseManager.DefaultDatabase = "ShowFloorDB"
DatabaseManager.Debug = "false"
DatabaseManager.DB.ShowFloorDB.ClassType = "Standard"
# DatabaseManager.DB.ShowFloorDB.ClassType = "Oracle"
DatabaseManager.DB.ShowFloorDB.JdbcDriver =
➥"org.enhydra.instantdb.jdbc.idbDriver"
# DatabaseManager.DB.ShowFloorDB.JdbcDriver = "oracle.jdbc.driver.OracleDriver"
# DatabaseManager.DB.ShowFloorDB.JdbcDriver = "sun.jdbc.odbc.JdbcOdbcDriver"
```

The debug mode dumps the SQL statements as they're sent to the database. You'll set the database class type to Standard because you're using the Enhydra InstantDB database engine. As you can see, there are class types specific to different databases, such as Oracle. The Database Manager is instructed to use the InstantDB JDBC driver.

Note that we've left a number of commented out Oracle references. It's quite possible that after you move the application to the staging environment, you will want to switch the Database Manager to point to the larger capacity Oracle database.

The InstantDB database comes with its own set of operations and configurations for conducting itself, such as debugging activities, conversion values, and so on. Here you set the connection URL to point to the InstantDB environment:

```
#DatabaseManager.DB.ShowFloorDB.Connection.Url =
➡"jdbc:idb:@OUTPUT@/discRack.prp"
DatabaseManager.DB.ShowFloorDB.Connection.Url =
➡"jdbc:idb:/enhydra/jack/jack/db/jack.prp"
```

Part of the Database Manager's role is to simply establish the connection with the database for the application. A user name and password are required, which are set to null here. Transparent to the user, this needs to occur only once during the lifetime of the application:

```
DatabaseManager.DB.ShowFloorDB.Connection.User = ""
DatabaseManager.DB.ShowFloorDB.Connection.Password = ""
```

The Database Manager can be told the maximum number of connections to hold in the connection pool. Setting it to 0 means that the Database Manager will simply wait until the database itself refuses any more new connections. Related to this, you can also allocate the time required before a timeout occurs while the Database Manager waits for a connection request to be satisfied by the database. During development time, all of this can be monitored in debugging mode, which is set to False here:

```
DatabaseManager.DB.ShowFloorDB.Connection.MaxPoolSize = 30
DatabaseManager.DB.ShowFloorDB.Connection.AllocationTimeout = 10000
DatabaseManager.DB.ShowFloorDB.Connection.Logging = false
```

Finally, the Database Manager can be configured to limit the number of object identifiers it retains in memory. Object identifiers refer to the data objects that are created:

```
DatabaseManager.DB.ShowFloorDB.ObjectId.CacheSize = 20
DatabaseManager.DB.ShowFloorDB.ObjectId.MinValue = 1000000
```

We'll walk through the complete inclusion of the InstantDB database for the ShowFloor application later in the book.

Enhydra DODS

At this point, let's return to discuss some of the Enhydra development tools. We've already covered AppWizard, and Enhydra XMLC is obviously addressed elsewhere. So let's focus on the tool for giving our application real persistence capability.

The Enhydra Data Object Design Studio, DODS, is a tool that offers a graphical, object-oriented user interface for creating schema definitions. DODS then generates the resultant definitions into

- SQL scripts for the definition, creation, and dropping of tables
- Java code for the third-tier data objects that will query and access the data objects represented by each row of the corresponding SQL table.

DODS is provided as a convenience by the Enhydra development environment. There's nothing that prevents the developer from generating their own query-building JDBC code or the SQL statements to manage the lifecycle of the database. But with the availability of DODS, there's little reason left to spend more time than required to churn out some data logic.

Figure 5.13 shows that we've used DODS to insert two packages, Product and Vendor. For each package, we've created two data objects, Product and Vendor. Data objects correspond to tables in the database. For each data object, we now start adding attributes. Each attribute corresponds to the column of a table.

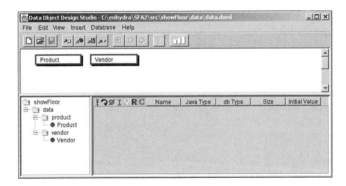

FIGURE 5.13

DODS with Product *and* Vendor *packages created.*

The relationship between Vendor and Product is a one-to-many relationship. In other words, a booth's vendor might have one or more products. To achieve this representation at the data object level, Figure 5.14 shows show we selected the VendorDO (vendor data object) as the "Java Type" attribute referenced from the Product data object.

FIGURE 5.14

Referencing the Vendor *data object from the* Product *attributes for a one (vendor)-to-many (products) relationship.*

After we've fully added the attribute, as seen in Figure 5.15, there's an arrow pointing from Product to Vendor, indicating that Product uses Vendor. The Vendor attribute in Product now references the Vendor data object.

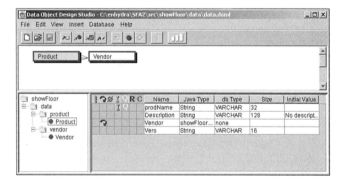

FIGURE 5.15

Product *data object with a reference to the* Vendor *data object.*

> **NOTE**
>
> When you create your data object (table), you can select the Cached option if you want the entire table loaded into memory during application start-up. The generated query object applies its operations directly to the cache, not the database. This approach, assuming it's an economically sized table, has obvious performance benefits. This is just an example of the many configuration options provided by DODS.

DODS saves all the generated information in the form of a DOML file. Our work is listed in Listing 5.7 as a DOML file.

LISTING 5.7   ./showFloor/src/data/data.doml

```xml
<?xml version="1.0" encoding="UTF-8"?>
<doml>
  <database database="Standard"
legal_values="Standard,InstantDB,Oracle,Informix,Msql,Sybase,PostgreSQL">
    <package id="showFloor">
      <package id="showFloor.data">
        <package id="showFloor.data.vendor">
          <table id="showFloor.data.vendor.Vendor">
            <column id="Address">
              <javadoc>/**
 * Address of Vendor's headquarters
 */</javadoc>
              <type dbType="VARCHAR" javaType="String" size="64"/>
            </column>
            <column id="venName" isIndex="true" usedForQuery="true">
              <javadoc>/**
 * Name of Vendor Company
 */</javadoc>
              <type dbType="VARCHAR" javaType="String" size="64"/>
            </column>
          </table>
        </package>
        <package id="showFloor.data.product">
          <table id="showFloor.data.product.Product">
            <column id="prodName" isIndex="true" usedForQuery="true">
              <javadoc>/**
 * Name of a product.
 */</javadoc>
              <type dbType="VARCHAR" javaType="String" size="32"/>
            </column>
```

LISTING 5.7   Continued

```
                <column id="Description">
                    <javadoc>/**
 * Description of the product.
 */</javadoc>
                    <type dbType="VARCHAR" javaType="String" size="128"/>
                    <initialValue>No description provided.</initialValue>
                </column>
                <column id="Vendor">
                    <javadoc>/**
 * Reference to Vendor data object
 * for one-to-many relationship.
 */</javadoc>
                    <referenceObject reference="showFloor.data.vendor.Vendor"/>
                    <type dbType="none" javaType="showFloor.data.vendor.VendorDO"/>
                </column>
                <column id="Vers">
                    <javadoc>/**
 * Version number of product.
 */</javadoc>
                    <type dbType="VARCHAR" javaType="String" size="16"/>
                </column>
            </table>
          </package>
        </package>
      </package>
    </database>
</doml>
```

Now select Build All from the DODS menu to generate the code that you'll use in your
ShowFloor data layer, as well as the SQL commands to create the corresponding SQL tables.
Table 5.11 lists the three files related to the Product table that DODS generates from having
processed the DOML file.

TABLE 5.11   Auto-Generated Files From Enhydra DODS

ProductDO.java	Represents a new or existing row in the Product table.
ProductQuery.java	Retrieves Product data objects for a row in the Product table.
ProductSQL.sql	Contains the CREATE_TABLE statement for building the Product table.

Initially limited to working with new tables only, DODS has been modified to support existing
tables as well.

QueryBuilder for Advanced Queries

QueryBuilder is a helper class used by all the DODS Query classes. If you want to go straight to the database and apply "where" clauses for advanced queries, use the QueryBuilder object. This is the preferred approach when performing tasks that simply read from the database, such as a report generation activity.

Debugging an Enhydra Application

There are many ways to debug an Enhydra application that go beyond the insertion of System.out.print statements. Of course, if you take advantage of Enhydra Kelp and your supported IDE environment, you can debug an Enhydra application just like any other Java application. The fact that you have source code to the Enhydra application server itself creates an even more thorough debugging environment.

Discussed earlier, built into every Enhydra application is the capability to write to a log file at different message levels, one of which is DEBUG:

```
public static void writeDebugMsg(String msg) {
        Enhydra.getLogChannel().write(Logger.DEBUG,msg);
}
```

To activate the DEBUG level, simple add the DEBUG name to the list of logging levels associated with the LogToFile keyword in the multiserver.conf file:

```
Server.LogToFile[] = EMERGENCY, ALERT, CRITICAL, ERROR, WARNING, INFO, DEBUG
```

This feature is great for post-deployment runtime debugging.

Admin Console Debugging

Another debug feature is provided by the Administration Console. From the control panel, selecting the Debug button pops up the Debug window, containing the only applet used in the entire Enhydra environment (see Figure 5.16).

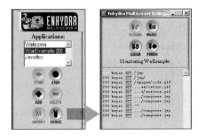

FIGURE 5.16

Entering Debug mode from the Administration Console.

In the figure, I've loaded the servlet 2.2/JSP 1.1 Number Guess game written by Jason Hunter and have started guessing numbers. Simultaneously, I've begun monitoring the GET requests as they appear over the HTTP channel.

Debug generates output under the tabs: REQUEST, TRACE, SESSION, and RESPONSE. Clicking on the GET link in the applet takes you to these tabs. The following lines show the initial servlet calls under the TRACE tab. Note the absence of parameter values, which is expected because I haven't yet entered my first guess:

```
getAttribute(javax.servlet.include.request_uri) = null
getParameterValues(jsp_precompile) = []
getQueryString() = null
getHeader(:aff:) = null
getAttribute(numguess) = null
getParameterNames() = {}
setStatus(200, OK)
addHeader(Date,Sun, 01 Jul 2001 19:12:47 GMT)
addHeader(Status,200)
addHeader(Content-Type,text/html)
addHeader(Servlet-Engine,Enhydra Application Server/3.1.1b1 (JSP 1.1; Servlet
2.2; Java 1.3.0_02; Windows 2000 5.0 x86; java.vendor=Sun Microsystems Inc.))
addHeader(Set-Cookie,JSESSIONID=yALY_3Vv-Ul-qh2iDlOJIiCy;Path=/examples)
getOutputStream() =
org.enhydra.servlet.connectionMethods.http.HttpOutputStream@7653ae
ServletOutputStream: write(byte[8192], 0, 566)
Elapsed time: 2163 milliseconds.
```

Having entered the first guess, 15, I click on the newly appeared GET for numguess.jsp. Now you can see that the JSP was passed the parameter guess with the value of 15:

```
getQueryString() = guess=15
getAttribute(numguess) = null
getParameterNames() = {
    Guess
}
getParameterValues(guess) = [
    15
]
setStatus(200, OK)
```

Deploying Enhydra Applications

So far you've been launching the SFA stub application from inside the development tree. Now you're going to go through the steps of migrating the application and its configuration file to the Enhydra application server environment. You will then launch the application in the same manner that an administrator would:

1. Copy ./output/archive/SFA.jar to /usr/local/enhydra3.1/lib/.

2. Copy ./output/conf/SFA.conf to /usr/local/enhydra3.1/apps/.

3. Comment out the first line of the Server.Classpath variable and uncomment the second line, so that it reads:

```
Server.Classpath[] = "/usr/local/enhydra3.1/lib/SFA.jar"
```

That's about it as far as "migration" goes. Now, let's launch the Multiserver, then the Admin Console:

1. Invoke the Enhydra application server with this command:

```
/usr/local/enhydra3.1/bin/multiserver&
```

2. From your browser, enter the URL http://localhost:8001 with the username as admin and using the password enhydra.

3. Click the Add button from the Control window.

4. Select SFA from the pop-up menu, then click OK. You will see a message indicating the successful addition of the SFA application.

You should now see a Status window focused on the status of SFA. The next step is to assign a connection method to SFA. To do this,

1. Select the CONNECTIONS tab.

2. Click Create. This will generate a pop-up dialog window called Add New Connection.

3. Select the default connection method of HTTP. This bypasses the need for a Web server/Director combination. Change the port number to 9002. (You can select any port, as long as it doesn't conflict with another application and, if you don't own root (Administrator) access, is greater than 1000. The highest value you can select is 65535.) Click OK. Click OK in the acknowledgement pop-up window that follows.

4. Now is the time to fire up the SFA application. Click Start in the control panel. You'll see the connecting URL, http://localhost:9002, become a live link. Select the link to bring up a new browser to access the SFA application.

You should now be viewing the SFA stub application.

Summary

If you still believed Enhydra was a lightweight server, by now you might have another opinion. Enhydra is clearly a complete application server. The number of development tools are modest but strategic. And where Enhydra punts on having its own IDE, it has a system for plugging into your favorite IDE.

I've attempted to introduce enough about Enhydra and the Enhydra Application Framework to establish a working knowledge of what it takes to build a Web application. Many of the topics that were introduced will be expanded upon in the remainder of the book.

XMLC Basics

IN THIS CHAPTER

It's true that much of the implementation details of HTML and XML show through the surface of XMLC programming. In the case of XML, this is not much of a problem, given XML's success as an evolving standard for transmitting data from one entity to another. HTML, on the other hand, shows no signs of going away. In fact, the HTML browser is playing a significant role in the evolution of display devices, and should therefore be taken seriously, despite its historical quirks.

The first half of this chapter addresses key topics in the relationships of HTML, XML, and the Document Object Model (DOM). These topics directly or indirectly affect the design of Enhydra XMLC, its features, and the look and feel of XMLC development. My hope is that by reading this chapter you will understand the "XMLC sandbox" to a depth that will assist you with circumventing typical conceptual issues that plague those who haven't looked beyond the API.

NOTE

During the writing of this chapter, it became clear to me that many of the questions asked about XMLC, XML, and DOM programming could easily be offset by a fundamental understanding of what XML and DOM development is all about. Be sure to take some time to browse the excellent documents at www.W3C.org to learn everything from the details of VoiceXML to historical facts on the origins of DOMs and HTML.

The second half of this chapter introduces XMLC features, capabilities, and concepts as organized by development time and runtime. We'll discuss the meaning of DOM templates, as well as highlight interesting XMLC methods and innovations, including how the XMLC compiler constructs the DOM-building Java logic. We'll wrap up with some of the more interesting XMLC innovations, including the performance-conscious LazyDOM. Many of these topics will set the stage for the introduction of the xmlc command and its command line options, described in Chapter 7, "The xmlc Command."

Chapter 2, "XMLC Development," was a crash course introduction of XMLC and DOM programming basics. Before we explore XMLC development in detail, we will now turn to the XML/HTML side of the equation and look back at how it relates to the DOM.

HTML in an XML World

As part of the widespread adoption of well-known Internet technologies, there are still a few places where historical artifacts continue to hinder the development tasks of designers and developers. One of these is HTML. In a perfect world, HTML would simply be another XML language. But it isn't. Because real-world HTML often violates the requirements of a well-formed XML document, browser parsers are expressly written to handle the idiosyncrasies of HTML markup.

To be fair, HTML was derived from the SGML world for the purpose of addressing the needs of browsers in the World Wide Web. The development of the DOM was inspired to first address representative HTML documents. XML came along later, with its new notion for defining well-formed documents. Combined with a presentation-free philosophy, XML made it possible to create markup without a special-knowledge parser to process it. A rapidly evolving device market and the success of XML has motivated the definition of XHTML, HTML's heir apparent.

The irony is that the most common reason for using XMLC, namely generation of HTML documents, is the "special case" when it comes to XMLC's support for multiple markup languages.

For the foreseeable future, HTML will remain king in the browser world, while XML takes on the mobile market. Luckily, the DOM specification, the middleman of XMLC, was originally developed with HTML in mind. Let's review XML and HTML to make this situation more clear, and explain how XMLC has adapted to this reality.

> **NOTE**
>
> With so much emphasis placed on HTML, is XMLC really better suited for HTML development? The answer is absolutely not. XML takes care of a lot of issues that make XMLC's life easier. HTML is more of a "squeaky wheel" situation that happens to still reflect the dominant Internet markup language.

XML Rules for Well-Formed Documents

XML establishes a set of rules for creating markup languages, referred to as "XML applications." VoiceXML, SVG (Scalar Vector Graphics), WML (Wireless Markup Language) and XHTML are examples of XML applications. These markup languages happen to be standards created by the W3C, the same group that delivered the XML and DOM specifications.

But XML is not just about creating standard XML languages. XML starts with rules that describe markup documents that can be understood by any XML compliant parser, without a pre-existing standard defining the document's language (that is, grammar). If the document conforms to these rules, then it is considered a *well-formed* document.

> **NOTE**
>
> If the term "XML application" throws you off, think of it in terms of the application of XML toward solving a particular problem, such as a set of business requirements, or how to define a standard document model for the parts list of rocking chairs.

The set of rules that guarantee well-formed XML documents include the following:

- An element containing text or elements must have start and end tags.
- An empty element must have a slash before the end bracket.
- All attribute values must be in quotes.
- Elements must not overlap.
- Isolated markup characters may not appear in parsed content.
- Elements are case-sensitive.
- Element names may only start with letters and underscores.

Compliance with these rules makes it practical for a world of generic XML parsers to parse well-formed XML without any prior knowledge of the XML language. Without well-formed documents, generic XML parsers can't parse. The consequence of non-conformance is reflected in the HTML industry, where custom parsers are required on a per-HTML basis. Even worse, HTML, which requires a DTD, doesn't always need one, because the custom parser already has built-in DTD knowledge. Imagine the version control issues!

Finally, XML focuses on data, not the presentation of that data. That makes XML applications highly portable when it comes to rendering XML content over a wide range of display devices. Use of a well-formed document means that a transformation language such as XSLT or XMLC can perform operations to turn a markup document from one format into another, a topic discussed earlier in Chapter 3, "Presentation Technologies."

Document Models and Standards

Describing a well-formed document is not always sufficient. Whether you're creating a standard XML language for an industry wireless standard, an inter-office communications standard within a corporation, or simply communicating cooking recipes, you must describe a *document model*. With a document model, your markup language approaches the XML promise of "self-describing data."

Defining a document model for an XML language is a prerequisite for standardization. Without a document model, your well-formed XML document would have an unlimited vocabulary, no limit on attribute usage, and no grammar rules to indicate, for instance, what an element can contain.

For instance, WML addresses the issue of delivering a pared-down set of user interface components that can be supported by the limited resources of mobile phones. WML and other industry standard XML applications, such as VoiceXML and XTHML, share the following common traits:

- They abide by basic rules defined by XML.
- They define a document model that formally defines their structure and grammar.

How do you create a document model? There are a number of ways, including creating XML schemas, which use an XML format for validating other XML documents. However, despite its antiquated, non-XML format, and until XML schemas are picked up by major standards efforts, the dominant method for defining document models is the Document Type Definition, or DTD. DTDs are an essential convention for the W3C specifications. DTDs share a common attribute with HTML in that they are both derived from the influence of the SGML world. DTDs address the following concerns:

- Defining the list of valid elements.
- Defining language grammar or content model, which describes the relationship of one element to another, such as which elements can reside in other specified elements.
- Defining the attributes for each element, including the attributes' possible values, data types, and behavior (for example, required or optional).

All the world's standard XML languages have document models by definition, and most of them are described in DTD format. The following example is a fragment from the WML DTD, defining the element card, which functions similarly to an HTML anchor. As you'll learn later in the book, WML supports the notion of decks of cards, with cards containing all the content you might fit into a mobile phone's display:

```
!ELEMENT card (onevent*, timer?, (do | p)*)>
<!ATTLIST card
  title           %vdata;        #IMPLIED
  newcontext      %boolean;      "false"
  ordered         %boolean;      "true"
  xml:lang        NMTOKEN        #IMPLIED
  %cardev;
  %coreattrs;
  >
```

In the case of a custom XML document that you might create, is the lack of a DTD a show-stopper for XMLC? Absolutely not. However, it does remove one of the more compelling advantages of XMLC programming. There are cases where you will create your own XML document, for example, to transmit structured data to and from a J2ME or Flash client, both of which are illustrated later in the book. You have the option of creating a DTD to define `id` and `class` attributes. Without the DTD, your application logic will have to work harder, taking on the overhead of basic DOM traversal, to accomplish simple changes to the document.

HTML, the Special Case

According to the rules of XML, HTML is a malformed XML document. Again, the reason lies in historical precedence. HTML was defined as a child of the SGML standard, before the well-formed influence of XML existed. XML is also an ancestor of SGML, with the basic rules added. And XHTML is the industry's attempt to correct this situation.

There are a number of situations that reflect HTML's divergence from XML's definition of well-formed, and why HTML assumes a specific parser will process it (for example, the Netscape browser parser):

- HTML is not case-sensitive. XML is.
- HTML does not require a slash before the right bracket in empty elements.
- HTML performs extra removal processing of new lines and white space, whereas XML preserves white space as part of the content. As we'll discuss later, this behavior often leads to the misuse of CDATA sections to coerce the generation of HTML.
- HTML does not support custom entity declarations, whereas XML does.

XML also promotes a philosophy of keeping display formatting data out of content in order to make data as portable as possible. This, too, is where XML and HTML diverge:

- HTML incorporates elements, such as <B> or <I>, that address presentation, not content.
- HTML relies somewhat on stylesheets for presentation and formatting. XML relies *exclusively* on stylesheets for presentation information.

It is the result of this divergence that partially explains why XMLC incorporates two HTML markup parsers, namely HTML Tidy and the Swing parser. Each takes its own approach to trying to deal with malformed markup.

> **NOTE**
>
> It's a fact that browsers as "display devices" are not going away. In fact, they're actually becoming more broadly accepted as they continue to prove their versatility. It turns out that browsers are the perfect display strategy for many of the newly emerging devices in our cars and homes.

There are more motivations for fixing HTML, rather than simply addressing its incongruity with XML. These include improved form handling, and the presence of too many variations of stylesheet implementations. There's also the task of defining a version of HTML that can service both tiny screens with simple needs as well as highly rich clients, by leveraging other emerging XML languages, including SVG. XHTML is the work in progress that will take advantage of the opportunity and need to get HTML in line with the rest of the markup world.

Selected XML Basics

There is an abundance of XML books for becoming well-versed in the topics of XML, DOM, and DTDs. Given that fact, we will confine our rapid review of the anatomy of XML documents to the topics that most directly affect XMLC programming.

XML presents a tree-based view to describe a document: how the document identifies itself, and how it structures its contents. But first, it must introduce itself, its document type, and perform some housekeeping chores to refer to any required resources (such as an externally located DTD).

Document Prolog

An XML document identifies itself with a document prolog located at the first line or lines of the document. The document prolog typically contains two declarations—the XML declaration and the document type declaration (DOCTYPE). For instance, the XML declaration

```
<?xml version="1.0"?>
```

brands the file as an XML document, and therefore not an HTML document. This is how an XML document indicates to a software application that it must be processed by an XML parser. The XMLC compiler reads the first line of the document prolog to load the appropriate parser.

Listing 6.1 shows the markup page for a WML stub application generated by the Enhydra AppWizard. This listing demonstrates how an expanded document prolog is used to identify the document type as WML, and the whereabouts of its document model described by a DTD.

Listing 6.1 Welcome.wml

```
<?xml version="1.0"?>
<!DOCTYPE wml
    PUBLIC "-//WAPFORUM//DTD WML 1.1//EN"
```

LISTING 6.1 Continued

```
    "http://www.wapforum.org/DTD/wml_1.1.xml">
<wml>
    <card id="card1" title="SFA6">
        <p>Server time:</p>
        <p>
            <em id="time">00:00:00</em>
        </p>
    </card>
</wml>
```

The PUBLIC identifier indicates the DTD to use, its name, and location.

A document prolog can also be expanded to reflect the document encoding. By default, XML encoding is set to UTF-8. The following markup shows how to override the default character set, in this case, to Chinese Big 5:

```
<?xml version="1.0"? encoding="Big5" standalone="yes"?>
```

Elements and Attributes

Elements, which are often and somewhat incorrectly referred to as "tags," are the building blocks of XML. They can be viewed as containers of content and other containers. Attributes are in-line, name-value pairs that give elements their personality. Structurally, one or more attributes, when used, appear to the right of an element, as seen here:

```
<name attr1="value1" attr2="value2">some content </name>
```

An attribute may modify the treatment that an element receives during processing. It can also be used to uniquely identify one like-named element from another. This is the typical roll of the id attribute as defined by HTML, and the id data type when indicated in an XML DTD.

For XMLC development, we are particularly interested in the attributes id and class for identifying XML and HTML elements targeted for runtime manipulation. The DTD entity for adding the id attribute to a DTD might look something like

```
<!ELEMENT Vendor (#PCDATA)>
<!ATTLIST Vendor id ID #IMPLIED>
```

where the element Vendor is defined, then assigned an optional id attribute by the ATTLIST declaration. The data type id has the special significance that ensures that any value associated with the attribute id is a unique value per instance of the Vendor element. In other words, you cannot use the value-pair id=blue more than once for the same element name.

XMLC BASICS

> **CAUTION**
>
> You must declare the `id` attribute in a DTD if you want XMLC to generate access methods using inserted `id` attributes. If you insert an `id` attribute into an XML file that you compile with XMLC and fail to define the `id` attribute in a DTD, then XMLC will generate an error.
>
> You can override the error by passing the `-validate no` option to XMLC, but no accessor methods will be generated.

Entities and Entity References

Entities are like constant values that define content that is substituted in entity references located elsewhere within a document. Adobe Illustrator, for example, takes advantage of entity values in order to reduce the complexity of files generated in SVG format, an XML application. Instead of repeating the same lengthy string of font information throughout the document, the SVG file defines a short entity name that represents the font, simplifying its use in the rest of the document.

Entities may be defined in a DTD or within the document itself, embedded as an "internal subset" in the document prolog:

```
<?xml version="1.0"?>
<!DOCTYPE booth SYSTEM "dtd/booth.dtd"
[
    <!ENTITY vendorName "SAMS Publishing, Inc.">
]>
<booth>
<sponsor>
<Description>&vendorName;</Description>
</sponsor>
</booth>
```

This sample document shows an internal declaration containing a single entity definition. It may be inserted in one or more places by entity references within the document using the form `&vendorName;`. An entity reference can be embedded in content, or even the value of a `class` attribute.

Selected HTML Basics

Because HTML still dominates the use of XMLC programming, I will invest some time to call out the features of HTML that differ from general XML. In essence, because HTML has its own required DTD (or in lieu of that DTD, a Netscape or Explorer browser parser that has built-in knowledge of HTML), we're really talking about the HTML document model.

HTML requires one of three DTDs: strict, transitional, or frameset (when frames are used). When a Web page refers to an HTML DTD, you will see the document project contain something like the following line:

```
<!DOCTYPE HTML PUBLIC "-//W3C//DTD HTML 4.01//EN"
➥"http://www.w3.org/TR/html4/transitional.dtd">
```

The following code fragment is from the `loose.dtd` at `http://www.w3.org/TR/REC-html140/loose.dtd`, and shows how the well-known attributes, including `id` and `class` attributes that are heavily leveraged by XMLC, are defined for HTML documents:

```
<!ENTITY % coreattrs
 "id          ID          #IMPLIED  — document-wide unique id —
  class       CDATA       #IMPLIED  — space-separated list of classes —
  style       %StyleSheet; #IMPLIED — associated style info —
  title       %Text;      #IMPLIED  — advisory title —"
  >
```

However, even more typically, there is no need for a DTD because the HTML parser already has the DTD knowledge built-in.

HTML is further distinguished from XML by its built-in support for presentation elements, such as input, forms, check boxes, buttons, and text fields. Unlike XML, HTML was clearly defined to support a particular style of user interface, primarily driven by the notion of forms-based data entry. This approach is very familiar to IBM 3270 mainframe users.

`id` and `class` Attributes

`id` and `class` attributes are defined by default for HTML documents. As defined by the `id` data definition, an `id` attribute's value must be unique within an HTML document. An `id` can be used for a stylesheet selector, a target anchor for hypertext links (when used in conjunction with the `name` attribute), a reference for accessing an element from a JavaScript, or for general purpose needs, as in the case of XMLC.

A `class` attribute, on the other hand, is used to associate elements with each other, by virtue of belonging to a common class. Therefore, the `class` attribute's value does not have to be unique within the document.

The following HTML fragment groups a list of booths as belonging to one of two classes:

```
<LI class="unassigned">Booth #3</LI>
<LI class="unassigned">Booth #4</LI>
<LI class="assigned">Booth #5</LI>
```

An earlier HTML `<style>` element, located in the head of the HTML page, defines `"unas-signed"` as a stylesheet selector. The result is that, for instance, the content is displayed with a font color of red, which has been chosen to visually represent unassigned booths. An example of how XMLC can take advantage of `Style` and `class` attributes is presented later in the book.

Note that because we do not control the HTML DTD, it is not possible, for instance, to specify the allowable values for the `class` attribute.

`class` attributes can be used for general purpose needs. They are commonly used to leverage the XMLC command line option `-delete-class` as an approach to removing mocked-up content from an HTML page. `"xmlc -delete-class deleteMe"` would do the trick on the following example, removing the entire element during compilation:

```
<LI class="vendor deleteMe">ACME Corporation</LI>
```

In this example, you can see that more than one class name can be identified, delimited by space characters. The class value `"vendor"` might have been used to reference a stylesheet selector during the design process and is no longer needed as mocked-up information.

DIV and SPAN Elements

HTML's `DIV` and `SPAN` elements add greater document structure and isolation to sub-HTML markup, a feature that designers and developers can use XMLC to take full advantage of. `SPAN` is used as an in-line element to isolate strings or characters within the content of other elements, such as a `<P>` element.

In this example, the class attribute value `"properName"` is probably a reference to a stylesheet selector:

```
<P>Welcome to the <SPAN id="confSponsor" class="properName">Enhydra</SPAN>
➥conference.
```

The `SPAN` tag is being used to isolate the stylesheet's influence to the in-line content, currently represented by the mocked-up data `Enhydra`. The presence of the `id` attribute means that the actual text content within the `SPAN` element may be altered by an XMLC-generated accessor method, in which case the new content will also be affected by the stylesheet selector.

`DIV`, on the other hand, accomplishes a similar purpose at the "block" level. Like `SPAN`, `DIV` can be used with `id` and `class` attributes to identify the block of markup and content in the `DIV` container, such as a set of buttons within a form, or collection of other related elements. This gives HTML designers the capability to control the layout of large or small blocks of content with respect to one another.

Entities and Entity References

HTML supports entities and entity references, described earlier in the XML section, with the major distinction that

- what entities exist are pre-defined for you; and
- you may not define additional entities with the HTML document.

An example of an entity is the non-blocking space character. HTML handles white space in a sometimes frustrating manner. For example, HTML will ignore all white space between a <P> element and the first real character. If you want to insert spaces before that character, the route you must often choose is to insert non-locking space characters. The non-blocking space character is inserted with the entity reference , the same format used by XML. How you accomplish inserting non-blocking space characters through the DOM interface is discussed later.

Selected DOM Topics

In XMLC programming, the DOM is the key to the separation of logic and markup. If you understand the strategy behind the DOM, then you'll spend less time trying to work around it; which appears to be a natural tendency, especially for those who are used to embedding markup in Java.

Rather than repeat the DOM discussion from Chapter 2, we're going to focus on some key concepts around the DOM, including the role of the Node interface and how HTML entities are handled.

DOM Structure

The DOM is an application programming interface for both HTML and XML documents. It supports all the pre-defined interfaces necessary to represent a complete markup-based document. It was designed with an object-oriented programming language in mind. The DOM is an API described by a set of interfaces defined in the package org.w3c.dom. The HTML extension of these interfaces is defined in the package org.w3c.dom.html.

The DOM instance is a object representation of the document. It doesn't contain any markup. It contains data, represented as Java strings, stored in an object hierarchy that has the semantic information that was captured from the markup document.

How you walk through the DOM, or write out the DOM to a client is not defined by the DOM. Instead, a parser such as Xerces from apache.org, originally contributed by IBM, defines it. Parsers are programs that can unmarshall XML data from a file into memory, as represented by a DOM structure. From there, the application's logic can work with the DOM. Xerces is one of three parsers supported by the XMLC compiler. The Swing parser (from Sun's Java Foundation Class) and JTidy (a project from SourceForge at `http://sourceforge.net/projects/jtidy`) are the others. We'll explore how XMLC takes advantage of their unique features later.

DOM Document

The DOM is a hierarchy of `Node` objects. `Node` objects are the representatives of markup entities (document declarations, elements, text, attributes, and so on), also referred to as "node types," found in a markup document. There are additional node types, such as the `DocumentFragment`, which are a handy and lightweight way to create a collection of new DOM tree elements, such as new rows in a table, and add them back to the tree in one simple operation.

The following code is generated by the `xmlc` compiler in order to build a DOM class. It reflects XMLC's approach to building a DOM, focusing first on initializing the document prolog, including encoding and calling another internal method, `buildSubDocument()`, to assemble the rest of the DOM-building code:

```
public void buildDocument() {
    org.apache.html.dom.HTMLDocumentImpl document =
        (HTMLDocumentImpl)fDOMFactory.createDocument(null, "HTML", null);
        setDocument(document,"text/html", "UTF-8");

        buildSubDocument(document, document);
}
```

We will discuss in greater detail the Java code generated by XMLC compilation later in this chapter.

The `Node`

The `Node` interface is the heart of the DOM API. Everything about the DOM API is there to manage the `Node`. `Nodes` represent the objects of markup languages, including elements, attributes and entities. Reminding yourself that they are the container of markup objects will make DOM and XMLC programming much easier to understand. Although XMLC greatly simplifies the task of traversing the DOM template to access targeted areas, you will likely rely on the DOM API to actually modify and enhance the template.

Table 6.1 lists all the legal node types. Some can have children and others, representing leaf nodes in a DOM structure, cannot.

TABLE 6.1   Node Types and Their (Possible) Children

Node Type	Possible Children
Document	Element (one only), PI, Comment, DocumentType (one only)
DocumentFragment	Element, PI, Comment, Text, CDATASection, EntityReference
DocumentType	None
EntityReference	Element, PI, Comment, Text, CDATASection, EntityReference
Element	Element, Text, Comment, PI, CDATASection, EntityReference
Attr	Text, EntityReference
PI	None
Comment	None
Text	None
CDATASection	None
Entity	Element, PI, Comment, Text, CDATASection, EntityReference
Notation	None

Each of these node types is represented by extensions of the Node interface. Obviously, these extensions are important because they reflect the distinguishing capabilities or aspects of what they represent in a markup language and how they are represented in a DOM tree. Text, for instance, cannot contain children. The Text interface inherits appendChild() from the Node interface. As an implementation of the Text interface, appendChild()'s behavior is modified to generate an exception if the program attempts to append a child. In contrast, appendChild(), as inherited by the Entity interface, would not generate an exception.

There are other interesting Node sub-interfaces not listed in Table 6.1 that act as container objects that you may or may not use at some point. Each of these interfaces offers an alternative to the standard tree view of a document. NodeList handles ordered lists of Nodes. Access to DOM nodes through NodeList gives the developer a linear view of the document elements. NamedNodeMap handles unordered nodes indexed by their name, making it ideal to contain a list of attributes and their associated values. These data structures are interesting, but not normally used for XMLC development.

Attr is another interesting Node sub-interface because it is often used by XMLC development. As Table 6.1 indicates, the Attr node can contain Text and EntityReference node types. This maps to the following example:

```
<booth company="Booth belongs to &companyName;"/>
```

The attribute company contains both an entity reference, companyName, and a string.

During the XMLC compilation process, entity references inside attribute values receive special pre-processing treatment. The replacement of the entity reference with the stated value of the entity takes place before the resultant text string is appended to the `Attr` node. The implication here is that no attributes will contain entity references. Entity references located in non-attribute text nodes are preserved.

`Attr` is also curious relative to other node types. You might expect the DOM to view it as a child of the `Element` node. Instead, it is a child of the Document node. This makes it possible for a set of attributes, such as `class` to be defined, then assigned for association to different elements as described in a DTD.

NOTE

The question is often asked why JDOM is not incorporated into Enhydra XMLC. JDOM is an alternative DOM that has the goal of being easier to use than the W3C DOM by virtue of its Java focus (as compared to the language-independent DOM). Some investigation was done into what would be required to support JDOM in XMLC.

Although JDOM is indeed easier to use, it doesn't necessarily raise the level of programming within the XMLC environment. You are still dealing with objects at the same conceptual level (elements, text, documents, etc).

What's really needed by those looking for a higher-level programming model are projects such as Enhydra's Barracuda, which abstracts the implementation details of DOM programming.

Node Versus Document

Comparing the `Node` and `Document` interfaces reveals a lot about the relationship between the DOM and the document. The `Node` interface deals in the world of generic DOM building and manipulation. Its interface methods include `appendChild()`, `cloneNode()`, `getFirstChild()`, `getNodeType()`, `getParentNode()`, and so on.

`Document`, on the other hand, is the interface that extends `Node` with knowledge of the XML or HTML domain. For example, `createElement()` and `createAttribute()` generate markup-specific objects. These methods return the objects that are specific to the `Node` sub-interface that they operate upon. `getDoctype()` associates the document with a DTD. `Document` is also responsible for all the factory methods that implement each `Node` sub-interface.

CDATA Section

In general, there are a couple of reasons why you might choose to use CDATA (Character Data) sections in your document:

- To get markup characters inside the document without using entity references; and
- to prevent the formatting of markup.

All too often, the CDATA section is treated as an unnecessary ripchord for inserting markup into a HTML (or XML) document. The DOM guarantees that its output will always be in the form of a well-formed document. The use of CDATA sections to pass markup through unprocessed can prevent this.

Later on, we'll review some of the situations when it is necessary to pass unprocessed markup directly from, for instance, a database to the client. CDATA sections are used to exempt blocks of text containing characters that, left unprotected, would be regarded and evaluated as markup. The CDATA section informs the parser that its contents contain no markup language, and should therefore be passed through as regular text.

CDATA sections are useful when <PRE> is not an option for identifying a body of unprocessed markup. The following example shows how CDATA can be used to protect in-line markup for parsing:

```
<P>The code looks like:<BR> <![CDATA[if (x<y) {echo "hello world!"}]]>
```

Too often, however, DOM programmers use CDATA sections as an easy way to address the frustrations of HTML development. The problem with using CDATA sections to smuggle in markup past the DOM's strongly-typed object representation of the document is that the DOM can no longer guarantee that a well-formed document will result.

How DOM Handles HTML Entities

The HTML implementation of the DOM interface greatly reduces the dependency on CDATA sections to crowbar strings of markup into the DOM result tree. As a true template environment that maintains complete separation of markup from programming logic, sending bits of "clear markup" from your Java code should be avoided.

How do you actually smuggle an element of HTML or XML markup past an HTML/XML parser and into the DOM's Text node?

> **NOTE**
>
> "There is no 'nice' way to put HTML markup into the DOM, because it is not what the DOM is designed to do. Specifically, the DOM contains an object representation of the data contained in an HTML or XML document, not the markup itself."—Mark Diekhans, XMLC inventor

The language-specific DOM implementations found in XMLC support pre-defined entities in their native Unicode format. HTML character entities all represent Unicode characters. These character entity references are all defined in Chapter 24 of the HTML 4 specification.

An example of such an entity is nbsp for HTML. More examples are listed in Table 6.2.

Definitions of HTML character entities and conversions between Unicode characters and HTML character entities are addressed in the following class:

```
org.enhydra.xml.io.HTMLEntities
```

TABLE 6.2 Selected HTML Entities

Field (static character)	Description
beta	Unicode character for entity beta (?)
Amp	Unicode character for entity amp (&)
cent	Unicode character for entity cent (¢)
acirc	Unicode character for entity acirc (â)
copy	Unicode character for entity copy (©)
frac12	Unicode character for entity frac12 (_)
hearts	Unicode character for entity hearts (?)
Gt	Unicode character for entity gt (>)
nbsp	Unicode character for entity nbsp ( )

If you take an HTML file with the line

```
<P>This book is <SPAN id=CopyRightMsg>legal goes here</SPAN>
```

then your presentation object might contain the following code fragment to modify the sample template:

```
// Load the HTML template created by the XMLC compiler
book = (bookHTML)comms.xmlcFactory.create(bookHTML.class);
book.setTextCopyRightMsg(org.enhydra.xml.io.HTMLEntities.copy +
➥"SAMS Publishing, Inc.");
comms.response.writeDOM(book);
```

The result is

```
© SAMS Publishing, Inc
```

Note that at no point did we do something like use CDATA to slip in a © entity reference. The DOM takes care of that for us by representing them through the DOM API.

Now, suppose you want to insert one or more instances of a markup character inside some content:

```
Warning!  Read the following excerpt >>>
```

The HTML templates for this might look like

```
<P>Warning! <SPAN id=Warning>Action goes here</SPAN>
```

You can do either of the following. One route is to embed the CDATA declaration directly in your string:

```
 welcome = (WelcomeHTML)comms.xmlcFactory.create(WelcomeHTML.class);
page.setTextWarning("Read the following information<![CDATA[>>>]]>");
```

Another approach is to use the DOM `Document` interface method `createCDATASection`. Or, you can use the DOM's HTML sub-interface to assist you with achieving the same result:

```
char gt = org.enhydra.xml.io.HTMLEntities.gt;
page.setTextWarning("Read the following information" + gt + gt + gt);
```

CAUTION	
	`createCDATASection` was created to address the requirement for delivering large blocks of markup from a database store. Although you are free to use it as you wish, be aware that you are bypassing one of the best values of DOM programming, namely the guarantee of a well-formed result tree.

The DOM API is key to XMLC's capability to support a clean interface between developer and designer. There is no markup language expected between XMLC and DOM. Instead, it's left up to the DOM to generate the correct markup language. It takes awhile for developers to understand that significance. On the mailing list, you'll often see developers instinctively revert to hardcoding an   in their code, rather than use the HTML DOM's representation.

XMLC Features and Functions

Although XMLC stands for "XML Compiler," there are really two completely distinct, yet linked, personalities to XMLC. One, of course, is the development time compiler. The other is the XMLC runtime environment. The runtime environment provides the developer with XMLC methods that, for example, make it possible to load the template DOM class, quickly access portions of the template, and control the output of the reworked DOM template.

These two sides of XMLC are linked by the runtime environment's dependency on key features of the XMLC compiler. XMLC is an intelligent, highly configurable compiler. It is more than just a bit of code that loads the appropriate markup parser. As we'll see, some of XMLC's features are the "hooks" inserted into the DOM template. Other features deal with how the resulting DOM class is structured.

The DOM gives XMLC more advantages than preserving clean separation between markup and Java. These advantages include the capability to insert accessor methods at key locations, and to present the developer with a page or "template object" that insulates the developer from the markup language the DOM contains.

XMLC's features and functions range from the simple to the profound:

- XMLC uses `id/class` attributes to auto-generate DOM accessor methods.
- XMLC extends the Xerces DOM for performance, leveraging the pre-knowledge of identified `id` and `class` attributes encountered during the DOM template's construction.
- XMLC supports type-specific DOM sub-interfaces and their implementations for major XML languages.
- XMLC can discard mocked-up data at compile-time.
- XMLC uses a specialized parser for assisting the developer with malformed HTML.
- XMLC can split compiled DOM templates into interfaces and implementations for runtime implementation selection.
- XMLC can support abstract classes that contain the method signatures generated by the XMLC compilation.
- Without programming intervention or application stoppage, XMLC can dynamically compile any newly updated markup page into a DOM class template during runtime.
- XMLC is highly portable to any modern servlet environment, Enhydra or otherwise.
- XMLC has extensive options for debugging and examining the generated DOM and output at any time in the process, including runtime.

Let's examine some of the details of these features as organized by their place in the Web application's lifecycle.

At Compile-Time

XMLC leverages `id` attributes to identify targeted areas of a markup page for dynamic manipulation by Java logic. This approach eliminates any need to introduce new elements (tags). JSP, of course, introduces JSP-specific tags as well as custom tags (Taglibs). We've already covered the many advantages of XMLC's strategy relative to other methodologies in Chapter 2.

At first glance, it might appear that you must learn the DOM API to work with XMLC. XMLC, however, has been developed to reduce the reliance on the DOM API without restricting those who are comfortable with DOM API programming.

The XMLC compiler generates Java methods to free you from significant DOM tree traversal and manipulation coding. These methods give direct access to elements and their textual content.

The compiler generates two forms of accessor methods. Each method satisfies different needs:

- `setText<AttributeValue>`
- `getElement<AttributeValue>`

`<AttributeValue>` is the value defined by the designer and/or developer, which is then assigned to the `id`. The attribute value must be a legal Java identifier.

Text-Setting Accessor Methods

`setText<AttributeValue>` methods let you change textual content without a single call to DOM-traversing methods. It is a direct-access form of DOM manipulation.

`<SPAN>` is an HTML tag discussed earlier in this chapter. Earlier versions of XMLC directly linked the creation of the `setText<AttributeValue>` accessor method to the `id`'s insertion in a SPAN tag.

Since the introduction of Enhydra XMLC 2.0, the algorithm for creating `setText<AttributeValue>` methods has disassociated its generation on the presence of a SPAN tag.

Any markup element that has

- an `id` attribute that can be converted to a Java identifier,
- a content model of PCDATA,
- and a text child in the template,

will generate a `setText<AttributeValue>()` method as a result of the XMLC compilation process. Examples of markup that will generate `setText` style methods include the following:

```
<P>Welcome to <span id=place>Chicago</span>.</P>
<P id=Greeting>Welcome to Chicago</P>
<LI id=CustomerName>John Doe</LI>
<BoothIndex id=boothNumber>857</BoothIndex>
```

The generated methods, respectively, are: `setTextPlace()`, `setTextGreeting()`, `setTextCustomerName()` and `setTextBoothNumber()`.

Element-Retrieving Accessor Methods

`getElement<AttributeValue>` methods, on the other hand, are useful for getting access to areas, or templates, of the larger DOM template. After the desired node is retrieved by this call, you can then use DOM calls for *cloning*, appending or deleting portions of the template. We will cover strategies for performing these type of runtime template-building activities in Chapter 8, "HTML Presentations."

```
<TABLE>
<TR id=customerRow>
<TD>John Doe</TD>
<TR>
```

The preceding HTML fragment would generate the accessor method `getElementCustomerRow`. If `customerDoc` is the variable containing the generated DOM class template, then the following code fragment

```
HTMLTableRowElement templateRow = customerDoc.getElementCustomerRow();
```

retrieves and stores the HTML table's row node; the node can now be cloned and turned into a template for generating new rows like a rubber stamp. Note how the first character of the attribute value is always converted to uppercase.

Accessor Methods for XML Documents

From a previous discussion, you know that HTML `id` and `class` attributes are defined for you, either by an HTML DTD or by built-in knowledge found in popular Web browser parsers. This is not necessarily the case with XML documents. Fortunately, it is a simple matter of creating the DTD declaration that will cause XMLC to generate the same accessor methods generated from HTML documents.

The DTD for declaring `id` and `class` attributes for XML documents is a simple one:

```
<!ELEMENT Vendor (#PCDATA)>
<!ATTLIST Vendor id ID #IMPLIED>
<!ATTLIST Vendor class CDATA #IMPLIED
```

XMLC generates accessors for elements containing attributes declared as type `ID` in the DTD. This is not the same as attributes named `id`. By convention, attributes of type `ID` are named `id`, although there is no requirement for this.

According to DTD syntax, an `ID` is a special type of attribute that serves as a unique qualifier for an element. In other words, there cannot be two or more `ID`s with the same name.

A Stable of Parsers for Flexibility

Command line switches and a selection of parsers give you the ability to control the XMLC compiler as desired.

It's easy to understand why there might be a selection of command line options. But the parser situation reflects our earlier discussion about HTML in an XML world. Enhydra XMLC uses two parsers for HTML parsing, and "one and a half" for XML parsing. Without a parser implementation to call upon, there is no object, because the DOM is just a specification that requires an implementation.

There are two general reasons for multiple parser support in XMLC:

- Input markup document type
- Performance characteristics

XMLC cannot tolerate malformed HTML during compilation. And there's a lot of malformed HTML out there, much of which is still constructed by hand. The reason a malformed document is a problem is that it's simply impossible to build a valid DOM tree.

So how does XMLC handle all that broken HTML? The chosen solution is the Java port of HTML Tidy. HTML Tidy parses and attempts to correct the source HTML. It doesn't always result in the HTML that renders the way the user intended, but it does give the designer/developer good information on how to fix their HTML.

HTML Tidy is an excellent, informative parser for malformed HTML and therefore owns the default position. The Java Foundation Class Swing parser is also included, but is primarily included for legacy support (when Swing was the only HTML parser included in earlier versions of XMLC).

But even when dealing with well-formed XML documents, there are still reasons for having a choice of parsers. Those reasons are performance and size of the memory footprint. The Xerces parser is used for parsing XML documents. In order to improve performance, this parser has been extended to take advantage of the pre-knowledge advantages of XMLC compilation to represent what Mark Diekhans calls the "LazyDOM." There are situations when the LazyDOM is not the best strategy for particular XML or HTML documents. For highly dynamic pages, it might be best to stick with standard Xerces parsing. We will discuss the LazyDOM strategy in the next few sections.

At Runtime

The XMLC runtime environment supports a collection of classes for creating dynamic presentations with the maximum amount of flexibility for implementing the best possible application architectures. This collection represents:

- XMLC factory and utility methods for debugging, DOM manipulation, and output formatting.
- Selected DOM methods from which to choose.
- Implementations of "type-specific" HTML and XML language sub-DOMs (for example, VoiceXML, XHTML).

During the running of the application, it is the responsibility of the application's code to load the template object. The application's code then uses the XMLC accessor methods and DOM API methods to locate, interrogate, and rework the template object. When all the modifications are complete, XMLC methods are used to take the updated DOM representation of the page, format it (including setting its encoding), and stream back the markup contents.

The XMLC-related classes and their supporting libraries are all contained within the Java class libraries listed in Table 6.3.

TABLE 6.3   XMLC Packages

javax.xml.parsers	org.enhydra.xml.xmlc.html
org.apache.xerces.framework	org.enhydra.xml.xmlc.reloading
org.apache.xerces.parsers	org.enhydra.xml.xmlc.servlet
org.apache.xml.serialize	org.w3c.dom
org.enhydra.wireless.wml	org.w3c.dom.events
org.enhydra.wireless.wml.dom	org.w3c.dom.html
org.enhydra.xml.dom	org.w3c.dom.range
org.enhydra.xml.io	org.w3c.dom.traversal
org.enhydra.xml.lazydom	org.xml.sax
org.enhydra.xml.xmlc	org.xml.sax.ext
org.enhydra.xml.xmlc.dom	org.xml.sax.helpers

Runtime Objects

A number of classes are part of the runtime XMLC environment and are worth calling out. Throughout the remainder of this book, the following classes will appear repeatedly:

XMLObject: This is the interface for all XMLC compiler-generated XML objects. Its methods include toDocument() and buildDocument(), which are discussed later in this chapter, when we address how XMLC constructs the Java source that builds the DOM class template.

XMLObjectImpl: This class implements the XMLObject interface, as well as Document and DocumentInfo. Document is an extension of the Node interface. Node is the signature of the building block of the DOM, and is the interface from which all element interfaces are derived (for example, HTMLSelectElement, VoiceXMLBlockElement, and WMLGoElement).

HTMLObject: This interface is derived from both XMLObject and HTMLDocument. Together, these interfaces give HTMLObject its capability to represent an HTML page.

DOMFormatter: toDocument is a method for generating markup from a completed DOM. It is, however, limited in its capability to support features such as URL-encoding (for avoiding session-based cookies). DOMFormatter and the outputoptions class give finer control over the formatting issues of converting the XMLObject (DOM) to a string of HTML/XML. writeDOM() serves a similar role (and is the default method generated by AppWizard). See Chapter 8 for more on this class.

XMLCFactory: This is the interface for factories generating instances of XMLC classes. It generates an XMLObject from a DOM class. When implemented by XMLCReloadingFactory, the application can take advantage of XMLC's capability to add new templates without recompiling the entire application.

XMLCContext: This class delivers XMLC support to the standard servlet environment, including XMLC features such as dynamic reloading, debugging, logging, and URL encoding. This class is discussed at length in Chapter 10, "Servlet Web Applications."

Dynamic Loading and Auto-Recompilation

A relatively recent feature of XMLC is the addition of the DOM factory method. By default, the XMLC compiler generates a single, complete Java class representation of the DOM template class. The XMLC compiler can also be instructed to generate two classes:

- A class interface definition
- An implementation of that interface (and the DOM class template)

To support this configuration, XMLC 2.0 has introduced the notion of a XMLC factory method used to create a DOM class from the loading of these XMLC-generated classes.

The result is that old style XMLC programming went from statically binding the DOM class to the application, as seen here:

```
welcome = new WelcomeWML();
```

to the loosely coupled approach of using a factory method for loading DOM classes and their implementations, as seen here:

```
welcome = (WelcomeWML)comms.xmlcFactory.create(WelcomeWML.class);
```

Support for dynamic loading gives the application designer a number of options, some of which include giving the application, during runtime, the capability to:

- Automatically compile, then load newly reworked markup pages.
- Automatically load class implementations that were recently generated by an invoked XMLC command.
- Make runtime determinations based on any number of conditions to load a particular class implementation.

We will discuss the details of how to use these features in Chapter 7, "The xmlc Command," as well as in subsequent chapters where we will show how generating interfaces and implementations of those interfaces can be used to support an ASP application, using ShowFloor as the basis for our examples.

Strong Document-Specific Type Safety

Enhydra XMLC provides additional programming value by supporting DOM implementations of particular DOM sub-interfaces, such as HTML and WML. To illustrate what this value actually is, take a look at this bit of markup:

```
<OL id="checkList" start="100">
<LI>
</OL>
```

This is an HTML-ordered list. The `start` attribute indicates that the numbering should start at 100, like ordering a new checkbook and indicating what the first check number should be. Without use of the OL-specific `HTMLOListElement` DOM sub-interface, you would use a generic DOM method such as the following to change the start number to 1000:

```
Element orderedList = myPage.getElementCheckList();
orderedList.getAttributeNode("start").setValue("1000");
```

As you can see, we were still able to take advantage of an id attribute and XMLC's generation of a convenient accessor method, `getElementCheckList()`. Now, let's apply the `HTMLOListElement` method to the same task:

```
Element orderedList = myPage.getElementCheckList();
orderedList.setStart(1000);
```

As you can see, the `HTMLOListElement` implementation offers a method for the specific purpose of updating the starting number. This eliminates the possibility of, for example, misspelling the `start` attribute.

NOTE

To date, Lutris has not made the DOM implementations of VoiceXML, cHTML or XHTML available to Enhydra.org. No indication has been given if or when this may occur, although nothing prevents an open source contribution from other parties or individuals.

Although a subclass DOM implementation of a specific XML language supports solid development, it is not a showstopper. In fact, it's not difficult at all, because, as we demonstrated earlier, you can still take advantage of using id attributes to get XMLC to generate accessor methods.

The flip side is that you are more exposed to the more generic APIs of the DOM API, losing the advantages of type-safe manipulation. Later in the book, we will show how you can use XMLC to build an SVG (Scalar Vector Graphic) presentation using this new XML language as defined by the W3C.

Writing Out the DOM

Your work might not be over after you've completed the reworking of the DOM template. There may still be problems that remain before streaming the output of the DOM back to the client as converted to HTML or XML. The XMLC runtime environment supports document formatting capabilities with methods and classes such as the following:

- `writeDOM`
- `DOMFormatter`
- `outputoptions`

For most applications, a simple call to `writeDOM()` will take care of converting the DOM to markup. But if, for instance, you want to reset the MIME type or encoding, then control is available using some combination of these classes. These features will be covered in subsequent chapters.

Working with Templates

In XMLC programming, the term *template* applies to both the HTML or XML markup document as well as the DOM class generated by the `xmlc` command. *Template* is a truly meaningful description, given that XMLC encourages a design process that starts with a solid approximation of how the end result will appear after the DOM class template has been generated during runtime execution.

With the help of some unique XMLC features, the designer can populate the initial template with mocked-up content in portions of the template that will be updated dynamically. There are many advantages to viewing the page as a template that can be made to look "real" with mocked-up data.

Template node is another term used to refer to a portion of the document, such as a block of check boxes, their labels, and the settings to be updated based on queries to a SQL database.

The fact is that the entire document can viewed as a template. Portions of it are static (that is, not targeted for dynamic replacement or modification). The remaining portions are dynamic, identified by the placing of `id` attributes to indicate their dynamic status to the XMLC compiler.

Templates can be used for more than just the internal organization of the page. They can also be used to represent multiple instances of a page on a per-language, per-device, or XML language basis. A French-Canadian Admin HTML document can serve as a template that is unique from the German version of the same presentation. As we'll see, XMLC utilities make it easy to load the appropriate template depending on one of many factors, including which language or device is involved.

How XMLC Constructs a DOM Class

When XMLC compiles a markup page into a DOM class or template, it generates an intermediate Java source file that contains the logic that is compiled into the Java class. The xmlc command option -keep instructs xmlc to leave the Java source file behind.

HTML Tidy parses the input markup file. XMLC then generates the DOM-building logic, using either the Xerces or the LazyDOM APIs. LazyDOM is the default parser. When the compiled DOM class is loaded during runtime execution, the Xerces or LazyDOM builds the DOM in memory.

Let's take a look at an extremely simple HTML source file and portions of the DOM-building Java source code assembled by the xmlc command:

```
<html>
<body>
<p>Hello World
</body>
</html>
```

You'll invoke the xmlc command , instructing it to "keep" the intermediate source file available for your examination. And, because we're not worried too much about performance in this example, you'll instruct xmlc to use the Xerces parser:

```
xmlc -keep -dom xerces hello.html
```

The generated Java source file is, by default, named hello.java. Inside there are a number of interesting areas:

```
public hello extends
org.enhydra.xml.xmlc.html.HTMLObjectImpl
implements
org.enhydra.xml.xmlc.XMLObject,
org.enhydra.xml.xmlc.html.HTMLObject {...
```

The DOM template is called hello. It is the extension of the abstract HTMLObjectImpl class, which is the basis of all XMLC-generated HTML DOM classes. hello also implements the XMLObject interface, representing the majority of the document-building methods, and the HTMLObject interface that defines the HTML-specific toDocument method.

The buildDocument constructor method builds the document starting with the document prolog. setDocument establishes the MIME type and the encoding. The rest of the work of building the document and the accessor methods is left to buildSubDocument:

```
public void buildDocument() {
    org.apache.html.dom.HTMLDocumentImpl document =
➥(org.apache.html.dom.HTMLDocumentImpl)fDOMFactory.createDocument
```

```
➥(null, "HTML", null);
    setDocument(document,"text/html", "ISO-8859-1");
    buildSubDocument(document, document);^M
    }
```

buildSubDocument is relatively straightforward, particularly because, for the sake of our expla-
nation, we chose to forgo the insertion of an id attribute. After examining the input document,
XMLC knows exactly how many Node and Element variables to declare and assign. Note the
impact of the HTML Tidy parser, having improved on the original HTML by adding the HEAD
element and TITLE elements.

This code uses the combination of createElement(), createTextNode() (referred to as factory methods), and appendChild() to construct a DOM tree. The first two methods are defined
by the DOM's Document interface. Each is used depending on the HTML type that is being
processed, in this simple case, an element or a text node. The latter, appendChild(), is defined
by the Node interface:

```
private void buildSubDocument(org.w3c.dom.Document document,
    .w3c.dom.Node parentNode) {
    Node $node0, $node1, $node2, $node3, $node4;
    Element $elem0, $elem1, $elem2, $elem3;
    $elem1 = document.getDocumentElement();
    document.createElement("HTML");
    $elem2 = document.createElement("HEAD");
    $elem1.appendChild($elem2);
    $elem3 = document.createElement("TITLE");
    $elem2.appendChild($elem3);
    $elem2 = document.createElement("BODY");
    $elem1.appendChild($elem2);
    $elem3 = document.createElement("P");
    $elem2.appendChild($elem3);
    $node4 = document.createTextNode("Hello World");
    $elem3.appendChild($node4);
}
```

You now have a relatively complete example of a DOM template that will be instantiated at
runtime; although not all that interesting to someone wanting to take advantage of XMLC's
more interesting features.

Now let's introduce an id attribute that will cause XMLC to create accessor methods for
accessing the portion of the DOM tree that is due for dynamic treatment:

```
<html>
<body>
<p id="Greeting">Hello World
</body>
</html>
```

Impact of Inserting an `id` attribute

The impact of the `id` attribute on the generated DOM-building logic is the addition of new node-creating statements, and two accessor method declarations.

First, in the `buildSubDocument` method, everything looks about the same as the previous example, until you complete the creation of the `"P"` element node:

```
$elem3 = document.createElement("P");
$elem2.appendChild($elem3);
$attr3 = document.createAttribute("id");
$elem3.setAttributeNode($attr3);
$node4 = document.createTextNode("Greeting");
$attr3.appendChild($node4);
$element_Greeting = (org.apache.html.dom.HTMLParagraphElementImpl)$elem3;
$node4 = document.createTextNode("Hello World");
$elem3.appendChild($node4);
```

The detection of the `id` attribute by the parser generates a `setAttributeNode` call in lieu of `appendChild`, because attributes are their own `Nodes`. The `attr` object is created and attached to the `"P"` element's node with `createAttribute()`, representing an object-oriented view of the `id` attribute. This is necessary because the DOM does not represent attributes as being directly associated with `element` type `Nodes`.

There is also a rather out-of-place statement that casts a value of type `HTMLParagraphElementImpl`:

```
$element_Greeting = (org.apache.html.dom.HTMLParagraphElementImpl)$elem3;
```

The statements that follow are key to the creation of both accessor methods, `getElementGreeting` and `setTextGreeting`:

```
public org.w3c.dom.html.HTMLParagraphElement getElementGreeting() {
    return $element_Greeting;}
```

and

```
public void setTextGreeting(String text) {
    doSetText($element_Greeting, text);
    }
```

These two methods appear painfully simple. `getElementGreeting` simply returns the reference to the `"P"` element, revealing its location in the tree. This is the advantage of XMLC's compiler approach—it leverages pre-knowledge of targeted areas of the DOM for manipulation.

`setTextGreeting` is greatly simplified by the helper method `doSetText` from the `XMLObjectImpl` class.

> **NOTE**
>
> Although we discuss how XMLC generates accessor methods later in the chapter, you can see how XMLC's compiler strategy creates an advantage based on pre-knowledge of the constructed DOM tree. This pre-knowledge gives XMLC the opportunity to "know where the action is" in the DOM tree. This knowledge is also used to create direct access methods, as well as a technique for only instantiating the targeted portions of the DOM. This latter technique is referred to as the LazyDOM.

Enhancing Performance with LazyDOM

DOM programming is often criticized for its relatively poor performance and large memory footprint when compared to embedded template JSP programming. Representing the entire document as a fully accessible tree has programming advantages, but also introduces potentially significant overhead as a consequence.

By default, the Xerces-generated DOM expands each node when it is loaded into memory. These nodes represent costly events, particularly if only small portions of the template are to be updated dynamically. The instantiation of nodes in static locations of the DOM makes little sense. But, it's understandable why the DOM was implemented with this behavior, because the DOM itself would not know which portions of its object representation were going to be manipulated.

> **NOTE**
>
> Performance can also be heavily influenced by design practices. Embedding one table into another might be necessary for the relative positioning of HTML elements, but it can have a significant affect on the performance of rendering markup inside the browser.

XMLC compilation, however, introduces a new element of DOM programming; namely, its reliance on id attributes for identifying areas of dynamic content changes the rules.

With the introduction of XMLC 2.0 in late 2000, Lutris defined a subclass of the Xerces DOM, ironically named LazyDOM. LazyDOM implements a strategy that takes advantage of XMLC's pre-knowledge of which nodes will be accessed. Using the information provided by the id attributes, LazyDOM will instantiate only those nodes that represent the elements under consideration. Targeted nodes are accessed without expanding parents. All nodes are referenced from an array, which keeps track of which node has been instantiated.

A Read-Only DOM Template for Reference

LazyDOM starts with a read-only DOM template with only the `Document` node instantiated. The read-only DOM is used to systematically create the "instance DOM," which is the result tree that is eventually returned to the client. The following rules and conditions describe how the LazyDOM handles changes and traversals in a manner that minimizes instantiation, keeping the memory footprint to a minimum:

- All other nodes remain unexpanded.
- A node can exist without an instantiated parent. This is made possible by the presence of an XMLC `id`, and has a direct impact on the improved performance of the `getElement<AttributeValue>` methods.
- Direct children of a node are expanded when any child is accessed.
- Attribute nodes are expanded only when the element it is associated with is expanded.
- When it's time to generate the markup from the DOM, special formatters traverse the unexpanded portions of the template without forcing instantiation of the traveled portions.

When LazyDOM Isn't the Answer

There is a certain amount of overhead to supporting the LazyDOM approach. As it turns out, if a page is highly dynamic, the overhead increases to the point where there is no longer a performance advantage. In this case, it is best to override XMLC's default usage of LazyDOM in order to use the standard Xerces DOM parser.

In the next chapter, you'll see how to measure the performance of each approach, in order to appraise which parser implementation will best serve your performance goals.

Summary

Our conceptual discussions of DOMs, DTDs, XML, and HTML are now finished. The goal of this chapter was to set the stage for the how-to remainder of this book by setting a conceptual picture that will enable you to take full advantage of XMLC and the strategies to make the most of XMLC's capabilities.

The magic of XMLC, besides taking advantage of the DOM's approach to representing markup in an object-oriented manner, is its compiler approach to making DOMs more self-aware of the intended use of their contents for dynamic manipulation. This affects everything from easing the chore of XMLC development to improving general DOM modification performance by virtue of the LazyDOM.

The `xmlc` Command

IN THIS CHAPTER

This chapter introduces the brass tacks of using the XMLC compiler to build presentation templates for Web applications, wired or otherwise. Having weathered the storm of conceptual discussions, it's time to explore the capabilities and conventions of the xmlc command.

It should be clear by now that the XMLC compiler has been designed to be highly flexible with its internal tools and classes in order to support the implications of compiling both well-behaved XMLC and problematic HTML. It should not be too surprising that XMLC supports an equally flexible set of compile-time options, including the formats in which they can take form.

XMLC supports traditional UNIX-style command line conventions as well as the new generation of XML languages for configuration information. xmlc command options are designed to influence everything from the choice of parser, the content of selected portions of the resultant DOM class, and even the behavior of the Java compiler.

XMLC is a highly portable environment, including the compiler and runtime package. But, as an Enhydra development tool, you'll see that there are extensions to the Enhydra make environment that support additional ways to specify xmlc command options.

Syntax and Formats

The XMLC compiler, in the form of the xmlc command, is a highly configurable software application. You have at least three methods for indicating the options you want xmlc to use. For example, the runtime options for the xmlc command can be indicated on the command line, from a make file variable or from an ASCII file. Even the options themselves can be expressed as a traditional UNIX-style -opt command, or as elements and attributes in an XML metadata file.

We will now walk through the different forms that xmlc command options can take in preparation for talking about the available options and their roles.

The xmlc command supports options, command line and otherwise, that can be used by the developer to affect XMLC's behavior, including

- where to store generated DOM class templates,
- changes to selected URLs inside the markup,
- which parser or parsers to use, and
- which compile-time information to display.

This is only a subset of what you can do with the xmlc command. As you'll see, the granularity of the impact represented by different options can even be applied on a per-DOM element basis.

Command Line Options

Options to the xmlc command can be specified in a number of ways. Options can take the form of traditional command line options, or as entries in an xmlc options file, *<your name>*.xmlc.

For instance, you'll see that the option -urlmapping can be used to rename URLs in the generated file in order to update the file that a URL points to. The xmlc command takes the following form:

```
xmlc [options] [optfile.xmlc ...] markupDocument
```

where *markupDocument* is the name of the HTML or XML file that you are processing, and options and optfile.xmlc are entirely optional. As you've seen earlier, if you want to process a markup file, keep the intermediate source file and have it list the names of the access methods that are created. Then, using the Xerces DOM-building API, the following line will do the trick:

```
xmlc -keep -methods -dom xerces hello.html
```

The `options.xmlc` Format

The options file, with the required extension .xmlc, is used to organize options when there are too many to include on the command line, or they are shared by multiple files. Option files can also be used in conjunction with options on the command line.

The typical contents of an options file might appear like the following:

```
-keep
-methods
-d ../../classes
```

The format for an options file is oriented as a series of one or more lines, processed line by line. There is one option per line, beginning with a hyphen (-) character. Blank lines are ignored. Each line is parsed into words based on white space delimiters. Comments begin with the hash (#) character. In addition:

- Words may be quoted with single (') or double (") quotes to prevent breaking into words.
- The usual escape sequences such as \n and \t are recognized and converted to single characters as a quoted string is parsed.

There is a well-stated order of precedence with respect to the ordering of option files and their relationship to any options listed on the command line:

- First, option files are processed from left to right.
- Then all options specified on the command line are processed, left to right.

There is also a stated behavior with respect to the nature of the intended use of options themselves:

- For options that have a single value, command line options override any specified in options files.
- For options that can be specified multiple times, the values are accumulated from the options files and the command line.
- If an option is repeated more than once and it was not designed to be specified multiple times, the last option found will be used.

The Enhydra AppWizard creates an `options.xmlc` file as part of the generation of the stub application environment. Its contents differ depending on the type of application it has been asked to initialize. For superservlet (EAF) applications, the contents of `options.xmlc` are

```
-urlmapping "Welcome.html" "/RedirectPresentation.po"
```

For standard servlets, the contents are

```
-urlmapping "Welcome.html" "/redirect"
```

The function of `-urlmapping` will be explained later in this chapter.

There is a third format or methodology for specifying options to the `xmlc` command. XMLC metadata is discussed later in the chapter, after you've had a chance to review most of the key `xmlc` command options.

xmlc Command Options

I'm going to take a task-oriented walk through the more interesting `xmlc` commands. The full listing of `xmlc` command options, in the conventional dashed `getopts` style, is located in Appendix A, "XMLC Command Line Options." For illustrative purposes, I'll confine the examples to the simple command line format.

Viewing the Intermediate Java DOM Source File

Using the `-keep` option, you can tell the XMLC compiler to preserve the Java source file that is assembled by XMLC and used to generate the template class file. The source file and the class file are given the same name.

Besides using this feature for debugging purposes, it's an excellent learning tool for understanding how the XMLC compiler goes about its work, including how it codes up the accessor methods, and how it builds the source code that will build the DOM tree after it is loaded by the application at runtime.

By default, XMLC keeps the source file in the current working directory from which the `xmlc` command is executed. To specify an alternative location, use `-sourceout`. For instance, the following line will create the file `/tmp/vendor.java`:

```
xmlc -keep -sourceout /tmp vendor.html
```

Selecting Parsers

The XMLC compiler employs the services of a number of parsing engines for a number of reasons. This is the strategy that XMLC uses to handle the problematic situation of malformed HTML documents. It's also how XMLC offers a choice of DOM-generating techniques that give the developer some tools to minimize the DOM's runtime footprint and performance profile.

HTML Tidy Versus Swing

There are two HTML parsers supported by the `xmlc` command. The default parser is JTidy. JTidy is a Java port of Dave Raggert's HTML Tidy, an HTML syntax checker and pretty printer. JTidy is used as a tool for cleaning up malformed and faulty HTML. As JTidy encounters markup problems during the processing of an input HTML document, it attempts to correct the markup, simultaneously generating a warning, or perhaps giving up and generating a fatal error message. Developers are encouraged to address the root cause of each warning message until they are no longer generated by JTidy.

The Swing parser that's bundled by Sun with the Java Foundation Classes was the original XMLC HTML parser. It is included for backward compatibility reasons. To use the Swing parser, you must specify the command line option in order to override the default use of JTidy:

```
xmlc -parser swing <filename>.html
```

Neither parser is perfect, because it is not possible to account for all the possible variations on HTML formatting that one can produce, especially given the fact that so much HTML is still created by hand.

LazyDOM Versus Xerces

The XMLC compiler uses the Xerces parser from Apache to construct DOM-building Java logic that will be executed by the application during runtime. LazyDOM, the default `xmlc` parser, is the Enhydra innovation on top of Xerces that adds the notion of a read-only template to minimize the per-node instantiation of the DOM template during runtime. It is a subclass extension of the Xerces interface. Why offer a choice of XML parsers if LazyDOM is so much faster than Xerces? As it turns out, this is not always the case. The results depend on your markup page's balance of static versus dynamic content:

- If your page is highly dynamic, requiring extensive runtime DOM manipulation, Xerces may be the preferred option.
- If your page is modestly to moderately dynamic, then LazyDOM might give your application the best performance and DOM-manipulating characteristics.

It is up to the developer to determine which strategy is best suited for a particular page. This can be determined by empirical evaluation using the `XMLC_DOM_STATS` message level described in the section "How to Measure DOM Behavior."

Changing URLs During the Development Process

Another real-world feature of XMLC is the capability to automatically map one URL to another. It's a commonplace situation that a page under development will point to other static, prototyped markup pages. These pages will eventually be replaced by dynamic presentation objects as they are implemented and refined. Until then, they are static pages as referenced from your working page in order to convey the flow of the application until it is fully functional.

URL mapping gives the developer the capability to update URL references from the `xmlc` command line, as opposed to reworking the URL references in the working page by hand. This makes it possible to define an application-wide system for updating individual pages in a systematic process.

URL changes can be accomplished by a set of URL mapping options, namely `-urlmapping`, `-urlregexpmapping`, and `-urlsetting`.

The option `-urlmapping` is the simplest of the three options, supporting simple mappings of *from* and *to* URL names:

```
xmlc -urlmapping adminVendor.html admin.po?admin=vendor admin.html
```

The following example uses the option `-urlregexpmapping` to write a single expression that performs all the necessary mappings. In this example, the filename's tail is simply replaced with a `.po` suffix. `-urlregexpmapping` is implemented with the `gnu.regexp` package introduced in Chapter 5, "Enhydra, Java/XML Application Server."

```
xmlc -urlregexpmapping "^(.*)\\.html$" "$1.po" vendor.html
```

There's also a way to change the value of the `href` attribute in an anchor tag using an `id` attribute. `-urlsetting` updates the `id`-referenced `href` attribute with a new value. If the initial markup in the fictitious markup file `vendor.html` looks like

```
<P><A id=vendorURL href=dummy.html>ACME Corp</A>
```

then the following `xmlc` command line will update the URL reference:

```
xmlc -urlsetting vendorURL "http://www.acmecorp.com" vendor.html
```

What if you just want to update URLs without creating a DOM template? -docout is the xmlc option that will save the updated markup to an ASCII file:

```
xmlc -urlsetting vendorURL "http://www.acmecorp.com" -docout vendorFinal.
➥html vendor.html
```

Discarding Mocked-Up Data

Giving designers the capability to leave mocked-up structure and content in a document is a distinguishing feature of XMLC. Mocked-up content gives the document template a live feeling that is highly useful to design reviewers.

There are a number of opportunities during development and runtime to remove mockup. However, the easiest way with the least impact is to use the xmlc command option -discard in combination with class attributes to identify unwanted mockup in the target document file.

Listing 7.1 contains an HTML table of vendors and vendor types. The first non-header row is the row template. This template will be used like a rubber stamp by the presentation object to insert new rows with real data. This is done by a cloning process described in Chapter 8, "HTML Presentations" The rows that follow the first row represent mocked-up content, serving a necessary role during the evaluation of the application's storyboards by the designer and, undoubtedly, the customer. But this content is useless to the runtime application.

LISTING 7.1   SFA/presentations/VendorList.html

```html
<html>
<head>
<title>Untitled Document</title>
<meta http-equiv="Content-Type" content="text/html; charset=iso-8859-1">
<link rel="stylesheet" href="listings.css" type="text/css">
</head>
<body bgcolor="#FFFFFF" text="#000000">
<table summary="Table of Vendors">
 <tr>
  <th>Vendor</th>
  <th>Vendor Type</th>
 </tr>
<tr id=VendorInfo>
  <td id=VendorName>ACME Corp</td>
  <td id=VendorType>App Servers</td>
</tr>
<tr class=DiscardMe>
  <td>Blue Corp</td>
  <td>Office Automation</td>
```

LISTING 7.1 Continued

```
</tr>
<tr class=DiscardMe>
  <td>Green Corp</td>
  <td>Operating Systems</td>
</tr>
</table>
</body>
</html>
```

The designer has inserted the class attribute `DiscardMe` in the last two rows of mockup content. There's no better time to remove these rows as when the DOM template object is being constructed by the `xmlc` command. The way to instruct the `xmlc` command to delete this information is as follows:

```
xmlc -delete-class "DiscardMe" vendorList.html
```

If you were to keep the intermediate Java source file, you'd see that all references to these rows are missing. This is because they were ignored by XMLC during construction of the DOM-building source code following the initial parsing of the input markup file.

Handling Multiple Classes

Classes can accept multiple values in the form of strings delimited with white spaces. If you need, for example, to use the class attribute for specifying a stylesheet selector in order to render the mocked-up document consistent in appearance, then you may do so simply by insuring that there's a space that separates it from the other string, `mockup`:

```
<tr class="rowColor mockup">
  <td>Green Corp</td>
  <td>Operating Systems</td>
<tr>
```

The string value that you select to indicate that the row or any other mocked-up document object will be discarded is up to you.

Why do we use the class attribute? Because class attributes can include values that are used elsewhere. `id` attributes cannot be used, given their requirement for uniqueness within a markup document.

Getting Progress Information and More from `xmlc`

Everything you would ever want to know about the compilation of your HTML or XML file can be gathered with the following invocation of `xmlc`:

```
xmlc -verbose -parseinfo -info -methods Listing01.html
```

Let's take a look at each of these options and their effect on the xmlc command.

What Methods Were Created by XMLC?

Use the -methods option to view the list of generated getElement<id value> and setText<id value> methods. For the HTML page listed in Listing 7.1, this option returns the following:

```
public org.W3C.dom.html.HTMLTableRowElement getElementVendorInfo();
public org.W3C.dom.html.HTMLTableCellElement getElementVendorName();
public void setTextVendorName(String text);
public org.W3C.dom.html.HTMLTableCellElement getElementVendorType();
public void setTextVendorType(String text);
```

Getting URL Info

The -info option will return additional compilation information regarding any URLs that are encountered:

```
Element IDs:
  VendorInfo => org.W3C.dom.html.HTMLTableRowElement
  VendorName => org.W3C.dom.html.HTMLTableCellElement
  VendorType => org.W3C.dom.html.HTMLTableCellElement
Document URLs:
  ../../../../../SFA/presentation/listings.css
```

As you can see, markup objects are fully resolved, including element types and the URL.

Getting Parser Information

Using -parserInfo will give you a detailed, structured review of how the input markup document was parsed. Tag labels are added for qualifying the nature of displayed node information, such as RootNode, DocTypeTag, TextNode and so on. The command

```
xmlc -delete-class DiscardMe -parserInfo Listing01.html
```

generates the following listing:

```
0>RootNode: ''
4>  DocTypeTag: 'html PUBLIC "-//W3C//DTD HTML 4.01 Transitional//EN"'
4>  StartTag: html
8>    StartTag: head
12>      StartTag: title
16>        TextNode: 'Listing 6.1 - Vendor Table'
12>      StartTag: meta content="text/html; charset=iso-8859-1"
➥http-equiv="Content-Type"
12>      StartTag: link type="text/css"
href="../../../../../Lutris/ChiefEvangelism/book/XMLCbasics/listings.css"
➥rel="stylesheet"
8>    StartTag: body text="#000000" bgcolor="#FFFFFF"
12>      StartTag: table summary="Table of Vendors"
```

```
16>         StartTag: tr
20>           StartTag: th
24>             TextNode: 'Vendor'
20>           StartTag: th
24>             TextNode: 'Vendor Type'
16>         StartTag: tr id="VendorInfo"
20>           StartTag: td id="VendorName"
24>             TextNode: 'ACME Corp'
20>           StartTag: td id="VendorType"
24>             TextNode: 'App Servers'
16>         StartTag: tr class="DiscardMe"
20>           StartTag: td
24>             TextNode: 'Blue Corp'
20>           StartTag: td
24>             TextNode: 'Office Automation'
16>         StartTag: tr class="DiscardMe"
20>           StartTag: td
24>             TextNode: 'Green Corp'
20>           StartTag: td
24>             TextNode: 'Operating Systems'
```

Watching the Progress of XMLC Compilation

Use -verbose to see the xmlc command's progress through parsing and code generation.
During parsing, it will echo the name of the DOM factory that was used for parsing the input
HTML/XML file:

```
>>> parsing Vendor.html
>>> using DOM Factory class:
org.enhydra.xml.xmlc.dom.lazydom.LazyHTMLDomFactory
>>> generating code
  creating class: Vendor.java
>>> compiling code
C:/jdk1.3//bin/javac Vendor.java
>>> completed
```

The LazyHTMLDomFactory refers to the class that constructs the DOM-building code using the
LazyDOM extensions to Xerces.

Dictating Generated Class Names

You can specify the qualified name of the DOM class file generated by XMLC with the
-class option. In lieu of using this option, XMLC takes the name of the input file and replaces
the file's tail with .class:

```
xmlc -class SFA.presentation.vendor Vendor.html
```

To specify a location outside the current working directory, you can specify the path to -d, which is passed directly to the Java compiler.

-validate and XML

You will probably always want a validating DTD to support the markup document you are processing with XMLC. There may be times, however, such as when you're offline and your DTD references a W3C URL. -validate can be used to override the use of DTDs:

```
xmlc -validate yes|no Vendor.html
xmlc -validate true|false Vendor.html
```

The default, of course, is to validate.

> **NOTE**
>
> -validate no is yet another example of the business requirements that went into the design of Enhydra and other Enhydra technologies. Discussed earlier in Chapter 5, the Enhydra Multiserver was designed to accept HTTP requests directly. This was done not to compete with Apache, but instead to simplify the task of consultants performing development on airplanes at 40,000 feet, so they wouldn't have to worry about an absentee network, or having to turn their laptops into enterprise-ready servers.

Character Sets and Encoding

Sometimes it's easy to forget that computers don't see or understand characters. They see the world and express results through numbers. They support the world's languages as data that is encoded in order to represent every symbol, whether it's a "½," "-," or a "®." Encoding is a form of Morse code, used to instruct the receiving operator, in our case a browser or an i-mode phone, how to map the code (numbers) into human-readable characters.

You can control encoding from both the XMLC command line and your application. By default, the DOM class template that is generated by XMLC lists ISO-8859-1 as the Western European character encoding for Unix. UTF-8, an 8-bit Unicode encoding type, and Shift_JIS for Japanese under Windows are other examples of encoding types. There's a nice list of the character sets used by various countries at http://www.w3.org/International/O-charset-lang.html.

The xmlc option -html:encoding is available when you want to override the default encoding that is used to build the DOM class template:

```
xmlc -html:encoding UTF-8 vendor.html
```

This example instructs the xmlc command to use UTF-8 encoding. This also becomes the default encoding to use when streaming the application-finalized DOM class template markup back to the client.

There's another opportunity at runtime to change the encoding in your final DOM document, using the class Outputoptions and its method setEncoding(). Actually, Outputoptions is used by the XMLC compiler as well, to format the initial DOM template.

The following XMLC-generated code was generated using the -html:encoding option with a value of UTF-8, and can be viewed by running xmlc with the -keep option:

```
....
private static final org.enhydra.xml.io.OutputOptions fPreFormatOutputOptions;
....
static {
  org.enhydra.xml.lazydom.html.LazyHTMLDocument doc =
➡ (org.enhydra.xml.lazydom.html.LazyHTMLDocument)fDOMFactory.createDocument
➡(null, "HTML", null);
  buildTemplateSubDocument(doc, doc);
  fTemplateDocument = new org.enhydra.xml.lazydom.TemplateDOM(doc);
  fPreFormatOutputOptions = new org.enhydra.xml.io.OutputOptions();
  fPreFormatOutputOptions.setFormat(org.enhydra.xml.io.OutputOptions.
➡FORMAT_AUTO);
  fPreFormatOutputOptions.setEncoding("UTF-8");
  fPreFormatOutputOptions.setPrettyPrinting(false);
  fPreFormatOutputOptions.setIndentSize(4);
  fPreFormatOutputOptions.setPreserveSpace(true);
  fPreFormatOutputOptions.setOmitXMLHeader(false);
  fPreFormatOutputOptions.setOmitDocType(false);
  fPreFormatOutputOptions.setOmitEncoding(false);
  fPreFormatOutputOptions.setDropHtmlSpanIds(true);
  fPreFormatOutputOptions.setOmitAttributeCharEntityRefs(true);
  fPreFormatOutputOptions.setPublicId(null);
  fPreFormatOutputOptions.setSystemId(null);
  fPreFormatOutputOptions.setMIMEType(null);
  fPreFormatOutputOptions.markReadOnly();
}
```

Some Runtime Options

Although most of this chapter has focused on compile-time options, there are some directly related runtime topics, most of which we will cover in the remainder of the book.

Runtime DOM Debugging

XMLC provides the -dump option for dumping the contents of the presentation template. This data is the result of compilation before the template has been loaded and manipulated by the presentation logic. What if you want to look at the DOM after it's been loaded by the factory method; or perhaps after the page's table template has been augmented with new rows?

The class DOMInfo has a number of fields for indicating which data to print; however, the printTree() method is the primary feature of this class.

This method has special handling for LazyDOMs to prevent expansion and avoid affecting the overall performance of the application. This can therefore be used as a nice debugging tool in a production situation:

```
import java.io.*;
import org.enhydra.xml.dom.DOMInfo;

public class SpacemanPresentation implements HttpPresentation {
public void run(HttpPresentationComms comms)
throws HttpPresentationException, IOException {

VendorHTML vendor;
NodeList nodeList;
  ...
 PrintWriter out = new PrintWriter(new OutputStreamWriter(System.out, "UTF8"));
 DOMInfo.printTree("SVG Tree Details", vendor, DOMInfo.PRINT_ATTR_DETAILS,out);
 comms.response.setContentType("image/wml");
 comms.response.writeDOM(vendor);
}
```

If you want to print just the named node, then you can turn recursion off by passing the static integer NO_RECURSION when invoking the DOMInfo constructor.

How to Measure DOM Behavior

The XMLC environment presents a number of options for dumping the contents and structure of the DOM from the point of view of both content and element and other markup interfaces. These options deal with both runtime as well as compile-time.

There is another view of the DOM that can help you watch and evaluate the runtime dynamic behavior of the DOM footprint from a more statistical format.

Setting the following in the Multiserver configuration file (under the AppWizard-generated source tree's /input directory) will generate some interesting runtime metrics regarding the state of the DOM tree:

```
Server.LogToFile = XMLC_DOM_STATS
```

The Multiserver will route formatted statistics to `./output/multiserver.log` unless you specify another location for the log file.

Setting the XMLC_DOM_STATS message level will cause the XMLC library to generate output that shows each node type, how many of each exists in the template, how many have been expanded, and which ones have been created dynamically (for example, added row nodes to a table template).

How do you interpret this data? If a large percentage of the nodes are expanded after manipulation of the DOM at runtime, then the LazyDOM might not be an advantage over the standard Xerces DOM. The data might also reflect a costly DOM strategy, even though a small part of the DOM is intended for dynamic updating.

Table 7.1 reflects the kinds of numbers generated by the simple loading of the DOM class template representing the SFAdminLogin screen (Figure 2.1 and Listing 2.1) from Chapter 2, "XMLC Development." As you might expect, there are only 2 of the 120 template nodes that have been expanded because no traversals or modifications have taken place. In Chapter 9, "Presentation Strategies," we'll show these numbers again after modification occurs.

TABLE 7.1 XMLC Metadata Directives

Node Type	Template	Expanded	New
Element	32	1	0
Attr	40	0	0
Text	48	0	0
CDATASection	0	0	0
EntityReference	0	0	0
Entity	0	0	0
ProcessingInstruction	0	0	0
Comment	0	0	0
Document	0	1	0
DocumentType	0	0	0
DocumentFragment	0	0	0
Notation	0	0	0
Total	120	2	0

Auto-Recompilation and Auto-Class Loading

Enhydra extends designer/developer independence one step further with support for automatic recompilation and the loading of markup pages. Auto compilation answers the question: "If I just want to make changes to the markup presentation, do I have to rebuild my presentation object?"

XMLC supports two options to enable applications to perform runtime auto-recompilation and DOM class loading:

- Build a DOM from markup, then load the resulting DOM class template.
- Load a pre-made DOM class template.

Both of these options key off of a source document or DOM class timestamp that can be used by the application to determine that auto-compilation and/or auto-loading should take place.

> **NOTE**
>
> The auto-recompilation feature is not nearly as interesting or dynamic as the application architecture implications of using the xmlc command to generate a DOM class in the form of an interface and an implementation.
>
> As we'll discuss in Chapter 9, using the -generate both option will give you the capability to employ factory methods that give you extreme flexibility in changing the behavior of document presentations.

Reasons for Using Auto-Recompilation

Why would you use auto-recompilation, particularly given that there is some processing overhead to support it?

- Your document's design is basically solid, but you want to make changes to the orientation of the document's organization.
- You want to make changes to the static areas and content of your markup document.
- You want to make a change to a URL embedded in the document to point to a new site (or away from a bad site).
- You want to cause the reloading of a server-side include (see later in this chapter) in order to update an advertisement area, a header, or the navigation bar.
- You want non-programmers to be able to change the presentation without having to involve you.

The ShowFloor application is a perfect example of why an application might take advantage of auto-recompilation. If your application has been designed well, and all the advertised services have been well received, then eliminating the need to tweak the application logic when there is a new show-hosting customer should be possible.

Designers can make changes to the document as long as they leave the id attributes intact (in relationship to their intended association). Or, a script can be executed that pre-compiles the HTML, placing it in a known directory located within the application server environment.

xmlc Options for Auto-Compiling and Auto-Reloading

To set the stage for enabling auto-compilation and/or auto-reloading, you must compile your document with one of the following xmlc command options:

- xmlc -for-recomp—For auto-recompilation and auto-classloading.
- xmlc -generate both—For auto-classloading only.

Auto-Compilation with -for-recomp

The -for-recomp xmlc option supports auto-recompilation by generating three files, using the vendor.html example shown in Figure 7.1:

- vendor.java is the Java Interface definition of the DOM class template. The naming convention is <document>.java.
- vendorImpl.java is the implementation of the DOM class template. The naming convention is <document>Impl.java.
- vendor.xmlc is the XMLC metadata file containing the necessary compile-time XMLC options that are associated with the document and its compilation.

Auto-Class Loading with -generate both

If the intended design scheme for your application is to automatically load new, pre-compiled DOM classes, then you will use the -generate both option for XMLC.

Figure 7.2 shows that this option simply generates the Java interface and implementation files for the document. No vendor.xmlc file is generated because there is nothing about XMLC metadata (that is, xmlc command options) that affects the runtime behavior of the generated DOM class.

The same file naming conventions are used as the Java files listed for -for-recomp.

7

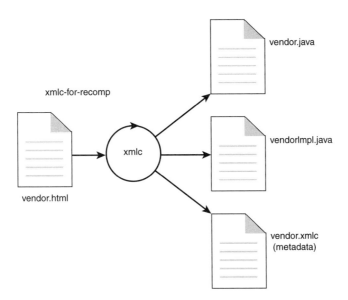

FIGURE 7.1

Output of the -for-recomp xmlc *option.*

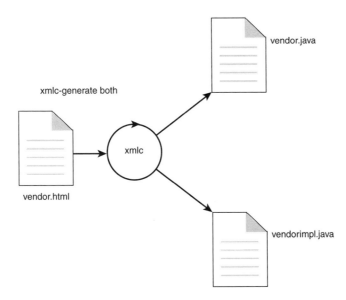

FIGURE 7.2

Output of the -generate both xmlc *option.*

Preparing the Application Environment for Auto-Recompilation

As we have discussed, there are any number of ways to pass XMLC options to the `xmlc` command. You can update `XMLC_HTML_OPTS` with `+= -generate both`; you can add the line `-generate both` to your `options.xmlc` file; or you can use the XMLC metadata approach, described later in this chapter.

There are other actions you must take in order to prepare the application's deployment organization to support the capability for the JRE to handle recompilation.

File Location Requirements

The auto-recompilation and class loading feature requires that DOM classes remain as classes and are not loaded into a jar file, as normally happens in the Enhydra environment. The markup document must also be stored in the same directory as the class files.

In your application's `config.mk` file, located at the root of the AppWizard-generated application source tree, set

```
XMLC_AUTO_COMP= YES
```

The impact of this `make` rule is to store your markup source document and associate DOM class in the application directory

```
./output/lib/classes
```

Configuration File Requirements

The following modifications must be made to your application's configuration files located under the `./input` directory:

- To enable auto-class loading only:

  ```
  Server.AutoReload = true
  Server.ClassPath[] = <location of the generated class file>
  ```

  Compile your document with the `-generate both` option.

- To enable auto-compilation and auto-class loading:

  ```
  Server.XMLC.Autorecompilation = true
  ```

  Compile your document with the `-for-recomp` option.

Monitoring Auto-Compilation and Auto-Class Loading

You can monitor the behavior of these runtime features in your application with the `xmlc` logging level. In your application configuration file, `./input/<application>.conf`, append the logging level `xmlc` to the `LogToFile` object:

```
Server.LogToFile[] = EMERGENCY, ALERT, CRITICAL, ERROR, XMLC
```

To check the auto-recompilation functionality of your application, launch the application, then refresh the browser (shift-refresh) to see output to the log file.

xmlcFactory at Runtime

In order to implement the auto-recompilation and auto-class reloading feature in your application, you must instantiate your DOM class template with the xmlcFactory method from your presentation object:

```
VendorHTML welcome = (VendorHTML)comms.xmlcFactory.create(VendorHTML.class);
```

There is a mild impact to runtime performance created by the use of xmlcFactory, because it accesses the file timestamps of the document markup files or the DOM class file in order to determine whether recompilation or reloading are in order.

NOTE

If auto-recompilation and auto-class loading are not turned on by the environment's configuration, then the create method defaults to using new(), and there is no performance impact as a result.

Auto-Recompilation for Non-Enhydra Environments

In Chapter 10, "Servlet Web Applications," we will show how you can use the XMLCContext class to configure the standard Web Container environment to access auto-recompilation and auto-class loading.

Server-Side Includes

Server-side includes (SSIs) are an excellent approach to achieving reusability of document fragments such as standard headers, footers, and navigation bars throughout your application. Pages that incorporate frames as a way of achieving similar goals are problematic for making your Web site search engine-friendly. SSIs componentize your pages without inadvertently confusing search engines.

A simplified version of the ShowFloor file `footer.ssi` would appear something like the following:

```
<— begin ShowFloorFooter.ssi —>
<table summary="ShowFloor Table" border="0" width="100%" >
<tr>
<td>
<a href="http://www.otterproductions.com/index.html
```

```
<img alt="Otter Productions" src="../media/otter.gif" border="0">
</td>
</tr>
</table>
<— end ShowFloorFooter.ssi —>
```

The SSI file is then requested by the host page using a syntax that is reflected in the following:

```
<!—#include file="ShowFloorFeader.ssi" —>
```

For most HTTP servers that support SSI, this would mean that the Web server is being instructed to load and integrate this file into the parent page at the time the parent page is requested.

In the case of XMLC, this behavior is more aptly described as a "compile-time include," where the XMLC compiler is being instructed to pull the named file into the parent page. XMLC is told to process server-side includes with the `-ssi` command line option.

Interfaces for Late-Binding Implementations

The role of your SSI file may range from a simple banner page with a URL reference or two to a fully dynamic navigational bar. This raises the question: How do you link the behavior or context of an SSI with the context of the currently displayed "main" page?

A way to accomplish this is to take advantage of XMLC's capability to generate two class files from a single compile. The first class is a Java interface that describes the SSI document fragment's accessor methods. The second class is the implementation of the interface. Using the command option `-generate both` generates these to files.

By compiling every document to implement this interface, you now have common code to manipulate the SSI. As part of the process of returning your manipulated DOM, you could follow the following algorithm:

```
if (mainDocument instanceof ShowFloorFooter) {
  UpdateFooter((ShowFloorFooter)mainDocument);
}
```

Because SSI is a compile-time phenomenon with XMLC, you might draw the conclusion that you would have to rebuild the application if you decide to change one of the included SSI files. This is not the case, because XMLC supports runtime class loading.

Again, we'll visit this strategy in greater detail in Chapter 9.

XMLC Metadata

XMLC compiler options can also be passed to `xmlc` in the form of an XML language called Enhydra XMLC metadata. Governed by XML rules and an XML Schema, XMLC metadata gives the developer greater control and flexibility to affect the behavior of the `xmlc` command.

Metadata applies directives that affect multiple document as well as sub-document levels. Not surprisingly, many of the directives and their sub-element options map directly to the effects of command line options. Metadata directives can be used to affect file compilation, groups of input markup files, and specific markup file elements.

Both options files and XMLC Document metadata files must end with the filename tail .xmlc. An XML document prolog tells the XMLC compiler that it is to be read as an XML metadata file.

Directives, Attributes, and Option Elements

There are eight directives, all of which are listed in Table 7.2. The directive <document> remains unimplemented at the time of this book's writing. The entire metadata schema is presented in Appendix B, "XMLC Metadata."

TABLE 7.2 XMLC Metadata Directives

Directive	Description
<compileOptions>	Specifies options for the xmlc compiler. Includes option elements such as printDOM, keepGeneratedSource, documentOutput, and processSSI.
<inputDocument>	Specifies the document that is to be compiled, and attributes such as the document format. Option element include is used in cases that combine auto-recompilation and SSI.
<parser>	Specifies the parser and parser options. Optional element xcatalog references external entities.
<html>	Specifies HTML-specific options. Option elements are htmlTagSet, htmlTag, htmlAttr, and compatibility.
<domEdits>	Specifies modifications performed on the DOM during compilation. Option elements include urlEdit, urlMapping, urlRegExpMapping, and deleteElement.
<document>	Specifies how a document is validated, as well as how source code is generated on specific elements. document *and its option elements* elementDef *and* tagClass *are not currently implemented.*
<documentClass>	Specifies properties of the XMLC document class to generate. Includes option elements such as generate, extends, and recompilation.
<javaCompiler>	Specifies information for the Java compiler. javacOption is an option element that specifies an option to send to the Java compiler.

Examples of Directive Usages

The XMLC metadata directive `compileOptions` addresses compile-time options. Each option is specified as an attribute name-value pair. The following sample metadata directs the `xmlc` command to generate the same output it would with the roughly equivalent command line options `-parseinfo`, `-keep`, `-dump`, `-methods`, and `-verbose`. As you can see, `compileOptions`'s attributes are generally more self-defining than their command line option equivalents (for example, `-keep` versus `keepGeneratedSource`).

```
<compileOptions
  verbose="true"
  printDocumentInfo="true"
  printParseInfo="true"
  printDOM="true"
  printAccessorInfo="true"
  keepGeneratedSource="true"\>
```

Instructions to manipulate the contents of the DOM during compilation are specified as sub-elements, or "option elements" contained by the `domEdits` directive. The following option elements, and their associated attributes, replicate the actions of command line options `-urlmapping`, `-urlregexpmapping`, and `-delete-class`:

```
<domEdits>
  <urlMapping url="admindemo.html" newUrl="admin.po"/>
  <urlMapping url="login.html" newUrl="admin.po?event=login"/>
  <urlRegExpMapping regexp="^(.*)\\.html$" "$1.po"/>
  <deleteElement elementClasses="DiscardMe"/>
</domEdits>
```

Slight Deviations Between Command Options and Metadata

A one-to-one mapping between command line options and XMLC metadata is not always the case. You will want to be careful to understand exactly which directive attributes or options elements to specify in order to get the desired configuration or effect.

The `DocumentClass` directive deals with the creation details of the output DOM class template. In order to use this metadata format for specifying, for example, that the DOM class should be prepared for auto-recompilation and auto-class reloading, the following three attributes must be called out:

```
<documentClass
  delegateSupport="true"
  createMetadata="true"
  generate="both" />
```

The attribute `delegateSupport` deals with the creation of a "delegate" whose role is to start up a new classloader. The fact that you cannot stop and restart a new class in the same classloader is one of the reasons why Enhydra's architecture supports multiple classloaders.

Building with Enhydra make Files

The Enhydra 3 make file system is unique to the Enhydra development environment. Because the XMLC development and runtime environments were designed to be highly portable, we'll focus on the added features of the Enhydra development environment.

Enhydra features a hierarchy of make files and make file variables that automate much of the process of building XMLC presentations. This feature was discussed in Chapter 5,"Enhydra, Java/XML Application Server." For each supported language (HTML and WML), the Open Source Enhydra 3 make rules use the *basename* of files in the format *basename.tail* to generate class names in the format *basename*HTML.

For example, if you create a markup page for WML called `Vendor.wml`, the make rules will cause `xmlc` to generate the DOM class template by the name of `vendorHTML.class`. This class file is placed in the classes directory within the application source tree hierarchy. The following command line is generated by the make rules of `stdrules.mk` when the make command is executed inside the application's source presentation sub-directory. The generated `xmlc` command passes the `-d` option to the `javac` command, indicating the resultant class' name and where it is to be installed:

```
/usr/local/enhydra3.1b1/bin/xmlc -d ../../../classes -class SFA.
➥presentation.VendorWML options.xmlc Vendor.wml
```

The central make file is `stdrules.mk`, located in `/usr/local/enhydra3.1b1/lib`. This is where the naming convention and the features of the language-specific variable names are defined.

Listing 7.2 illustrates a make file for processing our WML source file. This file was generated by AppWizard. The make file variable `XMLC_WML_OPTS_FILE` was created to dictate two things to the rules in `stdrules.mk`:

- the name of the options file that you use, and
- the markup language type, as indicated by the naming convention `XMLC_<MarkUpLanguage>_OPTS_FILE`.

LISTING 7.2   `./src/SFA/presentation/Makefile`

```
#
# Vendor.wml
#
```

Listing 7.2 Continued

```
# Copyright 2001 SAMS Publishing
#
ROOT = ../../..
PACKAGEDIR = SFA/presentation
WML_CLASSES = VendorWML
WML_DIR = .
CLASSES = VendorPresentation \
RedirectPresentation
SUBDIRS = media
XMLC_WML_OPTS_FILE = options.xmlc
include $(ROOT)/config.mk
```

By default, AppWizard specifies options.xmlc.

Table 7.3 explains the system of make variables specific to the rules found in stdrules.mk.

Table 7.3 Enhydra make File Variables for XMLC Compilation

WML_CLASSES	Names of DOM classes to be generated by XMLC.
WML_DIR	Name of directory containing the file(s) to be compiled by XMLC.
XMLC_WML_OPTS_FILE	Name of file containing options to pass to the xmlc command.
XMLC_WML_OPTS	List of options to pass to the xmlc command.

The make file variables XMLC_WML_OPTS_FILE and XMLC_WML_OPTS cannot co-exist in the same file. This makes sense because they are both used in the role of passing options to the xmlc command. You must pick which approach you want to take.

If you are compiling WML files, change the variable names where the language name appears: WML_CLASSES, WML_DIR, XMLC_WML_OPTS_FILE, and XMLC_WML_OPTS.

If you want to pass xmlc command options from the make file, then editing the XMLC_WML_OPTS variable as follows will do the trick:

```
XMLC_HTML_OPTS += -keep -dump
```

Again, the make files that compose the Enhydra development environment for building XMLC applications are unique to Enhydra. For non-Enhydra environments, you will have to define your own system, which is more than well-supported by the xmlc command, option files, and XMLC metadata files.

Summary

We've demonstrated the flexibility of the XMLC compiler environment and runtime environment from a number of perspectives. The manner in which the compiler can be instructed to effect different behaviors ranges from command line options, make file variables, and the use of an XML language composed of XMLC metadata. The application, as well, can be affected in its capability to automatically recompile documents and/or reload DOM class templates when either the document or class have been updated to reflect changes in the markup.

The XMLC feature of generating two Java classes and distinguishing the DOM's interface from the DOM's implementation is the key not only to automatic recompilation and class reloading, but to other interesting application runtime architectures as well. We will visit some of these possibilities in Chapter 9.

HTML Presentations

IN THIS CHAPTER

It's time to begin programming with XMLC. The obvious first target is the HTML markup language. HTML is still king. Its cleaned-up heir apparent, XHTML, is the choice of the WAP Forum and the i-mode standard to replace both WML and cHTML. The topics and strategies we will address will map well to other markup languages, including XHTML and WML.

This chapter addresses the topic of runtime manipulation of DOM templates representing typical HTML elements, including forms and buttons. We will describe some real-world goals for designing and developing Web presentations that illustrate some of the more common approaches to generating HTML presentations dynamically. Of course, these examples will be built on the features and capabilities of our working ShowFloor application.

The topics we will address include clearing the air on the use of generic DOM development versus the use of specific DOM sub-interfaces and their respective implementations.

By the end of this chapter and the next chapter, you will have a firm grasp of the XMLC development experience and some of the strategies from which you can choose that best fits your presentation design objectives.

> **NOTE**
>
> There we go again, throwing that word *template* around. By template, do I mean a document template? A table template? A form template? The answer is "yes" to all of the above. With XMLC, you can extract any portion of a DOM class template and define it as your "working template" whether it's a large template consisting of many markup elements, or just a simple table cell. We'll do our best to describe each template as you progress through the chapter.

To maximize your control of HTML manipulation, be sure to have the HTML 4.1 link bookmarked on your Web browser at `http://www.w3.org/TR/html4/#minitoc` for fingertip access to all the attributes and behaviors of HTML form and form control elements.

Since we're focused squarely on how to manipulate HTML form elements, the data we use will be mocked-up. The complete implementations, using real-time data, can be found on the book's CD. We will discuss, at some length, the use of business objects for delivering raw data to presentation objects using the Enhydra EAF framework.

Leveraging HTML DOM Implementation

Before we immerse ourselves deeply into HTML development with XMLC, let's take a few moments to clarify the value of leveraging DOM interfaces that are specific to the XML/HTML language that you are working with. Our goal is to highlight how this style of programming differs from generic DOM programming in the XMLC environment.

XMLC programming is a contrast of a strict DOM view of markup and extreme flexibility. At one end of the spectrum, it absolutely enforces the separation of Java from markup HTML and XML. At the other end of manipulating the DOM template, application architects enjoy extreme flexibility.

As we'll discuss later on, the strategies you can take to design and leverage the HTML or XML template document can vary in many ways. Similar flexibility exists when it comes to how your Java logic accesses and manipulates elements and attributes of the DOM template generated by the `xmlc` command.

Table 8.1 lists the supported sub-interfaces of the DOM's node interface. These interfaces reflect the support for type-safe development specific to HTML development. If you need to manipulate an `<li>` element, then you would leverage the `HTMLLIElement`. In addition to having its own specific methods, each sub-interface inherits the generic methods of `Node` and `Element`.

TABLE 8.1   DOM Sub-Class Interfaces of DOM's Node Interface

HTMLAnchorElement	HTMLAppletElement	HTMLAreaElement
HTMLBaseElement	HTMLBaseFontElement	HTMLBodyElement
HTMLBRElement	HTMLButtonElement	HTMLDirectoryElement
HTMLDivElement	HTMLDListElement	HTMLFieldSetElement
HTMLFontElement	HTMLFormElement	HTMLFrameElement
HTMLFrameSetElement	HTMLHeadElement	HTMLHeadingElement
HTMLHRElement	HTMLHtmlElement	HTMLIFrameElement
HTMLImageElement	HTMLInputElement	HTMLIsIndexElement
HTMLLabelElement	HTMLLegendElement	HTMLLIElement
HTMLLinkElement	HTMLMapElement	HTMLMenuElement
HTMLMetaElement	HTMLModElement	HTMLObjectElement
HTMLOListElement	HTMLOptGroupElement	HTMLOptionElement
HTMLParagraphElement	HTMLParamElement	HTMLPreElement
HTMLQuoteElement	HTMLScriptElement	HTMLSelectElement
HTMLStyleElement	HTMLTableCaptionElement	HTMLTableCellElement
HTMLTableColElement	HTMLTableElement	HTMLTableRowElement
HTMLTableSectionElement	HTMLTextAreaElement	HTMLTitleElement
HTMLUListElement		

So what does this buy the developer if you can do everything with generic DOM API methods? Let's look at some short examples to illustrate this topic.

Dealing with Boolean Attributes

Suppose you want to indicate that a check box is checked before displaying the page to the client:

```
<input type="checkbox" name="companyRole" value="executive">
<input type="checkbox" id="chkDemo" name="companyRole" value="employee"
checked>
```

For legacy reasons, the `checked` attribute is not a real attribute. It's a *Boolean attribute*, which means it has no assigned value. Unfortunately, that means you cannot set that attribute using the standard DOM API. This has been resolved by the W3C in the XHTML language. They simply eliminated all Boolean attributes so that `checked` is now `checked="checked"`.

With XMLC, thanks to its support for an implementation of the `HTMLElement` sub-interface of the DOM interface, you have a number of options. To set the other checkbox above, identified by `id="chkDemo"`, the following use of the `HTMLInputElement`'s `setChecked()` will work:

```
page.getElementChkDemo().setChecked(true);
```

Type-Safe Development

Let's take a look at the type-safe nature of XMLC development. The attribute `tabindex` is used in HTML markup to control the behavior of which HTML elements receive *keyboard focus* when the user hits the keyboard's tab key. For example, if you had a list of buttons in a form, you would set the `tabindex` attribute to the numeric value, such as `tabindex="1"`, `tabindex="2"` and so on to indicate the ordering of keyboard focus that is displayed when the user hits the tab key. This example here forces the focus that results from tabbing to move in reverse order, from the last button to the first. Note that this appears to work on Internet Explorer 6 only.

```
<input id="mybutton" type="button" name="green" value="green" tabindex="3">
<input type="button" name="blue" value="blue" tabindex="2">
<input type="button" name="yellow" value="yellow" tabindex="1">
```

If you want to set the tab ordering dynamically, perhaps because you're building the list of button elements on-the-fly, there are a couple of ways to set the `tabindex` attribute:

- Use standard DOM methods to access the `Button` element, then use a generic DOM method to update the attribute's value.

  ```
  page.getElementMyButton().setAttribute("tabindex","3");
  ```

- Use the HTML-specific DOM interface to set the `tabindex`.

  ```
  page.getElementMyButton().setTabIndex(3);
  ```

In the second example, it should be apparent that there are a number of advantages to using the HTML-specific `setTabIndex()`, a method defined by `HTMLInputElement`. First of all, the `setTabIndex()` signature requires a parameter of type `int`, so there's no chance for an illegal value to cause an exception at runtime. Secondly, there's a reduction in the likelihood for errors caused by, for example, misspelling the attribute name. Finally, there's no chance of inserting an unsupported attribute in the targeted element, because the method wouldn't be supported.

The flexibility of XMLC will require fingertip access to the DOM, HTML, and XMLC APIs as described by the JavaDoc provided with Enhydra XMLC.

Preparing for Examples

Let's prepare the stage for how the examples in this chapter are organized. Since the examples we'll examine are all Enhydra superservlet EAF-style applications designed to fit into this chapter, we didn't worry too much about creating an official naming hierarchy, such as `com.otterpod.sfa.presentation.*`.

So, instead, you'll see the package name `examples.presentation` at the top of the presentation objects, resulting in the naming convention of

```
./classes/sfa/examples/presentation
```

in the output class hierarchy, created during the Enhydra `make` process. Under the presentation directory located below the `src` branch, we created a single sub-directory for each group of related examples in order to keep things simple and easy to find. For example, two of the examples seen here illustrate this convention:

Example	Package
VendorDetails	sfa.examples.presentation.vendor.VendorDetails
VendorListing	sfa.examples.presentation.vendor.VendorListing

AppWizard was to create the basic Enhydra EAF environment. The project directory was named `SFA`, and `examples` was listed as the package name. To create each example, the following set of changes were made to the `make` files, in this case to `VendorDetails`:

1. Go to `examples/presentation` and create the subdirectory `vendor`.
2. Edit `presentation/Makefile` to add the references to the `vendor` directory to `SUBDIR`.
3. Copy `presentation/Makefile` to `vendor/Makefile`.

Now that we've created the basic sub-directory layout, it's time to update the `make` file in the vendor directory. Here are the modifications to make:

1. Add one more level for ROOT, so that it reads ROOT=../../../../

2. The HTML page is named VendorDetails.html. Therefore, the Enhydra environment will automatically generate the XMLC DOM class using the name VendorDetailsHTML. This name should be added to the HTML_CLASSES make file variable.

3. Enhydra uses the name of the presentation object source file to name the presentation object class. Therefore, since we named the source file VendorDetailsPresentation.java, we added VendorDetailsPresentation to the make file's CLASSES variable.

4. Update the PACKAGEDIR variable to incorporate the vendor sub-directory.

The modified examples/presentation/vendor/Makefile should appear as follows:

```
ROOT = ../../../..

PACKAGEDIR = examples/presentation/vendor

HTML_CLASSES = VendorListHTML VendorDetailsHTML
HTML_DIR = .

CLASSES = VendorListPresentation VendorDetailsPresentation

SUBDIRS = media
XMLC_HTML_OPTS_FILE = options.xmlc
include $(ROOT)/config.mk
```

Back at the top presentation level, we've provided the main menu examplesPresentation.po for conveniently launching each example application in this chapter. This PO can be found on the book's CD.

A single cascading stylesheet file was created and stored in examples/presentation/media. In order to achieve a common look and feel across all the examples, each HTML template references the vendors.css file in that media directory. An example is shown here:

```
<head>
<title id="vendorTitle">Questionnaire from Company A</title>
<meta http-equiv="Content-Type" content="text/html; charset=iso-8859-1">
<link rel="stylesheet" href="../media/vendors.css" type="text/css">
</head>
```

Common DOM Operations

A basic level of DOM programming is an essential aspect of XMLC development. We're going to spend this section reviewing the most commonly required DOM API methods.

In XMLC development, the developer adds dynamic content to an HTML document template by adding and manipulating DOM objects. DOM objects represent everything from large sub-documents containing other DOM objects to small rows in a table.

Using XMLC command line options, static `href` attributes in `form` elements can be replaced with references to presentation objects or servlets. Prototype table rows can be used as small templates to stamp out dynamically-generated rows.

As we discussed earlier, there's a balance between taking advantage of XMLC's capability to use `id` attributes to generate direct access methods, and relying heavily on the low-level DOM API methods. And for anyone who monitors the XMLC mailing list at Enhydra.org, it doesn't take long to realize that everybody has their own preference of how to balance the two strategies.

We're going to take a task-oriented view to discuss some of the more common approaches to traversing or manipulating a DOM template. As we'll see, relying on `id` attributes can reverse the reliance on the DOM API for traversing the DOM. But, when it comes to modifying and expanding the template with new HTML or XML objects, the DOM API is a must.

When No Sub-DOM Is Available

The same discussion applies to XML languages that are not represented by a specific extension of the DOM interface, such as the HTML and WML sub-DOMs that are available with the standard XMLC distribution. In Chapter 11, "Wireless Markup Presentations," we will review how easy it is to work with "unsupported" languages such as W3C's SVG XML language.

You can still take full advantage of the insertion of `id` attributes to generate access methods during XMLC compilation. You can also use all the other XMLC features as well, both during compilation time and runtime. The only loss is the type-safe nature of element-specific classes.

Querying a Node

Let's begin the discussion of useful DOM methods. There are a number of DOM API methods for accessing and querying DOM nodes. Recall that nodes are objects that represent different types of markup, such as `Element`, `Attr`, or `Text`.

- `getNodeType()`—This method returns the node type. If the node is an `Attr` node, then the value `ATTRIBUTE_NODE` is returned. Other possible values include `TEXT_NODE`, and `ELEMENT_NODE`.
- `getNodeName()`—Let's say we know that the element is of type `ELEMENT_NODE`. But what kind of element is it? This method returns the name of the node, such as `TABLE`, `TD`, or `OPTION`. If it's an attribute, then `getNodeName()` might return `id` or `class`. In the case of SVG, it might be `font` or `circle`.

- `getNodeValue()`—This method only returns a value when it makes sense. For example, if there is an `Attr` representing `class=executive`, then `getNodeValue()` will return the value of `executive`. This also works for values represented by nodes of type `TEXT`. However, no value is returned for nodes of type `ELEMENT_NODE`.

Gathering Nodes

Traversing through a DOM is a bit like finding one's way around a large university campus. You rely on the goodness of one stranger to guide you with one set of instructions to another stranger to get your next set of instructions, finally reaching your destination. As long as you know where you are, these methods will find a nearby node relative to your current position.

- `getParentNode()`—This method will return the parent node of your current node. For example, if you are operating from the node that was returned by an XMLC-generated `getElement<AttributeValue>` command, then `getParentNode()` would return the parent of that node.

- `getFirstChild()` and `getLastChild()`—Relative to your current node, these methods, as they suggest, access the parent's first or last child nodes respectively. If your current node is named `TR`, then assuming there are cells in this row, `getLastChild()` will return the last cell element.

- `hasChildNodes()`—How do you know if the current node has children? This method returns `true` or `false`.

Once you've moved to that first or last child, you can now move horizontally with the two methods `getNextSibling()` or `getPreviousSibling()`.

When you want to move away from the tree orientation of the DOM, the DOM API provides a convenient array structure for collecting nodes, `NodeList`. `getChildNodes()` and `item()` are specific to the `NodeList` view of a DOM's nodes:

- `getChildNodes()`—This method returns a `NodeList` containing all the child nodes of the current parent.

- `item()`—To access a child in the `NodeList`, the `NodeList` object's `item()` method will return it.

DOM Manipulation

Let's now address the methods that we're most likely to encounter in our examples of manipulating a DOM template class.

- `appendChild()`—This method, as you'll see, is essential for adding new child nodes to an element, such as adding option items to a Select control, adding rows to a table, or adding cells to a row.

- `removeChild()`—When it's time to remove your template clone, for a table's row for instance, `removeChild()` does the trick. More information on cloning will be covered later.

`insertBefore()` and `replaceChild()` can also come in handy, but are not as commonly required. These methods might become useful where selective changes within an existing set of nodes is required.

Gaining Access to Attributes

So far, none of the DOM accessing methods we've reviewed are useful for accessing the attributes associated with an element. That's because the DOM treats nodes of type `Attr` as independent from the node tree, even though they are associated with elements in markup.

The DOM addresses this by defining attribute-accessing methods as a part of the Element interface API:

- `getAttribute()`—When provided with the name of the attribute, this method returns its value.
- `setAttribute()`—Sets the value of the named attribute.
- `removeAttribute()`—Removes the attribute associated with the element. Why would you need this? As we'll discuss later, this method is used to ensure that the browser is not confused by the multiple inclusions of `id` attributes with the same value.
- `getAttributeNode()`—Returns the node representation of the attribute.

XMLCUtil—A Little Help from XMLC

A small suite of useful utility methods complement XMLC's generation of access methods. `XMLCUtil` methods perform commonly needed functions that would otherwise require multiple calls to DOM methods.

- `findFirstText()`—Finds the first text descendent node of an element.
- `getElementById()`—Recursively searches the tree for an element identified by the given `id` attribute value.
- `DOMInfo()`—Convenient runtime class for dumping the contents of the DOM at any point during execution. Excellent for before-and-after comparisons.
- `getFirstText()`—Finds the first text descendent node of an element.

Later in this chapter, we'll see how `findFirstText()` can conserve on DOM-traversal calls.

Cloning and Templates

The nature of the dynamic manipulation of HTML ranges from straightforward, localized content replacement to the making of wholesale changes to the structure of the document. In this section, we will walk through strategies for using cloned portions of a DOM template to build new DOM structure and content.

Content Substitution

Template manipulation can take the form of simple replacement of placeholder or mockup content. Taking advantage of the role of the id attribute in XMLC programming turns this into a trivial task:

```
<HTML>
<BODY>
<P>Street Address: <SPAN id=vendorAddress>111 AAA Way</SPAN>.
</BODY>
</HTML>
```

In this simple HTML example, no additional markup is actually being created or reworked. Our intent is to simply update the DOM template with a small amount of content using a minimum of Java logic, illustrated in this standard servlet example (we'll discuss standard servlet development with XMLC later in Chapter 10, "Servlet Web Applications"):

```
import examples.business.VendorBO;

public class WelcomeServlet extends HttpServlet {
 public void doGet(HttpServletRequest request, HttpServletResponse response)
  throws ServletException, IOException
 {
  XMLCContext xmlc;
  SimpleDocHTML page;
  VendorBO vendor = new VendorBO();

  //XMLCContext is for supporting XMLC in standard servlet programming.
  //It contains a factory method for loading XMLC generated templates.
  xmlc = XMLCContext.getContext(this);
  page = (SimpleDocHTML) xmlc.getXMLCFactory().create(SimpleHTML.class);
  page.setTextVendorAddress(vendor.getStreet);
  xmlc.writeDOM(request, response, page);
 }
}
```

page is a variable of the type containing the generated DOM class, SimpleHTML. The SimpleHTML class was created from the XMLC compilation of the HTML example. The mocked-up data associated with the id value vendorAddress is replaced with the string returned by the fictitious vendor.getStreet(), where vendor is a business object representing vendor data.

> **NOTE**
>
> A heavy reliance on SPAN tags was encouraged by older versions of XMLC that keyed on the association of a SPAN element with an id attribute in order to determine if a setText<attributeValue> method should be generated. This is no longer a requirement as discussed in Chapter 6, "XMLC Basics."

Cloning for Stamping New Markup

Dynamic manipulation can also take the form of an orderly, systematic construction of portions of a DOM template. A table might be enhanced with the addition of new rows of content. To make things even more interesting, each row or cell may be enhanced with additional elements of HTML controls, reviewed later in this chapter.

The rows of a table may require different templates of HTML objects depending on the context of, for example, an online survey that is updated dynamically with new questions and question types (yes, no, textual, checkboxes, and so on). We will construct such a document later in this chapter.

The DOM interface defines the method cloneNode(). It is implemented by HTMLObjectImpl, the HTML-specific implementation of the DOM interface. cloneNode() creates an orphaned duplicate of a selected template. The template might be any of the following:

- a table row
- a table cell
- a collection of yes/no radio boxes
- a complex collection of HTML elements and static text

The duplicate node that results from the cloneNode() operation inherits copies of all the copied node's attributes and their respective values. The operation looks like this:

```
Node copiedNode = templateNode.cloneNode(false);
```

cloneNode() also supports the capability to perform *deep cloning*. With deep cloning, indicated by the Java Boolean true as a parameter, the node copy will inherit all text node information as well. Listing 8.1 demonstrates the results of the cloneNode(true) operation as applied to an HTML-ordered list. The input HTML follows:

```
<ol>
 <li id=VendorInfo>Vendor A
 <ol>
  <li>Product A
  <li>Product B
 </ol>
</ol>
```

The sample source code in Listing 8.1 is an Enhydra EAF servlet. It takes advantage of the XMLCUtil class DOMInfo to display the state of the DOM during execution.

LISTING 8.1   vendor/vendorInfo.java

```java
// Enhydra SuperServlet imports
import com.lutris.appserver.server.httpPresentation.HttpPresentation;
import com.lutris.appserver.server.httpPresentation.HttpPresentationComms;
import com.lutris.appserver.server.httpPresentation.HttpPresentationException;

// Added for our demo.
import org.w3c.dom.*;
import org.w3c.dom.html.*;
import org.enhydra.xml.dom.DOMInfo;

import java.io.*;

public class VendorInfoPresentation implements HttpPresentation {

 public void run(HttpPresentationComms comms)
   throws HttpPresentationException, IOException {

  VendorInfoHTML welcome;
  page = (VendorInfoHTML)comms.xmlcFactory.create(VendorInfoHTML.class);

  PrintWriter out =
   new PrintWriter(new OutputStreamWriter(System.out, "UTF8"));

 Node tmp = welcome.getElementVendorInfo().cloneNode(false);
 DOMInfo.printTree("Shallow Node",
    tmp, DOMInfo.PRINT_ATTR_DETAILS,out);

 Node tmp2 = welcome.getElementVendorInfo().cloneNode(true);
 DOMInfo.printTree("Deep Node",
    tmp2, DOMInfo.PRINT_ATTR_DETAILS,out);

  comms.response.writeDOM(page);
 }
}
```

The output of the `DOMInfo printTree()` method shows the contrasting results of the shallow and deep clone operations.

```
Shallow Node:
 HTMLLIElementImpl: LI
  Attributes:
   AttrImpl: id
    TextImpl: VendorInfo
Deep Node:
 HTMLLIElementImpl: LI
  Attributes:
   AttrImpl: id
    TextImpl: VendorInfo
  TextImpl: Vendor A
  HTMLOListElementImpl: OL
   HTMLLIElementImpl: LI
    TextImpl: Product A
   HTMLLIElementImpl: LI
    TextImpl: Product B
```

The output shown here represents the structure and content of clones of the original DOM template. Shallow or deep cloning can be used as a strategy to control how much of any sub-document template is used by an XMLC application.

Flow of a Typical Cloning Operation

Let's analyze a more interesting use of cloning. It's a common task to add more than one item to an HTML object that's acting as a container of other objects. For example, the rows of a table can be used to contain a vendor's name. Or the options in a `Select` element representing an Option Menu might be added dynamically as well.

In XMLC programming, the common approach to performing this task is to extract a mini-template from the larger DOM class template and use that template as a "mold" to "cast" freshly acquired data in the shape of the original template.

Figure 8.1 attempts to graphically represent the individual steps representing the process.

This mini-template is an HTML `Row` element containing two cell elements. Our goal is to use this as a template to reproduce identically structured rows with new content. Some of the following numbered steps correspond to the actions performed on the template and the parent HTML table.

1. Fetch the template, typically using an XMLC-generated `getElement<attributeValue>` method. In this case, it's `getElementVendorRow()`.

2. Clone the template element with `cloneNode()`.

3. Remove the id attributes. You'll see how to do this later in this section.

4. Step through an iteration of generating a new dynamic value or set of values for insertion into the cloned object.

5. Replace cloned values with new value(s).

6. Append the clone to the parent element.

7. Return to Step 4, if new values remain.

8. Having no further need for the template, delete it so that it doesn't appear in the final markup.

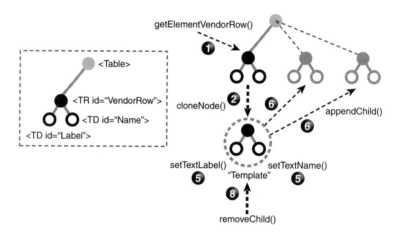

FIGURE 8.1

Simple static-dynamic vendor detail page.

This may appear as a very rigid process, but there are plenty of ways to tailor the dynamic elements of your algorithm to suit your goals. In fact, there are no rules that prevent you from dynamically introducing new DOM components, even though the intent is not captured in the original template document.

For example, you might decide to change the background color of every fifth row in a table. Or you might decide to insert a small graphic in the same cell to indicate that the vendor is a sponsor. It really comes down to using algorithms and strategies that make Web presentations that are easy to maintain or rework over time.

> **CAUTION**
>
> Although it's easy to introduce new elements without the aid of template cloning, your presentation may generate unexpected side effects when rendered simply from, for example, unanticipated overcrowding. Using templates as storyboards will help to avoid these issues. Another way to approaching adding new elements dynamically is to simply include them in the storyboard template to begin with, with the option of not incorporating them in the final result.

Removing `ids`

In Step 3 of the cloning algorithm we just reviewed, you remove the reference to the `id` attribute that was inherited by the clone. Your first impression may be that this is a bit of unnecessary housecleaning. In fact, it's essential to remove `id` attributes because of their potential impact on HTML browsers.

Recall that `id` attributes are defined as representing unique instances of an HTML element. By that definition, they're not being used properly if more than one attribute with the same value appears in more than one instance of a particular element.

Because we're using the template to replicate copies of it, it will introduce multiple occurrences of an `id` with the same value. The DOM interface method `removeAttribute()` takes care of this important operation.

Conversely, removal of class attributes is not necessary at all, because 1) if they were used for the purposes of mockup data, they were removed using the `-delete-class` option during compilation; or 2) they are being used for some other purpose, such as a stylesheet reference, and should therefore not be removed.

Later in this section, you will work an example that shows the entire cloning process as applied by the ShowFloor application.

Options for Extreme Dynamic Manipulation

By no means does the cloning process we've described thus far represent the upper end of the dynamic capabilities of XMLC programming. As you'll see in the next chapter, it's possible to build an entirely new DOM template from other DOM classes in order to achieve the greatest amount of control and partitioning of Web pages leading to simplified maintenance and future redesign.

Perhaps the ultimate flexibility in the dynamic nature of XMLC programming is reflected in the capability to load, at runtime, different implementations (or "behaviors") that deal with the same template. This approach to runtime polymorphic behavior is made possible by the XMLC command line option -generate. This will be discussed in greater detail in Chapter 11.

You'll see that it's possible to make wholesale changes to the DOM tree that deliver practical values in the areas of maintainability, time savings, and internationalization support.

Different Strokes

The XMLC compiler gives you your template and some convenient access hooks into targeted areas of the template. The presentation logic can now manipulate both the content and the structure as you choose.

In Chapter 2, we discussed the fact that the design of the login page could be handled differently depending on your particular strategy. We chose the route of building a single template with all the possible dynamic sub-templates, including the error message for a failed login. Others might choose to have multiple admin templates, or to simply treat the error message as an HTML element that's created programmatically without the use of a template row identified by an id. Instead, create it on-the-fly, adding the row, and the error message it contains, to the resultant DOM template if needed.

The same flexibility of options applies to the strategy one takes when manipulating the DOM template. Some may want to minimize the use of DOM programming as much as possible. Others may enjoy the generic flexibility of DOM programming. In this chapter, for instance, our view is to maximize the use of XMLC-generated methods because we want to emphasize the highest level of XMLC abstraction possible, and convince you that you don't need the DOM API as much as you might think. Once you're comfortable with this approach, then the world's your oyster if you choose to start diving deeper into the DOM API.

Take the simple example of referencing the top of a table template. The top, of course, is represented by a node of type HTMLTableElement. We may need that node to, for example, append a new table row of type HTMLTableRowElement.

There are at least two ways to locate that table element. One way is to take the template row that you are working with and simply ask for its parent with a DOM API method:

```
Node vendorTbl = templateRow.getParentNode();
```

Another approach is to insert an id attribute into the markup to begin with. <table id=vendorTbl> would trigger the xmlc command to generate a custom accessor method giving us direct access to the parent node that contains the Table element:

```
Node vendorTbl = getElementVendorTbl();
```

It doesn't particularly matter which route you choose. We've already stated that we're going to maximize the XMLC conveniences, in turn minimizing our reliance on the DOM API. Others may choose to use the lower-level DOM methods in order to insert more logic portability into the design process.

Loosening `id` Bindings with `getElementByID()`

So far, we've talked exclusively about the use of the XMLC-generated `getElement` `<AttributeValue>` methods for indexing the location of the DOM that's been targeted for dynamic manipulation. However, there is another way that also bypasses the need for DOM traversal. `getElementById()` is available from the DOM API, as inherited and implemented by the `XMLObjectImpl` and `HTMLObjectImpl` classes, to return an element that is associated with a unique id. Implemented by the `HTMLObjectImpl` and `XMLObjectImpl` XMLC classes, this method takes advantage of access to the internal table of `id`s created by the Xerces parser to avoid performance penalties, as compared to the performance of the equivalent XMLC-generated access methods

```
HTMLTableElement vendorTbl = page.getElementByID("VendorTbl");
HTMLTableElement vendorTbl = page.getElementVendorTbl();
```

that are functionally equivalent. So what distinguishes them?

- When using the `getElement<AttributeValue>` approach, compile-time error messages are generated if the method is referenced but has somehow been omitted by the designer. This condition might be the result of a designer misspelling the `id` attribute value.

- When using the `getElementById()` approach, the programmer can check for the existence of such a tagged element without having to worry about the existence of the actual generated method.

The sum total of their difference has to do with the tightness of the binding between the document and the presentation logic. With `getElementById()`, the linkage between the XMLC template-building and the runtime logic is reduced.

There's more to these different approaches than catching misspelled `id` attribute values. The developer can use `getElementById()` to easily check for a non-null value, indicating the attributed element is not present and therefore can be bypassed in this presentation logic.

This is an important design strategy to consider if your application is being designed to leverage auto-recompilation. Imagine a designer updating an HTML or XML file and forgetting to insert a particular `id`. If your application relies on the accessor methods, then the recompilation will still complete successfully; but after the class is auto-loaded, references to the class will result in an exception.

8

In order to address this possibility, you may install a policy that requires that only pre-compiled classes that have been tested are made available for auto-loading. Or, you may want to require the use of `getElementById()` to enable runtime checking for the existence of the `id`, and therefore gracefully handle the error condition.

Building Tables

The emerging theme of this chapter seems to reiterate the fact that XMLC supports an incredible amount of flexibility and variation of implementation strategies, while still delivering on its promise of supporting highly maintainable Web presentations.

In this section, we're going to focus on perhaps the most common chore of all, updating an HTML table. We'll do this by looking at two cases representing different levels of dynamic manipulation. In the first example, we will perform an in-place content update of a statically-formatted table. In the other, we'll add new rows and content to that same table.

Static Tables with Dynamic Content

Let's address the ShowFloor page that will display information about a single vendor to the viewer. This page, `VendorDetails`, is generated by the selection of an individual vendor from a list of vendors in a previous page, `VendorList`. The strategy for this page is to simply display a table containing two columns. In the first row, we'll span the two columns with the vendor's name. We will then use the first column to label the contents of the adjoining column. Since we know the nature of the data in the second column, the first column's content will be pre-existing template content.

In Listing 8.2, the document `VendorDetails.html` contains a single table. We've inserted `id` attributes in the right column of cells to generate the access methods we'll need to deliver the dynamic content. Class attributes are used for stylesheet control.

LISTING 8.2   vendor/VendorDetails.html

```
<html>
<head>
<title>Vendor List</title>
<meta http-equiv="Content-Type" content="text/html; charset=iso-8859-1">
<link rel="stylesheet" href="../media/vendors.css" type="text/css">
</head>

<body bgcolor="#FFFFFF" text="#000000">
<table width="20" border="0" cellspacing="4" cellpadding="0" id="VendorTable"
➥ class="vendorLabels">
 <tr>
  <td colspan="2"><img src="../media/spacer.gif" width="400" height="2"></td>
```

LISTING 8.2   Continued

```
</tr>
<tr bgcolor="#00FF00">
 <td colspan="2" class="vendorTitle" id="VendorName">AtomicPoweredLinux
➥Company</td>
</tr>
<tr>
 <td width="10" align="right" class="vendorLabels"> Street:</td>
 <td width="230" class="vendorInfo" id="vendorStreet">1991 AlphaWave
  Avenue</td>
</tr>
<tr>
 <td align="right" width="10" class="vendorLabels"> City:</td>
 <td width="230" class="vendorInfo" id="VendorCity">Santa Cruz</td>
</tr>
<tr>
 <td align="right width="10" class="vendorLabels"> State:</td>
 <td width="230" class="vendorInfo" id="VendorState">CA</td>
</tr>
<tr>
 <td width="10" class="vendorLabels" align="right"> Country:</td>
 <td width="230" class="vendorInfo" id="VendorCountry">USA</td>
</tr>
<tr>
 <td width="10" nowrap class="vendorLabels" align="right">
➥ <span class="vendorLabels">Category</span> </td>
 <td width="230" class="vendorInfo" id="VendorDesc">Sub-atomic appliances</td>
</tr>
<tr>
 <td width="10" class="vendorLabels" align="right">Product </td>
 <td width="230" class="vendorInfo" id="VendorProduct">The Appliance</td>
</tr>
<tr>
 <td width="10" class="vendorLabels" align="right"> Description:</td>
 <td width="230" class="vendorInfo" id="VendorProdDesc">Great sub-atomic
➥application
  server for small devices.</td>
</tr>
<tr>
 <td colspan="2" class="vendorLabels"><img src="../media/spacer.gif"
➥width="80" height="10"></td>
 </tr>
</table>
</body>
</html>
```

We've added two additional rows to contain references to adjustable "spacer" GIF image files. This is a standard designer technique to control the displayed dimensions of the table. Believe it or not, tables are not very well-behaved in the area of taking geometric instructions. We'll take advantage of this later in the chapter to illustrate how to effect attribute changes in generated HTML.

Now let's take a look at the presentation object that is going to replace the mockup in VendorDetails.html. In this very simple slide, we take advantage of all the setText<attributeValue> methods generated during the XMLC compilation. This is a straightforward process with no requirement for iterations through data or references to DOM elements. Instead, our Enhydra EAF presentation object, VendorDetailsPresentation.java, carries out the operation described in Listing 8.3.

Listing 8.3   vendor/VendorDetailsPresentation.java

```
package examples.presentation.vendor;

//Import the associated business object.
import examples.business.vendor.VendorBO;

import java.util.*;
import com.lutris.xml.xmlc.*;
import com.lutris.appserver.server.httpPresentation.*;
import org.w3c.dom.*;
import org.w3c.dom.html.*;

public class VendorListPresentation implements HttpPresentation {

 public void run(HttpPresentationComms comms)
  throws HttpPresentationException {

  //Get the vendor selected in VendorList. Ignore error checking.
  String vendorName = comms.request.getParameter("VendorName");

  //Hypothetical business object returns details of the Vendor.
  VendorBO vendor = new VendorBO(vendorName);

  //Load the template page representing VendorDetails.HTML
  VendorDetailsHTML vendorPage =
   (VendorDetailsTML)comms.xmlcFactory.create(VendorDetailsHTML.class);

  vendorPage.setTextVendorName(vendor.name());
  vendorPage.setTextVendorStreet(vendor.street());
  vendorPage.setTextVendorCity(vendor.city());
  vendorPage.setTextVendorCountry(vendor.country());
```

Listing 8.3   Continued

```
vendorPage.setTextVendorDesc(vendor.description);
vendorPage.setTextVendorProduct(vendor.product());
vendorPage.setTextVendorProdDesc(vendor.prodDescription());

comms.response.writeHTML(vendorPage);
 }
}
```

In `VendorDetailsPresentation.java`, we only need to know the name of the vendor that was selected in the previous page, `VendorList.html`. This is accomplished with a call to `getParameter()`, which retrieves the value returned by the form object in the `VendorList` page. We'll see more about how this works later in the chapter.

> **Note**
>
> It might be tempting to add `id` attribute assignments to each label in the `VendorDetails` example in order to programmatically update the page with localized translations of the labels, such as `Product:`. That's certainly a legitimate strategy, but as we will review in Chapter 9, "Presentation Strategies," there are a number of strategies from which to choose.

To access the details of that particular vendor, we rely on a business object, `VendorBO`, which is specifically written to provide that information. To get to that object, we've imported it with the following statement:

```
import example.business.vendorBO;
```

After creating an instance of `VendorBO`, for Vendor Business Object, we then invoke its public methods to return the strings we need to populate the right-hand column of the table template. Following from our discussion of Enhydra EAF development, `VendorBO` formulates its responses after fetching the raw data by invoking one or more data objects in the data layer. These objects encapsulate the required SQL queries of the attached database.

> **Note**
>
> To keep our emphasis on XMLC development, all references to data objects and most of the business objects are left to the reader to explore more deeply. These objects can be found in the ShowFloor application source tree located on the book's CD.

Figure 8.2 illustrates the generated result of `VendorDetailsPresentation.java`.

FIGURE 8.2
Simple static-dynamic vendor details page.

Dynamic Tables, Content and All

Let's add a wrinkle to the same vendor details page in order to expand the table's dimensions with new, interesting, variable content. We will restructure the page and the code to support the capability to add more than one product, because many vendors will have more than a single product. Simply put, to add more than one product, we'll need to append more rows to the table.

The HTML markup below is extracted from Listing 8.1. Retaining the existing id attributes, we've inserted additional id attributes to identify each row. We are doing this in order to turn each of the three rows (ProductRow, ProdDescRow, and SpacerRow) into three templates that we can use to clone after adding new data, then append to the bottom of the table.

```
<tr id="ProductRow">
<td width="10" class="vendorLabels" align="right">Product </td>
<td width="230" class="vendorInfo" id="VendorProduct">The Appliance</td>
</tr>
<tr id="ProdDescRow">
<td width="10" class="vendorLabels" align="right"> Description:</td>
<td width="230" class="vendorInfo" id="VendorProdDesc">Great sub-atomic
➥application
  server for small devices.</td>
</tr>
<tr id="SpacerRow">
<td colspan="2" class="vendorLabels"><img src="../media/spacer.gif"
➥width="80" height="10"></td>
</tr>
```

We've introduced the row SpacerRow to visually represent a separation between two products for clarity and readability.

TIP

The conventions that you use when naming id attribute values is up to you. We like to refer to their type; that is, the type of HTML element they're referencing. We find that it helps with the clarity of the presentation logic and more closely aligns the Java code with the markup document in a self-documenting manner.

With the updated HTML in hand, let's reflect these changes in the presentation object. We will replace the statements

```
vendorPage.setTextVendorProduct(vendor.product());
vendorPage.setTextVendorProdDesc(vendor.prodDescription());
```

with a looping statement that will append groups of cloned rows containing representations of one or more products:

```
//Fetch the table and table's row templates.
HTMLTableElement table = vendorPage.getElementVendorTbl();
HTMLTableRowElement productRow = vendorPage.getElementProductRow();
HTMLTableRowElement prodDescRow = vendorPage.getElementProdDescRow();
HTMLTableRowElement spacerRow = vendorPage.getElementSpacerRow();

Node clonedRow;
String height = "20"; // for our spacer row.
VendorProduct product;

//Fetch product list and enter a loop
Enumeration products = vendor.productList());
while (products.hasMoreElements()) {
  if ( ! products.hasMoreElements()) {
    height = "10";
  }
  //Fetch the image's height attribute.
  Element img = (Element)spacerRow.getLastChild();
  img.setAttribute("height", height);

  product = products.next();

  clonedRow = spacerRow.cloneNode(true);
  table.appendChild(clonedRow);

  vendorPage.setTextVendorProduct(product.name());
```

```
        clonedRow = productRow.cloneNode(true);
        table.appendChild(clonedRow);

        vendorPage.setTextVendorProdDesc(prduct.description());
        clonedRow = prodDescRow.cloneNode(true);
        table.appendChild(clonedRow);

    }

    // get rid of the row templates now that we're done with them.
    table.removeChild(productRow); // removes the template
    table.removeChild(prodDescRow); // removes the template
    table.removeChild(spacerRow); // removes the template

    comms.response.writeHTML(vendorPage);
}
```

The result of this change is shown in Figure 8.3.

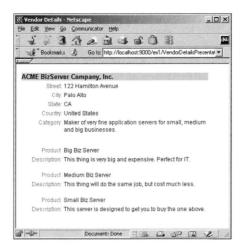

FIGURE 8.3
The revised simple static-dynamic vendor detail page.

Dealing with Vestigial Templates

If you forget to remove the template rows used for cloning, you'll certainly find out the first time you successfully run your application. You'll immediately discover that the presentation object displays the cloned row and its mock content right along with the newly processed dynamic data. This is why we rely on the DOM method removeChild() to do a little house-keeping before turning the enhanced DOM template into HTML that's ready for display back to the client.

Part of the removal process requires a reference back to the parent node of the template table rows. Our intent for inserting an id attribute into the table element might not have been clear at first:

```
<table id=vendorTbl>
```

By doing this, it's a quick call to get to the row's parent node and remove all traces of the template rows. As we explained earlier, the table variable could have also been set by a call to getParentNode(), relative to the row node. The following statements address the operating of removing the original row templates used for cloning:

```
HTMLTableElement table = GetElementVendorTbl();
....
table.removeChild(productRow);
table.removeChild(prodDescRow);
table.removeChild(spacerRow);
```

You now have a DOM template with all vestiges of the original row-building templates removed.

Changing Attribute Values

The spacer.gif static image used in the VendorDetails page is a designer's trick to guarantee an absolute width or height of a table, row, or cell. A single GIF image can be referenced from many locations within an HTML file. At each location, it can be instructed to assume different dimensions depending on the setting of the height and width attributes associated with the IMG element.

We inserted an id attribute in the row element containing the spacer.gif reference. However, the id and its value spacerRow are associated with the table's row element, and not with the IMG element directly. So, we had at least two options for getting access to the IMG element's height attribute:

- Insert an id attribute into the IMG element, or
- Use DOM methods to access the IMG node and its height attribute.

In the first option, if you inserted an id with the value spacer, you could then use any of the following non-inherited methods from HTMLImageElement to make the update: setWidth(), setVspace(), setUseMap(), setSrc(), setName(), setLowSrc(), setLongDesc(), setIsMap(), setHeight(), getSrc(), getName(), getLongDesc(), getHeight(), and getBorder(). The appropriate method for use in this example is setHeight():

```
Element spacer = vendorPage.getElementSpacer()
spacer.setHeight(20);
```

If we go with the second option, then the following calls would be required:

```
HTMLTableRowElement SpacerRow = vendorPage.getElementSpacerRow();
Node img = (Element) SpacerRow.getFirstChild();
spacer.getAttributeNode("height").setValue("20");
```

This is the strategy we went with in Listing 8.1. But note that using a DOM method that relies on relative positioning can lead to problems down the road in the event that the template is reworked by the designer. Perhaps the first option, where we associate an id directly with the IMG element, might be the safest route to take.

Wading Through In-Line Presentation Information

HTML does not follow the general XML philosophy of structuring data independent of information that indicates display-specific requirements. HTML was heavily used before the general acceptance of stylesheets, so it's not surprising that its one-stop-shopping markup approach would incorporate the heavy use of <B>, <I>, <strong>, and other elements that influence the browser in the presentation department.

Earlier, we advocated the use of stylesheets as a means of loosely coupling the displaying of content to the content itself. We also enjoy taking advantage of class-defining stylesheet selectors in order to more easily influence programmatically the display attributes of the manipulated DOM template. This loose coupling also means that it would be easier to ship different stylesheet-defined "skins" for all sorts of reasons, including the needs of individuals who require high-contrast user interfaces in order to better distinguish between fonts and the browser's background color.

So let's get off our soapbox and back to reality. There's a ton of markup out there with plenty of in-line instructions for controlling the display of content. The HTML fragment here is from the real world:

```
<td id="restaurant"><b><i>Jack's Hamburgers</i></b>
```

The problem that we're presented with is how to get access to the text node represented by Jack's Hamburgers from the table cell element td. Doing so will require some code to traverse past the <b> and <i> elements.

Earlier, we introduced XMLCUtil. Another one of its methods, findFirstText(),was created to solve the problem we're currently trying to address.

Rather than working your way down a DOM branch, you can instead use this method to simply indicate that you want the first text node that findFirstText() encounters as it walks through the children of the td element. The following fragment returns the value Jack's Restaurant:

```
TestHTML testPage = (TestHTML)comms.xmlcFactory.create(TestHTML.class);
HTMLTableCellElement cell = testPage.getElementRestaurant();
Text txt = XMLCUtil.findFirstText((Node)cell);
System.out.println("value: " + txt.getNodeValue());
```

Working with Stylesheets

Stylesheets are an essential tool for maintaining a consistent look and feel across the pages of a Web site, such as ShowFloor, with a minimum of work. Once a stylesheet is established, it's just a matter of associating individual styles with elements using class attributes.

The HTML fragment here is from the ShowFloor `VendorList` page. The page, as the name suggests, lists the vendors participating in the show from which the visitor can select in order to get access to the `VendorDetails` page.

```
<br>
<table id="VendorListTbl" width="200" border="0" cellspacing="0"
➥cellpadding="0">
 <tr>
  <td><img src=../media/spacer.gif width="300" height="1"></td>
 </tr>
 <tr id="vendorListRow">
  <td class="vendorListGreenBG" id="VendorNameCell">Vendor Company A</td>
 </tr>
 <tr class="mockup">
  <td class="vendorListBlueBG">Vendor Company B</td>
 </tr>
 <tr class="mockup">
  <td class="vendorListGreenBG">Vendor Company C</td>
 </tr>
 <tr class="mockup">
  <td class="vendorListBlueBG">Vendor Company D</td>
 </tr>
</table>
```

The HTML for `VendorList.html` alternates the background colors used for each row containing the vendor name. Style selectors, specified with the class attribute, indicate the background color to use. This makes it possible for the ShowFloor administrator to modify the look and feel of how the alternating behavior is realized by modifying the cascading stylesheet file.

Listing 8.4 demonstrates how the `VendorListPresentation.java` PO can manipulate the class references to selectors on a row-by-row basis.

LISTING 8.4   vendor/VendorListPresentation.java

```java
package examples.presentation.vendor;

import java.util.*;
import com.lutris.xml.xmlc.*;
import com.lutris.appserver.server.httpPresentation.*;
import org.w3c.dom.*;
import org.w3c.dom.html.*;

public class VendorListPresentation implements HttpPresentation {

  public void run(HttpPresentationComms comms)
    throws HttpPresentationException {

    String vendors [] = {"Apple Computer", "Anderson Paint",
➥"Anne's Software Shop", "Alex Software","Annex Systems",
➥"AghMeister Systems"};

    VendorListHTML vendorPage =
    (VendorListHTML)comms.xmlcFactory.create(VendorListHTML.class);

    // find our way to the DOM nodes representing the table
    // and the row element.
    HTMLTableElement table = vendorPage.getElementVendorListTbl();

    //Fetch the row templates.
    HTMLTableRowElement vendorRow = vendorPage.getElementVendorListRow();
    HTMLTableCellElement cell = vendorPage.getElementVendorNameCell();
    vendorRow.removeAttribute("id");
    cell.removeAttribute("id");

    Node clonedRow;
        //Fetch vendor list and enter a loop
    for (int i = 0; i < vendors.length; i++) {
      cell = vendorPage.getElementVendorNameCell();
      if (i % 2 == 0) {
        cell.getAttributeNode("class").setValue("vendorListGreenBG");
      } else {
        cell.getAttributeNode("class").setValue("vendorListBlueBG");
      }
    vendorPage.setTextVendorNameCell(vendors[i]);
    clonedRow = vendorRow.cloneNode(true);
    table.appendChild(clonedRow);
  }
  // get rid of the row templates now that we're done with them.
```

LISTING 8.4 Continued

```
table.removeChild(vendorRow); // removes the template

comms.response.writeHTML(vendorPage);
  }
}
```

Working with Forms and Controls

With the advent of the PC some 20 years ago, the old world of forms-based data entry seemed to be a style of user interface interaction that was relegated to the 3270 half-plex terminals of IBM Mainframe glasshouses. The PC introduced full-plex and gave us things like WordStar, MultiCalc, and Lotus 1-2-3. Today, their conquering ancestors, Word and Excel, have to share the desktop with the re-emergence of form-style user interfaces, thanks to the success of request/response Internet applications.

Forms are containers of controls enhanced with static and dynamic content organized to carry out a task, such as registering a user or logging in an administrator. Forms are often designed as static content, but we want to focus on those that have some dynamic content as well, tailoring the presentation to either the individual, or to data fetched for a database.

HTML controls consist of buttons, check boxes, radio boxes, option menus, and single- and multi-line text boxes. The form acts as a "widget container" for presenting a cohesive interaction with the user and then sending the collected interaction back to the HTTP server. As shown here, it is also responsible for routing the results of the form interaction back to a script or servlet as specified with its action attribute. The event is caused by the default behavior of the Submit button:

```
<FORM action="/vendor/questionnaire.po" method="post">
...HTML with one or more controls...
  <INPUT type="submit" value="Send">
</FORM>
```

For the purposes of the next few discussions, we will ignore the client-side validation and processing role that JavaScript can bring to forms processing. Instead, we will focus on how to use XMLC programming to generate dynamically composed HTML forms. Server-side validation will be addressed in the next chapter.

Controls and Access to Control Results

HTML controls reflect some of the typical inconsistencies within the overall environment of HTML programming. Controls do not always reflect a consistent interface. And some effects, such as buttons, can be accomplished by a couple of controls, such as the button and input elements.

Controls are given a name by their `name` attribute, which is used by a post-processing agent, such as a servlet or CGI script, to access the values gathered by the form. The `value` attribute is usually used to specify the control's initial value. Again, be sure to have access to an HTML document to verify how each control addresses its initial value. For example, instead of using `value`, a `textarea` control establishes its initial value as whatever content it is originally provided with. The initial values are an important topic when it comes to use of the `reset` button for starting over. The initial value is considered the control's current value until it is changed by the user or by a client-side script.

The values of controls in a form are returned to the script or servlet as specified by the `form` element's `action` attribute. Most of the control values, modified or otherwise, are returned along with the name. Thus, the presentation object (servlet) can decompose the submitted form with calls such as the following:

- `getParameter(name)`—Returns a string containing the lone value of the specified query parameter, or null if the parameter does not exist.

- `getParameterNames()`—Returns the parameter names for this request as an enumeration of strings, or an empty enumeration if there are no parameters.

- `getParameterValues(name)`—Returns the values of the specified query parameter for the request as an array of strings, or a `0` length array if the named parameter does not exist.

When a form is submitted for processing, some controls have their name paired with their current value and these pairs are submitted with the form. Using the methods above, we can perform the following whether it's an Enhydra PO

```
String value = comms.request.getParameter("age");
```

or a standard servlet

```
String value = request.getParameter("age");
```

Building a Dynamic Questionnaire Form

Let's get back to the ShowFloor application and construct a questionnaire feature we'll call VendQuest.

To illustrate the more common HTML controls and how they can be integrated within a single form, VendQuest will be designed to serve as an automated questionnaire service, provided to vendors by ShowFloor. This service will give vendors the opportunity to easily generate dynamic questionnaires in order to generate feedback from visitors to the ShowFloor Web site. It will be so dynamic that a vendor can easily update their questionnaire while the SFA service is running and the show is in progress. Multiple and single-choice as well as textual questions can be asked of visitors regarding their interests, roles, feedback, and any other question that the vendor might be interested in. VendQuest will also provide the capability to rank items, such as the vendor's favorite show topic.

As we will discuss in the next chapter, VendQuest will support an XML environment for the authoring and generation of vendor-defined questionnaires. For example, a fragment of the input XML document may result in an HTML questionnaire that asks the user the following question:

```
<Question type="SC">
<Prompt>What is your role at your company?</Prompt>
<Choice>Engineer</Choice>
<Choice>Executive</Choice>
<Choice>Writer</Choice>
<Choice>Gopher</Choice>
</Question>
```

This question is assigned the type attribute value of SC, indicating that it is a "single choice" question requiring that only one choice be selected. You can envision the choices presented to the visitor as a group of radio boxes or an options menu. The approach we take will be dictated by the HTML template that we design later.

However, for now, we are going to demonstrate just enough business logic to generate these questions in code. In the next chapter, we'll show how Zeus, the data-binding project from zeus.enhydra.org, can be used in concert with XMLC to produce a highly dynamic Web application in which XML is used to drive XMLC presentations.

The VendQuest Template

The template we'll be working from is shown in Figure 8.4. All the labels, questions, and choices are mock information. Even the page title, "Questionnaire From Company A," is storyboard mockup.

We have kept the form's organization relatively simple in order to keep the code behind the example simple. For instance, we will put each choice or option on a single row, rather than try to put two or three across. That's another exercise for you to attempt on your own.

The HTML will take full advantage of id attributes. The strategy behind how each id is leveraged will be reviewed. The HTML appears in Listing 8.5.

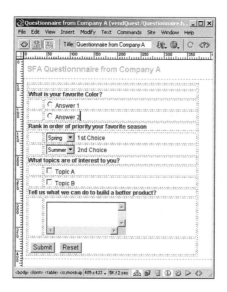

FIGURE 8.4

The VendQuest template.

LISTING 8.5   vendQuest/Questionnaire.html

```
<html>
<head>
<title id="vendorTitle">Questionnaire from Company A</title>
<meta http-equiv="Content-Type" content="text/html; charset=iso-8859-1">
<link rel="stylesheet" href="../media/vendors.css" type="text/css">
</head>
<body bgcolor="#FFFFFF" text="#000000">
<p id="title" class="regTitle">SFA Questionnaire from <span id="vendorName">
➡Company A</span>
<form name="form1" method="post" action="ProcessQuestions.po">
 <table id="QTable">
  <tr id="SpacerRow">
   <td colspan="2" class="regLabel" nowrap><img src="../media/spacer.gif"
➡width="358" height="8"></td>
  </tr>
  <!— Single Choice Template —>
  <tr id="PromptRow">
   <td colspan="2" id="PromptCell" class="regLabel" nowrap>What is your
➡favorite    Color?</td>
  </tr>
  <tr id="SCRow">
   <td class="regField" width="30"><img src="../media/spacer.gif" width="30"
```

LISTING 8.5   Continued

```
➥height="20"></td>    <td id="SCInputCell" class="regField" width="325">
   <input id="SCInput" type="radio" name="radiobutton" value="radiobutton">
   <span id="SCInputLabel"> Answer 1</span></td>
 </tr>
 <tr class="mockup">
  <td class="regField" width="30"> </td>
  <td class="regField" width="325">
   <input type="radio" name="radiobutton" value="radiobutton">
   Answer 2</td>
 </tr>
 <!— Rankings Template —>
 <tr class="mockup" >
  <td colspan="2" class="regLabel" nowrap>Rank in order of priority your
➥favorite    season</td>
 </tr>
 <tr id="RankRow">
  <td class="regField" width="30" height="21"><img src="../media/spacer.gif"
➥ width="30" height="20"></td>
  <td class="regField" width="325" height="21">
   <select id="RankSelect" name="select">
    <option id="RankOption">Spring</option>
    <option class="mockup">Summer</option>
   </select>
   <span id="RankSelectLabel">Choice #1</span></td>
 </tr>
 <tr class="mockup">
  <td class="regField" width="30"> </td>
  <td class="regField" width="325">
   <select name="select2">
    <option value="Spring">Spring</option>
    <option value="Summer" selected>Summer</option>
   </select>
   Choice #2</td>
 </tr>
 <!— Multiple Choice Template —>
 <tr class="mockup">
  <td colspan="2" class="regLabel" nowrap>What topics are of interest to
➥you?</td>
 </tr>
 <tr id="MCRow" >
  <td class="regField" width="30"><img src="../media/spacer.gif" width="30"
➥height="20"></td>
   <td id="MCInputCell" class="regField" width="325">
    <input id="MCInput" type="checkbox" name="checkbox" value="checkbox">
    <span id="MCInputLabel">Topic A</span></td>
```

LISTING 8.5 Continued

```
   </tr>
   <tr class="mockup">
    <td class="regField" width="30"> </td>
    <td class="regField" width="325">
     <input type="checkbox" name="checkbox2" value="checkbox">
     Topic B</td>
   </tr>
   <!— Comment Text Area Template —>
   <tr class="mockup">
    <td colspan="2" class="regLabel" nowrap>Tell us what we can do to build
    a better product?</td>
   </tr>
   <tr id="CommentRow">
    <td width="30"><img src="../media/spacer.gif" width="30" height="20"> </td>
    <td width="325">
     <textarea id="CommentTextArea" name="textfield" rows="3"
➡cols="30"></textarea>
    </td>
   </tr>
  <tr id="SubmitRow">
    <td colspan="2">
     <input type="submit" name="Submit1" value="Submit">
     <input type="reset" name="Submit2" value="Reset">
    </td>
   </tr>
  </table>
 </form>
 </body>
 </html>
```

There are a couple of things to note about this listing. First, we've inserted a number of class attributes for those parts of the document that we can throw away before the template is generated by xmlc. We're creating a healthy reliance on the use of class attributes to specify selectors for certain presentation attributes, such as font and font color. We're also using class attributes such as class="mockup" to identify mock template and content that will be thrown away by specifying -delete-class mockup in the options.xmlc file.

How do we know which HTML markup to label as mockup? First, wherever there is a row containing a redundant input element acting as the second checkbox or radio box can be eliminated. Also, wherever a row contains a second option element or second select statement, that element can be marked as mockup as well. To see the effect of removing the elements identified as mockup, try the command

```
xmlc -delete-class mockup -docout q.html Questionnaire.html
```

This `xmlc` command will stop short of generating a class file, and instead create an HTML file that can be viewed with a browser using the trimmed-down template shown in Figure 8.5.

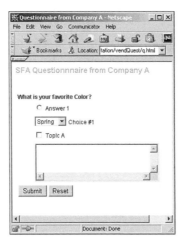

FIGURE 8.5

The VendQuest template with mock content and HTML removed.

You'll notice right away that all the question prompts were removed, except one, `What is your favorite Color?` The other question prompts were classified as mockup since they and the row that contained them were identical with respect to one another. So, we only need one surviving question prompt template to serve our needs.

The Business Object

Since this book focuses primarily on XMLC development and less so on Enhydra programming, we haven't stressed business and data object construction. But let's take this opportunity to describe a possible business object that we'll rework to use Zeus in the next chapter.

`QuestionnaireBO.java` is the primary business object. Its responsibility is to furnish the presentation object, `QuestionnairePresentation.java`, with a list of question objects. The presentation object will decompose the list, using XMLC and DOM methods to match questions, types of questions, and choices with the appropriate DOM HTML template.

Building the question objects at the business layer means you can later swap out the short term implementation for a Zeus-based implementation later on.

One of the helper objects, `SC.java`, shown in Listing 8.6, is responsible for collecting and representing a single question that represents a single-choice question. Possible choices are accrued in a linked list and then associated with a question prompt.

LISTING 8.6   examples/business/SC.java

```java
package examples.business;

public class SC {
  private String prompt;
  private java.util.List choiceList;
  private static final String TYPE = "SC";

  public SC() {
    this.choiceList = new java.util.LinkedList();
  }

  public void setPrompt(String p) {
    this.prompt = p;
  }

  public String getPrompt() {
    return this.prompt;
  }

  public String getType() {
    return TYPE;
  }

  public void addChoice(String choice) {
    this.choiceList.add(choice);
  }

  public java.util.List getChoiceList() {
    return this.choiceList;
  }
}
```

There are similar helper classes for multiple choice questions (MC), ranking questions (Rank) and simple comment questions (Comment). For our purposes, we're going to populate a linked list of questions with helper objects. The code fragment here is an example of how we instantiated and populated a single-choice question within a business object.

```java
public class QuestionnaireBO {

  private List questions;
  private Vendor vendor;

  public QuestionnaireBO() {
```

```
vendor = new Vendor("Lutris Technologies");
questions = new LinkedList();

// SC question #1
SC sc = new SC();
sc.setPrompt("What is your role?");
sc.addChoice("Engineer");
sc.addChoice("Executive");
sc.addChoice("Buttkicker");
sc.addChoice("None of the above");
questions.add(sc);
```

We have the capability to create multiple questions of type SC and an unlimited mixture of types of questions. There will be no restrictions on the number of questions the vendor may construct. For example, the vendor might want to ask five single-choice questions only.

The VendQuest Presentation Object

We now have worked out enough about the business object to know where the data is coming from and in what format. Now we need a strategy for extracting the templates we need from the Questionnaire.html template, generated by the xmlc command. That template will be populated by our presentation object with the vendor's questions.

Before we dig deeply into code, let's review what we're going to do with the question objects. First of all, after extracting the mock content and its containing table information, the table template is now whittled down to the minimum set of templates we need to format all the new questions and their associated choices or text fields. What we're going to do is

1. add new content to the row template,
2. clone the template, remove the id attribute, and
3. append the cloned row to the table.

For each question, we're going to extract the question prompt. We'll then use the template row identified by the PromptRow id attribute to first add the question "What is your role?"

If you look at the PromptRow table row, you'll see that it contains a cell that spans the two columns and contains the id attribute PromptCell. XMLC turns that id into the method setTextPromptCell(), which we can use to update the template cell with a new question before cloning it and appending the question to the table as a new row. Again, since all the question prompts and the cells and rows that contain them look the same, there's no point in preserving more than one of these rows as a template.

```
HTMLTableRowElement promptRow = qPage.getElementPromptRow();
qName = ("Q:" + new Integer(questionCount));
qPage.setTextPromptCell(qName + " " + sc.getPrompt());
```

The algorithm we'll use is explained in the pseudo-code here. The outermost loop iterates through the linked list of question objects returned from the `QuestionnaireBO` business object. Each question object is checked for its type (`SC` for single-choice, `Rank` for ranking question, and so on.). When there's a match, the question-specific logic takes over, using its associated template row.

```
QuestionnaireHTML qPage =
➥(QuestionnaireHTML)comms.xmlcFactory.create(QuestionnaireHTML.class);

HTMLTableElement table = qPage.getElementQTable();
QuestionnaireBO qbo = new QuestionnaireBO();
List qList = qbo.getQuestions();
int questionCount = 0; //Number each question asked.
for (Iterator i = qList.iterator(); i.hasNext(); ) {
  questionCount++;
  Object q = i.next();
  if (q instanceof SC) {
    ...template modifying code...
     for (Iterator j = choiceList.iterator(); j.hasNext();) {
      ...template modifying code...
  } else if (q instanceof MC) {
    ...template modifying code...
     for (Iterator j = choiceList.iterator(); j.hasNext();) {
      ...template modifying code...
  } else if (q instanceof Rank) {
    ...template modifying code...
     for (Iterator j = choiceList.iterator(); j.hasNext();) {
      ...template modifying code...
  } else if (q instanceof Comment) {
    ...template modifying code...
  }
}
....final changes to the table and page
comms.response.writeHTML(qPage);
```

Once the list of questions have all been processed, the remaining code reattaches the orphaned `SubmitRow` row containing the `Submit` and `Reset` buttons as the last row in the table.

HTML Controls

All the HTML-specific DOM extensions are defined by the package `org.enhydra.xmlc.html`. Illustrated earlier, this XML/HTML language-specific implementation of the HTML sub-interface greatly simplifies and makes type-safe the process of XMLC development for HTML documents. Similar implementations of DOM sub-interfaces exist for WML in the open source Enhydra XMLC.

Input Elements

Input elements are a strange animal, in that they are manifested as user interface widgets depending on the indicted type, such as: "text," "password," "checkbox," "radio," "submit," "reset," "file," "hidden," "image," or "button."

Table 8.2 lists all the methods introduced by HTMLInputElement. Some are clearly specific to particular manifestations of the input element depending on the indicated type. The method setSrc(), for example, is dedicated to indicating the path to the location of an image.

TABLE 8.2 Methods of HTMLInputElement

blur()	click()	focus()	getAccept()
getAccessKey()	getAlign()	getAlt()	getChecked()
getDefaultChecked()	getDefaultValue()	getDisabled()	getForm()
getMaxLength()	getName()	getReadOnly()	getSize()
getSrc()	getTabIndex()	getType()	getUseMap()
getValue()	select()	setAccept()	setAccessKey()
setAlign()	setAlt()	setChecked()	setDefaultChecked()
setDefaultValue()	setDisabled()	setMaxLength()	setName()
setReadOnly()	setSize()	setSrc()	setTabIndex()
setUseMap()	setValue()		

Clearly, we can take samples of methods such as getValue(), getValue(), and setDefaultChecked() to dynamically query and define the state of the checkboxes and radio boxes in the presented questionnaire. Using getType(), for example, we can query the template to determine if we are working with a button or an image.

Radio and Check Boxes

Recall from the previous section that the VendQuest presentation object, QuestionnairePresentation.java, iterates through a list of question objects, accesses question information in order to systematically construct a questionnaire form. The code that we're about to walk through addresses the conversion of a single-choice question object into single-choice question presentation logic for generating a list of radio box choices described by a question prompt.

We've extracted the SCRow template from the Questionnaire.html source listed earlier in Listing 8.1. The row contains two cells (or columns). The first cell is used for padding to shift the options to the right. The second cell, SCInputCell, contains the template input control of type radio. It is also accompanied by a text label that describes the radio choice. It is captured as a easy-to-reference inline template by an HTML scan element, SCInputLabel.

```
<tr id="SCRow">
  <td class="regField" width="30"><img ➥src="../media/spacer.gif"
➥width="30" height="20"></td>
  <td id="SCInputCell" class="regField" width="325">
   <input id="SCInput" type="radio">
   <span id="SCInputLabel"> Answer 1</span></td>
</tr>
```

Note the absence of name and value attributes in the input element. Because we're going to generate those attribute-value pairs dynamically, there's no point in cluttering the template; unless, of course, you want the storyboard to show some predicted behavior when demonstrated.

Before we begin processing the question object, the first task is to grab the templates represented by the SCRow and SCInput identifiers. The code below uses the XMLC accessor methods, getElementSCRow() and getElementSCInput(), to locate and record the nodes they represent in the overall document DOM tree template.

```
//Grab the SC table row and input templates
HTMLTableRowElement scChoiceRow = qPage.getElementSCRow();
HTMLInputElement scInput = qPage.getElementSCInput();
```

Before we get to these templates, we first define a string that will be used for two purposes. One is to preface the question prompt with a question number, such as Q1 or Q2. We're storing it in a variable in order to also use it to set the name attribute shared by each radio type input element. This will give us a convenient way of identifying the answer (to Q1) when the form is submitted and processed by the question processor, QuestionProcessor.java.

```
if (q instanceof SC) {

  SC sc = (SC) q;
  qName = ("Q:" + new Integer(questionCount));
```

This code will generate a string such as Q2: What is your favorite programming language? In the next fragment, we are bringing the question number string and the prompt together, then using the accessor method generated by XMLC, setTextPromptCell(), to easily update the question prompt template. It is then cloned and the clone is appended to the table. We now have our first new dynamic content installed in the table template.

```
// Set the question prompt, clone it and append to the table.
qPage.setTextPromptCell(qName + " " + sc.getPrompt());
clonedRow = promptRow.cloneNode(true);
table.appendChild(clonedRow);
```

Now we're ready to update the template row containing the radio box input element, clone it, and stamp out a series of choices. In the following code, the first thing we do is reference the name attribute in the input element with scInput.setName. Here we set the attribute with the

Q1 value, uniquely identifying the collection of radio attributes as belonging to the same question group. Then, as we extract each choice from the SC question object, we set their value attributes with unique values to label the choice that will eventually be returned to QuestionProcessor.java. The format we use to set the value attribute is value=Choice:#, where # is the number assigned to each choice. We also use the XMLC accessor method setTextInputLabel() to simultaneously label the current choice.

```
scInput.setName(qName);
// Grab the row containing the control and stamp out
// new rows for every choice encountered.
//
choiceList = sc.getChoiceList();
choiceCount = 0;
for (Iterator j = choiceList.iterator(); j.hasNext();) {
  choiceCount++;
  scInput.setValue("choice:" + new Integer(choiceCount));
  qPage.setTextSCInputLabel((String)j.next());

  clonedRow = scChoiceRow.cloneNode(true);
  table.appendChild(clonedRow);
}
```

Once the choice template is populated with a new set of dynamic data and attribute values, the entire row is cloned and the copy is appended to the table.

In this example, we've demonstrated the use of HTMLInputElement's setValue() and setName() to dynamically name and identify the choices that are represented by radio-style input elements. Since the only difference between the radio (SC) and check box (MC) templates in terms of logic are the template id values and the setting of the input element's type, we've sufficiently covered both types of questions.

Select/Option Menus

Perhaps the most complex row template in the VendQuest template represents the ranking question. To make the best use of space, we're using option menus to represent each set of choices. The array of option menus then represent a "ranking" from top to bottom. The user makes a choice from each menu to indicate first, second, third choice, and so on.

Option menus are created by the combination of a single select element containing multiple option elements. select can be instructed to allow single- or multiple-choice behavior. The nice thing about option menus is that they conserve a lot of display space, featuring scrolling to get to each option. Table 8.3 lists some of the methods that are supported by the HTMLSelectElement DOM sub-class.

8

TABLE 8.3 Additional Methods of `HTMLSelectElement`

getLength()	getMultiple()	getOptions()
getSelectedIndex()	getSize()	setDisabled()
setMultiple()	setSelectedIndex()	setSize()

We've kept the features of this type of question relatively simple. For every possible answer, there is an `option` control. Each set of options is contained within a `select` element. The markup following fragment composes the row template, identified by the `id RankRow`:

```
<tr id="RankRow">
 <td class="regField" width="30" height="21">
➥<img src="../media/spacer.gif" width="30" height="20"></td>
  <td class="regField" width="325" height="21">
   <select id="RankSelect" name="select">
    <option id="RankOption">Spring</option>
    <option class="mockup">Summer</option>
   </select>
   <span id="RankSelectLabel">Choice #1</span></td>
 </tr>
```

Our goal is to replicate this row for every one the ranking menus. If there are three items, there will be three option menus, labeled "Ranking 1," "Ranking 2," and "Ranking 3," respectively. The following code sets the table, so to speak, grabbing the `row` element, the `select` element, and the `option` element templates.

```
HTMLTableRowElement rkRankRow = qPage.getElementRankRow();
HTMLSelectElement rkSelect = qPage.getElementRankSelect();
HTMLOptionElement rkOption = qPage.getElementRankOption();
rkRankRow.removeAttribute("id");
rkSelect.removeAttribute("id");
rkOption.removeAttribute("id");
```

After determining that we're working with a ranking question object, we extract the ranking question and add it to the cloned question prompt template.

```
} else if (q instanceof Rank) {
 Rank rk = (Rank) q;

 //Get the Q # to prepend the prompt string with.
 qName = ("Q:" + new Integer(questionCount));

 //Set the prompt string.
 //Clone and add back to the table.
 qPage.setTextPromptCell(qName + " " + rk.getPrompt());
 clonedRow = promptRow.cloneNode(true);
 table.appendChild(clonedRow);
```

Here's where we get a bit tricky. Not necessarily clever, just tricky. For each choice, we're going to eventually deliver an option menu. Repeating our goal, if there are three choices, there will be three option menus.

This code picks off the choices, such as `apples`, `oranges`, and `kiwis`. It uses the `rkOption` template, containing the `option` element, to add values, then make a copy by cloning it. Then, rather than add it to the parent `select` element, we instead add it to a linked list of `option` elements. `optionNodes` is the linked list.

```
choiceCount = 0;
choiceList = rk.getChoiceList();

for (Iterator j = choiceList.iterator(); j.hasNext();) {
  choiceCount++;

  value = (String)j.next();

  rkOption.setLabel(value);
  rkOption.setValue(value);
  qPage.setTextRankOption(value);

  optionNodes.add(rkOption.cloneNode(true));
}
```

So we now have a set of orphan `option` elements stored in the linked list. We're ready for building the `select` elements and adding these stored options. We're going to enter an iteration that will loop once for each stored option. Each iteration will build one new `RankRow` containing the `select` element, and append the options as children to the `select` element.

```
checkedCount = 0;
for (int m = 0; m < optionNodes.size(); m++ ) {

  checkedCount++;
  checked = false; // set flag for assigning "selected" opt.
  optionCount = 0;
  for (Iterator k = optionNodes.iterator(); k.hasNext();) {

   option = (HTMLOptionElement)k.next();
   optionCount++;
   if (!checked && (optionCount == checkedCount)) {
     option.setSelected(true);
     checked = true;
   } else {
     option.setSelected(false);
   }
   rkSelect.appendChild(option);
  }
```

With a `select` element populated with `option` elements, we now do some post processing, setting the `select` element's name attribute and label. Finally we clone the row, appending it to the table.

```
//Set the Select's "name" attribute value
rkSelect.setName(qName + ":" + (m + 1));

//Assign a label to the option menu.
qPage.setTextRankSelectLabel("Choice #" + (m + 1));

//So now I have a full select with options.
//clone it and append it.
clonedRow = rkRankRow.cloneNode(true);
table.appendChild(clonedRow);
}
//clear for next iteration, if another rank question comes up.
optionNodes.clear();
```

Error Checking

This template certainly introduces all kinds of scenarios for possible error conditions. Perhaps the visitor gives two choices the same ranking. With server-side validation, we can send a highly dynamic response that can:

- Include an textual error message indicating the problem.
- Deliver a presentation with only the ranking question. When the Submit button is selected, the entire page is resent, rankings and all, for the user to double check for completeness, deciding to either resubmit or resume answering questions.

We'll demonstrate in the next chapter how to do server-side validation using this very example.

textArea

There are two types of text input controls. Using the `input` element with the `type` attribute set to `text`, you can display a single line. For multi-line boxes, like the one we'll want to use in the VendQuest questionnaire, HTML provides the `textarea` element.

Table 8.4 lists the methods introduced by the `HTMLTextAreaElement` class. With the column and row-related methods, we can dynamically control the dimensions of the text area template. With `select()`, we can select the text displayed in the text area control for easy deletion by the user.

TABLE 8.4 Methods Introduced by `HTMLTextAreaElement`

getCols()	getRows()	select()
setCols()	setRows()	

After visiting the more complex algorithm we defined for the ranking question, the `textarea` question, which we've called the `Comment` object, is relatively simple.

```
HTMLTableRowElement cmRow = qPage.getElementCommentRow();
HTMLTextAreaElement cmTextArea = qPage.getElementCommentTextArea();
cmRow.removeAttribute("id");
cmTextArea.removeAttribute("id");
```

First we fetch the table row containing the `textarea` element. Then we grab the node representing the `textarea` template, storing it in `cmTextArea`.

```
} else if (q instanceof Comment) {
  Comment cm = (Comment) q;

  qName = ("Q:" + new Integer(questionCount));

  qPage.setTextPromptCell(qName + " " + cm.getPrompt());
  clonedRow = promptRow.cloneNode(true);
  table.appendChild(clonedRow);
  //
  cmTextArea.setName(qName);

  clonedRow = cmRow.cloneNode(true);
  table.appendChild(clonedRow);
}
```

Again, we first update the question prompt template with the `Comment` question, such as "How can we improve on our booth for next year?" The `textarea` element is fetched from the template and cloned. It's assigned a name with `setName()`, a method of the HTML.

Working with the Document Head

The class `HTMLDocument` holds everything there is to know about the markup page. How pragmatic this information is for your application depends on your presentation strategy. `HTMLDocument` defines methods that return an `HTMLCollection` of document objects representing forms, links, images, and applets. An `HTMLCollection` is simply a list of nodes.

At the top of the document resides the document's `head` element. Among other things, including JavaScript, the `head` element contains the document's `title` element. The content associated with the `title` element is usually presented in the browser's main window bar and is used as the title in a history mechanism. The name of the `title` needs to be meaningful; because the page is often referenced out of context to how the user got there. This is the case particularly if, for example, it's a link referenced in somebody else's page.

For our needs in VendQuest, we're simply looking to update the document's `title` element.

```
String vendor = qbo.getVendor();
qPage.setTextVendorTitle("Questionnaire from " + vendor);
```

The preceding code first retrieves the vendor's name from the `VendorObject`, provided by `QuestionnaireBO.java`. Then we take advantage of an `id` attribute, `vendorTitle`, that's been placed in the document's `title` element. One approach to setting the `title` is to take advantage of the `HTMLTitleElement` class, using the `setTitle()` method.

```
HTMLTitleElement pageTitle = qPage.getElementVendorTitle();
pageTitle.setText("Questionnaire from " + vendor);
```

Or, we can simply use the `setTextVendorTitle()` method, generated by `xmlc`.

The VendQuest Presentation Object

Now that we've examined key sub-algorithms and their respective strategies, let's take a look at the entire listing in Listing 8.7. Although we could have delegated more complex tasks to helper POs, for demonstration's sake, we went with a fairly flattened presentation object.

LISTING 8.7   vendQuest/QuestionnairePresentation.java

```
package examples.presentation.vendQuest;

import examples.business.QuestionnaireBO;
import examples.business.SC;
import examples.business.MC;
import examples.business.Rank;
import examples.business.Comment;
import com.lutris.appserver.server.httpPresentation.HttpPresentation;
import com.lutris.appserver.server.httpPresentation.HttpPresentationComms;
import com.lutris.appserver.server.httpPresentation.HttpPresentationException;
import java.io.*;
import java.util.*;
import com.lutris.xml.xmlc.*;
import org.w3c.dom.*;
import org.w3c.dom.html.*;

public class QuestionnairePresentation implements HttpPresentation {

  public void run(HttpPresentationComms comms)
    throws HttpPresentationException, IOException {
```

LISTING 8.7 Continued

```
QuestionnaireHTML qPage =
➥(QuestionnaireHTML)comms.xmlcFactory.create(QuestionnaireHTML.class);

//Grab the overall table template, a.k.a. the Parent Node.
HTMLTableElement table = qPage.getElementQTable();

//Grab the spacer row.
HTMLTableRowElement spacerRow = qPage.getElementSpacerRow();

//Grab the prompt row and cell elements.
HTMLTableRowElement promptRow = qPage.getElementPromptRow();
promptRow.removeAttribute("id");

//Grab the SC table row and input templates
HTMLTableRowElement scChoiceRow = qPage.getElementSCRow();
HTMLInputElement scInput = qPage.getElementSCInput();
scChoiceRow.removeAttribute("id");
scInput.removeAttribute("id");

//Grab the MC table row and input templates
HTMLTableRowElement mcChoiceRow = qPage.getElementMCRow();
HTMLInputElement mcInput = qPage.getElementMCInput();
mcChoiceRow.removeAttribute("id");
mcInput.removeAttribute("id");

//Grab the Rank table row, select and option templates
HTMLTableRowElement rkRankRow = qPage.getElementRankRow();
HTMLSelectElement rkSelect = qPage.getElementRankSelect();
HTMLOptionElement rkOption = qPage.getElementRankOption();
rkRankRow.removeAttribute("id");
rkSelect.removeAttribute("id");
rkOption.removeAttribute("id");

//Grab Comment
HTMLTableRowElement cmRow = qPage.getElementCommentRow();
HTMLTextAreaElement cmTextArea = qPage.getElementCommentTextArea();
cmRow.removeAttribute("id");
cmTextArea.removeAttribute("id");

//Assorted counters and placeholders.
HTMLOptionElement option;
List choiceList;
Node clonedRow = null;
int choiceCount;
int checkedCount;
```

LISTING 8.7 Continued

```
int optionCount;
String value;
String qName;
boolean checked;

//Instantiate the business object.
QuestionnaireBO qbo = new QuestionnaireBO();

//for Ranking questions (Select/Option elements).
List optionNodes = new LinkedList();

//Fetch the list of question objects from the business object.
List qList = qbo.getQuestions();

int questionCount = 0; //Number each question asked.

for (Iterator i = qList.iterator(); i.hasNext(); ) {

 questionCount++;
 Object q = i.next();

 if (q instanceof SC) {

  SC sc = (SC) q;
  //Set this string for prepending question prompts
  //with a number.
  // e.g., "Q3: What is your favorite bird?"
  qName = ("Q:" + new Integer(questionCount));

  // Deal with the prompt first. Update the template row.
  // Then clone it. Then add the clone back to the table.
  qPage.setTextPromptCell(qName + " " + sc.getPrompt());
  clonedRow = promptRow.cloneNode(true);
  table.appendChild(clonedRow);

  // Name the input element name attribute using the Q number.
  scInput.setName(qName);

  // Grab the row containing the control and stamp out
  // new rows for every choice encountered.
  choiceList = sc.getChoiceList();
  choiceCount = 0;
  for (Iterator j = choiceList.iterator(); j.hasNext();) {
   choiceCount++;
   scInput.setValue("choice:" + new Integer(choiceCount));
   qPage.setTextSCInputLabel((String)j.next());
```

LISTING 8.7   Continued

```
      clonedRow = scChoiceRow.cloneNode(true);
      table.appendChild(clonedRow);
     }

  } else if (q instanceof MC) {
   MC mc = (MC) q;

   qName = ("Q:" + new Integer(questionCount));

   // Update the question prompt.
   qPage.setTextPromptCell(qName + " " + mc.getPrompt());
   clonedRow = promptRow.cloneNode(true);
   table.appendChild(clonedRow);

   // Name the input element name attribute using the Q number.
   mcInput.setName(qName);

   choiceList = mc.getChoiceList();
   choiceCount = 0;
   for (Iterator j = choiceList.iterator(); j.hasNext();) {
    choiceCount++;
    mcInput.setValue("choice:" + new Integer(choiceCount));
    qPage.setTextMCInputLabel((String)j.next());

     clonedRow = mcChoiceRow.cloneNode(true);
     table.appendChild(clonedRow);
    }

  } else if (q instanceof Rank) {
   Rank rk = (Rank) q;

   //Get the Q # to prepend the prompt string with.
   qName = ("Q:" + new Integer(questionCount));

   //Set the prompt string.
   qPage.setTextPromptCell(qName + " " + rk.getPrompt());
   clonedRow = promptRow.cloneNode(true);
   table.appendChild(clonedRow);

   // grab the choices, build the option list, then
   // add to the select element.
   choiceCount = 0;
   choiceList = rk.getChoiceList();

   for (Iterator j = choiceList.iterator(); j.hasNext();) {
```

LISTING 8.7 Continued

```
choiceCount++;

value = (String)j.next();
// Be sure to avoid putting "selected" in the html
// template... otherwise you either have to remember
// to remove it, leave it ... probably just easier
// to add it.
rkOption.setLabel(value);
rkOption.setValue(value);
qPage.setTextRankOption(value);

optionNodes.add(rkOption.cloneNode(true));
}

checkedCount = 0;
for (int m = 0; m < optionNodes.size(); m++ ) {

checkedCount++;
checked = false; // set flag for assigning "selected" opt.

optionCount = 0;
for (Iterator k = optionNodes.iterator(); k.hasNext();) {

option = (HTMLOptionElement)k.next();

optionCount++;
if (!checked && (optionCount == checkedCount)) {
 option.setSelected(true);
 checked = true;
} else {
 option.setSelected(false);
}

rkSelect.appendChild(option);
}

//Set the Select's "name" attribute value
rkSelect.setName(qName + ":" + (m + 1));

//Assign a label to the option menu.
qPage.setTextRankSelectLabel("Choice #" + (m + 1));

//So now I have a full select with options.
//clone it and append it.
clonedRow = rkRankRow.cloneNode(true);
```

LISTING 8.7 Continued

```
      table.appendChild(clonedRow);
    }
    //clear for next iteration, if another rank question comes up.
    optionNodes.clear();

  } else if (q instanceof Comment) {
    Comment cm = (Comment) q;

    qName = ("Q:" + new Integer(questionCount));

    qPage.setTextPromptCell(qName + " " + cm.getPrompt());
    clonedRow = promptRow.cloneNode(true);
    table.appendChild(clonedRow);
    //
    cmTextArea.setName(qName);

    clonedRow = cmRow.cloneNode(true);
    table.appendChild(clonedRow);
  }
  //Append a spacer row for seperate questions.
  clonedRow = spacerRow.cloneNode(true);
  table.appendChild(clonedRow);
}
//And last, but not least,
//let's append the Submit/Reset buttons row, so that it
//appears at the bottom of the form.
HTMLTableRowElement submitRow = qPage.getElementSubmitRow();
clonedRow = submitRow.cloneNode(true);
table.appendChild(clonedRow);
table.removeChild(submitRow);

//Now let's remove all of those template rows.
table.removeChild(promptRow);
table.removeChild(scChoiceRow);
table.removeChild(mcChoiceRow);
table.removeChild(rkRankRow);
table.removeChild(cmRow);

//Name the title and page title.
String title = qbo.getVendor();
qPage.setTextVendorTitle("Questionnaire: " + title);
qPage.setTextVendorName(title);

comms.response.writeHTML(qPage);
  }
}
```

There are other ways to accomplish the same task. This is the route we took.

One final note: In ProcessQuestions.java, for demonstration purposes, we've added code that simply dumps the parameter names and their associated value(s):

```
for (Enumeration enum = comms.request.getParameterNames();
➥enum.hasMoreElements();) {
  name = (String)enum.nextElement();
  value = comms.request.getParameter(name);
  System.out.println("paramName: " + name + "[" + value + "]");
}
```

The results of answering all the questions from the questionnaire shown in Figure 8.4 are as follows:

```
paramName: Q:5[I would love to see dancing bears.]
paramName: Q:6:3[oranges]
paramName: Q:4[The show is great.]
paramName: Submit1[Submit]
paramName: Q:6:2[apples]
paramName: Q:3[choice:1]
paramName: Q:6:1[kiwis]
paramName: Q:2[choice:3]
paramName: Q:1[choice:2]
```

Working with JavaScript

JavaScript, or the use of it, has been responsible for much of the client-side dynamic behavior of modern Web presentations. Its role ranges from the client-side validation of user-provided information to supporting wild animations by Flash and the dynamic manipulation of browser layers.

It has become a regular feature of emerging markup standards to specify bindings to JavaScript for the purpose of client-side manipulations and processing. The new SVG standard from the W3C, for instance, incorporates JavaScript bindings for supporting the client-side manipulation of graphical objects, such as bar charts.

However, there's a small problem in the relationship of XMLC and JavaScript programming. While the HTML implementation of the DOM specification does represent the SCRIPT element node type, it does not recognize the JavaScript language other than as a text node. In other words, there is no JavaScript DOM or DOM element:

```
<html>
<head>
<script id="passwordScript">
```

```
    <! script for checking the minimum length of a password goes here. !>
</script>
</head>
<form>
```

We can take advantage of XMLC's support for `HTMLScriptElement` and the auto-generation of the `setTextPasswordScript()` method, keying off the preceding `id` value, to perform a whole-sale replacement of the JavaScript contained within this `<script>` element.

Let's take a look at two approaches to solving the dynamic construction of JavaScript during runtime operation.

Using Hidden Fields

There are generally three ways for Web applications to save information, such as session keys or the session itself. This is an important topic in a world that is inherently stateless.

Hidden fields have been traditionally used to pass information from one page request to another in order to maintain session state during a client transaction. Hidden fields can also pass additional information when associated with a form's Submit button.

Hidden fields are also a way to squirrel away session information, alleviating the need for fancy session failover schemes. This works for simpler application designs.

We can make use of HTML hidden fields to pass information that affects the behavior of a document's JavaScript. In Listing 2.1 from Chapter 2, "XMLC Development," we're using a simple JavaScript to verify that an administrator has entered in the minimum number of letters when creating their password. Hidden fields are created with `<input>`. They include only three properties; namely `name`, `type`, and `value`. The `value` is passed with the hidden field:

```
<form name="loginForm">
<input type="hidden" name="passwordLength" value="8" id="PasswordLen">
</form>
```

The JavaScript accesses the data in the hidden field with the following code:

```
<script language="javascript">
document.write("Required password minimum is:"
➡ + document.loginForm.passwordLength.value + "<br>");
</script>
```

Listing 8.8 demonstrates how the `input` element's attribute `value` is accessed and updated. The hard-coded value could just as easily have been fetched from a database.

LISTING 8.8   Example of How to Pass Dynamic Information to a JavaScript Variable

```
package examples.presentation.ex2;

import java.util.*;
import com.lutris.xml.xmlc.*;
import com.lutris.appserver.server.httpPresentation.*;
import org.w3c.dom.*;
import org.w3c.dom.html.*;

public class HiddenFieldPresentation implements HttpPresentation {

  public void run(HttpPresentationComms comms)
    throws HttpPresentationException {

    HiddenFieldHTML hiddenPage =
      (HiddenFieldHTML)comms.xmlcFactory.create(HiddenFieldHTML.class);

    //Fetch the input element, then update the "value" attribute.
    HTMLInputElement input = hiddenPage.getElementPasswordLen();

    input.getAttributeNode("value").setValue("16");

    comms.response.writeHTML(hiddenPage);
  }
}
```

As you might guess, there are other approaches to XMLC and JavaScript as well. Our next topic involving merging multiple sub-documents together can also be applied to introducing runtime-selected JavaScripts.

Generating Output

At some point, a servlet or presentation object completes its manipulation of the DOM template. It's then time to convert the DOM to an HTML (or XML) document and stream the markup as a string back to the client that made the original HTTP request.

So far, in all the examples you've used `writeDOM()`. `writeDOM()` is a convenient method that, among other things, supports URL encoding with session data required to preserve state from page request to page request.

For Enhydra EAF-style presentation objects, `writeDOM()` is defined as a method belonging to

`com.lutris.appserver.server.httpPresentation.HttpPresentationResponse`

and the `writeDOM` signatures are

```
writeDOM(XMLObject)
writeDOM(OutputOptions, XMLObject)
```

For standard servlet development, as defined by

```
org.enhydra.xml.xmlc.servlet.XMLCContext
```

the writeDOM signatures are

```
writeDOM(HttpServletRequest, HttpServletResponse, OutputOptions, XMLObject)
writeDOM(HttpServletRequest, HttpServletResponse, XMLObject)
```

So far, the examples have kept things pretty simple, not yet taking advantage of the class OutputOptions to exert more control over the formatting of the DOM conversion. Before we explore this option, let's explain what this means.

Complete control over the conversion of the DOM to a resultant string can be directed by the use of the classes DOMFormatter and OutputOptions. DOMFormatter formats XML and HTML DOM templates into documents. It relies on the class OutputOptions for the actual control of the formatting. Both classes are part of the parent class org.enhydra.xml.io. With these two classes, you can construct your own DOM-formatting class, called just before you use writeDOM to stream back the resultant DOM.

> **NOTE**
>
> Often you'll see developers who've discovered the toDocument() method implemented by HTMLObject and XMLObject. On the surface, the simplicity of this method makes it the apparent choice for streaming back strings of HTML or XML as extracted from the working DOM. Unfortunately, toDocument() simply calls DOMFormatter to format the DOM into a string. And that's it. The problem with this is that it doesn't, for example, address features such as the URL encoding of session information.

At the time of this writing, the pretty-printing options were not yet implemented by XMLC.

OutputOptions supports three fields for indicating which type of output document is to be generated.

- FORMAT_AUTO—Constant indicating format should be determined automatically from examining the document object.
- FORMAT_HTML—Constant indicating HTML format.
- FORMAT_XML—Constant indicating XML format.

The code below represents a simple use of OutputOptions and DOMFormatter to set formatting and set the output document's encoding:

```
OutputOptions opts = DOMFormatter.getDefaultOutputOptions(doc);
opts.setFormat(org.enhydra.xml.io.OutputOptions.FORMAT_AUTO);
opts.setEncoding("ISO-8859-1");
writeDOM(opts, page);
```

The possible formatting options are relatively robust. To illustrate the list of possible formatting actions, the following list was extracted from a DOM template Java class, generated by an xmlc compilation. The -keep option was used to preserve the Java source file representing the DOM template class:

```
fPreFormatOutputOptions = new org.enhydra.xml.io.OutputOptions();
fPreFormatOutputOptions.setFormat(org.enhydra.xml.io.OutputOptions.FORMAT_AUTO);
fPreFormatOutputOptions.setEncoding("ISO-8859-1");
fPreFormatOutputOptions.setPrettyPrinting(false);
fPreFormatOutputOptions.setIndentSize(4);
fPreFormatOutputOptions.setPreserveSpace(true);
fPreFormatOutputOptions.setOmitXMLHeader(false);
fPreFormatOutputOptions.setOmitDocType(false);
fPreFormatOutputOptions.setOmitEncoding(false);
fPreFormatOutputOptions.setDropHtmlSpanIds(true);
fPreFormatOutputOptions.setOmitAttributeCharEntityRefs(true);
fPreFormatOutputOptions.setPublicId(null);
fPreFormatOutputOptions.setSystemId(null);
fPreFormatOutputOptions.setMIMEType(null);
fPreFormatOutputOptions.markReadOnly();
```

So, it's unlikely that you will need OutputOptions for much more than setting the encoding value and the mimetype. But it does come in handy for some unusual situations, such as WML development. It turns out that some devices cannot handle the typical XML header in which encoding is specified, so XMLC was enhanced with the capability to remove the encoding specified in the XML prolog. This is done with setOmitEncoding(false).

> **NOTE**
>
> Pretty-printing has not been implemented yet. The best way to debug these pages is to save the generated file (from the browser) and then run it through the Tidy program (check www.w3.org for the C version; the Java version is included in Enhydra).

XHTML

XHTML is the W3C's reformulation of HTML to comply with XML and its requirements for well-formed documents. The impact on XMLC development is mostly felt by the designers. <li>, <Li>, and <LI> are now three different elements, because case sensitivity is introduced to elements by the XHTML DTD. Here is a simple survey of some of the key distinctions between HTML and its heir apparent, XHTML.

- **Correctly nested elements**

  HTML forbids the nesting elements that don't make sense inside other elements, but it doesn't enforce them. For example, you can stick an `img` element inside a `pre` element. You can also overlap `b` and `i` elements, such as `<b>Push or <i>pull</b> to open</i>`. You can't do either of these with XHTML.

- **End tags and empty elements**

  With HTML, you can use `<LI>` to list things, but you don't have to terminate with an `</LI>`. You do with XHTML. Elements with no content, such as `<hr>`, are expressed with a trailing `/`, as in `<hr/>`, which opens and closes this single tag.

- **Case sensitivity**

  `<a>` and `<A>` have different meanings.

- **Quoted attribute values**

  With HTML, you can get away with forgetting the quotes when expressing attribute values. That's not allowed with XHTML.

- **Attributes require values**

  HTML supports a number of Boolean attributes, which are attributes with no values. In the example earlier, we used `selected` to indicate which option was selected by default. In order to set this value, we were required to go through the `HTMLOptionElement` and its `setDefaultValue()` method. With XHTML, `<option selected>` becomes `<option selected="selected">`. We can therefore use standard DOM attribute methods for setting values instead. Other examples include the following:

  `<select multiple>` is now `<select multiple="multiple>`

  `<textarea readonly>` is now `<textarea readonly="readonly">`.

- **`id` for name attributes**

  XHTML replaces the use of the name attribute with the `id` attribute for dealing with anchor elements within a page.

- **Special characters**

  Whereas inserting a `&` in the middle of a string might work with HTML, it will require a `&amp;` in XHTML. XHTML places a higher reliance on CDATA for hiding scripts and hidden values. With standard HTML, this was done using `<! —` comments. For example, it's common to place JavaScript within comments. With XHTML, CDATA must be used:

```
script language="javascript">
<![CDATA[
```

```
    ...javascript here...
]]>
</script>
```

The good news is that XHTML should represent little impact on designers and developers, which only makes sense because the effort behind XHTML is to make it more XML-compliant. Because XHTML is an XML language, the idiosyncrasies of HTML-style development are virtually eliminated, paving the way for a blurring of the line between HTML markup and its integration with other interesting XML languages, such as SVG.

Summary

XMLC programming doesn't sacrifice flexibility in order to support complete separation of Java from markup languages such as HTML. Even within the flexible side of XMLC development, one can choose to rely almost exclusively on DOM programming or, alternatively, minimize pure DOM programming by relying heavily on XMLC utility methods and the supported DOM extensions for HTML and WML provided by XMLC.

We've demonstrated a portion of the wide range of design strategies using HTML templates. We've shown how to perform in-place updates of HTML templates with dynamically processed data. And we've shown how to take multiple templates within a single questionnaire template and turn it into a data-driven application for creating on-the-fly custom questionnaires.

In the process of presenting these examples, we've addressed the dynamic generation and manipulation of only a small percentage of the available HTML controls and static elements. Our hope has been to use the handful we selected in order to convey the flexibility and strategies for maneuvering through a DOM template and accessing its sub-templates to rebuild the overall DOM to address the application design goals.

As we'll explore in the next chapter, there are higher levels of XMLC flexibility and dynamic design strategies to take advantage of.

Presentation Strategies

IN THIS CHAPTER

It's one thing to manipulate isolated bits of HTML wrapped in a form. It's quite another to create a presentation environment that orchestrates the interaction of multiple sub-views in a cohesive, error-free manner. Take into account that each sub-view represents different contributors, data sources, behaviors and policies, and you have quite a challenge.

The goal of this chapter is to address some key topics in the presentation architecture of larger scale Web applications. In some ways, we will be setting the stage for the discussion of a real presentation framework for Enhydra XMLC presented in Chapter 13, "Barracuda Presentation Framework."

In this chapter, we will review the topic of event-driven application design and how it can be used to organize ShowFloor presentation logic into a controller for vectoring client requests to the appropriate presentation object.

We'll begin by discussing the `BasePO` strategy for defining a standard presentation object (PO) abstract class and standard methods from which your application can be extended. As a low-level presentation technology, XMLC does not support a standard event-model or a lot of pre-defined presentation framework elements. The `BasePO` approach gives you a template from which to work and develop a set of helper POs in a consistent manner.

We'll also address the topic of composite views, featuring discussions on server-side includes and the more dynamically interesting use of `importNode`. Both have the capability to bring DOM sub-documents together, simplifying the task of site maintenance and design rework. In exploring support for multiple presentation personalities and localized presentations, we'll also review how to use XMLC's capability to turn markup into multiple DOM implementations, all in support of a single markup class interface.

Lastly, we'll close out our earlier discussion about Zeus and the VendQuest application begun in the previous chapter. Zeus and XMLC are closely related in their capability to import markup into a Java application. We'll show how to update the business object `QuestionnaireBO` to use Zeus to establish a tight, DTD-defined binding between the business object and the vendor questions—only this time formatted as an XML language.

A Presentation Architecture

Enhydra XMLC is a presentation technology that introduces new capabilities on top of DOM development to make it possible to completely separate Java logic from HTML and XML markup. It intentionally stops short of a presentation framework by virtue of the tasks left up to the presentation architect and developer.

The role of presentation frameworks is to do the following:

- Abstract the more mundane details of what transpires deep in the enabling presentation technology.
- Support a set of standard interfaces and concepts for implementing a model for presentations and presentation transactions. Common presentation concepts that are supported address event handling, form validation, and integration of the presentation with the data model.

This book ends with a discussion of Barracuda, a true presentation framework for XMLC development. It represents an option for presentation development that you might find beneficial. In the meantime, there's absolutely nothing to prevent you from diving into XMLC development to get the Web presentation task done.

So, what are we left with? Lots of room to move in terms of custom strategies. This is both good news and bad. But, no matter which way we go, we'll always have a complete separation of Java from markup.

The Base Presentation Object

Enhydra developers often leverage the concept of a *base presentation object*, or BasePO. Not surprisingly, the BasePO is an abstract class with many of the methods left for implementation by the developer. As an abstract class, it defines an extensible signature that influences the design and functionality of the helper presentation objects that are responsible for accessing the model to generate page views. In effect, the BasePO approach supports a type of "delegated controller" architecture, wherein each presentation object inherits the role of controller.

Per-page presentation objects are sub-classed from the BasePO class. What they inherit is a set of methods that address event handling, session handling, user management, and runtime debugging. If you are, for example, creating a Visitor screen, you would sub-class your Visitor.po from the BasePO class.

Defining the BasePO as an abstract class gives you the flexibility to handle functionality that is unique to your application. For example, a particular method might make sense to a typical HTTP request for an HTML page view, but make no sense if the request is coming from a J2ME phone, a "smart client" capable of handling its own presentation chores. In this case, you would add methods that reflect the required interaction between J2ME and your application.

The BasePO Class

BasePO is designed as an abstract class with the methods listed in Table 9.1. It is declared as follows:

```
public abstract class BasePO implements HttpPresentation
```

9

As you can see from the table, some aspects are particular to the ShowFloor application, but the general structure is very portable to other applications. The entire BasePO.java listing is described in Appendix D, "The Base Presentation Object."

TABLE 9.1 BasePO Methods

Method	Returns
handleDefault()	XMLObject
getComms()	HttpPresentationComms
getSessionData()	ShowFloorSessionData
rerouteForContent()	Void
run(HttpPresentationComms comms)	Void
handleEvent(HttpPresentationComms comms)	Void
handleLogout()	XMLObject
getPage(String event)	XMLObject
getApplication()	ShowFloor
writeDebugMsg(String msg)	static void

Let's take a look at some of these methods, describing each method's role in the ShowFloor application:

- handleDefault()—When no event is specified along with the client request, this method must be supported by the application. Its role is to return the XMLObject that is the resulting page view.

- getComms()—Returns HTTPPresentationComms, containing everything associated with the current HTTP request.

- run()—This is the familiar doGet() Enhydra EAF method required by every presentation object that is ultimately responsible for handling an HTTP request. run() is located by the Enhydra Multiserver, then invoked with the HTTP request.

    The run() method, as defined by the BasePO class, looks for an event parameter and then calls handle<EventName>. If the event parameter is not defined, then the handleDefault() method is called in the child class.

- rerouteForContent()—This method detects the nature of the client making a request. Is it a WML client? A J2ME client?

- getPage()—Using the event passed by the HTTP request, getPage() returns the page requested by the HTTP request.

- `handleLogout()`—The user's session is deleted by this method, forcing the user to log in again. Usually associated with a timeout:
  ```
  SessionManager sessionManager = myComms.session.getSessionManager();
  sessionManager.deleteSession(myComms.session);
  ```

- `getApplication()`—This method returns the application object. Recall that the application object contains information about the application's name, status (running or stopped), logging channel, and its configuration file.

- `writeDebugMsg()`—Simple debugging method that uses the debug log channel to write output to a multiserver log file when the `DEBUG` level is listed.

Flow of Control with `BasePO`

An HTTP request comes in, invoking a particular presentation object. The flow of control continues as follows:

1. The `run()` method is invoked, which fetches the `event` parameter to determine whether an event value has been provided.

2. `run()` invokes `handleEvent()` to process the request. Either `handleDefault()` or `handle<EventName>()` is called.

3. The presentation object processes the event. If an error is detected during form validation, the presentation object uses `showPage()` to update the current page's template representation with error messages.

4. If no errors are detected, the presentation object might choose to invoke `ClientPageRedirectException(<PO name>)` in order to continue processing to the next page.

All these pathways can be followed in the ShowFloor application source code, found on the book's CD.

initSessionData()

Compensating for the Web's inherently stateless nature, the role of `initSessionData()` is to initialize the hash table variable `comms.sessionData` that is used to pass session information from request to request. Invoked from the `run()` method, this method sets the table for all session data related to the particular page:

```
protected ShowFloorSessionData session = null;

protected void initSessionData(HttpPresentationComms comms)
    throws ShowFloorPresentationException

    this.myComms = comms;
```

```
try {
  Object obj = comms.sessionData.get(ShowFloorSessionData.SESSION_KEY);

  //If session data found, save it in a private data member
  if (obj != null) {
    this.session = (ShowFloorSessionData) obj;
  } else {
    // No session data was found; create a new session data instance
    this.session = new ShowFloorSessionData();
    comms.sessionData.set(ShowFloorSessionData.SESSION_KEY,
      this.session);
  }
} catch (KeywordValueException ex) {
  throw new ShowFloorPresentationException("Trouble initializing user",
    ex);
}
}
```

SESSION_KEY is a hash key used to associate the session information with the particular client. With a session variable in hand, you now have the capability to save session from page to page.

Tracking Session

The class ShowFloorSessionData, found in ShowFloorSessionData.java, is an application-specific, developer-defined class containing everything from the session key used to retrieve the session object related to the application, to all methods related to setting and retrieving bits of session information. This might include the visitor's name and login status (for My ShowFloor). The BasePO code fragment that follows shows, in part, how ShowFloorSessionData is used to store and retrieve business objects (for example, vendor) to and from sessionData:

```
import com.otterpod.showfloor.business.Visitor;
import com.otterpod.showfloor.business.Vendor;
import com.otterpod.showfloor.business.Booth;

private Visitor visitor = null;
private Vendor vendor = null;
private Booth booth = null;
private int AUTHORIZATION = ShowFloorConstants.VISITOR;

public class ShowFloorSessionData [
  proc void setVendor(Vendor vendor) {
    this.vendor = vendor;
  }
  proc Vendor getVendor() {
    return vendor;
  }
```

```
  public void setUserAuth(int auth) {
    this.AUTHORIZATION = auth;
  }
  public int getUserAuth() {
    return AUTHORIZATION;
  }
}
```

Elsewhere in the code, when a new HTTP request has been received, you simply recover the existing Vendor object with a call to

```
Vendor vendor = getSessionData().getVendor();
```

Authorization levels are established elsewhere in the ShowFloor source tree, in a class we've defined as ShowFloorConstants. They are as follows:

```
public static final int VISITOR_USER = 0;
public static final int MYSFA_USER = 1;
public static final int VENDOR_USER = 2;
public static final int ADMIN_USER = 3;
```

handleEvent()

The run() method uses handleEvent() to begin processing HTTP requests for its child presentation object. As stated earlier, if no event type is detected, it simply invokes the presentation object's handleDefault() method and lets the rest of the PO take it from there. HandleEvent(), of the BasePO.java abstract class, appears as follows:

```
public void handleEvent(HttpPresentationComms comms) throws Exception {

  String  event = comms.request.getParameter("event");
  XMLObject returnDoc = null;

  try {
    if (event == null || event.length() == 0) {
      returnDoc = handleDefault();
    } else {
      returnDoc = getPage(event);
    }
    comms.response.writeDOM(returnDoc);

  } catch (Exception e) {
    throw new Exception("Exception turning DOM template:" + e);
  }
}
```

If an event value is detected with the request, then getPage(<EventName>) is called, which builds and calls the more targeted handle<EventName> method. The presentation object should have a method that matches the generated handle<EventName> acting as a simple "listener" for the event.

For example, the method handleBrowse() is generated from the following URI request:

```
showFloor/ListVendor.po?event=browse
```

where the ListVendor is the targeted ShowFloor presentation object and the event is browse. Of course, the example is not a true *event type*, an event that is represented as a Java class. Instead, we're literally reading a string with predefined significance.

As you can see, handleEvent() is also responsible for streaming the DOM template back to the client with writeDOM().

getPage()

This method makes use of the Java reflection API to construct and then invoke a method that incorporates the name of the event. This approach gives you the capability to more easily extend the application with event-driven pages without having to expand the definition of the BasePO:

```
public XMLObject getPage(String event) throws Exception {
  try {
    Method method = this.getClass().getMethod(toMethodName(event), null);
    XMLObject thePage = (XMLObject) method.invoke(this, null);

    return thePage;
  } catch (InvocationTargetException ex) {
...
```

toMethodName(), also a part of the BasePO, constructs the method, prepending handle to the event name.

> **NOTE**
>
> As you can see, this approach to indicating events is a bit primitive, relying on the recognition of strings. In Chapter 13, you'll see how Barracuda uses true Java classes to represent event types.

Assembling Composite Views

Now that the Internet has had some time to evolve since it really started to roar in the mid-90s, familiar patterns of portal-style Web pages have emerged. Pages of developer sites, online financial services, news sites, and corporate and nonprofit sites typically contain a recognizable collection of headers, footers, main windows, page-context navigation bars, or a global top navigation bar of site-wide menu categories.

Each sub-page or sub-view represents areas of different rates of change with respect to monthly, weekly, or daily maintenance. Some sub-views might represent entirely different data sources. And each sub-view might be managed by a different set of individuals, policies, or data sources, depending on how the project is organized. And finally, the sub-view might change according to role-based permissions, reflecting who the client visitor is—you, me, or the boss.

For instance, a header view might be purely driven by the automatic generation of ad content, posted according to the nature of the ad transaction (for example, posted every third page view). A main window sub-view might be entirely handcrafted by a newsroom of individuals, looking forward to automatically-generated pages of current news.

Enhydra XMLC supports a number of strategies for assembling composite views from multiple sub-views or pages.

Strategies for Composite Views

When designing and building a site that makes extensive use of headers, footers, and navigational bars, the last thing you want to do is recreate these elements with every page you create. Instead, the ideal is to create each element once, then reference them from within the current document. There are good reasons for doing this, including reducing the impact of change if you need to do such tasks as the following:

- Update the navigational bar with a new menu item.
- Change the header to reflect the hosted company in the ShowFloor application.
- Add new compelling graphics and/or behaviors to portions of each page, without putting the rest of the page at risk for errors.
- Build a library of common sub-documents, such as search objects or member login objects.
- Import from a library of HTML documents containing JavaScript.
- Load template implementations that are sub-document specific, instead of the entire page. We'll discuss the use of the XMLC -generate option to separate DOM template implementations from their interface in the next chapter.

There are at least two approaches you can take to support the efficient design of multi-part documents requiring headers, footers, and navigational bars: SSI and composite view integration.

SSI

In Chapter 7, "The xmlc Command," we introduced the xmlc command option -ssi for server-side includes. In reality, the more appropriate term for this feature is *compile-time includes* because real server-side includes rely on runtime support from the Web server. XMLC SSIs are addressed during xmlc compilation, incorporating each referenced sub-document. They are not applicable at runtime. But the format of the server-side include markup conforms with standard server-side format:

```
<!--#include virtual="../media/TopBanner.ssi"-->
```

The following markup shows how .ssi files are referenced from inside its host markup. For replacement to occur during compilation, the xmlc command must be used with the -ssi option in order for the compile-time includes to occur:

```
<html>
<head>
<title>Air Sent: Customer Login</title>
<link href="../media/airsent.css" rel="styleSheet" type="text/css">
</head>
<body bgcolor="#FFFFFF" text="#000000" link="#0000FF" vlink="#800080">
<form action="Login.html" method="POST">
<input type="HIDDEN" name="event" value="login">
<!--#include virtual="../media/TopBanner.ssi"-->
<!-- Main Layout -->

<!-- Main Window Table goes here -->

<!-- End Main Layout -->
<!--#include virtual="../media/Footer.ssi"-->
</form>
</body>
</html>
```

An example of Footer.ssi is shown in Listing 9.1. Note that it is a subset of typical markup because the form, body and html elements are already specified in the host HTML file.

LISTING 9.1 Footer.ssi

```
<!— Begin Footer —>
<table width="100" border="0" cellspacing="5" cellpadding="0" height="74">
 <tr>
  <td width="60"><img src="../../media/otterPodLogoXsmall.gif" width="35"
➥height="35"></td>
  <td width="83" class="footerFont" valign="top"><a href=
➥"http://www.otterpod.com/about.html" target="away">About
   SFA and OtterProd Productions</a></td>
  <td width="2" class="footerFont" valign="top"><a href=
➥"http://www.otterpod.com/dogshow.html">Watch
   for TheDogShow, an OtterPod Production, 11 June 2003</a></td>
  <td width="1" class="footerFont" valign="top"><a href=
➥"http://www.otterpod.com/bitbucket.html">Give
   us your feedback</a></td>
 </tr>
 <tr>
  <td width="60"> </td>
  <td width="83"><img src="../../media/spacer.gif" width="120" height="1"></td>
  <td width="2"><img src="../../media/spacer.gif" width="120" height="1"></td>
  <td width="1"><img src="../../media/spacer.gif" width="120" height="1"></td>
 </tr>
</table>
<!— End Footer —>
```

At first, this feature might appear to be limited to simply economizing on the inclusion of content that doesn't change very often. SSIs are ideal for Web applications that remain relatively static over a one-to-three year lifecycle. They're not so ideal for portals that require changes in units like hours.

However, a great deal of value is still here because you are minimizing redundant markup. Changes made to a header.ssi file are propagated to any other markup file that includes that header.ssi file. However, to cause that propagation, you must re-compile all the affected files.

SSIs and XMLC's Runtime Auto-Class Loading

A SSI strategy can be made quite a bit more dynamic when combined with XMLC runtime features. A clever system can be designed to take advantage of the runtime auto-class loading feature of XMLC.

By enabling the auto-class loading feature in the runtime XMLC environment, SSI changes can be made, for instance, once every night, causing the rebuild of all affected markup, and therefore the DOM templates.

This approach improves on other systems that do performance-costly runtime checks for loading new content. However, if an SSI file is used throughout an application, the first users of the system will detect a discernible performance impact. But, this only affects the users who first cause the auto-class loading to take place. After this event, there is no further performance delay. In addition, this approach is not very efficient for sub-views that change frequently, such as advertisements that constantly rotate or are subject to complex contractual terms.

There are other effects in terms of how your production system is coordinated. Again, it goes back to the nature of your Web application and the staging environment (of building new DOM templates leveraging SSIs) that you are willing to build.

Runtime Composite View Integration

Let's discuss a strategy for building composite views (of sub-views) using the capability of DOM programming to make copies from multiple DOM trees and import them into target DOM templates.

In many cases, what you really want is the capability to grab markup for different sources at runtime, reducing the need to rebuild the entire presentation environment. More significantly, what you really want is the capability to make runtime decisions about which sub-views to incorporate and when, based on the user's push of a button or selection of a menu item.

Figure 9.1 represents a typical composite view that you might encounter at a site offered by your bank or credit card company. The topmost menu is a category navigation bar, used to organize macro tasks within the Web application. Depending on the nature of the site, categories take on different meanings, such as a product company that promotes its "products," "services," and "news."

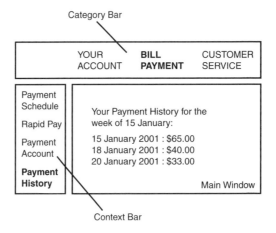

FIGURE 9.1

Typical menu-driven Web presentation.

In Figure 9.1, the vertical context navigation bar represents the topics that pertain to the currently selected category, Bill Payment. With Payment History selected, the main window is presenting the content associated with the visitor's payment history.

Let's review what is happening behind the scenes in the application's presentation logic to support the interaction of these three sub-views:

1. The user clicks on the main category of Bill Payment. Steps 2, 3, and 4 immediately occur.

2. The context navigation bar is updated to reflect the pre-built sub-view of bill payment options.

3. The main category window is replaced with a view that highlights the Payments button, indicating it's the working category.

4. The main window is updated with general information about payment features.

5. The user clicks on Payment History.

6. The main window is updated with payment history information.

Clearly, some of these actions can be handled by JavaScript development. We'll rely on server-side Java to take care of the bulk of these tasks.

importNode and XMLC

One approach you might take to manage all these views is to take advantage of the importNode() method of the DOM API. This will give you the capability to dynamically build the resultant DOM template presentation from multiple DOM classes that you load dynamically.

With importNode(), you can take advantage of the DOM API's capability to extract sub-documents as represented in different DOM template classes and import them into another DOM template document. Actually, this is a "read" copy behavior because you cannot legally relocate a sub-tree from one DOM into another.

Figure 9.2 illustrates this strategy. For SFAPresentation.java, the composite view consists of the three general sub-views we discussed earlier; namely, a main window, a category navigation bar, and a context navigation bar. This strategy uses importNode() to copy the tables contained in three other DOM templates, marked by their respective id attributes, CategoryTbl, ContextBarTbl, and MainContextTbl. The copies are then placed in the table SFA.html, which acts as the layout table for the overall view.

Figure 9.3 represents the DOM view of the importNode manipulation, showing the importation of the MySFA-specific context bar from the DOM template, generated from MySFAcontextBar.html, to the DOM template represented by SFA.html.

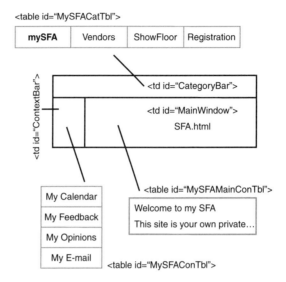

FIGURE 9.2

Strategy for extracting three tables from separate DOM templates.

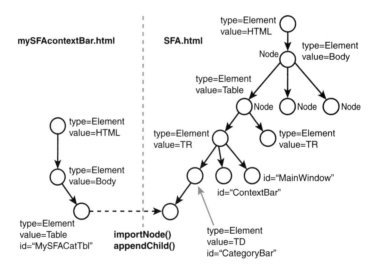

FIGURE 9.3

How importNode() *copies* MySFAContextBar's *table into* SFA.html.

The point of this strategy is to give your presentation logic the capability to choose tables from any number of available DOM templates, based on where the visitor is in terms of the navigational situation within SFAPresentation.java. Potentially, you could insert all the possible table representations of, for instance, the MySFA category, into a single HTML file and therefore a single DOM template, then select them based on their id attribute value.

Listing 9.2 shows the presentation logic used to load each DOM, copy the sub-views represented by each table, and append them to the layout table.

LISTING 9.2   SFAPresentation.java

```
package examples.presentation.ex5;

import java.util.*;
import com.lutris.xml.xmlc.*;
import com.lutris.appserver.server.httpPresentation.*;
import org.w3c.dom.*;
import org.w3c.dom.html.*;

public class SFAPresentation implements HttpPresentation {

  public void run(HttpPresentationComms comms)
    throws HttpPresentationException {

    //Grab the DOM Template that represents the compositive view's layout
    SFAHTML mainPage = (SFAHTML)comms.xmlcFactory.create(SFAHTML.class);

    //Grab each DOM Template, representing each view.
    MySFAcontextBarHTML contextBarView =
➥(MySFAcontextBarHTML)comms.xmlcFactory.create(MySFAcontextBarHTML.class);
    MySFAcategoryBarHTML categoryBarView =
➥(MySFAcategoryBarHTML)comms.xmlcFactory.create(MySFAcategoryBarHTML.class);
    MySFAMainIntroHTML mainWindowView =
➥(MySFAMainIntroHTML)comms.xmlcFactory.create(MySFAMainIntroHTML.class);

    //Grab the locations in the host table that we're going
    //to hang the new content from.
    HTMLTableCellElement catBarCell = mainPage.getElementCategoryBar();
    HTMLTableCellElement conBarCell = mainPage.getElementContextBar();
    HTMLTableCellElement mainWinCell = mainPage.getElementMainWindow();

    //Pluck the table that we want from each page.
    //importNode() just makes a copy of the node.
    Node catBarNode = mainPage.importNode(categoryBarView.
➥getElementMySFACatTbl(), true);

    Node conBarNode = mainPage.importNode(contextBarView.
➥getElementMySFAConTbl(), true);
    Node mainWNode = mainPage.importNode(mainWindowView.
➥getElementMySFAMainConTbl(), true);
```

LISTING 9.2   Continued

```
    //Attached the copied nodes.
    catBarCell.appendChild(catBarNode);
    conBarCell.appendChild(conBarNode);
    mainWinCell.appendChild(mainWNode);

    comms.response.writeHTML(mainPage);
  }
}
```

In order to focus on the task of importing nodes, Listing 9.2 forgoes the conditional logic of determining tables to import based on the visitor's position relative to the overall navigational path. Figure 9.4 displays the visible results of this integration.

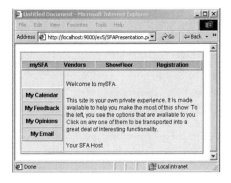

FIGURE 9.4
The resulting page after integrating three DOM template views into one.

SSIs Versus `importNode()`

It's probably self-evident that the flexibility of using this `importNode` strategy is greater than accomplishing the equivalent with server-side includes. Although a similar effect can be accomplished by having DOM templates of pre-integrated views, the flexibility of `importNode` makes a great deal of sense when applied to highly dynamic news portals, for instance.

The use of `importNode()` does introduce a performance overhead. Some of this can be offset with a combination of pre-compiled composite views, isolating the need for using `importNode()` to deal with highly dynamic components, such as advertisement views that are often subject to creative contractual terms such as being displayed every third page view.

As with much of our discussion of XMLC strategies, the sky is the limit regarding the integration of strategies that you can use. Typically, the tradeoffs involve upfront pre-configuration that stresses the stage-setting XMLC compilation process against the performance-impacting flexibility of runtime sub-view integration.

Interface-Implementations for ASPs and Skins

Up to this point, we've painted a generally one-to-one mapping of pages to DOM templates. It's now time to break that pattern and demonstrate one of the more intriguing capabilities of XMLC to introduce a flexible approach to presentation polymorphism.

Many business models, including the ASP model we're using for ShowFloor, require the capability to reuse individual pages with different personalities. The ASP business model makes sense when a minimum amount of labor is required to support each new client.

A bank that delivers financial applications to its member banks wants to give their members the capability to show their own *fingerprint*, or brand, to their end users. Some of this presentation customization might even remove all traces of the parent bank's originating role, making it appear to patrons of the child bank that the application is a feature only provided by the one bank.

Also, an increasingly popular feature of Web applications is to offer a selection of *skins* to the client. This has caught on particularly with trendy, highly customizable Web sites. Using cascading stylesheets can address some of this presentation polymorphism, but it's limited to a relatively small set of features, such as font, font colors, and background colors.

To support the capability to build the application presentation logic once, but have it generate in the form of many presentation identities, XMLC provides built-in support for the UML bridge pattern from the Gang of Four's (Erich Gamma, Richard Helm, Ralph Johnson, and John Vlissides) book *Design Patterns: Elements of Reusable Object-Oriented Software* (Addison-Wesley, 1995). Access to it requires the use of the `xmlc` command line options `-generate both` and `-implements`.

The bridge pattern, shown in Figure 9.5, reflects the use of an interface class to define a pattern or signature for a particular class of HTML, WML, or XML page. One of these classes might represent a standard registration page, a login form, or a report page. The page's interface signature is represented by the auto-generated `getElement<attributeValue>` and `setText<attributeValue>` methods created when the `xmlc` compiler is run. With that interface signature defined, all subsequent DOM implementations must support those methods.

A page's implementation is the DOM template that is specific to a particular design of the HTML page. Two implementations can differ, for example, by the placement of images, HTML controls, or the language. How an individual page is implemented is up to the designer and developer, but it must support the established interface.

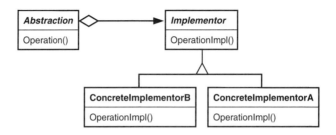

FIGURE **9.5**
The Gang of Four's bridge pattern.

What are the implications of taking this approach to presentation development?

- Multiple implementations of a page can represent multiple skins of the same page. The nature of the skin goes well beyond the capabilities of simply pointing to a different cascading stylesheet. For instance, static buttons might be replaced with more dynamic rollover capability.

- Multiple implementations can represent different page layouts of the same HTML or WML elements with respect to each other.

- A page can be implemented that is identical to the original reference implementation page, but in a different language.

- A page's interface assures conformance to the dynamic requirements. In other words, a page interface class introduces compile-time checking to prevent introduction of runtime errors.

- Compile-time checking is enforced by the presence of the interface class, ensuring that each page implementation supports the interface and therefore the id attributes and their xmlc-generated methods. The end result is the addition of a layer of error checking that will reduce the occurrence of runtime errors.

Perhaps the most interesting implication of separating interface from presentation is the capability to continually rework presentations, ensuring that they conform to the interface, and add them to the pool of available presentations for runtime execution. The use of runtime class loading combined with clever uses of the reflection API can make this absolutely dynamic, requiring no changes to the presentation logic.

Figure 9.6 illustrates the creation of a "pool" of page implementations that could be used by the ShowFloor application to, for instance, load a vendor-specific information request page that reflects the branding (for example, colors, images, wording) of individual vendors. In this case, we're loading the IBM-specific implementation of this generic information request page.

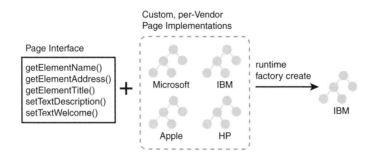

Custom, per-Vendor
Page Implementations

Page Interface

getElementName()
getElementAddress()
getElementTitle()
setTextDescription()
setTextWelcome()

Microsoft   IBM

Apple   HP

runtime
factory create

IBM

FIGURE 9.6

Selecting the IBM-branded page at runtime in ShowFloor.

> **NOTE**
>
> As Nick Xidis, longtime XMLC supporter, and others have pointed out, there's a discernible pattern of pages to different types of Web sites. Registration pages, for example, tend to follow a particular flow that can be captured as a standard interface, then implemented to reflect the desired design. This offers a real approach to project architects for enforcing standard interfaces for different types of page patterns.

Generating Multiple Implementations

Let's walk through the process of using the xmlc command to generate a single DOM template interface and two DOM implementations that support that interface. The implementations will differ in how the resultant HTML is expressed in terms of layout. Their differences can be seen in Figure 9.1. What do these implementations have in common?

- They have the same id attributes associated with the same elements. Therefore, they share the same interface as generated by xmlc.

How do these implementations differ?

- The layout of the DOM tree differs based on the design layout of the HTML, background colors, non-id attributes of the table (for example, thicker borders). In other words, a different skin. This could be done in reaction to the visitor configuring their MyShowFloor profile by selecting from different look and feel configurations, such as "cool," "hot," and "extreme."

The sequence of steps to build the interface and implementations begins with:

```
xmlc -keep -generate both Question.html
```

The `-generate both` option instructs `xmlc` to create two files:

- `Question.java`—an interface file
- `QuestionImpl.java`—an implementation file

`QuestionImpl.java` implements the interface described in `Question.java`.

At this point, you have what you need to begin development of the presentation servlet. This initial implementation can be used as a reference implementation to begin application development because the Java logic that will be created will be the same no matter which subsequently-generated DOM template implementation is loaded and manipulated. The only implementation-specific code in the presentation servlet deals with determining which implementation to load.

To create two more implementations that use the same interface in `Question.java`, the HTML designer would probably do something like load the original HTML file into GoLive or Dreamweaver and make the layout or language changes as required. Then, the developer would take the reworked HTML and apply the `xmlc` command:

```
xmlc -keep -implements classname Question_IBM.html
xmlc -keep -implements classname Question_Lutris.html
```

The `-implements` option instructs XMLC to use the interface represented by its class name and use it to ensure that the generated implementations representing `Question_IBM.html` and `Question_Lutris.html` conform to the interface. Errors occur if any of the `ids` have been changed in terms of omission or changed attribute values.

NOTE

If your use of `-implements` is causing an error, it could be because of the `xmlc` command's inability to locate the interface class generated earlier. The solution can probably be found by ensuring that your classpath contains the location of the interface class file.

Loading and Executing an Implementation

Now that you have your two implementations, let's take a look at Figure 9.7 and see how their manifested look and feel change when loaded and rendered by `QuestionPresentation.java`.

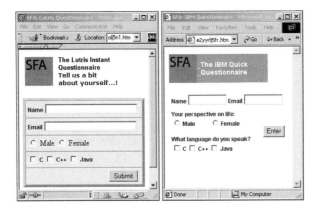

FIGURE 9.7
Two implementations of HTML files supporting the same id *attributes.*

One or the other implementation's DOM template is loaded using xmlcFactory.create(), depending on conditions tested by the surrounding logic.

The capability to define a standard page interface that is supported by multiple implementations reflects the beauty of a fully object-oriented view of building Web applications. With every resource represented as classes, many things become possible, including the capability to support complex aggregations of pages, yet exert full control over their behavior and interactions. XMLC's view of HTML pages as DOM template classes makes all this possible.

Internationalization

Internationalization, like security, is often a left-for-later discussion. XMLC, however, benefits as an open source project by the fact that the members are from across the world, where highly localized applications, many of which come from the United States, are a must.

As usual, there are a number of ways to approach internationalizing your XMLC presentations:

- Create a separate HTML template for each locale supported.
- Create one HTML template and substitute all text in the template during runtime with the localized equivalent.
- Both of the above, depending on the situation.

As you read the preceding list, you probably saw some issues right away. First, if you are building an application that must satisfy the language requirements of a worldwide community, then the first option is pretty daunting. It might be easy to implement using an interface/implementation strategy, but any changes that you might make to the layout of the page will cause a huge ripple effect throughout the other pages. In other words, your designers would have to go through each page, one by one, and make the necessary changes. This strategy is probably more workable if, for example, you are the state of California and you have mandated that the State Web site support both Spanish and English.

The first option becomes even more daunting when you are responsible for a Web application that must serve different devices, such as WML and cHTML, as well as standard HTML.

The second option scales better because, when changes are required, you need only modify the one HTML document. However, this introduces the performance overhead of replacing every localizable area with a string during runtime, and can prove too costly for complex Web sites, such as news sites.

> **NOTE**
>
> Barracuda, the open source presentation framework for XMLC, cleverly blends the use of an Ant taskdef and Java resource bundles to "spawn" localized DOM templates from a single markup source file. This is discussed in some detail in Chapter 13. The good news here is that Barracuda's localization capability can be used as a standalone module if you choose to forgo the other Barracuda modules.

Our discussion has by no means addressed all the possible strategies you can take. The next section on JavaScript highlights just one strategy, proposed by David McCann of MindWork Software in Vienna, Austria, that brings out one of many strategies for localizing your presentations.

JavaScript and Internationalization

JavaScript is always a topic of discussion for localization because it lies outside the DOM API. The solution usually involves DOM substitution of <SCRIPT> nodes for this, but that can get messy when there is a lot of code.

As you'll see, the best strategy is usually structuring your JavaScript to meet XMLC halfway. Consider the following:

```
<script id="validateScript" language="JavaScript">
<!—
function checkForm(form)
{
  var   errorMsg = "";
  if(form.UserId.value == "")
    errorMsg += "Please input a valid user ID" + "\n";
  // other validation code goes here ...
  if(errorMsg != "") {
```

```
        alert(errorMsg);
        return false;
    } else
        return true;
}
//-->
</script>
```

Now you don't want to have to substitute all this stuff on a per-locale basis, especially if checkForm() is complex, and/or is required in lots of pages.

The first step would be to split up the validation code like this:

```
<script id="localizedScript" language="JavaScript">
<!--
  badUserIdStr = "Please input a valid user ID";
  // ... Other error strings etc ...
//-->
</script>

<script id="validateScript" language="JavaScript">
<!--
function checkForm(form) {
  var errorMsg = "";
  if(form.UserId.value == null)
    errorMsg += badUserIdStr + "\n";
  // ... other validation stuff ...
  if(errorMsg != "") {
    alert(errorMsg);
    return false;
  } else
    return true;
}
//-->
</script>
```

In this case you only need to substitute the localizedScript node. All other <SCRIPT> elements in the same page referencing localized strings (or whatever) can be made locale-independent.

To avoid cluttering up the HTML with in-line scripts, the following will do the job:

```
<script id="localizedScript" language="JavaScript"
src="js/localized.js"></script>
<script id="validateScript" language="JavaScript"
src="js/checkForm.js"></script>
```

The advantage here is that browsers can cache the scripts. Reuse of the script fragments avoids runtime inclusion or error-prone cutting and pasting into multiple files. It also reduces the deployed code size of your application jar files. However, it still doesn't address the fact that you can't dynamically create a JavaScript entry in the jar file at runtime.

An approach that addresses runtime localization uses the fact that the src attribute is a URL, and not a static filename. So the src URL for the first fragment can be a presentation object as well:

```
<script id="localizedScript" language="JavaScript"
src="LocalizedJavaScript.po"></script>
<script id="validateScript" language="JavaScript"
src="js/checkForm.js"></script>
```

The presentation object LocalizedJavaScript.java simply needs to return JavaScript instead of HTML/XML:

```
public class LocalizedJavaScript implements HttpPresentation {
  public void run(HttpPresentationComms comms) throws
HttpPresentationException
  {
    Locale loc = LocaleUtil.getPreferredClientLocale(comms);
    try {
      // Output localized strings for use in static scripts
      // referenced by the containing PO.
      StringBuffer buffer = new StringBuffer(1024);
      buffer.append("badUserIdStr = \"");
      buffer.append(LocaleUtil.getText(loc, "javascript.badUserId"));
      buffer.append("\";\r\n");

      // More internationalized strings ...
      buffer.append("\";\r\n");
      //Make sure we set the correct content type and length
      comms.response.setContentType("text/javascript");
      comms.response.setContentLength(buffer.length());
      comms.response.getOutputStream().println(buffer.toString());
      comms.response.flush();
    } catch(Exception ex) {
      ErrorHandler.handle(ex);
    }
  }
}
```

You can use POs to address localization in all kind of creative ways.

Integrating Data Binding with XMLC

You might be wondering why, if we have already described how XMLC can be used to build a dynamically generated questionnaire presentation, we would want to discuss the back end component. The reason is that this provides an excellent opportunity to discuss the role-based differences of XMLC and Zeus, a data binding framework, and both Enhydra.org projects. Folks on the mailing list often ask about the differences, so let's complete the VendQuest discussion and flesh out a few distinctions.

> **NOTE**
>
> JAXB is Sun Microsystem's XML Binding API, similar to Zeus. In fact, Zeus incorporates JAXB, so how is it different? Perhaps the single most interesting enhancement is that Zeus makes it possible to generate Java classes without requiring the JAXB framework. The benefit is that there is no version dependency on any framework—JAXB, Zeus, or otherwise. Zeus-generated classes are completely autonomous, requiring only a SAX-compliant parser, not a Zeus or JAXB framework.

In Chapter 8, "HTML Presentations," we used Enhydra XMLC running in an Enhydra EAF environment to update a VendQuest markup page that is presented as the vendor-specific questionnaire. The environment required that the design be highly dynamic, updating the template with new questions if the vendor chooses to update the input XML question file. Our goal in choosing Zeus reflected in part our desire to accomplish the following:

- Validate the XML file, ensuring a well-formed document that conforms to an XML language definition.
- Parse the XML file and bring it into the VendQuest application.
- Bind the input data in a way that makes the use of XMLC and the generated presentation DOM template easier.

Validating and Parsing the XML

In a trade for providing an incredibly flexible runtime feature to the vendor, the application will need to take steps to ensure that the vendor generates an input document that conforms to a prescribed format. An ill-formatted input file could result in hours of delay before the desired questionnaire is put into operation.

This is where you want to take full advantage of XML's language-defining attributes. You want a well-formed document, as well as content that conforms to a grammar that will simplify the design and implementation of your processing logic.

The DTD that we used to create the VendQuestXML dialect, listed in Listing 9.3, supports three types of questions: SC (single choice), MC (multiple choice), and comment (text answer).

LISTING 9.3   ./src/showFloor/VendQuest/VendQuest.dtd

```
<!ELEMENT Questionnaire (Question+)>
<!ELEMENT Question (Prompt, Choice+, Default)>
<!ATTLIST Question type (MC|SC|comment) #REQUIRED>
<!ELEMENT Prompt (#PCDATA)>
<!ELEMENT Choice (#PCDATA)>
<!ELEMENT Default (#PCDATA)>
```

The DTD describes a language that supports the capability to describe one or more Question elements, each question containing the prompt What is the favorite letter?, and one or more choice elements A, B, C. Optionally, one of the choices can be listed as the default answer.

It should be obvious that this DTD can become much more complex and powerful, but for our purposes, we'll keep it simple.

Using Zeus for XML Data Binding

The selection process for finding the optimal XML manipulation tool was a bit daunting. Certainly, Enhydra's support for XSLT could handle our needs, but the goal for this book was to limit the number of programming languages necessary to build Web presentations to one—Java. JDOM, Xerces, and SAX were other obvious options, but I was hoping to find something a little more high-level to avoid having to resort to a lot of low-level DOM programming.

Ironically, the perfect choice comes from another Enhydra project called Zeus. Zeus is located at zeus.enhydra.org, where it is chaired by its founder, Brett McLaughlin, co-developer of JDOM (www.jdom.org) along with Jason Hunter. Zeus is sometimes described as a Java-to-XML data binding tool. As this label doesn't necessarily imply, Zeus supports bi-directional interaction between Java and XML documents:

- Turns Java objects into XML
- Turns XML into Java objects
- Presents XML language-specific methods for accessing and manipulating XML content.

Zeus reads a DTD document to generate a Java object that supports the language described by the DTD. This represents the act of *binding* Java to XML. The relationships of elements to other elements or attributes to elements, all described by the DTD, are captured in the behavior and structure of the generated Java object. In other words, the targeted XML language's grammar is now represented in Java with classes that describe, as Brett likes to put it, "the constraints of the document."

Let's review the bi-directional nature of Zeus data binding, namely marshaling and unmarshaling:

- Marshaling—This is the process, described by Zeus, of generating an XML document from Java using the Java object created by Zeus.

- Unmarshaling—This is the process of reading an input XML document and populating Java objects with its content. The content can now be manipulated.

Unmarshaling is the strategy we are interested in for VendQuest. It will give us the capability to read the document written in `VendQuestXML` and present its contents to the VendQuest application. A future feature that we might consider adding to VendQuest is a friendly forms-based HTML editor tool with which the vendor can manage their VendQuest XML document. But for now, direct editing of the XML file will have to suffice.

The selling point for me was Zeus' capability to present the contents of the XML document with Java methods that were generated and specifically tuned to the DTD. All the other technology options were generic DOM representations at best. With Zeus, I can use XMLC-like, generated setter and getter methods, such as `getChoiceList()` or `question.getType()`.

There is a great deal more to learn about Zeus' methodologies and features. However, you have enough to move forward with your immediate needs. Be sure to consult `zeus.enhydra.org` for more details about this up and coming technology innovation.

Generate Binding Logic with Zeus

Let's examine how to generate the logic that you'll need in order to populate a Enhydra business object with the unmarshaling logic it will need to serve the needs of the presentation layer. The strategy is to first download and build the Zeus environment. You'll use the DTD to generate the Java classes. The following instructions will generate the binding, marshaling, and unmarshaling logic, which you can then test against the questionnaire XML file before migrating to the Enhydra environment:

1. Download the Zeus source distribution and build it by executing the provided `./build.sh` or `./build.bat` files.

2. Set your classpath to include the following. These instructions assume that you installed the Zeus distribution under `/Zeus on Unix/Linux`:

   ```
   CLASSPATH=/Zeus/lib/dtdparser113.jar:/Zeus/lib/jdom.jar:../Zeus/lib/
   ➥xerces.jar:/Zeus/build/classes:/Zeus/samples/output
   ```
   or, for Windows,
   ```
   setCLASSPATH=\Zeus\lib\dtdparser113.jar;\Zeus\lib\jdom.jar;\Zeus\lib\
   ➥xerces.jar;\Zeus\build\classes;\Zeus\samples\output
   ```

3. Compile `TestDTDBinder.java` with the first of the following Java commands:

```
cd /Zeus/samples
javac -d /Zeus/build/classes TestDTDBinder.java
```

4. The next two steps will first generate a collection of source code files representing the Java interface classes and their associated implementation classes. The DTD file is all Zeus needs to create these bindings. The second step will then turn the source files into Java classes that you'll use later on:

```
javac samples.TestDTDBinder -file=q2.dtd
javac output/*.java
```

You are now ready to migrate all the classes you need over to the Enhydra environment:

1. Place the jars located in `Zeus/lib` (namely `jdom.jar`, `optional.jar`, `dtdparser113.jar`, and `xerces.jar`) in the Enhydra classpath, `$ENHYDRA_HOME/lib`.

2. Copy the source and class files under `/Zeus/samples/output` into the business directory:

```
cp /Zeus/samples/output/* $MYAPPROOT/examples/business
```

You now have everything you need to rock and roll inside the Enhydra environment.

Building the Business Object

It's important to take advantage of the multi-tier philosophy of Enhydra development. So we're going to focus on the business layer to use the Zeus-generated binding logic to return the values required by the presentation layer.

Let's take a look at the Java interface for the element <Questionnaire> generated by Zeus, seen in Listing 9.4. Some of the methods, such as `addQuestion()`, are not of much use until you build a questionnaire generation tool, but we'll leave that as an exercise for the reader.

LISTING 9.4   `./src/examples/VendQuest/`

```
public interface Questionnaire {
  public static final String ZEUS_XML_NAME = "Questionnaire";
  public static final String[] ZEUS_ATTRIBUTES = {};
  public static final String[] ZEUS_ELEMENTS = {"Question"};
  public java.util.List getQuestionList();
  public void setQuestionList(java.util.List questionList);
  public void addQuestion(Question question);
  public void removeQuestion(Question question);
}
```

The interesting method is `getQuestionList()`. The business object can make this available to the presentation object to loop through the list of questions, interrogating each one to methodically build the output document template.

Aside from adding the read-only methods to the business object, there is now little for you to do, other than bind the presentation logic to the business object methods. This was performed in Chapter 8.

The only remaining chore is to update the Enhydra environment with the location of the `VendQuestXML` files representing the questions of each vendor. With Zeus business objects in place, these files can be read on-the-fly during runtime without interruption to the running SFA application. You have succeeded in creating the most dynamic application possible.

Summarizing XMLC Versus Zeus

When I considered using XMLC to process the input VendQuest document, I began to see the unique problem-solving applicability of Zeus. I couldn't use `id` attributes to generate accessor methods, because there were multiple instances of each element, such as `<Question>`. As you'll recall, `id` attributes guarantee a unique representation of each element it they are attributed to.

In general, XMLC has more dedicated features to support DOM templates that serve as the layout manager for a Web presentation. Zeus is much more generic, moving the language-constraining role of the DTD inside Java, where it can process XML-conforming language without the need to recompile. The data it processes can be treated as a stream of a well-formed XML language, but formless in presentation structure. Combining the roles of XMLC and Zeus seemed to make the perfect soup-to-nuts solution.

Summary

Once again, the name of the game in XMLC development and architectures is flexibility. XMLC delivers flexibility at the cost of pre-defined, framework-like structure. Despite this characteristic, XMLC never sacrifices its inherent capability to keep Java logic out of XML or HTML markup.

We've addressed the use of the DOM API's `importNode()` and XMLC's compile-time use of server-side includes to address the flexibility that's required when a presentation is made up of two or more sub-views. These very different approaches each come with their limitations, so the decision will reflect the flexibility, or lack thereof, of your development and production environment.

One of the more exciting aspects of XMLC development features the built-in bridge pattern for separating implementations of the same markup interface, addressing the needs of ASPs, localization, and modern sites that give their visitors a great deal of control with skins to select.

In our discussion of internationalizing your Web application, we've kept things relatively high-level, because Java 2 Standard Edition is relatively internationalized to begin with. We also set the stage for the discussion of the Barracuda Framework in Chapter 13, which features a very nice localization mechanism worth considering.

Servlet Web Applications

IN THIS CHAPTER

The Java 2 Enterprise Edition (J2EE) specification is taking on the magnitude of the old saying: "Nobody ever got fired for buying IBM." From IT executives to line engineers, this alphanumeric acronym is unquestioningly uttered as the baseline requirement for application server standards, even though a servlet or Web container strategy is more than sufficient for solving most Web application building needs.

This chapter will refrain from addressing human psychology and instead focus on how to employ Enhydra XMLC as an alternative to JavaServer Pages in the construction and deployment of Web presentations using J2EE platforms. Thanks to the defined divisions of the J2EE Blueprints, we can restrict the focus to the J2EE component known as the *Web application.*

To establish XMLC's applicability to standard servlet and J2EE development, we'll address the topics of Web application archives and the construction of XMLC applications in two J2EE environments, Lutris EAS 4 and WebLogic 6.1. We'll also take this opportunity to explore the heir apparent to the Unix make system, namely the XML-based Apache Jakarta technology, Ant. Ant has been adopted by both the WebLogic and EAS platforms.

This chapter will alleviate the concerns of those who mistakenly believe that XMLC is an Enhydra-only technology. XMLC has been engineered as both an integral part of Enhydra application server technology as well as an easily portable presentation technology for Java servlet environments. In fact, xmlc.enhydra.org was created just for the purpose of evolving and advocating Enhydra XMLC as the servlet/J2EE platform de facto standard.

Servlets and Web Applications

The J2EE architecture defines three tiers in the J2EE environment. The back-end tier is for legacy applications and databases. The client tier is where Web browsers, Web servers, and thin and thick clients sit, making requests of the middle tier. The middle tier is where EJB and Web containers reside. The Web container is the focus of this chapter.

The Web container execution environment is responsible for communicating with the outside world, whether it's via TCP/IP sockets or HTTP. Web applications reside within the Web container, consisting of servlets, JSPs, HTML, documents, images, and other presentation resources. It is here where servlets incorporating XMLC technology also reside.

The Web container can operate independently of the rest of the J2EE environment. As requirements may or may not dictate, it has access to enterprise beans in the EJB container and/or other J2EE services, including JNDI, JMS, and JavaMail. More often than not, many will find that simply having access to JDBC will accommodate most of their functional requirements for connectivity to the back-end database tier.

Web Application Archive

It takes more than a collection of standard programming APIs to define a standard platform. The other side of the equation addresses standard deployment, packaging, and installation constructs that minimize the installation issues of deploying an application from one implementation of that platform to another.

J2EE specifies a standard file structure for the arrangement of runtime logic components. The Web application is organized and distributed as a Web Application aRchive (WAR) file. Along with HTML documents, images, and other application resources, its standard sub-directory WEB-INF includes an XML-based deployment descriptor file, Java classes, and libraries.

The WEB-INF directory is the name of the parent directory for these immediate servlet components. It contains servlet components in the form of jar files or individual classes. Like a manifest in a jar file, WEB-INF contains the metadata that describes the contents of this directory as their relationship:

- /WEB-INF/lib/ for jar files
- /WEB-INF/classes for Java classes
- /WEB-INF/web.xml for the deployment descriptor
- / for JSPs and static content, such as HTML, WML, and media.

Supporting resources, such as applets, images, and static HTML pages sit at the same directory level as WEB-INF.

WAR Files

Web applications can be processed by the Web container as a hierarchy of files on disk, or the same collection of files captured in a single file, in the form of a jar-archived file. WAR is the artificial name given to a jar file containing a Web application. The only visual distinction between a jar and a WAR file is the .war extension.

The immediate benefit of this prescribed organization is that you can build a Web application on one application server and easily transplant it to another. This becomes a handy feature when, for example, business issues require the swapping of one application server vendor for another.

web.xml for Configuration

The web.xml file is the Web application's *deployment descriptor*, located immediately underneath WEB-INF/. It is the XML document with all the configuration information required to present the preferred configuration of the Web application to the hosting application server.

The information expressed in the deployment descriptor ranges from how the target servlet is mapped to one or more URLs, to the parameters that are passed to it when the Web application is loaded for execution. Table 10.1 lists some of the possible directives in a typical web.xml deployment descriptor.

TABLE 10.1 Selected web.xml Elements

<servlet-name>	Establishes a name for the servlet that can be referenced from elsewhere within the file.
<servlet-mapping>	Maps the URLs to the servlet relative to the base path. Sub elements are <servlet-name> and <url-pattern>.
<servlet-class	Specifies the fully qualified pathname for the servlet.
<init-param>	Lists initial parameters for the servlet, made available to the servlet with the ServletConfig class.
<welcome-file-list>	Lists names that eliminate the requirement that the visitor, for example, explicitly include index.html or index.htm as part of the URL.

As we'll see later on, <init-param> is key to the enabling of Enhydra XMLC runtime features such as dynamic recompilation and class reloading.

Portable Enhydra XMLC

Enhydra XMLC is a portable presentation technology. xmlc.enhydra.org is dedicated to spreading the use of Enhydra XMLC across every Java application server platform that supports standard servlet containers.

There are two key components to the portable Enhydra XMLC development kit. The first is the XMLC distribution that is downloadable from xmlc.enhydra.org and is available with this book's CD as well. The xmlc2.0.1 distribution contains the following three files in addition to an extensive set of JavaDoc user documentation:

- ./bin/xmlc
- ./lib/xmlc.jar
- ./xmlc-config

xmlc is, of course, the XMLC command for compiling markup documents into DOM class templates. xmlc.jar is composed of the DOM, HTML, WML, and XMLC classes you will need to refer to from servlet applications. This includes the Xerces and Tidy parsers and DOM sub-interfaces. It also contains the XMLC classes needed to support dynamic recompilation and class loading.

`xmlc-config` is a setup script. Its role is to set up the XMLC development environment, pointing to the Java JDK and the `xmlc.jar`.

XMLCContext for Web Application Servlet Development

`XMLCContext` was specifically created to assist with the development and runtime deployment of HTTP servlets using an XMLC strategy. `XMLCContext` brings with it the capability to use standard Enhydra XMLC features, including the following:

- Session URL encoding
- Dynamic recompilation
- Dynamic class reloading
- Runtime logging

Other than the convenience of developing in the friendly confines of the Enhydra application server, there is little you sacrifice by deploying your Enhydra Web application on other Java application servers, with one exception regarding the classloader implementation. The classloader issue is discussed later in this chapter.

> **NOTE**
>
> As many experienced Java developers will tell you, Java's classpath mechanism for locating imported classes is both a blessing and a curse. Depending on the manner in which the contents of `xmlc.jar` and your servlet platform overlap, you might have to juggle the ordering of classes and jars in your classpath to successfully run XMLC servlets. This has become more of an issue as developers take advantage of technologies from other open source projects that use differing versions of overlapping technologies, such as `xerces.jar`, which is used by a large number of technologies.

An instance of the `XMLCContext` object and the standard servlet `ServletContext` object are allocated to a single Web application. `XMLCContext` builds upon `ServletContext` to access important parameters located in the application's `web.xml` deployment descriptor file.

The following list describes the methods of the `XMLCContext` class. These methods support the complete lifecycle of the care and feeding of a DOM class template. Their functions support factory-based creation, development time debugging, and the formatting and writing out of the resultant DOM tree.

This method creates an `OutputOptions` object for a document:

```
createOutputOptions(HttpServletRequest request, HttpServletResponse response,
➥ XMLObject document)
```

This method obtains the XMLCContext for the current application, creating it if it doesn't exist:

```
getContext(HttpServlet servlet)
```

This method returns XMLCContext.SessionURLEncodingMode:

```
getSessionURLEncoding()
```

This method gets the XMLC factory object associated with the context:

```
getXMLCFactory()
```

This method sets the session URL encoding mode and returns void:

```
setSessionURLEncoding(XMLCContext.SessionURLEncodingMode mode)
```

This method explicitly sets the XMLC factory and returns void:

```
setXMLCFactory(XMLCFactory factory)
```

This method outputs a DOM document object and returns void:

```
writeDOM(HttpServletRequest request, HttpServletResponse response,
➥OutputOptions outputOptions, XMLObject document)
```

This method outputs a DOM document object and returns void:

```
writeDOM(HttpServletRequest request, HttpServletResponse response,
➥XMLObject document)
```

Controlling XMLC Runtime Features with web.xml

getContext() is key to the configuration of the behavior of the XMLC runtime. It fetches servlet parameter values as they are stored in the Web application's web.xml deployment descriptor file.

In the following sample XML fragment, the web.xml sets parameter values to indicate that the application is configured only for dynamic loading of new DOM class templates:

```
<web-app>
 <servlet>
  <servlet-name>VendorAdmin</servlet-name>
  <servlet-class>com.otterpod.vendor.presentation.admin</servlet-class>
  <init-param>
    <param-name>xmlcReloading</param-name>
    <param-value>reload</param-value>
  </init-param>
 ...
```

param-name: `xmlcReloading`

These parameter values influence the runtime behavior of the servlet to perform dynamic compilation and class loading:

- `off`—No automatic reloading or recompilation (default).
- `reload`—Automatic reloading of modified class files.
- `recompile`—Automatic recompilation of classes that are out-of-date relative to their source files and reloading of modified class files.

Auto recompilation is not a slam dunk outside of the Enhydra application server environment. The reason is that the classloader mechanisms for different servers are different. And classloaders do not reveal all the information that is required to support class reloading.

XMLC reloading/recompilation requires an adapter class, implementing

`org.enhydra.xml.xmlc.reloading.ResourceLoader`

for each classloader implementation it interacts with. `XMLCReloadingFactory` is the factory class that creates instances of XMLC-generated class with automatic recompilation if the class is out-of-date relative to a source file.

`ResourceLoader` is an interface definition that must be implemented for the target servlet container, such as newer versions of Tomcat. The implementation of what XMLC calls a *selective classloader* obtains the classpath that will be searched, and creates an instance of a classloader that will load the re-generated DOM. Some have implemented this by grabbing the latest version of

`org.enhydra.xml.xmlc.reloading.ClassEntry`

from the Enhydra XMLC CVS source tree.

By the time you read this, contributed implementations may be part of the distribution found at xmlc.enhydra.org. You should check out this site for news before spending time on your own implementation.

param-name: `xmlcSessionURLEncoding`

URL encoding is a technique that embeds information within the URL from servlet response to HTTP request. The encrypted session ID is extracted from the HTTP request and used by the servlet to query the environment about the particular session. Typically, URL encoding is used as an alternative to tracking sessions with the use of cookies, the ultimate Internet kludge.

These parameter values specify the servlet's handling of session ID encoding:

- auto—Automatically enable session URL encoding as needed (default).
- always—Always enable session URL encoding. This does not work on most servers because of conflicts in the uses of both cookies and URL encoding.
- never—Never enable session URL encoding.

The default setting auto works best across different possible application servers, turning on URL encoding as needed.

param-name: xmlcLogging

The parameter values listed here dictate what runtime information XMLC logs. The value is a space-separated list of one or more of the following values:

- INFO—Logs basic information about notable events, such as recompiling or reloading classes.
- DEBUG—Logs debugging information. Mostly related to recompiling and reloading.
- STATS—Logs statistics information useful in debugging performance problems. Currently writes information about each DOM that is written. This is especially useful in looking at how much of a Lazy DOM has been expanded.

The default behavior of XMLC logging is set to INFO.

Building Web Application Servlets with Enhydra 3

In Chapter 5, "Enhydra, Java/XML Application Server," we discussed how the Enhydra AppWizard presents the option to select from two types of servlet frameworks. One is the Enhydra Application Framework, EAF. The other is the standard servlet 2.2 Web application framework or Web application.

When you indicate to the AppWizard that you intend to build a Web application, a different distribution of source and configuration files is created and the generated stub application takes on a new appearance. If you are an experienced servlet developer visiting Enhydra for the first time, you'll feel right at home.

Listing 10.1 shows how the stub application employs the use of the XMLCContext class introduced earlier. We gave the AppWizard the project name of WebApp and the package name example.

LISTING 10.1 WelcomeServlet.java

```java
package example.presentation;

// XMLC imports
import org.enhydra.xml.xmlc.servlet.XMLCContext;

// Servlet imports
import javax.servlet.ServletException;
import javax.servlet.http.HttpServlet;
import javax.servlet.http.HttpServletRequest;
import javax.servlet.http.HttpServletResponse;

// Standard imports
import java.io.IOException;
import java.util.Date;
import java.text.DateFormat;

public class WelcomeServlet extends HttpServlet {

  public void doGet(HttpServletRequest request, HttpServletResponse response)
    throws ServletException, IOException
  {
    XMLCContext xmlc;
    WelcomeHTML welcome;
    String now;

    now = DateFormat.getTimeInstance(DateFormat.MEDIUM).format(new Date());
    xmlc = XMLCContext.getContext(this);
    welcome = (WelcomeHTML) xmlc.getXMLCFactory().create(WelcomeHTML.class);
    welcome.setTextTime(now);
    xmlc.writeDOM(request, response, welcome);
  }
}
```

The statement

```java
xmlc = XMLCContext.getContext(this);
```

fetches the <init-parameter> content contained in the web.xml deployment descriptor in preparation for invoking the getXMLCFactory() method.

Invoking the make command generates two new high-level sub-directories: classes and output.

```
./classes/example/presentation/RedirectServlet.class
./classes/example/presentation/WelcomeHTML.class
```

```
./classes/example/presentation/WelcomeServlet.class
./classes/Generated Source/example/presentation/WelcomeHTML.java

./output/boot.properties
./output/conf/bootstrap.conf
./output/content/index.jsp
./output/content/media/Enhydra.gif
./output/java.policy

./output/lib/WebApp.war

./output/run
./output/run.bat
```

The final leg of the make session invokes the toolbox to generate the WAR file and WEB-INF distributions. The distribution of the generated files into classes and content sub-directories makes it particularly easy for the Enhydra toolbox to sort out the needed files and file types to construct the WAR file and WEB-INF distribution:

```
exec "C:/jdk1.3/bin/java" -jar "C:/usr/local/enhydra3b1.1/tool/lib/
➥toolbox.jar" -archive \
  -webArchive \
    -classpath ./classes \
      ./output/content \
      ./output/content/WEB-INF/web.xml \
      ./output/archive/WebApp.war
```

The build uses the project name to name the generated WAR file. Examining the contents of the WAR file, the command jar -tvf WebApp.war generates the following:

```
index.jsp
media/Enhydra.gif
WEB-INF/classes/example/presentation/RedirectServlet.class
WEB-INF/classes/example/presentation/WelcomeHTML.class
WEB-INF/web.xml
```

NOTE

Despite the fact that the generated Web application is a legitimate servlet 2.2 implementation, it is not quite ready for deployment on other application servers, such as Tomcat or BEA. The reason has to do with the need for a specialized class-loader enabling the auto-recompilation feature of XMLCContext. This was discussed earlier in the section on XMLCContext.

index.jsp for `<welcome-file>`

Enhydra AppWizard automatically generates the `index.jsp` file in the initial source tree, despite the fact that this is a servlet application configured for Enhydra XMLC development. If you take a look at `index.jsp`, it's not particularly impressive, other than the fact that it is extensively commented. Taking a look at the bottom of file you'll see the JSP directive

```
<%
    pageContext.forward( "/redirect" );
%>
```

This is Enhydra's approach to mapping the URL slash to a servlet name for a Web application. Note that it's just a coincidence here that the servlet is called `welcome` and the deployment descriptor element is also called `<welcome-file>`.

The reference to `/redirect` in `index.jsp` directs the application server to load the class `RedirectServlet.class`. Listing 10.2 shows how `RedirectServlet` plays "hot potato" by grabbing the request and its possible parameters and "redirecting" it to the servlet we're really interested in, namely `WelcomeServlet`.

This bit of trickery enables you to use the `<welcome-file>` mapping in the deployment descriptor. `<welcome-file>` specifies the possible URL mappings that can be associated with your servlet, such as the URL www.otterpod.com mapping to www.otterpod.com/welcome/. Without this approach, the `<welcome-file>` directive in `web.xml` would have no effect.

LISTING 10.2 Presentation/RedirectServer.java

```java
public class RedirectServlet extends HttpServlet {

  /*
  * There is the only function needed in order to be a servlet
  */
  public void doGet(HttpServletRequest request, HttpServletResponse response)
    throws ServletException, IOException
  {
    StringBuffer redirect = HttpUtils.getRequestURL(request);
    int start = redirect.toString().lastIndexOf("/redirect");
    int end  = redirect.length();
    redirect.replace(start, end, "/welcome");
    response.sendRedirect(redirect.toString());
  }
}
```

As you can imagine, the deployment descriptor for the Welcome stub application is relatively simple. Listing 10.3 lists the contents of `web.xml`. First the two servlets, `WelcomeServlet` and

10

RedirectServlet, are named with <servlet-name> and associated with Java class names they will represent using <servlet-class>. From there, the mappings of the URLs to each servlet are established using <servlet-mapping> and <url-pattern>.

LISTING 10.3   web.xml for the Stub Application

```
<?xml version="1.0" encoding="ISO-8859-1"?>
<web-app>
 <servlet>
  <servlet-name>welcome</servlet-name>
  <servlet-class>example.presentation.WelcomeServlet</servlet-class>
 </servlet>
 <servlet>
  <servlet-name>redirect</servlet-name>
  <servlet-class>example.presentation.RedirectServlet</servlet-class>
 </servlet>
 <servlet-mapping>
  <servlet-name>welcome</servlet-name>
  <url-pattern>/welcome</url-pattern>
 </servlet-mapping>
 <servlet-mapping>
  <servlet-name>redirect</servlet-name>
  <url-pattern>/redirect</url-pattern>
 </servlet-mapping>
</web-app>
```

So, what does all this accomplish? To put it simply, you've configured the application server to launch the class example.presentation.WelcomeServlet when the URL http://localhost:<port#>/welcome is sent from the client via HTTP.

Constructing the VendorCategory XMLC Servlet

We're now at the point where it's time to demonstrate what's involved in deploying XMLC-driven WAR applications from one environment to another. Let's construct a simple single-servlet Web application that we can use to illustrate what kind of modifications are required to go from an Enhydra 3 stub Web application to a relatively dynamic, real-world application. We'll then use this example to show how to migrate from the venerable Enhydra 3 environment to the Lutris EAS 4 and BEA WebLogic application servers supporting the J2EE APIs.

VendorCategory is a screen, shown in Figure 10.1, created for the EventHostAdmin to present the opportunity to select and set a default value that will be listed when creating vendor booths. Elsewhere in the application, this default value will be assigned when the EventHostAdmin is adding new vendors to the list of booth assignments.

FIGURE 10.1

The Set Default Vendor Web presentation.

This presentation is generated by the `VendorCategory` servlet. It loads the DOM class template generated from the XMLC compilation of `VenCat.html` in Listing 10.4. The mocked-up option rows are removed at XMLC compile-time by specifying the option `-delete-class` `"dummyOptions"`.

LISTING 10.4   VenCat.html

```
<html>
<head>
<title>Vendor Default Category</title>
<meta http-equiv="Content-Type" content="text/html; charset=iso-8859-1">
<link rel="stylesheet" href="SFA.css" type="text/css">
</head>

<body bgcolor="#FFFFFF" text="#000000" class="vendorHeading1">
<table width="80%" border="0" cellspacing="0" cellpadding="4" align="center">
 <tr>
  <td class="vendorHeading1">Set Default Vendor Category</td>
  <td><img src="media/otterPodLogo.jpg" width="100" height="100"></td>
 </tr>
 <tr>
  <td class="bodytext">This is the official list of Vendor Categories.
Select the default value that will be applied to all new vendors
 subject to getting
   overridden.</td>
  <td> </td>
 </tr>
 <tr>
```

LISTING 10.4 Continued

```
<td class="bodytext" valign="middle">
 <form name="form1" method="get" action="VenCat.html">
  Categories:
  <select id=vendorOptsMenu name="select" class="bodytext">
   <option id="vendorCategory" value="dummyA" selected>type A</option>
   <option class="dummyOption" value="dummyB">type B</option>
   <option class="dummyOption" value="dummyC">type C</option>
  </select>
  <input type="submit" name="Submit" value="Go">
 </form>
</td>
<td> </td>
</tr>
<tr>
 <td class="bodytext" valign="middle">
  <div align="right">Current Default Category: <span id=defaultVendorCategory>
➥<span class="defaultValue">UNASSIGNED</span></span></div>
 </td>
 <td> </td>
</tr>
</table>
</body>
</html>
```

This document employs a single form containing three form objects (or HTML controls): Select, Option, and Button.

In the servlet, we'll first update the vendor category list. The list will be hardcoded. In normal practice, this list would be configured by the EventHostAdmin, a role introduced in Chapter 4, "The ShowFloor ASP Application," and delivered by a business object, discussed in Chapter 5, "Enhydra, Java/XML Application Server," to display the vendors that reflect the type of industry show that they are hosting.

When the user makes a selection, you'll update the same page to indicate the current default value, then redisplay the page.

The servlet logic shown in Listing 10.5 should reflect a familiar algorithm by now, having reviewed it in Chapter 8. We take the first Option element, turn it into a template, clone the result, and append it as a child to the Select element. When the building operation is complete, the template Option element is removed.

LISTING 10.5   VendorCategoryServlet.java

```java
/*
 * sfa
 * Copyright SAMS Publishing, Inc.
 */

package vendor.presentation;

// XMLC and DOM imports
import org.enhydra.xml.xmlc.servlet.XMLCContext;
import org.enhydra.xml.xmlc.*;
import org.enhydra.xml.xmlc.html.*;
import org.w3c.dom.*;
import org.w3c.dom.html.*;

// Servlet imports
import javax.servlet.ServletException;
import javax.servlet.http.HttpServlet;
import javax.servlet.http.HttpServletRequest;
import javax.servlet.http.HttpServletResponse;

// Standard imports
import java.io.IOException;

public class VendorCategoriesServlet extends HttpServlet {

 public void doGet(HttpServletRequest request, HttpServletResponse response)
    throws ServletException, IOException
  {
  XMLCContext xmlc;
  VenCatHTML vendorC;
  //Hardcoded vendor categories
  String categoryList [] = {"Application Servers",
    "Databases", "Desktop Applications", "Open Source", "Imaging"};

  //Get the servlet context
  xmlc = XMLCContext.getContext(this);

  //Load the DOM template
  vendorC = (VenCatHTML) xmlc.getXMLCFactory().create(VenCatHTML.class);

  //XMLC Access Method to retrieve the Select element.
  HTMLSelectElement catSelect = vendorC.getElementVendorOptsMenu();

  //Use another XMLC Access Method to grab the template option element.
  HTMLOptionElement templateOpt = vendorC.getElementVendorCategory();
```

LISTING 10.5 Continued

```
//Clone it.
//Enter a loop to stamp out options of categories.

for (int i=0; i<categoryList.length; i++) {

  //Set the Option's content.
  vendorC.setTextVendorCategory(categoryList[i]);

  // Set the value attribute to represent the category.
  templateOpt.setValue(categoryList[i]);

  //Make a copy of the template.
  Node clonedOpt = templateOpt.cloneNode(true);

  //Use the HTMLSelectElement "add" method to append
  //the new Option element.
  catSelect.add((HTMLElement)clonedOpt, null);
} // end for
// get rid of the Option template now that we're done with it.
catSelect.removeChild(templateOpt);

//Grab the URL parameter representing the Select element's name
// to determine the chosen category.
String select = request.getParameter("select");
if (select != null) {
  vendorC.setTextDefaultVendorCategory(select);
}
xmlc.writeDOM(request, response, vendorC);
}

}
```

We used AppWizard to create the initial servlet environment, choosing Web Application as the application type. This type causes AppWizard to create an additional src sub-directory called resources, which sits alongside the standard Enhydra presentation, business, and data sub-directories. Controlled by the make file located in presentation, resource is intended as the home for markup files and media, making it easy for the build environment to migrate these files to the content portion of the output tree. After the content directory is populated, the make process can then build the WAR file, a collection of files migrated from the directories and subdirectories of contents and the classes.

The `classes` directory contains these files:

```
RedirectServlet.class
VendorCategoriesServlet.class
VenCatHTML.class (DOM class template)
```

The files under the `output` directory contain the content files and directories, as well as the resultant WAR file and Enhydra runtime-specific configuration file, log file, and start script:

```
./multiserver.log
./start

./archive/SFA.war

./conf/servlet/servlet.conf

./content/index.jsp
./content/media/otterPodLogo.jpg
./content/sfa.css
./content/WEB-INF/web.xml

./work/sfa/_0005cindex_0002ejspindex.class
./work/sfa/_0005cindex_0002ejspindex_jsp_0.java
```

The last two files listed are the signature of the Tomcat environment and are of no concern to us. Also, the `servlet.conf` file, specific to Enhydra 3, is ignored in the creation of the `SFA.war` file.

Modifications

We had to make a number of modifications to the files and file contents of the servlet layout:

- `/src/WEB-INF/web.xml`—References to the welcome servlet were changed to `vendorcat`. The servlet class was renamed from `WelcomeServlet` to `VendorCategoryServlet`.

- `/src/presentation`—We renamed `WelcomeServlet.class` to `VendorCategoryServlet.class`. Made internal changes to the class name as well as adding our DOM template manipulating code. Reworked the filenames referenced in `Makefile`, included those referenced in the resources directory.

  Edited `RedirectServlet.java`, replacing the occurrence of servlet name `/welcome` with the `/vendorcat`. This satisfies the Enhydra mechanism of using the `index.jsp` to address `web.xml`'s `<welcome-file>` configuration.

- `/src/resources`—Replaced `Welcome.html` with `VenCat.html`. Added the associated stylesheet file, `sfa.css`.

  Added the option `-delete-class` to discard HTML Option elements belonging to the class `dummyOptions`. The `make` file in presentation was updated to reflect the name changes.

You now have your `SFA.war` file, containing the `VendorCategory` Web application, ready to deploy.

Deploying XMLC WARs on Lutris EAS 4

Lutris EAS 4 is Lutris Technologies' commercial version of the Enhydra Enterprise project for the implementation of J2EE services. As might be expected, it too features XMLC development. It is also the platform we will use in this book for the examples of cHTML, XHTML, and VoiceXML development with XMLC. At the time of this writing, the DOM interface implementations for these markup language standards is not implemented in Enhydra 3.

If you have had the opportunity to start using the Enhydra AppWizard, then you have probably already experienced most of what it takes to establish a Web application in the EAS 4 environment. We'll take the next section to review the source tree generated by the EAS version of AppWizard before showing the steps for taking our existing `SFA.war` and adding it to the EAS platform.

Web Application Source Tree Under EAS 4

The following file hierarchy is created by EAS 4's AppWizard when Web Application is selected. Much of the structure is familiar to EAF developers. `input`, `presentation`, `business`, and `data` directories are still used. To those who develop standard Web applications with Enhydra 3, this listing appears even more familiar:

```
./build.xml
./readme.html

./input/boot.properties.in
./input/conf
./input/conf/bootstrap.conf.in
./input/java.policy.in
./input/run.bat.in
./input/run.in

./src/example/business
./src/example/data
./src/example/presentation/options.xmlc
./src/example/presentation/RedirectServlet.java
```

```
./src/example/presentation/WelcomeServlet.java
./src/example/resources/index.jsp
./src/example/resources/media/Enhydra.gif
./src/example/resources/Welcome.html

./src/WEB-INF/web.xml
```

The most significant difference with respect to Enhydra 3 Web applications is the replacement of the make framework of make file and config.mk files with Ant's build.xml. Both of the target J2EE platforms support this powerful new open source build and deploying utility. After our review of Lutris EAS deployment is concluded, we'll spend some time with a short introduction of Ant.

Initializing the EAS 4 Environment

Lutris EAS 4 goes much further than earlier Enhydra implementations to support both the Windows and non-Windows environments. If you want a Unix/Linux-like environment on your Windows environment, then you can take advantage of the companion Cygnus tools for creating a Bash shell environment.

The next two sets of commands set up the runtime environment for Lutris EAS, particularly addressing the CLASSPATH and compiler environments. At this point, we're assuming that you've followed the instructions on the CD for installing Lutris EAS 4.

If you want to stick with pure Windows, then execute these commands:

```
cd lutris-eas4
setup.bat
```

For a Unix/Linux environment, or Windows with Cygnus Tools:

```
cd lutris-eas4
source setup.bash
```

With configuration now addressed, you can start the application server by finding the directory /lutris-eas4/bin and executing the command

```
./multiserver
```

When you see the message

```
InitializationManager,STATUS: All services loaded. Enhydra is up.
```

you'll know that the application server is ready to accept requests. You can now use the default Web-based Admin Console to add your Web application to the server.

Adding the SFA.war to Lutris EAS

EAS features two administration consoles. We'll work with the baseline Web browser version. In fact, this is an enhanced version of the Enhydra Admin Console that we introduced in Chapter 5.

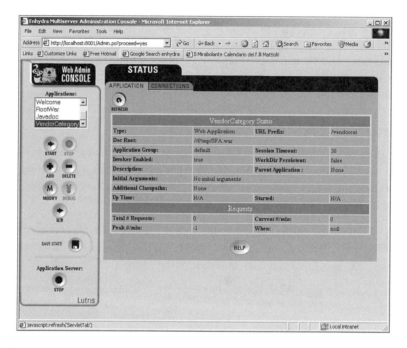

FIGURE 10.2

EAS Web Admin Application and Connection Status Window.

To bring up the Admin Console, enter the URL http://<machine>:8001. To install the WAR application, follow these steps:

1. Copy the SFA.war file into the directory lutris-eas4/webapps.

2. Click the Add button.

3. In the Add New Application/Servlet window, select the WAR radio button. This will expand the existing dialog to include more WAR-specific parameters.

4. In the this dialog, give the value SFA to the fields Name and URL Prefix. In the text field labeled Path To WAR File, enter the path

   /lutris-eas4/webapps/

You're now ready to start the application. In the main window of the Admin Console, you can see that SFA now appears in the list box. Click the Start button. If you encounter any problems, such as with the console's capability to find the path to the directory containing the WAR, just click the Modify buttons to make changes to the configuration.

> **NOTE**
>
> After deployment, you should consider moving your images and static HTML pages where the Web server can find them. Web servers are optimized for superior caching of static resources. This leaves the dynamic portions of your applications, EAF or Web application style, for the application server to process. This will improve the overall performance characteristics of your application.

Now select the Connections tab to see how the WAR is going to be reached from the outside world. You will see that the Admin Console automatically associated the WAR with a URL. You can change this if you want by removing and creating a new connection using the Create button. Selecting the indicated URL will launch the VendorCategory application.

Ant, the Java/XML Alternative to make

This might appear to be a strange place to introduce a new system for design and performing coordinated builds of Java applications. But Ant, a sub-project of the Apache Jakarta Project, happens to be the engine behind the build environment for both of the J2EE application servers included with this book's companion CD, Lutris EAS 4 and BEA WebLogic 6.1. It's also only a matter of time before the entire Enhydra project is Ant-based. Already, members of the Enhydra.org community have contributed Ant-based build environments that are likely to replace the existing Enhydra 3 system of make files.

Ant builds on many of the attributes of make, popularized by UNIX C development environments. Both systems take advantage of target file modification timestamps of files, or files that are required by other files. If no changes have been made to the file or the files upon which it depends since the previous make or Ant session, then they are left alone. Clearly, this supports a more efficient use of your computer's CPU, particularly if you've touched a couple of files in an application environment represented by hundreds of files. These systems also make sure that files are compiled that, although they have been untouched directly, are dependent on another file that has.

But Ant goes a few steps further than make. First, it's a Java implementation, making it friendlier to Java systems. Entire collections of Java files are sent to the compiler at once, rather than one-by-one. Extending Ant with new features is a matter of sub-classing existing Ant classes, then announcing the new functionality via an XML configuration file.

build.xml

Ant is an environment of pure Java and XML. Distinctively named `build.xml` files serve as an instant clue that you're looking at an Ant environment. The `build.xml` file contains a *project*, representing the series of *tasks* that have been selected and organized to build the project. Tasks are built-in Ant logic representing the more common functions you would need in a Java application-building environment.

- `copy`—Copies everything from files to directories.
- `war`—Generates a WAR file.
- `jar`—Generates a jar file.
- `mail`—Sends e-mail to individuals depending on the achievement of specified events.
- `cvs`—Checks files in and out of a CVS version control system.

Both BEA and Lutris application servers extend Ant's default set of tasks with additional ones. As you might expect, Lutris EAS incorporates an `xmlc` task:

```
<target name="xmlc" depends="prepare">
  <xmlc srcdir="${dir.src}"
    sourceout="${dir.xmlc}"
    packagedir="${dir.package}/presentation"
    includes="${dir.package}/resources/**/*.html"
    options="${dir.src}/${dir.package}/presentation/options.xmlc" />
</target>
```

This is an example of a *target*, which is a collection of one or more ordered tasks. Targets list the dependencies they have on other targets using the `"depends"` attribute. The `xmlc` task lists attributes that describe everything the XMLC compiler will need to build DOM classes, including where to find the `options.xmlc` file.

A property is another element of the `build.xml` file. It supports the definition of name-value pairs that are later referenced by targets and tasks. As shown in the following Lutris EAS example, the property element can be used to name all the areas of the source build and deploy environment:

```
<!— Set up application values —>
<property name="project.name"  value="SFA"/>
<property name="project.package" value="example"/>
<property name="project.version" value="1.0"/>
<property name="project.year"  value="2001"/>

<!— directory locations —>
<property name="dir.package"  value="example"/>
<property name="dir.classes"  location="classes"/>
<property name="dir.input"    location="input"/>
<property name="dir.java"     location="${java.home}/../" />
```

```
<property name="dir.src"     location="src"/>
<property name="dir.output"  location="output"/>
<property name="dir.project" location="."/>
<property name="dir.content" location="${dir.output}/content"/>
<property name="dir.lib"     location="${dir.output}/lib"/>
<property name="dir.javadocs" location="${dir.output}/javadocs"/>
<property name="dir.xmlc"    location="${dir.classes}/Generated Source/"/>
```

The following target is given the name `"prepare"`, which will be referenced as a dependency by other targets, such as our earlier `xmlc` target example. This target plays the essential role of creating directories that will serve as the destination locations for classes, resources, and WAR files that are generated during the build:

```
<target name="prepare">
  <mkdir dir="${dir.lib}"/>
  <mkdir dir="${dir.content}"/>
  <mkdir dir="${dir.classes}"/>
  <mkdir dir="${dir.output}"/>
  <mkdir dir="${dir.xmlc}"/>
</target>
```

There's obviously a great deal more detail to the Ant environment that we're not going to cover here. For more information, including the full set of built-in tasks, download the documentation available at `http://jakarta.apache.org/ant/manual/index.html`.

For more information about platform-specific extensions to the `ant` command, consult the respective documentation from the Lutris and BEA products.

Deploying an XMLC WAR on BEA WebLogic

BEA System's WebLogic application server dominates the data centers of enterprise IT. Chances are that you or a colleague are WebLogic developers. We're going to spend this section explaining how you can take an open source technology like Enhydra XMLC and offer an excellent alternative to JSP presentation development for a leading commercial product. The straightforward deployment of an Enhydra 3-built WAR should demonstrate the portable nature of Enhydra and Enhydra XMLC technology.

Let's see what happens when we take our `SFA.war` file, containing the `VendorCategory` Web application built by a 100% open source platform, and deploy it on top of an industry standard platform with costs as far from open source as you can get.

WebLogic Installation

The Windows version of BEA's trial version of WebLogic 6.1 was downloaded from `http://www.bea.com` for the purpose of this exercise. From the installation wizards, we chose Server Only, indicating that we didn't want all the provided examples.

During the installation of WebLogic 6.1, you will be asked for a small set of configuration parameters; namely, the administration domain name, the name of the server instance, and the port the server instance will listen on. We chose to keep the configuration very simple (that is, on a single Windows 2000 laptop as the target server). We provided the following values:

```
weblogic admin domain name: aptos
server name: nicole
listen port: 7001
```

Our WebLogic server will be called `nicole`, and will be managed within the domain name of `aptos`. All references to resources under the local host must include the port number 7001, a default value that you may override. The secure port, by the way, is 7002.

Server File System

There are a number of WebLogic server file configurations provided, including one that's pre-configured with a number of simple servlet and enterprise application examples. For our purposes, we're going to go straight to the configuration that was created in response to our earlier answers.

The root of the default WebLogic application server installation resides at `/bea/wlserver6.1/config`. From this directory, you'll find such sub-directories as `examples`, `petstore`, and the domain we're interested in, `aptos`. Under `aptos`, we have all the configuration and startup scripts we need, as well as the `applications` directory, the eventual site for the deployment of the `SFA.war` file:

```
./aptos/config.xml
./aptos/logs/access.log
./aptos/logs/weblogic.log
./aptos/setEnv.cmd
./aptos/startWebLogic.cmd
./aptos/applications/certificate.war
./aptos/applications/DefaultWebApp
./aptos/applications/DefaultWebApp/images
./aptos/applications/DefaultWebApp/images/built_bea_web.gif
./aptos/applications/DefaultWebApp/images/redarrow.gif
./aptos/applications/DefaultWebApp/index.html
./aptos/applications/DefaultWebApp/WEB-INF
./aptos/applications/DefaultWebApp/WEB-INF/web.xml
```

config.xml

To install `VendorCategory`, you'll use the WebLogic administration console, because it provides an interface that can accomplish the WAR deployment with a few button clicks. More importantly, it updates the key file `config.xml` for you, avoiding the possibility of corrupting the file and preventing the server from running at all. After it's been updated, the `config.xml` file will contain the following additional content:

```
<Application Deployed="true" Name="sfa" Path=".\config\aptos\applications">
  <WebAppComponent Name="sfa" Targets="nicole" URI="SFA.war"/>
</Application>
```

If you're new to WebLogic, I would highly recommend that you follow the steps that we take, avoiding shortcuts that could delay this process and potentially lead to the necessity of having to reinstall to get back to square one. And if you can resist whipping out your vi editor, then be sure to make a backup copy of the file before proceeding. At that point, you're on your own.

Preparing the WebLogic Server for XMLC

As you might expect, it doesn't take much to launch the server. This is done by executing the script `startWebLogic.cmd`, located just under the `aptos` directory. But before you do that, you need to ensure that the XMLC runtime library of classes can be found by the WebLogic server.

Take the following steps to set up WebLogic for an XMLC runtime environment:

1. Copy an instance of the `xmlc.jar` file, contained in the xmlc2.0.1 distribution, to the `lib` directory, located just under `/bea/wlserver6.1`.
2. Change directories to the `aptos` directory. Copy `startWebLogic.cmd` to `myWebLogic.cmd`.
3. Open `myWebLogic.cmd` for editing. Search for the string `CLASSPATH`. Append the location of the `xmlc.jar` file to the end of the line that sets the `CLASSPATH` environment variable so that it appears as

   ```
   set CLASSPATH=.;.\lib\weblogic_sp.jar;.\lib\weblogic.jar;.\lib\xmlc.jar
   ```
4. Close the file.

Launching the WebLogic Server

We're now set for launching the XMLC-ready WebLogic server. To do this, type the name of the modified script from the Windows command line:

```
myWebLogic
```

The script will do a number of things. First, it will echo lines of its script as they are executed. You should be able to see that the `CLASSPATH` is set with the reference to `.\lib\xmlc.jar`. The script will ask you for a password, one that you decided on when prompted during the initial installation.

When you see the following message, you'll know that the server is ready to accept requests:

```
<Notice> <WebLogicServer> <Started WebLogic Admin Server "nicole" for domain
➥"aptos" running in Production Mode>
```

Deployment Through the WebLogic Server Console

With a running server, the server console can now be brought up. The following URL will invoke the server console.

```
http://localhost:7001/console
```

The WebLogic Server Console is shown in Figure 10.3. The left frame contains an applet that displays the server hierarchy, including servers, services and deployed applications. Under "Web Applications," you will see two default applications.

FIGURE 10.3
Initial WebLogic Server Console.

To begin deployment, right-click on the Web Applications label. You'll see a pop-up menu. Select Install a New Web Component.

The right frame of the server console is updated to indicate the types of files that can be uploaded. At the bottom of the frame, you'll find an Upload/Browse dialog. Use it to find the `SFA.war` and load it.

After this task is complete, you'll see (in Figure 10.4) that the `SFA.war` containing the `VendorCategoryServlet` has been added to the Web application.

FIGURE 10.4
The WebLogic Server Console displaying a deployed SFA Web application.

Running the `VendorCategory` Servlet

At this point, the application has been loaded by the server, and all that remains is to make a request to it with the following URL:

```
http://localhost:7001/SFA/vendorcat
```

This will bring up the application, looking very much like the version displayed in Figure 10.1.

XMLC for Ruby

As with any great technology, the concept of XMLC transcends the implementation itself. As an example of this, a port of XMLC is connected to the Ruby programming language, enabling the power of XMLC to be combined with the dynamic and expressive nature of Ruby. Its authors sought to bring the decoupled nature of XMLC from the Java world into their Web-based Ruby programming (where semi-equivalents of JSP already exist).

Just as XMLC is the product of a group of great existing concepts combined with some out-of-the-box creativity, the Ruby language is a creative meld of several great technologies that came before it. Created by Yukihiro Matsumoto and now maintained as an open source project at http://www.ruby-lang.org, Ruby has combined the extreme object-orientation of Smalltalk, the practicality and power of Perl, and the best practices from numerous other languages into one powerfully expressive language to which users are often fervently devoted. It is available for free on the project Web site for a number of platforms, including UNIX and Windows.

The Ruby XMLC port is available at http://sourceforge.net/projects/rubyx/.

Summary

Hopefully, you now have enough knowledge at your fingertips to understand the basics of building portable XMLC Web applications. The different strategies range from building them on the Enhydra 3 application server as WAR files; or simply building them on the target servlet/J2EE platform of your choice, with the aid of the XMLC distribution (xmlc2.0.1.zip or xmlc2.0.1.jar) from Xmlc.enhydra.org or the book's CD.

As a by-product of the development and deployment of the VendorCategory servlet, we have addressed the topics of Web applications and the role of WAR files and their organization. We've also introduced the emergence of Apache's Ant, an open source modern alternative to the venerable but old-world make system.

Wireless Markup Presentations

IN THIS CHAPTER

It's now time to visit all things wireless. In this chapter, we'll examine how Enhydra XMLC supports this extremely diverse new wireless world and its rapid evolution.

There is a single major reason that XMLC is able to support the major devices of the world: XML. The world seems to have gotten it right this time. Starting with Phone.com's move to make HDML XML-compliant—and re-dub it *Wireless Markup Language* (*WML*)—the wireless industry, including the voice recognition folks, did us all a favor by using XML constructs to define their take on presentation markup.

The XML fervor has marched into the voice market as well. This market addresses the reticent few who have yet to go wireless. A whole new industry, led by TellMe, Nuance, and Voxeo, are making it simple for any business that has existing Web technology to reach the audience that is neither mobile phone- nor browser-connected. As we'll see, it takes only a few moments to use Enhydra to access completely free voice activation and voice generation technology, presenting verbal forms over phones both rotary and wireless.

Although Enhydra XMLC is quite capable of supporting XHTML and NTT DoCoMo's i-mode/cHTML, this chapter will focus on development with the Enhydra XMLC wireless and voice representative technologies WAP and VoiceXML. Many, many books are available on the generic nature of wireless and voice development, so we'll introduce just enough of each language to set the stage for explaining and demonstrating what it means to generate presentations with Enhydra XMLC.

Wireless Domains

Reflecting a relatively new market, wireless development must take into account the mish mash of standards and proprietary extensions, both in software and hardware. If you're developing wireless applications for the consumer market, there's a lot of per-vendor idiosyncrasies to consider. If you're an IT developer for a company that has selected devices from one or two vendors, your job is going to be much easier.

The good news is that there are only two major wireless technologies in the entire world: WAP and i-mode. Each of these phone standards supports a markup language and, in yet more good news, both standards are headed toward supporting XHTML Basic as a presentation language.

WAP Phones, WAP Gateways

Most of us have now heard of the *Wireless Application Protocol (WAP)* and the WAP Forum, a consortium of carriers and handset manufacturers. The WAP Forum set out to deliver a mobile device- and carrier-independent standard that could support mobile phones of all types, as well as all varieties of private networks. A protocol had to be defined that could work effectively over old style circuit networks as well as modern TCP/IP-capable, packet-switched networks.

Wireless Markup Presentations

CHAPTER 11

325

11

WIRELESS
MARKUP
PRESENTATIONS

The key to carrier network and handset independence is the required presence of a WAP gateway. The WAP gateway is not an application server, nor is it a Web server. Instead, it is a specialized device that supports both a private and public interface. This interface represents the "gated garden" of each proprietary, private carrier network of mobile devices.

Illustrated in Figure 11.1, the WAP gateway receives and transmits HTTP request/responses from and to the Internet, performing various tasks such as *transcoding*. At this point the gateway will rework HTML, and sometimes munge WML, into what it believes will be meaningful to, for example, a Nokia or Ericsson phone.

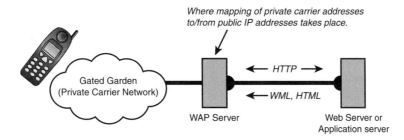

FIGURE 11.1

WAP servers as gateways between the Internet and carrier networks.

WML is the markup language promoted by the WAP Forum. Nokia, Motorola, Ericsson, and many other handset makers support WAP-enabled phones capable of rendering WML presentations.

NOTE

If ever there was a reason for supporting the coming of IPv6, the proliferation of mobile devices is a big one. Imagine if the millions of phones that have already been deployed had their own IP addresses. WAP phones luckily share one IP, that of their carrier. The carrier's private network has its own proprietary address mechanism for finding the right phone. As clumsy as this IP-to-private address mapping might seem, it's a blessing for now until IPv6 becomes widespread.

WAP servers can be problematic. They don't all behave consistently, requiring the knowledge of coding and configuration tricks on the part of the application developer. For instance, one well known WAP server strips the user agent information from the heading, requiring some algorithmic sleight-of-hand by the application to determine the client type (that is, the phone type). Turning off handset caching is another.

The Wireless Markup Language

WML was not always an XML language. WML is derived from Openwave's (formerly Phone.com) HDML language. In its wisdom, the WAP Forum decided to move HDML to a real XML language, namely WML. It is well-formed XML and is formalized by its DTD.

Once again, XML is the underlying theme. In Chapter 1, "Enhydra and XMLC," we told the story of how long before WAP publicly entered the U.S., developers of WAP applications from Taiwan and Sweden turned Enhydra and Enhydra XMLC into a wireless, WML application-serving technology in mid-1999. Their contributions took the form of the WML-specific extensions of the DOM API, making it possible to perform "type-safe" DOM template programming in the XMLC environment.

WML adopts a subset of HTML elements as well as some specialized markup designed to provide meaningful functions when hosted by a small phone that can be off-line or out-of-range of a server at any time. In order to give a WML document a fighting chance of giving a user a pleasing, useful experience, a single document, referred to as a *deck*, might contain multiple *cards*. Each card is a possible display interaction, chosen based on user interactions in previous cards. This paradigm allows for a meaningful amount of user interaction before another deck is required.

cHTML and i-mode

The largest rival to WAP is the i-mode protocol for mobile devices. i-mode and its "compact HTML" language, cHTML, take advantage of the packet-based i-mode network and an "always on" environment to better mimic browser-like behavior. Another major advantage of i-mode development reflects the standard construction of i-mode handsets. Every i-mode device is assured of the same amount of presentation space: 16 characters-by-6 lines. WAP has almost no standardization in this respect. And every i-mode phone has an IP stack that supports SSL for secure connections.

If you're wondering why WAP hasn't required the same of its handset makers, there's one answer: The i-mode environment is dominated by one large carrier and device vendor rolled into one—NTT DoCoMo.

The final thing to consider about cHTML/i-mode development is that it dominates the wireless world, representing more than half of the world's wireless market. The flip side to this statistic is that the vast majority of i-mode clients are in the Japanese market, whereas wireless is more pervasive in the rest of the world. Although this might be sufficient reason to stick to WAP programming, be sure to keep an eye on the eventual proliferation of i-mode to other areas of the world.

Wireless Markup Presentations

CHAPTER 11

327

11

WIRELESS
MARKUP
PRESENTATIONS

i-mode isn't perfect. There's no client scripting language, like WML's WMLscript. But there are still very clear advantages:

- No requirement exists for a gateway device, such as a WAP server.
- Applications can be written to assume an "always on" environment.
- Far fewer per-device tricks are required for supporting i-mode phones.

We will not be addressing cHTML development in this book, but Enhydra XMLC is quite capable of supporting i-mode development.

Perusing the WML Language

On the surface, the WML language will look familiar to an HTML developer. To accommodate the constrained memory and uncertain connection characteristics of WAP phones, WML reflects a "deck of cards" metaphor. The deck is the entire markup page, containing a collection of cards. Individual <card> elements represent the portion of the larger deck that is currently displayed. A card is rendered when it is called upon by an internal event, an anchor using href attributes, a "relative" movement directive that moves through a page history stack, or a WMLscript command.

This strategy saves on the use of an already constrained bandwidth by pre-loading many of the pages (or cards) that will be displayed in a multi-card navigation. It also means that the user can continue performing a useful task, even though the connection has been lost.

Cards are referenced by a URL, much like the use of ids and anchors in HTML. For example,

```
<card id="vendors>
```

might be referenced by

```
http://www.otterpod.com/mySFA.wml#vendors
```

where mySFA.wml is the name of the application. A typical "hello world" WML page might look like the following:

```
<?wml version="1.0">
<DOCTYPE wml PUBLIC "-//WAPFORM//DTD WML 1.1//EN"
    "http://www.wapformum.org/DTD/wml_1.1.xml">
<wml>
 <card id="Hello" title="Hello World">
  <p>
   <small id="Greeting">Hello There</small>
  </p>
 </card>
</wml>
```

The id attribute uniquely identifies each card element. The title attribute value represents the card's title, and is automatically displayed by (most) handsets at the top of the display. The title is also used for the handset's bookmarks.

Event Bindings

WML supports the notion of *events*. Events are registered with the <onevent> or <do> elements. The <do> element associates the actions of the handset's menu systems and keys with browser functions. The following fragment instructs the browser to display the next card, friends, when the Accept button has been clicked by the user:

```
<do type="accept">
  <go href="#friends" />
</do>
```

The <onevent> element deals with the effect of, for instance, advancing to the next card. Another way of putting it is that <onevent> registers actions (quasi-"listeners") that are set in motion when one of a number of standard events occurs. The following

```
<onevent type="onenterbackward">
  <go href="#otherfriends" />
</onevent>
```

will cause the loading of the card otherfriends if the user should scroll backwards. Table 11.1 lists the <onevent> event types.

TABLE 11.1 WML Event Types

Event	Description
onenterbackward	Specifies a URL to access when the card is entered from a <prev> task
onenterforward	Specifies a URL to access when the card is entered from a <go> task
ontimer	Specifies a URL to access when a timer, set by <timer>, expires
onpick	Specifies a URL to access when you select or deselect an item defined by an <option> element

Events are bound to *tasks*, described in the following code fragment. For instance, you can use <onevent> to bind an <ontimer> event to a <refresh> task, which resets a WML card and resets any values:

```
<card>
  <onevent type="ontimer">
    <refresh/>
  </onevent>
</card>
```

User Tasks

Tasks are actions taken by the microbrowser based on some user action. In Table 11.2, we've already used the <go> element task with our event examples.

TABLE 11.2   WML Tasks

Task	Description
<go>	Loads a specified URL
<prev>	Loads the previous card
<noop>	Behaves like it sounds
<refresh>	Redisplays cards; resets variables

Using the <onevent> element, you can assign a task to an event. You can also assign a task to a user interface element. To do this, you use the <do> element, as in

```
<do type="prev">
  <accept/>
</do>
```

which, in this case, maps the accept soft key to the <prev> event. The supported user interface elements for mobile devices are the following: accept, delete, help, options, prev, and reset.

Variables

WML supports the concepts of variables:

```
<setvar name="vendor" value="HP">
<p>Vendor is $(vendor)
```

These two lines demonstrate how to set the variable vendor, then access the variable's contents.

Formatting Elements

Given the focus on supporting very simple mobile devices, WML provides a small but flexible group of formatting elements. Attributes of each element are listed in parentheses in Table 11.3.

TABLE 11.3 WML Formatting Elements

Element	Description
`<b>`	Boldface text
`<big>`	Large font
` `	Line break
`<em>`	Emphasis
`<i>`	Italicized text
`<img>`	An image (`alt`, `src`, `localsrc`, `height`, `width`, `align`)
`<p>`	A paragraph (`align`, `wrap`)
`<small>`	Small font
`<strong>`	Same as emphasis
`<table>`	A table (`columns`, `align`, `title`)
`<td>`	A table cell
`<tr>`	A table row
`<u>`	Underlined text

In general, you'll make heavy use of these elements to coerce the most consistent behavior possible in a world of handset devices supporting four to eight lines of display, and characterized by inconsistent implementations of button and choice selections.

For example, it's probably no surprise that the font-reducing behavior of the element `<small>` is used often to offset the size of the display as much as possible. `<anchor>` and `<br/>` elements are often your best choice for building a menu of selections that will appear consistently across devices.

The WML Development Environment, Kinks and All

Not too many of us can afford to have a lab of every handset configuration on the market. Luckily, it's easy to find handset device emulators, each capable of emulating multiple devices. To simplify the issues of establishing a wireless development environment, the phone vendors have been wise enough to provide free phone emulation tools, some written in Java, that are often capable of assuming multiple device personalities.

Figure 11.2 demonstrates the Openwave emulator and development environment. With its URL set to `localhost:9000`, you can see that it's displaying the Enhydra stub application as adapted to WML. This application was created by the Enhydra AppWizard, selecting WML in the

Wireless Markup Presentations

CHAPTER 11

331

11

WIRELESS
MARKUP
PRESENTATIONS

Client Type pop-up menu. This phone emulator, as well other emulators and development environments from Nokia, Pixo, and other handset makers, can be downloaded (usually at no cost) from the companies' respective Web sites.

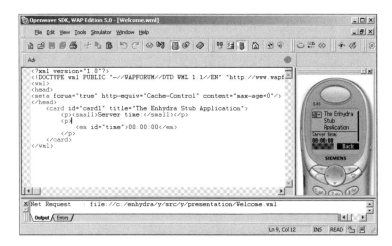

FIGURE 11.2

Openwave SDK and microbrowser emulator, displaying the Enhydra stub application.

Forget Cookies

Most microbrowsers do not support cookies, so we'll want to rely on URL encoding to give Enhydra the capability to maintain session for the wireless application. To override Enhydra's default behavior of using cookies for storing session keys, we'll want to update the application's configuration file to read the following:

```
SessionManager.SessionEncodeUrlState = auto
```

Using `writeDOM()` is also key to URL encoding, so be sure to use it when you're ready to write out the DOM.

Disable Document Caching

Document caching is something that microbrowsers take advantage of to conserve on bandwidth. For a dynamic application, this is an undesirable feature, so we'll want to find a way to turn off this behavior. One way is to use the META element in the document's HEAD element, using the WML-specific forua ("for user agent") attribute:

```
<meta forua="true" http equiv="Cache Control" content="max age=0"/>
```

And There's More...

Keep your eyes and ears peeled for the idiosyncrasies that characterize a lot of phones out there. We've listed a few things to watch for, but as you can imagine, implementers of micro-browsers have had to integrate support for the small environment of mobile devices with desktop technologies that assume there's a lot of memory space. And even if you can squeeze all the well-known functionality into a small device, that technology must be adapted to address the fact that mobile devices are on, then off, in and out of contact with the back office server and the rest of the network.

Watch out for strange caching and other unexpected behaviors. For example, some developers have standardized the insertion of a timestamp in phone URLs to account for buggy caching. Other tricks abound to account for the fact that there are WAP servers that strip the header information before passing on the client request in an HTTP request header.

Luckily, there's a lot of information out there. Get on a Nokia or open source mailing list and take notes.

WML Template Generation with `xmlc`

Mentioned earlier, Enhydra XMLC gets its WAP awareness from the inclusion of a DOM extension that is specific to the WML DTD. Everything WML in Enhydra can be found in the following packages:

```
org.enhydra.wireless.wml
org.enhydra.wireless.wml.dom
```

The first package addresses the WML DOM factory that is specific to generating WML DOM templates. The class WMLDomFactory is defined as an extension of the standard XercesDomFactory and performs WML-specific housekeeping chores, such as setting the correct MIME type:

```
setDocument(document,"text/vnd.wap.wml", "UTF-8");
```

XMLC must be told to use the WMLDomFactory, which can be done at the command line:

```
xmlc -dom-factory org.enhydra.wireless.wml.WMLDomFactory
```

When you use Enhydra AppWizard to build your WML client type, it automatically adds this -dom-factory option and value to the generated options.xmlc file. For standard servlets, you'll want to set the MIME type with the following:

```
response.setContentType("text/vnd.wap.wml");
```

Again, if you use AppWizard to build a standard servlet, this will be taken care of for you.

DOM API Extensions for WML Programming

Enhydra XMLC incorporates a WML-specific extension of the DOM API. Each element is represented by its own DOM interface, as listed in Table 11.4.

TABLE 11.4 WML DOM Element Interfaces

MLAccessElement	WMLAElement	WMLAnchorElement
WMLBElement	WMLBigElement	WMLBrElement
WMLCardElement	WMLDocument	WMLDoElement
WMLDOMImplementation	WMLElement	WMLEmElement
WMLFieldsetElement	WMLGoElement	WMLHeadElement
WMLIElement	WMLImgElement	WMLInputElement
WMLMetaElement	WMLNoopElement	WMLOneventElement
WMLOptgroupElement	WMLOptionElement	WMLPElement
WMLPostfieldElement	WMLPrevElement	WMLRefreshElement
WMLSelectElement	WMLSetvarElement	WMLSmallElement
WMLStrongElement	WMLTableElement	WMLTdElement
WMLTemplateElement	WMLTimerElement	WMLTrElement
WMLUElement	WMLWmlElement	

WMLCardElement supports 15 methods, some of which set up event behavior:

- setOnEnterBackward()—Specifies the event to occur when a user enters a card using a go task.
- setOnEnterForward()—Specifies the event to occur when the user enters a card using a prev task.
- setOnTime()—Specifies the event to occur when a timer expires.

Device Detection

As you might expect, information about what type of device is accessing your application can be deciphered by inspecting the HTTP request header. Note that there are still WAP servers out there that strip this information, so you'll need to perform some validation with the client if there's an uncertainty.

The ShowFloor application is designed to support multiple devices where it makes sense, again taking advantage of the fact that HTML, WML, and other wireless markup languages can all be served by XMLC-generated DOM templates. The getPageName() method takes advantage of the DOM template class-naming convention enforced by the Enhydra make file system, where the name of the markup page is appended with the language it represents. For example,

- mysfa.html becomes mysfaHTML.class
- mysfa.xml becomes mySFAXML.class
- mysfa.wml becomes mysfaWML.class

As we'll see in Chapter 12, "Client-Server Development with J2ME and Flash," the XML file will become important for delivering a custom XML dialect to a J2ME phone.

getPageName() reads the Accept string in the HTTP request header to determine the type of content required by the wireless client. After it has been determined, it takes the presentation object name, stored in poName (for example, mysfa), and appends the preferred language name (for example, XHTML) to the string that is returned (for example, mysfaXHTML). The string is then used to load the DOM template reflecting, by naming convention, the expected markup language. getPageName() is implemented as follows:

```
public static String getPageName(HttpPresentationComms comms, String poName)
    throws ShowFloorPresentationException {

  String header = null;
  String userAgent = null;
  String flashClient = null;

  try {
    flashClient = comms.request.getParameter("flash");
    userAgent = comms.request.getHeader("User-Agent");

    if (flashClient != null) {
      comms.response.setEncoding("ISO-8859-1");
      return poName + "XML";
    } else if(userAgent != null && userAgent.indexOf("RIM") != -1) {
      return poName + "HTML";
    } else if(userAgent != null && userAgent.indexOf("UP.") != -1) {
      return poName + "WML";
    } else if ((header = comms.request.getHeader("Accept")) == null) {
      return null;
    } else if (header.indexOf("text/xml") != -1) {
      return poName + "XML";
    } else if (header.indexOf("wap") != -1) {
      return poName + "WML";
    } else if (header.indexOf("text/xhtml") != -1) {
      return poName + "XHTML";
    }
    else {
      //Defaulting to html.
```

Wireless Markup Presentations

CHAPTER 11

335

11

WIRELESS
MARKUP
PRESENTATIONS

```
      return poName + "HTML";
    }
  } catch (Exception e) {
    throw new ShowFloorPresentationException("Trouble rerouting header:"
➥+ header, e);
  }
}
```

As you'll discover, a good number of WAP and i-mode phones are quite good at handling HTML, so it makes a good default language type in the event that no match is made.

The mySFA Vendor Notes Application

It's time to apply this brief introduction to WAP and WML to the implementation of a ShowFloor service. What we will do is give the mySFA subscribers, having logged into their account, the capability to browse the list of notes they made earlier, associating each one with a "must see" vendor. They will use these notes to make sure they don't forget to see vendors they had a specific interest in.

Using their mobile phone, they can

- Select from a list of mySFA applications.
- Having selected Vendor Notes, they can then scroll vendor-by-vendor through a list of notes associated with the current vendor.

Listing 11.1 is the WML markup that will display the list of mySFA applications from which to select. Our application is Vendor Notes.

LISTING 11.1 mysfa.wml

```
<?xml version="1.0"?>
<!DOCTYPE wml PUBLIC "-//WAPFORUM//DTD WML 1.1//EN" "http://www.wapforum.org/
➥DTD/wml_1.1.xml">
<wml>
<head>
<meta forua="true" http-equiv="Cache-Control" content="max-age=0"/>
</head>
  <card id="mySFAmenu" title="mySFA Apps">
    <p>Your apps:<br/>
      <anchor>Schedule
       <go href="http://localhost:9000/mySFAPresentation.po?event=sched"/>
      </anchor><br/>
      <anchor>Vendor Notes
       <go href="http://localhost:9000/mySFAPresentation.po?event=notes" />
      </anchor><br/>
```

LISTING 11.1 Continued

```
        <anchor>Booth Lookup
         <go href="http://localhost:9000/mySFAPresentation.po?event=lookup" />
         </anchor><br/>
       </p>
      </card>
</wml>
```

Each application selection is made active by its inclusion in <anchor> elements, and is associated with specific href attributes pointing to the mySFAPresentation presentation object (servlet) using the <go> element.

We're now faced with a design issue. We could list the first vendor and associated notes, then use <do href=<anchor reference>> to fetch the next vendor. Or, we could just send the whole set of vendor notes over as a set of cards, one card per vendor. We've chosen the latter for purpose of this demo; although careful thought should be given to just how much space the targeted phone is capable of handling.

The mySFA.wml DOM Template

Fundamentally, there is little difference between WML and HTML development with XMLC. Other than the strangeness of some of the newly introduced WML elements, the mySFA.wml markup in Listing 11.2 probably looks somewhat like a typical XMLC template.

One thing to note is that we're going to cast an overloaded light on the significance of the use of the id attribute to identify card1. In this example, card1 will result in the creation of an xmlc-generated accessor method, getElementCard1(). It will also serve within the WML microbrowser environment as an attribute that uniquely identifies the first card in the deck.

LISTING 11.2 mysfa.wml

```
<?xml version="1.0"?>
<!DOCTYPE wml PUBLIC "-//WAPFORUM//DTD WML 1.1//EN"
➥"http://www.wapforum.org/DTD/wml_1.1.xml">
<wml>
<head>
<meta forua="true" http-equiv="Cache-Control" content="max-age=0"/>
</head>

  <card id="card1" title="IBM" >
    <p id="PrevAndContent"><small>See if Joe Smith, the VP is there.
      <anchor> <br/>[Next]<go id="NextGo" href="#card2"/></anchor>
      <anchor> [Previous]<prev/> </anchor>
      </small>
```

Wireless Markup Presentations

CHAPTER 11

337

11

WIRELESS
MARKUP
PRESENTATIONS

LISTING 11.2   Continued

```
    </p>
  </card>

  <card id="card2" title="ACME" class="mockup">
    <p><small>Check out the new server.
      <anchor> <br/>[Next]<go href="#card3"/></anchor>
      <anchor> [Previous]<prev/> </anchor>
      </small>
    </p>
  </card>

  <card id="card3" title="Peabody" class="mockup">
    <p><small>Here's everything I know about Peabody.
      <anchor> <br/>[Next]<go href="#card1"/></anchor>
      <anchor> [Previous]<prev/> </anchor>
      </small>
    </p>
  </card>
</wml>
```

As you can see, we're going to discard the second and third cards in our stack because they bring nothing new to the template, other than serving as good content and navigation targets for a proof-of-concept or design review. The following will remove the mockup as identified by the class attributes:

```
xmlc -dump -delete-class mockup mySFA.wml
```

The mySFA Application

mySFAPresentation.java in Listing 11.3 is responsible for the generation of live content, using the DOM template generated by xmlc from mySFA.wml. We've chosen to forgo the use of the BasePO approach to show this demonstration application as fully functioning with a minimal amount of code (and hard coding of vendor and vendor notes data).

LISTING 11.3   mySFAPresentation.java

```
package x.presentation;

import org.w3c.dom.*;
import org.enhydra.wireless.wml.dom.*;
// Enhydra SuperServlet imports
import com.lutris.xml.xmlc.*;
import com.lutris.appserver.server.httpPresentation.*;
```

LISTING 11.3 Continued

```java
import com.lutris.appserver.server.httpPresentation.HttpPresentation;
import com.lutris.appserver.server.httpPresentation.HttpPresentationComms;
import com.lutris.appserver.server.httpPresentation.HttpPresentationException;

// Standard imports
import java.io.*;
import java.util.*;
import java.io.IOException;

public class mySFAPresentation implements HttpPresentation {

  public void run(HttpPresentationComms comms)
  throws HttpPresentationException, IOException {

    HttpPresentationRequest req = comms.request;
    String menuItem = req.getParameter("event");
    if (menuItem.equals("notes")) {
      DisplayNotes(comms);
    } else if (menuItem.equals("schedule")) {
     // Display the mySFA user's schedule
    } else if (menuItem.equals("lookup")) {
     // Display the mySFA user's booth lookup page
    }
  }

  public void DisplayNotes( HttpPresentationComms comms)
  throws HttpPresentationException, IOException {

    HttpPresentationRequest req = comms.request;
    String vendors [] = {"Nokia", "Ericcson", "Motorola", "Pixo"};

    String vendorNotes [] = {"See if Charlie still works there.",
➡"See if they have a J2ME phone.", "Ask about their developer program",
➡"Ramp up on i-mode."};

    mySFAWML mySFAdeck;
    mySFAdeck = (mySFAWML)comms.xmlcFactory.create(mySFAWML.class);

    // Grab all of the id references we need; not forgetting
    // to remove the id attributes, with the exception of
    // the card ID!
    WMLCardElement card = mySFAdeck.getElementCard1();

    // Grab the parent. We'll need it for removing the template
    // later on.
    Node parent = card.getParentNode();
```

LISTING 11.3 Continued

```java
WMLPElement note = mySFAdeck.getElementPrevAndContent();
note.removeAttribute("id");

WMLGoElement go = mySFAdeck.getElementNextGo();
go.removeAttribute("id");

String vTitle = "";
for (int i = 0; i < vendors.length; i++ ) {
  vTitle = vendors[i] + " (" + (i + 1) + " of " + vendors.length + ")";
  card.getAttributeNode("title").setValue(vTitle);
  card.setTitle(vTitle);

  // Set the card's ID, incrementing it by one.
  card.getAttributeNode("id").setValue("card" + (i + 1));

  mySFAdeck.setTextPrevAndContent(vendorNotes[i]);

  // Update the go element's href value to point to the next card.
  //
  if ((i + 1) == vendors.length) {
    // reset the deck to point to the top card.
    go.setHref("#card1");
  } else {
    // set the current card to point to the next one.
    go.setHref("#card" + (i+2));
  }
  Node clone = card.cloneNode(true);
  parent.appendChild(clone);
}
//Remove the card template.
parent.removeChild(card);

comms.response.writeDOM(mySFAdeck);
  }
}
```

If you've read Chapter 8, "HTML Presentations," the algorithm applied by this example is straightforward. After loading the DOM template, we immediately use the xmlc-generated accessor methods getElementCard1(), getElementPrevAndContent(), and getElementNextGo() to access the portions of the DOM template that are to be dynamically updated, then cloned. We also want to, with the exception of the card id attribute, remove id attributes where they're no longer needed. Redundant ids by definition might cause the device's microbrowser to fall over.

We then enter a loop, updating the template with fresh content for every vendor that has been noted. The `ids` for each card are guaranteed to be unique for our use of incrementing the number appendix to the "card" name, for example, `card2`, `card3`, and so on.

After removing the original template, the only task left is to invoke `writeDOM()` to return the updated WML markup to the client device. Again, because we used the WML DOM factory, there's no need to worry about updating the MIME type.

Enhydra AirSent Demo

If you or the folks you work with are still trying to figure out the possible impact of supporting wireless, mobile, and small footprint devices in your Web application design, the publicly available demonstration site `http://www.airsent.com` is implemented with Enhydra and Enhydra XMLC to suggest some possible scenarios for bringing HTML, WML, CHTML, J2ME, and Flash together within a single business application.

AirSent is a speculative implementation of a fictional Fed-Ex-like delivery business that picks up and delivers small packages and letters using bicycle messengers, presumably operating in the financial district of San Francisco. Be sure to note where the roles of browsers and phones make sense. Afterwards, see whether you can then walk through your existing Web application and determine if and where wireless, Flash, or even voice presentations make sense.

VoiceXML

The promise of voice recognition technology has been around for quite a while. It now appears to be ready to plug into the Internet backbone of application servers and Enhydra XMLC is up to the task. The XML language of voice, according to the W3C specification, is VoiceXML. The rest of this chapter will be spent on explaining VoiceXML and how you might incorporate it into a Web application—where it makes sense!

On March 7, 2000, the VoiceXML Forum released the VoiceXML 1.0 specification as a standardized programming interface for speech and telephony applications. During its May 10-12, 2000 meetings, the Voice Browser Working Group of the W3C agreed to adopt VoiceXML 1.0 as the basis for the development of a W3C dialog markup language.

Voice Portals

There's a new concept called the *voice portal*, providing development and voice technology services that make it easy for anyone with a browser and a VoiceXML book to process voice presentations at little or no cost. Throw in an open source application server like Enhydra, and you're on your way to building highly dynamic voice-driven applications.

Let's consider the role of a voice portal, illustrated in Figure 11.3, and how it plays into the Web picture.

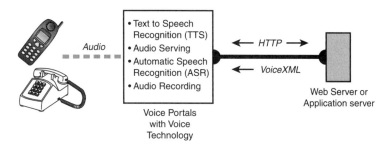

FIGURE 11.3

The role and functionality of voice portals.

A person dials a special telephone number that connects through a telephone switch into a voice portal. A voice portal is a hardware device that connects a telephone line to the Internet, and provides speech recognition, text-to-speech, speech recording, and digital sound playback functionality. The voice portal interfaces over the Internet to a VoiceXML server, which provides the actual application that the user is accessing through the other interfaces. The VoiceXML server provides VoiceXML to the voice portal and the business logic and database access. Multiple machines can replace the single VoiceXML server to distribute the layers, the load, and the functionality.

IBM, Nuance, L&H, and SpeechWorks are some of the voice portal software providers. Voice portals are expensive to set up and maintain, so many third party companies provide voice portal services, most of which are free of cost when used for development purposes. Examples include TellMe, BeVocal, and Voxeo. These sites provide impressive online development environments that provide the following services:

- The opportunity to specify a URL, representing the location of your Enhydra XMLC application, which the voice portal site will link to a specific phone number. When somebody dials the number, your application is activated.

- An HTML text area control for entering "quick check" VoiceXML. This is fun and useful for getting your feet wet with static VoiceXML, until you're ready to program.

- A debug window to monitor, step by step, how the site's VoiceXML processor is handling your markup.

- Extensive online documentation, including sample code, tutorials, discussion groups, and in some cases, hyperlinks.

- Best of all, a phone number with ID code is provided to you with which to test your VoiceXML application.

Using the Voxeo system at `http://community.voxeo.com`, it took me fewer than 20 minutes from the point I started registering as a developer to receive my login ID and password, at no cost. Other systems provide similar services with a quick turnaround in setting up your account.

The VoiceXML Language

Your first question of VoiceXML might be, "What can I actually do, other than speak some words electronically, or interpret some words the caller might utter?" The answer is, "A lot!" I felt a bit like Rip Van Winkle as I learned just how much can be done today with voice technology. My first clue was seeing that VoiceXML is a W3C specification.

A quick glance at VoiceXML reflects many capabilities that are similar to HTML development, including the use of forms and menus.

The flavor of the VoiceXML programming model is similar to HTML development, making it clear that mapping the parts that can take advantage of voice technology is relatively straightforward, where it makes sense. It is also similar to WML development in its reliance on registering events that are associated with tasks.

The following example is the familiar Enhydra stub application, as expressed in the VoiceXML dialect:

```
<?xml version="1.0"?>
<!DOCTYPE vxml
  PUBLIC "-//Lutris Technologies//DTD VXML 1.0 + Lutris Ids//EN"
  "c:/ lutrisvoicexml1-0.dtd">
<vxml version="1.0">
 <form>
  <block>Welcome to voice XML from Lutris Technologies</block>
  <block>The time is now </block>
  <block id="time">00:00:00</block>
 </form>
</vxml>
```

In this case however, you "view" this presentation by dialing a phone number and listening to the phrase, "Welcome to VoiceXML from Lutris Technologies. The time is now *(current time)*." Of course, the current time is inserted by the manipulation of the VoiceXML DOM template using XMLC development.

Grammar

Most speech recognizers work by matching up a recorded speech utterance with a list of words. The way of expressing the words to match with rules for the match is defined by a *grammar*. Because speech recognizers and their grammars existed prior to the VoiceXML specification, how the grammar maps into the specification varies from vendor to vendor, and from the various voice portal services and VoiceXML emulators. Additional features such as menu operations are dependent on and tied to the grammar. For this reason, writing VoiceXML for Voxeo differs from writing VoiceXML for IBM or TellMe.

XMLC Accessor Methods and VoiceXML

Because `id` attributes are necessary in the creation of the accessor methods, you must check for the definition of `id` attributes as defined by the DTD. Each voice portal, depending on their own preferences and the telephony equipment they use, has a uniquely defined VoiceXML. (Okay, so it takes awhile for a standard to become comprehensively implemented in a standard way.)

Without the accessor methods, the items can still be modified using a more complex, DOM tree-walking methodology. But you probably want to go beyond tree walking to take advantage of XMLC's features. Make a copy of your publicly available voice portal's preferred VoiceXML DTD to your server environment. Making the following addition of the following modification will do the trick:

```
<!ENTITY % enhydraid "id  ID   #IMPLIED">
```

Then, elsewhere in the DTD, incorporate references to `enhydraid` for any elements that you will be identifying with `id` attributes for the `xmlc` command to find during compilation:

```
<!ATTLIST prompt
    bargein        %boolean;    #IMPLIED
    cond           %expression; #IMPLIED
    count          %integer;    #IMPLIED
    timeout        %duration;   #IMPLIED
  %enhydraid; >
```

Then be sure to update your VoiceXML file to point to your custom DTD:

```
PUBLIC "-//My Company//DTD VXML 1.0 + Enhydra Ids//EN" "c:/
➥enhydravoicexml1-0.dtd">
```

This same philosophy of enhancing a DTD with an `id` declaration applies to any XML language, including the new SVG specification from W3C, discussed in Chapter 12.

mySFA as a VoiceXML Application

We're going to take advantage of VoiceXML's support for Dual Tone Multi Frequency (DTMF) to take the mySFA Vendor Notes application discussed earlier and turn it into a more convenient application. Small presentation screens aren't a concern when you can rely on voice technology.

DTMF is the standard behind the tones produced by the keys in a telephone handset. DTMF grammars using the element <dtmf> or the dtmf attribute can be associated with voice prompts and choices to rely less on the spoken word and more on simple touches of the keypad. Sorry, for those of you hanging onto the 60s, there's no princess phone support at this time.

Listing 11.4 generates a voice prompt that describes the three keypad buttons that can be pressed to launch our three mySFA applications. The number 2 key will launch Vendor Notes. As you can see, this VoiceXML file employs the familiar form, then stores the user's response in a value variable. The filled element is an aspect of VoiceXML's Form Interpretation Algorithm (FIA). <filled> is an implicit navigational element that takes over the form when a value has been chosen. In our case, it's the push of the 2 button on the user's key pad.

LISTING 11.4   mySFAwelcome.xml

```
<?xml version="1.0"?>
<!DOCTYPE vxml PUBLIC '-//Nuance/DTD VoiceXML 1.0b//EN'
          'http://community.voxeo.com/vxml/nuancevoicexml.dtd'>
<vxml version="1.0">
<form id="mysfaapps">
 <prompt>
 Welcome to my S F A. Please select one of the three applications
➥ using 1 for Schedule, 2 for Vendor Notes and 3 for booth look up.
 </prompt>

 <option dtmf="1" value="sched">
 Schedule
 <option>
 <option dtmf="2" value="notes">
 Vendor Notes
 <option>
 <option dtmf="3" value="booth">
 Booth Location
 <option>

 <filled>
  <submit next="http://www.otterpod.com/mySFAPresentation.po"
      method="post"
      namelist="mysfaapps" />
 </filled>
```

Wireless Markup Presentations

CHAPTER 11

345

11

WIRELESS
MARKUP
PRESENTATIONS

LISTING 11.4   Continued

```
</form>
</vxml>
```

What happens at this point is the activation of the `<submit>` element to pass execution control back to the Enhydra application server and the `mySFAPresentation` presentation object. The `namelist` variable contains the VoiceXML variable `value`, which will be sent with the HTTP request along with its value, `notes`.

Listing 11.5 is the template we'll generate with `xmlc` and modify with `mySFAPresentation.java`. Because it is so similar to Listing 11.3, let's review the unique portions of the code.

LISTING 11.5   `mySFAVendorNotes.xml`

```
<?xml version="1.0"?>

<!DOCTYPE vxml
  PUBLIC "-//Enhydra//DTD VXML 1.0 + Enhydra Ids//EN"
  "c:/enhydra/x/src/x/presentation/enhydra.dtd">

<vxml version="1.0">
 <form>
  <block>
    <prompt id="Greeting">
  Here are your Vendor Notes
    <prompt>
    <goto nextitem="vendor1">
  </block>

  <block id="vendor1">
    <prompt id="vendorNotes">
  For IBM, see the man about a blue suit.
    <prompt>
    <goto id="nextItem" nextitem="vendor2">
  </block>

  <block id="vendor2" class="mockup">
    <prompt id="vendorNotes">
  For Apple, check out those cool development boxes.
    <prompt>
    <goto nextitem="vendor1">
  </block>

 </form>
</vxml>
```

First of all, we'll leave the first `block` element intact. All it does is introduce the caller to the page. We can, however, update the greeting to indicate how many vendor notes are about to come:

```
page.setTextGreeting("Here are your " + vendors.length + vendor notes.");
```

Later on, we enter a loop, making use of the generated `setTextVendorNotes()` method to update each prompt with the current vendor's vendor note. To generate `<goto>` elements pointing to additional, dynamically-added vendor blocks such as this

```
<goto id="nextItem" nextitem="vendor2">
```

we use the following operations:

```
element nextItem = page.getElementNextItem();
nextItem.setAttribute("nextitem", "vendor" + (i + 2));
```

Having completed and deployed the presentation object, the mySFA subscriber can now simply listen to the application describe each vendor's note as a stream of spoken information, with no further voice or keypad actions required.

Developing Without a VoiceXML DOM Extension

The open source version of Enhydra XMLC has no VoiceXML-specific DOM at the time of this writing. We therefore must rely on standard DOM programming and general DOM `Element` classes. But, as we've seen, because we still have access to `xmlc`-generated accessor methods, there's very little need to expose our code to heavy DOM API methods or DOM traversal algorithms. The only real price we pay in the absence of a VoiceXML DOM is the lack of VoiceXML-specific-type checking during runtime.

This has been a rapid introduction to the VoiceXML language, providing a very narrow view of its overall capability. Our goal has been to demonstrate how easy it is to manipulate VoiceXML content with Enhydra XMLC. Having a common basis in XML makes it almost trivial to design and drive a VoiceXML application with XMLC. Be sure to check out *Voice Application Development with VoiceXML* from Sams Publishing for a complete review and appreciation of the capabilities and potential of VoiceXML.

Summary

In this chapter, we've introduced both the good and bad news about wireless presentation development. The good news is that mobile computing has embraced XML as a means of tapping into and extending Internet applications. The bad news is that it's an early adopter industry, characterized by a lot of diverse devices implemented in non-standard ways, in order to address their unique, small footprint environments.

Enhydra XMLC makes it very easy to adapt new and existing Web applications to the mobile client. This is due in large part to the common language of XML and the emulation of browser displays by the mobile industry.

We've also touched on VoiceXML, which impressively adapts old technology to the new ways of Web development. Again, thanks to the common underpinning of XML, Enhydra XMLC is an excellent technology for building and driving dynamic VoiceXML presentations, taking advantage of the wide variety of highly accessible voice-enabling technologies.

This chapter was in no way intended to be a comprehensive discussion of these technologies, or the design implications of their integration into Web applications. Hopefully, we've provided sufficient flavor to using wireless and voice markup technology for you to judge their applicability for using Enhydra XMLC with your Web applications.

Client-Server Development with J2ME and Flash

IN THIS CHAPTER

Browsers, as PC or mobile clients, are really operating system-independent "desktops" with a modest amount of built-in intelligence. The addition of JavaScript, combined with browser manufacturer-specific features, gives them the capability to do some pretty clever things. But they lack the capability to save information between sessions and operate meaningfully when there's no Internet connection. There are inconsistent versions and implementations across operating systems, and their manufacturers continue to compete with different markup extensions (and behaviors).

After introducing the topic of wireless and voice presentations in Chapter 11, we're now going to look at client technology that casts XMLC in a different role. In this chapter, we'll spend most of our time focusing on smart clients represented by Java 2 Micro Edition (J2ME) and Macromedia's wildly popular Flash, both capable of manipulating and structuring their own presentations.

J2ME and Flash are similar in their capability to take care of the visual business on the client side, leaving little reason for server-side preparation of a structured display. J2ME and (surprisingly) Flash 5 offer new capabilities in the tradition of the "heavy client" client/server development of the late 1980s.

There are a great deal of articles and books that go into great detail to explain J2ME, such as Yu Feng and Jun Zhu's *Wireless Java Programming with J2ME* (Sams Publishing). With that in mind, we will focus on the J2ME components, as well as an open source contribution from kxml.enhydra.org, that are relevant to turning Enhydra XMLC into a core communications tool for integrating J2ME-enabled smart phones and PDAs into enterprise clients for modern application servers.

We'll wrap the chapter up with another new spin on markup that makes it still a compelling proposition, even with the emergence of J2ME and Flash. Scalar Vector Graphics, the new graphics markup language from W3C, will expand our imagination regarding the role that graphics, already a heavily influence on browser application design, will take in the very near term.

Java 2 Micro Edition

Everything about Java has been made possible by the fact that computers, starting with typical Intel desktops, are faster and bigger. What would have been unheard of a short decade ago is made possible by the continual raising of the bar representing the minimum memory footprint and computing power of desktops. The same can be said of mobile devices and appliances.

There's a new style of consumer device application development that takes advantage of a new generation of devices, incorporating yet another edition of the ever-expanding Sun Java 2 platform. Typically, a technology like Java will have its limits, operating only in the environments that make sense. Sun Microsystems has, however, defined a flavor of the Java runtime environment and API for the small environments of mobile devices and appliances.

J2ME defines a pared-down version of the J2SE environment to account for the rarified dimensions of mobile devices, such as phones, PDAs, and car navigational units, as well as plugged-in home appliances. But this is only part of the scope of J2ME. It also addresses the real-world topics of deploying J2ME applications and their security model. And because they are clearly well-suited to the needs of both small and large enterprises that support field personnel, as well as the connected consumer, J2ME addresses an API that is rich in network capabilities.

J2ME in the Wireless Space

Assuming you believe that Java can run effectively on mobile devices, there are some real advantages of the microbrowser-driven applications we discussed in Chapter 11:

- Security—J2ME supports the HTTPS protocol for secure Internet connections.
- No gateways—J2ME devices support a complete IP stack. Each device has its own IP address.
- Standard GUI—J2ME features a standard graphical user interface across the devices that it supports. These GUI components will be familiar to Java Foundation Class (Swing) developers.

However, even J2ME has its downside. It is, after all, a brand new technology driven by a growing number of handset makers including Motorola, Nextel, and NTT DoCoMo:

- Existing HTML sites/solutions must be rewritten.
- The number of GUI components is somewhat limited at this point. Generally, text, text boxes, check boxes, and low-level graphics are supported.
- With browsers, installation is a no-brainer, as long as the application and your browser are compatible. With J2ME, there is a device installation element to consider. The good news is that over-the-air installation will be available soon, although it will be on a per-vendor basis for now.
- J2ME requires a different kind of UI designer, one who is familiar with JFC-style development. HTML designers add little value in developing J2ME presentations. If you're using XMLC to drive multiple presentations, you're faced with new challenges when J2ME and/or Flash are part of the mix.

The J2ME Device Environment

Although J2ME addresses devices with a capacity of much greater than 2 MB, we will focus on the small devices powered by the J2ME-defined K Virtual Machine. The KVM is designed and tuned to operate in environments of less than 1MB.

J2ME configurations are defined to reflect the realistic capabilities of devices with small memory, small screens, and small keyboards (or even smaller keypads). For instance, the profile of a typical J2ME phone and its operating environment is assumed to be the following:

- 128KB to 1MB of memory
- 16- or 32-bit CPU
- Low bandwidth
- Intermittently connected

Below a certain size, devices tend to take on wildly different capabilities, and therefore, applications or roles. As a result, specifications that reflect particular devices and the industries that they serve (for example, consumer, medical, automobile) are necessary in order to define Java libraries and APIs that maximize, not underpower or overwhelm their intended environment:

- CLDC— The Connected, Limited Device Configuration profile defines the lowest common denominator reflected by J2ME phones, such as Motorola's iDEN. It comprises the more generic core Java APIs for developing wireless applications. It is essentially a slimmed down version of the Java 2 Standard Edition (J2SE) tailored for small devices.
- MIDP—The Mobile Information Device Profile builds on the CLDC to make it possible to develop and operate very modern applications for mobile devices. MIDP specifies the Java libraries that address GUI, timers, persistent storage, and networking.
- Vendor—The J2ME specification permits device manufacturers to add their own proprietary APIs. These features give application developers more device-specific options, such as querying the environment for remaining power and signal strength.

The rest of our discussion will focus on the MIDP profile for developing mobile applications.

XML for J2ME Client/Server Communication

The extension of the Java 2 platform to mobile devices creates a natural association that conjures up images of smart devices roaming the countryside, checking in on a regular basis with application servers back at home. In fact, as we'll discuss soon and as illustrated in Figure 12.1, a similar scenario applies to mobile devices, such as the Palm PDA, supporting Flash applications powered by an XML engine, introduced in Flash 5.

Also, the reality of the last 20 years is that devices get smaller, faster, and grow in internal capacity. The implications of these circumstances and industry trends have been recognized by the Enhydra project.

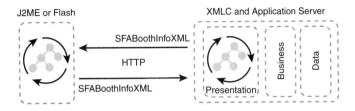

FIGURE 12.1
XML-driven data linking the J2ME/Flash client and the application server.

J2ME provides a network package that features the Generic Connection framework that supports HTTP requests and responses over both packet-based and circuit-switched networks. This functionality is sufficient for others to support mechanisms that define application specific protocols to support client/server style application architectures.

Leveraging Enhydra XMLC as an XML generation tool, the Enhydra.org project has grown to enhance the J2ME environment with the tools necessary to support XML as the basis for client/server protocols. Figure 12.1 illustrates the role that XMLC, as well as a J2ME client(or Flash client, as we'll discuss later), can serve in communicating over HTTP using an XML protocol that is application-specific in its knowledge, but generic in its use of XML as a language foundation.

Let's discuss some of the missing technology pieces required to support this scenario, all of which are addressed in the Enhydra.org open source project.

EnhydraME and XMLC

Established in August 2001, the EnhydraME (Enhydra Micro Edition) project at me.enhydra.org is an effort that is defined to unify a set of related sub-projects that collectively target two goals:

- Enable the integration of Java micro devices with the back-end of enterprise computing, represented by application servers.

- Define a self-sufficient "micro application server" capable of serving other devices in a highly distributed environment. This configuration also enables J2ME devices to gain access to the new world of SOAP-based Web services.

EnhydraME is a collection of many projects that compose the EnhydraME framework, all tuned for the unique attributes of tiny devices. Some of these technologies include the following:

- kXML—A complete XML parser for micro Java environments. kXML incorporates kDOM for representing parsed XML in a DOM view.

- kSOAP—A fully capable SOAP messaging component for wireless devices.
- kHTTP—An HTTP server for sending and receiving HTML on wireless devices.

There are numerous other projects under the umbrella of EnhydraME, including kJMS and kUDDI, but they are too new to focus on at this point. Our interest is in kXML and kDOM as the missing pieces in a client/server scenario involving J2ME devices.

Enhydra kXML

Much of the design of EnhydraME is based on the assumption that XML will be the custom dialect-enabling protocol that links client and server.

Predictably, we are not interested in building standalone J2ME applications. Instead, we want to leverage the best of what these new devices have to offer to enhance the value of the ShowFloor application. How are J2ME devices different than the WAP mobile devices we've talked about thus far?

- They have their own GUI library for rendering a simple set of "widgets," such as forms, text boxes, buttons, and lists, as well as low-level graphics that turn them into excellent "monitoring" tools.
- They have the capability make data locally persistent, using the built-in J2ME persistence library. Access a server, download data and, if you disconnect, you still have the data you need.
- Although devices that support WML can leverage WMLscript, the J2ME device can simply do more logically and be more easily extended within the space that it has, with new functionality. An example of this would be business-specific Java classes.

It is probably no great shock that we want to leverage XML and Enhydra XMLC to communicate with a J2ME phone. After all, we do the same with WAP and i-mode devices.

What is different in the J2ME-to-Enhydra scenario is that the computational aspects of the overall application are a cleaner division between business logic, as composed and processed on the server, and display logic, as generated by the J2ME application. The role of XMLC will be to generate and process XML that has a pure data view, as opposed to markup intended to drive a browser. The display work will be done by the J2ME application.

A Lean XML Parser for J2ME

Each client, whether it's an application or a mobile phone, must contain an XML parser in order to decompose or generate an XML object. A number of options exist. We will use kXML from the EnhydraME project on the J2ME device end of the pipe to Enhydra and Enhydra XMLC. Between the two, we will create a J2ME application as driven by data from an application server using XMLC.

kXML is a lean XML API for the Java 2 Micro Edition (J2ME). It was originally developed at the AI Unit of the University of Dortmund as a side product of the COMRIS project. It now lives at `kxml.enhydra.org`, where it is chaired by Stefan Haustein, co-author of *Java 2 Micro Edition (J2ME) Application Development* from Sams.

kXML is different than other XML parsers in that it avoids the overhead and large footprint of building a full DOM. It also avoids the heavy processing requirements of an event-based model, like the SAX parser.

Pull Versus Push Parser

kXML is a *pull-based processor* that gives the application direct control of XML data as it is read. The application takes control, parsing the tree recursively, rendering the entire DOM quickly and efficiently.

In contrast, the well-established SAX XML parser employs a *push model*, where events are generated and sent to the application. Events correspond to the encountering of an element or characters. In this "throw over the wall" manner, no actual data structure is created, leaving the application to come up with its own processing strategy. The application must also figure out where it is at before acting on the event.

The kXML parser is driven by the application. Its interface is a bit more modular in comparison to SAX, designed to be taken over by the application. Recursion and the use of the application's own variables are used to collect data. The result is a smaller footprint, thanks to the absence of a self-driven parser and the additional code required of the application to determine what to do with the data.

DOMs on Pilots?

An optional kDOM library is provided by kXML for those who want that pre-built tree view of incoming data. As you might have guessed, this is a pared-down DOM parser that was designed to operate within the restricted set of MIDP-defined classes. Its design center also assumes the tightest restrictions on available memory. Perhaps as MIDP is expanded to account for the improved capacity of these devices, JDOM (`http://www.jdom.org`) might become an option as well.

The ShowFloor Admin Application

Let's introduce a mobile application of the ShowFloor application. This application demonstrates some basic J2ME capabilities, such as using the high-level user interface library and the network connection package. But, in this chapter, we're going to review the portions of the application that do the following:

- Define an application-specific protocol based on XML
- Use kXML to parse XML delivered from Enhydra XMLC
- Communicate with an application server from a J2ME client

Defining `FloorAdmin` and `BoothInfoXML`

Every show must have administrators, floating from booth to booth, fixing problems that vendors might be experiencing, such as connectivity to the Internet. Let's look at some of the components of a midlet application that give mobile ShowFloor administrators the capability to look up booth information on a per-vendor basis. This information will include contact person, booth number, and assigned IP address.

Using their J2ME phone, a "Floor Admin" will be able to enter the name of a vendor and receive the formatted data back from the SFA server in the back office. As a two-way client server application, the Floor Admin can update any incorrect information that he or she discovers.

To connect the J2ME client with the rest of the application residing on the application server, we'll define a protocol language, shown in Listing 12.1, in the form of an XML dialect defined by the DTD `BoothInfoXML`. Data, organized to conform to this protocol, will be processed by a kXML parser on the client, and XMLC in the server presentation object. The DTD describes one to many vendors.

Listing 12.1 BoothInfoXML.dtd

```
<!—- This DTD is dedicated to serving the BoothRater Application>
<!ELEMENT FloorAdmin (Vendor+)>
<!ELEMENT Vendor(Name, Contact, BoothNum, IPadd, Href)>
<!ATTLIST Vendor id ID #IMPLIED>
<!ELEMENT Name (#PCDATA)>
<!ATTLIST Vendor id ID #IMPLIED>
<!ELEMENT Contact (#PCDATA)>
<!ATTLIST Contact id ID #IMPLIED>
<!ELEMENT BoothNum (#PCDATA)>
<!ATTLIST BoothNum id ID #IMPLIED>
<!ELEMENT IPadd (#PCDATA)>
<!ATTLIST IPadd id ID #IMPLIED
     HREF CDATA #IMPLIED>
```

This could easily be redefined to represent a collection of vendors that could be downloaded at once, taking advantage of MIDP's persistence library. This capability would give our Floor Admin a significant advantage over flaky mobile connections deep in the bowels of the San Jose Convention Center.

`BoothInfoXML` is sufficiently defined to standardize the data required by the J2ME application. We've introduced `id` attributes as the hooks we'll use for Enhydra XMLC to populate the XML template. The last element, `HREF`, gives us some flexibility by binding the URL with the data in the event we relocate. For example, the Floor Admin might update the IP address for the booth. The `HREF` attribute would contain the URL representing the presentation object or servlet back on the server that would process the request to update the IP address.

Elements of the `FloorAdmin` Midlet

Let's examine `FloorAdmin` and the source code examples that best illustrate how a J2ME device issues a request to the server, then processes the response.

Listing 12.2, `FloorAdmin.java`, builds the display that will ask the Floor Admin to enter a vendor name into a J2ME textbox. `commandAction()` processes the answer when the user selects OK.

LISTING 12.2   FloorAdmin.java

```
import javax.microedition.midlet.*;
import javax.microedition.lcdui.*;

public class FloorAdmin extends MIDlet implements CommandListener {
  private TextBox textbox;
  private Display display;
  private Command okCommand okCmd = new Command("OK", Command.OK, 1);
  private Command exitCommand exitCmd = new Command("Exit", Command.EXIT, 1);

  public BoothAdmin() {
    textBox = new TextBox("Enter vendor name:");
    textBox.addCommand(okCmd);
    textBox.addCommand(exitCmd);
    textBox.setCommandListener(this);

    display = Display.getDisplay(this);
  }

  pubilc pauseApp() {}

  public void destroyApp(boolean unconditional) {
    textBox = null;
    okCmd = null;
    exitCmd = null;
    display = null;
  }
```

LISTING 12.2   Continued

```java
public void commandAction(Command c, Displayable d) {
  if (d == textbox && c == okCmd) {
    //Retrieve the string representing the vendor's name.
    String t = textBox.getString();
    if (t.length() > 0) {
      BoothInfoScreen(t);
    }
  } else if (c == exitCmd) {
    destroyApp(true);
    notifyDestroyed();
  }
}
}
```

BoothInfoScreen() in Listing 12.3 is an extension of a form and does two things. First, it makes a request for the vendor data by passing the request-specific URL to handleBooth(). Then, with data in hand (in the form of a Vector), it populates a displayable StringItem that presents a label "BoothInfo:", followed by the vendor information.

LISTING 12.3   BoothInfoScreen.java

```java
public class BoothInfoScreen extends Form {
  private StringItem boothInfo = new StringItem("BoothInfo:", "");
  private Vector boothData = new Vector();

  private int VNAME_FIELD = 0;
  private int VCONTACT_FIELD = 1;
  private int VBOOTHNUM_FIELD = 2;
  private int VIPADD_FIELD = 3;

  public void loadDetails(String ven) throws SFAException {
    String url = "http://www.otterpod.com/sfa/FloorAdmin.po?vendor=" + ven);
    try {
      // Fetch vector with vendor booth information.
      boothData = services.handleBooth(url);
      // Populate StringItem (Label...followed by vendor info)
      populate();
    } catch (Exception ex) {
      throw new SFAException(ex);
    }
  }

  }
  public void populate() {
    if (boothData != null && boothData.size() >= 4) {
```

LISTING 12.3 Continued

```
      boothInfo.setText((String) boothData.elementAt(VNAME_FIELD) + "\n"
    + (String) boothData.elementAt(VCONTACT_FIELD) + "\n"
    + (String) boothData.elementAt(VBOOTHNUM_FIELD) + "\n"
    + (String) boothData.elementAt(VIPADD_FIELD));
  }
 }
}
```

The method handleBooth() is responsible for taking the kDOM document generated by the getDocumentFromURL() method as a result of decomposing the HTTP request, and delivering it in the BoothInfoXML dialect. Before we look at handleBooth(), the method getDocumentFromURL() is shown here:

```
public static Document getDocumentFromURL(String url) throws Exception {
  Document doc = null;
  try {
    HttpConnection hc = (HttpConnection) Connector.open(url);

    // Set the request method and headers
    hc.setRequestMethod(hc.GET);
    hc.setRequestProperty("Accept", "text/xml");
    hc.setRequestProperty("Content-Language", "en-US");

    // Opening the InputStream will open the connection
    // and read the HTTP headers.
    InputStream is = hc.openInputStream();
    DefaultParser parser =
      new DefaultParser(new InputStreamReader(is));
    doc = new Document();
    doc.parse(parser);

    if (is != null) {
      is.close();
    }
    if (hc != null) {
      hc.close();
    }

  } catch (Exception ex) {
    throw new Exception("Error connectoing to server " +
            ex.getMessage());
  }
  return doc;
}
```

Using the J2ME network library, getDocumentFromURL() formats the HTTP request, then opens a stream to wait for the response. The kDOM DefaultParser() reads the BoothInfoXML input stream. The parse() method of Document() converts the BoothInfoXML content into a DOM that is then returned to HandleBooth, shown in Listing 12.4.

LISTING 12.4   The handleBooth Method

```
// This method is written to assume that only one vendor is
// included in the XML file.
// DefaultElement is kDOM's version of the standard DOM's Element
public Vector handleBooth(String url) throws SFAException{
  Vector boothInfo = new Vector(4, 1);
  int childIndex = 0;
  String errorMessage = null;
  try {
    // Fetch data via HTTP request back to Enhydra.
    Document boothInfoDoc = getDocumentFromURL(url);
    DefaultElement root = (DefaultElement) boothInfoDoc.getRootElement();
    DefaultElement child;
    //Vendor name
    child = (DefaultElement)root.getChild(childIndex++);
    boothInfo.addElement((String)child.getChild(0));
    //Contact name
    child = (DefaultElement)root.getChild(childIndex++);
    boothInfo.addElement((String)child.getChild(0));
    //Booth number
    child = (DefaultElement)root.getChild(childIndex++);
    boothInfo.addElement((String)child.getChild(0));
    //IP Address
    child = (DefaultElement)root.getChild(childIndex++);
    boothInfo.addElement((String)child.getChild(0));
    // From the HREF associated with IPaddress, pointing
    // back to the servlet/pres object that can update the IP address.
    boothInfo.addElement((String)((Attribute)child.getChild(childIndex).
➥getAttribute("href")).getValue());

  } catch (Exception ex) {
    return null;
  }

  return boothInfo;
}
```

handleBooth() systematically extracts the data from the DOM document object into a Vector that is eventually returned to loadDetails(), which invokes populate() to update the StringItem for eventual display.

The output from the `StringItem` variable `boothInfo` looks something like the following:

```
BoothInfo:
Compaq
Jack Doe
334
127.0.0.1
```

Building a J2ME Application

Everything you need to build a J2ME application is downloadable from Sun's J2ME Web site. The site also references how to develop applications for third party handset vendors, such as Palm, RIM, or Motorola. The Sun J2ME Wireless Toolkit provides the following components:

- Device emulators that mimic the behavior of selected actual phone devices.
- A simple graphical development environment called KtoolBar.
- A bytecode pre-verifier that pre-verifies byte code prior to packaging.

For fans of the Forte IDE, a J2ME Wireless Module plug-in is also provided.

Compiling and Deploying the Application

The compilation of midlets reflects the general J2SE scheme for turning Java source code into classes and jar files of classes:

```
javac –g:none -d /tmp/j2meclasses –boothclasspath /usr/local/jwmewtlkt/lib/
➥midpapi.zip -classpath /tmp/j2meclasses;classes <SRCFILES>
```

There are, however, a few J2ME-specific features. The pre-verification process of J2SE and the JVM is normally hidden from the developer. It's how the JVM optimizes the bytecode for performance gains. In order to keep the kJVM (micro JVM) as small as possible for J2ME devices, this process is performed prior to deployment in order to offload this task from the kVM.

The preceding compilation uses `/tmp/j2meclasses` to hold the unverified classes. After the compiled classes are verified, the `preverifier` will store them in the classes directory.

Another J2ME wrinkle is the *Java Application Descriptor (JAD)* file. Unlike the manifest that is part of the jar file of midlet classes, the JAD remains outside the jar and is key to the eventual emergence of over-the-air midlet deployments. The JAD for the FloorAdmin application is the following:

```
MIDlet-Name: FloorAdmin Application
MIDlet-Version: 0.1
MIDlet-Vendor: David H. Young and Sams Publishing
MIDlet-Description: Demo of SFA Floor App and J2ME
```

```
MicroEdition-Profile: MIDP-1.0
MicroEdition-Configuration: CLDC-1.0
Connection-address: tcp://0.0.0.0:3369/
MIDlet-1: FloorApp,com.otterpod.sfa.floorApp
```

Can I Download a J2ME Application Over the Net?

You might assume that a J2ME specification would address wireless installation of J2ME midlets. However, this is a topic that currently the handset industry has yet to deal with. Application loaders are a typical offering from vendors such as Motorola and Nextel.

Having said that, *wireless provisioning* is the proposed new buzz phrase that addresses how MIDp applications are distributed to wireless devices. A Sun Java Community Process (JCP) MIDP expert group called JSR 37, "Mobile Information Device Profile for the J2ME Platform," is in the process of addressing wireless provisioning. "Over-the-Air User Initiated Provisioning for Mobile Information Device Profile," is a JSR 37 document that describes how provisioning works.

For a complete description and implementation of the FloorAdmin application, be sure to refer to the CD.

Flash

We're all familiar with Flash graphics and animation. Like any tool, in the right hands it can add excellent value to Web sites. However, we've also seen examples of how it can be used to turn any Web site into something ponderous and overwhelming.

But there's a new angle to Flash that makes it very interesting to application architects. With the release of Flash 5 came an embedded XML parser. This simple but powerful development promises to expand the role of Flash clients in any environment that requires client/server application development.

As with our J2ME discussion, XMLC now finds itself in the role of delivering application-specific XML protocols between the presentation layer of a Java application server and the XML parser on the client side.

Flash ActionScript

Another nice development with Flash 5 is the more JavaScript-like flavor of ActionScript, the Flash scripting language. ActionScript is what gives Flash its animation pizzazz, programmatically glueing Flash elements (graphics, animations, and audio) together in a non-linear fashion to make possible high-end, professional grade movies and user interactions.

Client-Server Development with J2ME and Flash
CHAPTER 12

363

12

CLIENT-SERVER
DEVELOPMENT
WITH J2ME AND
FLASH

With access to XML-formatted information from back office servers, ActionScript and Flash are capable of delivering real-time presentations and interactions, reducing the need to deploy new Flash applications.

Let's take a brief introductory look at how XML parsing is accomplished from ActionScript.

First of all, let's look at an application-specific XML dialect, incorporating its DTD in file, that is generated by XMLC to literally deliver the news to a Flash application:

```
<?xml version="1.0"?>
<!DOCTYPE sfanews [
<!ELEMENT eFolks (newsitem+)>
<!ELEMENT newsitem (title,story)>
<!ELEMENT title (#PCDATA)>
<!ELEMENT story (#PCDATA)>
]>
<sfanews>
 <newsitem id="newsitem">
  <title id="title">IBM announces Web Services!></title>
  <story id="story">IBM has made Web Services available as... </story>
 </newsitem>
 <newsitem class="mockup">
  <title>Microsoft announces Web Services!></title>
  <story>Microsoft has made Web Services available as... </story>
 </newsitem>
</sfanews>
```

This XML file is compiled into a DOM template, updated with current news by the servlet or presentation object using XMLC access methods (for example, `getNewsitemElement()`, `setTextTitle()`, or `setTextStory()`).

On the client side, ActionScript has the capability to request the news feed from the server's presentation servlet. This can be done with a Flash timer event or the release of a button. Let's assume that an SFA visitor is pushing an Update News button at a kiosk on the show floor. The Flash *frame* (as in a series of frames that represents a movie) that is associated with the button executes the ActionScript:

```
on (release) {
  gotoAndPlay (2)
}
```

The (2) refers to a second frame that contains the following script, responsible for fetching the news feed:

```
newsXML = new XML();
newsXML.load("http://www.otterpod.com/SFA/newsfeed.po");
display= "Stand by for News!..."
newsxML.onload = extractNews;
```

This script sets the stage for invoking the ActionScript function `extractNews` to process the XML after it is fully loaded from `newsfeed.po`. `XML()` is the constructor object. `newsMXL` is the object that stores the XML data. `onload` indicates the method to call when loading is complete.

The variable `display` is associated with a text field on the Flash screen, keeping the user informed. The `extractNews` function is located in the same frame:

```
function extractNews() {
 rootNode = new XML();
 newsList = new Array();
 rootNode = this.lastChild;
 newsList = rootNode.childNodes;
..for (i=1; i<=newsList.length; i += 2> {
  display += newsList[i];
 }
}
```

This tight little script grabs each news item and delivers it to the Flash movie. `rootNode`, as it implies, is allocated to store the root node of the document. The root node is found by using the last child's node name. That's because the closing tag's element name, `</newsitem>`, is the same as its matching element `<newsitem>`. Therefore,

```
rootNode = this.lastChild
```

does the trick. Now we can add the child nodes to the array with

```
newsList = rootNode.childNodes;
```

The preceding loop then extracts the array's elements to identify the child nodes (`<title>` and `<story>`) of each `<newsitem>` element. Again, the variable `display` is the pipeline back to the Flash movie into which the contents of the news items are dumped.

A nice implementation feature of the Flash XML parser is that it runs in its own thread. Other user interactions or timed events can go their own way while other parts of Flash can periodically or spontaneously fetch updated news information.

Here's a quick review of the key methods for integrating Flash with an XMLC-driven application:

- `XML.send`—Sends the XML object back to a URL. The response is displayed in the browser window.

- `XML.load`—Downloads XML from a URL, placing the content in an ActionScript XML object.

- `XML.sendAndLoad`—This method is key to developing a two-way protocol connection with an application server. It sends the XML object back to a specified URL, such as `processVisitorResponse.po`, or any standard servlet that might also be powered by

XMLC. The response that comes back from the servlet is stored in an ActionScript XML object to determine the success of the exchange.

Keep an eye on Flash. Macromedia is now working with PDA and other handset makers to support Flash on mobile devices. In some ways, it's easier to use Flash than J2ME, thanks in large part to its excellent design studio tools, an area where J2ME has much catching up to do.

Dynamic Graphics with SVG and XMLC

Have you ever tried making a dynamic graph with an HTML table, manipulating its width, height, and color attributes, wishing you didn't have to resort to such a kludge? There is now a new W3C-standard XML language for generating high-end graphics.

Scalar Vector Graphics (SVG), is a language for generating rich, two-dimensional graphical content. Because it is written in XML, SVG content can be generated from server-side sources of real-time information, such as diagnostics or e-commerce statistics.

SVG supports three types of graphic objects:

- Vector graphic shapes (for example, path of lines and curves)
- Images
- Text

SVG then gives you the capability to manipulate all these objects, changing their attributes color, stroke, and so on, as well as performing high-end transformations, such as rotation.

It's also possible to build SVG presentations that are interactive and highly dynamic. The interactive side is best driven by JavaScript extensions of the SVG language. For the dynamic side, we want to use Enhydra XMLC.

One project that makes extensive use of the client-side, dynamic portion of SVG is Batik, an open source Apache project hosted from `xml.apache.org/batik`. This project is developing a set of modules that can be mixed and matched to provide SVG solutions using Java. Sample modules are SVG parsers, SVG generators, and SVG DOM implementations.

The W3G folks have included an extensive SVG DOM API extension. As of this writing, however, there is no Enhydra XMLC implementation. However, as we demonstrated with VoiceXML, there's nothing to stop us from taking advantage of the `id` attribute and the use of a few low-level DOM APIs to build incorporated SVG elements into our SFA application. The most recent release of the SVG specification, including DTD and DOM API descriptions, can be found at `http://www.w3.org/TR/2001/REC-SVG-20010904/`.

To demonstrate an extremely simple use of SVG, we'll build a simple graph generator presentation, illustrating how XMLC and SVG can be used to create compelling, data-driven dynamic graphs. But first, let's review a subset of the SVG language.

SVG Versus Raster Images

There are at least two views of how graphical images can be described. One is the world of raster formats, represented by JPEG, GIF, and PNG. These are "as-is" graphics, describing every pixel of the graphic. When you zoom in on a raster image, you soon see a distortion effect often referred to as *pixelation* caused by the fact that a raster image can't react or adjust to the changes in the rendering landscape.

Vector graphics, on the other hand, represent a descriptive language where objects are represented by the paths of lines and curves. Additional information describes their relative orientation, making it simple for these objects to "react" in a zoom condition in order to present themselves accurately at closer inspection. *Scalar* refers to their ability to scale. A handy feature of vector graphics and SVG is that you can incorporate raster images when the need arises.

SVG has the ability to turn mundane HTML development into something very interesting with Enhydra XMLC. There are many aspects of SVG that make it a useful component when designers and developers sit down to consider presentation strategies:

- An SVG graphic is stored as text-based instructions, all of which are interpreted at the time it is rendered. Because it's text-based, it's editable!
- It's a Web-tailored technology.
- It's easy to localize. Even a string embedded in a graphic can be programmatically updated from English to German.
- Tools like Adobe Illustrator generate SVG output, making it easy to create high-end graphics, save them as SVG, insert `ids`, compile it into a DOM template, then manipulate it as an Enhydra presentation.
- It's vastly more scalable in terms of resolution quality, as compared to bitmap images that have no adaptive capability. This makes SVG applicable to all sizes of devices. It also takes up less bandwidth as compared to bitmap images when transferred by HTTP to a client.

Perhaps the most exciting potential of SVG is that, as an XML language, it will integrate seamlessly with other XML languages, including HTML.

Let's take a quick look at SVG, then we'll describe some of the more common, useful elements:

```
<!DOCTYPE svg PUBLIC "-//W3C//DTD SVG 1.0//EN"
    "http://www.w3.org/TR/2001/PR-SVG-20010719/
    DTD/svg10.dtd">
<svg width="300" height="200">
<rect x="0" y="0" width="20" height="40" style="fill:blue;stroke:green;"/>
</svg>
```

The preceding SVG XML defines a 300x200 pixel canvas with the `<svg>` element. On that canvas, it draws a rectangle with the dimensions and style specified in the `<rect>` element. The rectangle is filled with blue and its outside path is outlined by a green-colored stroke.

Normally, colors are specified in hexadecimal. However, SVG also recognizes 128 pre-defined color names.

A Quick Introduction to the SVG Language

Let's review some representative elements of the SVG language, listed in Table 12.1. You'll need only a small portion of the language to achieve the generation of some pretty impressive graphics.

TABLE 12.1   Selected SVG Elements

Element or Attribute	Description
`<svg>`	This is the base element that establishes the initial viewport. You define the initial height and width of the SVG image.
`<g>`	Used for grouping several `<svg>` elements, `<g>` is used to transform the objects it contains, changing their rotation, shape, size, and position.
`<desc>`	This is a handy, non-displayable element for describing the objects in the file.
`<defs>`	Use this element for code re-use by grouping one or more graphics elements that can then be referenced one or more times from other parts of the document.
`<use>`	This element is used to reference a `<symbol>`, `<g>`, `<svg>`, `<rect>`, `<line>` or other elements defined elsewhere in the document. `<use>` references each of these by their id attribute.
`<image>`	This element references bitmap graphics files, such as PNG, GIF, or JPEG. Also used for importing other files of type `text/xml+svg`.
viewbox	This is not an element, but an attribute of `<svg>`. viewbox provides a view on the infinite size of the SVG canvas. The first pair of x, y coordinates indicates the upper-left corner of the view box; the second pair defines the lower-right corner.

A Demo Report Generator

We've covered a small portion of the SVG elements and their capabilities. We're now going to create a small demonstration application using `<svg>` and `<rect>` for describing rectangles.

Recall that in Chapter 11, "Wireless Markup Presentations," we discussed the mySFA application that gave subscribers the capability to enter notes on a per-vendor basis, which they could later retrieve by voice or phone. The Vendor Interest report will generate a bar chart that indicates the number of notes entered per vendor, suggesting to a vendor how they did in terms of general interest in their presence at the show.

The Vendor Interest report is composed of two presentation objects. The first, `ReportPresentation.po`, dynamically generates the hosting HTML content. It refers to the second presentation object, `TableReport.po`, using the HTML `<object>` element.

Listing 12.5 shows how we're using an HTML table to host the SVG graphic, integrated into the HTML document using the `<object>` element.

LISTING 12.5   Report.html

```html
<html>
<body>
<p>Welcome to the "Vendor Interest" report. This report
graphically displays the amount of interest in each vendor
based on the number of notes entered by mySFA subscribers.
<p>Of the <span id="VendorTotal">100</span> vendors participating
in the show, there were an average of <span id="AverageNotesEntered">
10</span> notes entered by subscribers.
<p>
<table border=5>
<tr>
<td>
<object width="200" height="100"
data="http://localhost:9000/ex6/TableReport.po"
type="image/svg+xml">
To view this graphical report, you must download an SVG Viewer.
You can find one at <a href="http://www.adobe.com/svg/">Adobe</a>.
</object>
</td>
</tr>
</table>
</body>
</html>
```

The SVG template that we've created to represent a bar graph is listed in Listing 12.6. The <svg> element defines the overall dimensions of the graphic. A rectangle element is used to represent a bar, which is accompanied by a vendor name in alignment with the bar at the far right.

LISTING 12.6 TableReport.svg

```
<?xml version="1.0" encoding="iso-8859-1"?>
<!DOCTYPE svg PUBLIC "-//W3C//DTD SVG 20000303 Stylable//EN"
➡  "http://www.w3.org/TR/2000/03/WD-SVG-20000303/DTD/svg-20000303
➡-stylable.dtd">
<svg width="300" height="200">
  <rect id="meterTemplate" x="0" y="0" width="80" height="16"
➡style="fill:orange;stroke:none;"/>
  <text id="vendorName" x="85" y="12" style="fill:black">
Vendor A</text>
</svg>
```

TableReport.java is the presentation object that will manipulate the SVG template, adding new bars for each vendor included in the report. Shown in Listing 12.7, we'll generate four bars using hard-coded data. We've added a wrinkle to the application that renders the color of the bar in green or red, depending on whether the bar's value falls below or exceeds the arbitrarily chosen value of 40.

LISTING 12.7 TableReport.java

```
package examples.presentation.ex6;

import java.util.*;
import com.lutris.xml.xmlc.*;
import com.lutris.appserver.server.httpPresentation.*;
import org.w3c.dom.*;
import org.w3c.dom.html.*;

public class TableReport implements HttpPresentation {

  public static final String REDBAR = "fill:red;stroke:black";
  public static final String GREENBAR = "fill:green;stroke:black";
  public static final int VERTICAL_TEXT_PADDING = 12;
  public static final int VERTICAL_BAR_SPACING = 24;
  public static final int HORIZ_TEXT_SPACING = 5;

  public void run(HttpPresentationComms comms)
    throws HttpPresentationException {
```

LISTING 12.7 Continued

```java
// hardcoded values.
String vendors[] = {"Company A", "Company B", "Company C", "Company D"};
int vendorNoteCount[] = { 38, 80, 20, 44 };

TableReportHTML table =
  (TableReportHTML)comms.xmlcFactory.create(TableReportHTML.class);

//Retrieve DOM locations from the xmlc-generated accessor methods.
Element rect = table.getElementMeterTemplate();
Element textElem = table.getElementVendorName();

Node parent = rect.getParentNode();

int verticalSpacing = 0;
int vspace = 0;

for (int i = 0; i < vendors.length; i++) {
  //Deal with the <rect> element template first.
  //x=0 always... to start from left margin.
  //y=<vertical amount>
  rect.setAttribute("y","" + verticalSpacing);

  //width: length of bar.
  rect.setAttribute("width", "" + vendorNoteCount[i]);

  //Having some fun with color... 40 is an arbitrary value.
  rect.setAttribute("style",GREENBAR);
  if (vendorNoteCount[i] < 40) {
   rect.setAttribute("style",REDBAR);
  }

  //Now, let's deal with the Text Element.
  //The idea is to keep the text in line with the bar.
  table.setTextVendorName(vendors[i]);

  //x defines the horizontal...
  int s = vendorNoteCount[i] + HORIZ_TEXT_SPACING;
  textElem.setAttribute("x", "" + s);

  //y defines the vertical...
  vspace = verticalSpacing + VERTICAL_TEXT_PADDING;
  textElem.setAttribute("y", "" + vspace);
  verticalSpacing = verticalSpacing + VERTICAL_BAR_SPACING;
```

LISTING 12.7   Continued

```
      //remember. <rect> and <text> are peers, so you must
      //clone both of them.
      Node clone = rect.cloneNode(true);
      parent.appendChild(clone);
      clone = textElem.cloneNode(true);
      parent.appendChild(clone);
    }
    parent.removeChild(rect);
    parent.removeChild(textElem);

    //Because we're not using an SVG XMLC factory, we've got to
    //update the DOM with the correct MIME type.
    comms.response.setContentType("image/svg+xml");
    comms.response.writeDOM(table);
  }
}
```

As we've seen repeatedly, the algorithm for updating the DOM template representing the SVG graph is relatively straightforward. id attributes are defined in the SVG DTD, and therefore support XMLC's generation of accessor methods.

Because there is no make rule for SVG files, we've coerced Enhydra into simply treating the SVG file as an HTML file during XMLC compilation. Another more elegant route would have been to edit the Enhydra make file system with an SVG-specific build rule. Also, there is no SVG DOM factory, so we've updated the document's content type with a MIME of type svg+xml.

Figure 12.2 shows the results of our demonstration application.

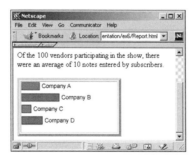

FIGURE 12.2
Report with dynamically-generated SVG graph.

You will need an SVG Viewer for your browser. There are multiple sources, including

- `http://www.adobe.com/svg/`
- `http://sis.cmis.csiro.au/svg/`
- `http://xml.apache.org/batik/dist`

The recognized SVG MIME types are `image/svg+xml`, `image/svg-xml`, and `image/svg`.

Summary

The goal of this chapter was to introduce a different role for XMLC development, using it to generate application-specific, XML-based protocols. Requiring an XML parsing and processing capability at both ends, the need for smart clients such as J2ME and Flash becomes very interesting, bringing to mind more traditional client/server application development.

Although the industry will determine whether J2ME is to achieve the acceptance of the rest of the Java 2 specifications, Flash has clearly become a common component of high-end Web sites. By adding XML parser support to Flash, Macromedia has put a new light on the role of Flash, and as Flash becomes more prevalent on PDAs, for example, an interesting smart client competition may emerge.

Wrapping up, we've thrown another technology into the mix. SVG is also something to watch. Vastly superior to bitmap graphics, SVG's scaling capability makes it an interesting candidate for supporting browser-based clients, in part because of its capability to scale to a wide range of presentation footprints with little loss in rendering quality. In general, when blended with HTML, its use makes for an interesting alternative to the reliance on the costly overhead of unwieldy raster graphics.

Barracuda Presentation Framework

IN THIS CHAPTER

It seems only fitting that this last chapter should address the probable next step in the evolution of Enhydra XMLC. Enhydra Barracuda is a presentation framework that goes further than XMLC to present a set of easy-to-use modules based on a component view of presentation development. Starting with the traditional view of client/server development tools, Barracuda builds on the fundamental value of XMLC to natively separate markup from Java logic to abstract away the low-level detail work of DOM manipulation.

The open source Barracuda project resides at Barracuda.enhydra.org, where it is chaired by its founder, Christian Cryder. Christian has defined the Barracuda framework to address six areas of common presentation needs, including forms validation, client-side properties, event-handling, and localization, as well as a component view for linking the Model portion of MVC directly to areas of the DOM template.

For developers of Swing (Java Foundation Class), Motif, or Windows user interfaces, the concepts of Barracuda development will look very familiar. There's no way to do justice to everything that Barracuda has to offer, so this chapter will do its best to bring out some of the key functional aspects of Barracuda development and how it simplifies the task of XMLC presentation programming.

> **NOTE**
>
> This was probably the easiest chapter to write, thanks to the incredibly complete repository of online documents, including tutorials, javadoc, and FAQs located in the documentation section of Barracuda.enhydra.org. In fact, it became a little intimidating as I realized that I could never do justice to Barracuda in attempting to present it comprehensively. Therefore, I hope this chapter serves to pique the reader's interest and at least convey the essence of what Barracuda is about and how it picks up where XMLC leaves off.

XMLC: Where the Value Is

XMLC makes no excuses for its low-level approach to supporting presentation development. It is a simple, elegant approach to ensure complete separation of logic and content. With a low-level approach, there is great flexibility. You have many options for a basic presentation architecture. If your application requires support for multiple XML languages representing many display devices, then XMLC is a solid option.

XMLC does not provide a lot of task-insulating abstraction, except that provided by the accessor methods, the implemented DOM sub-interfaces (for example, HTML and WML), and some of the methods in the XMLCUtil class.

As a by-product of its simplicity, XMLC requires that you roll up your sleeves and think out a number of issues, depending on the complexity and project goals of your Web application. Another way of looking at this is that XMLC, by virtue of its relatively policy-thin approach to presentation development, makes an excellent platform upon which to build real presentation frameworks that solve specific problems.

Its simplicity also makes it an excellent platform for the collection of *best practices* often discussed in the XMLC development community. Web site creation can be achieved in a multitude of ways. Best practices reflect the approaches that seem to pay off in the long run, reflecting, for example, minimal cost of long-term maintenance. Some best practices make sense at one stage of evolution, but lose favor over time as technology changes or the dimensions of the challenge change. JSP made more sense when Web site building projects were constructed primarily by programmers who knew enough HTML and graphics creation to get the job done. Today's Web building standard requires a cleaner separation of roles, supporting the best talent possible. Some believe that JSP is not necessarily the best practice in this modern model.

XMLC is an enabling platform. By virtue of its elegant approach to bridging logic and content, it sets the stage for presentation frameworks to be built upon it. And it establishes a fundamental philosophy of disallowing the intermixing of Java and markup. Any future presentation framework that builds on XMLC—whether it's an open standard or an in-house developed enterprise standard—by definition will support the same demarcation between Java and markup.

So, other than expose the low-level DOM APIs every now and then, where does XMLC punt and leave the rest to the presentation architect?

- XMLC defines no server-side event mechanism.
- A localization strategy is up to you.
- There is no standard mechanism for handling forms and server-side validation of forms.

There are tens of thousands of Visual Basic developers out there, just getting their arms around Java. Is it really necessary to become a DOM expert to take advantage of XMLC development?

A Presentation Framework for XMLC

Presentation frameworks are higher-level technologies that sit on top of presentation technologies such as JSP. They present a layer of abstraction that simplifies the many tasks that involve the management and generation of the presentation lifecycle. In the Web application world, this lifecycle is the request-response activity of displaying and responding to the activity of a page display.

Barracuda is a comprehensive presentation framework that offloads and standardizes the chore of developing Web presentations. It is a collection of features that will be recognized by anyone who has performed presentation development as extremely useful when it comes to solving typical presentation building tasks. Barracuda is the best candidate going to make XMLC a possibility for all those Visual Basic developers making the transition to Java and Web development.

The Barracuda framework is cleverly structured to integrate the multiple capabilities of event handling, form validation, and so on. At the same time, Barracuda is a framework of loosely coupled capabilities, none of which require the other or the overall framework. For those who want the complete set of framework features, Barracuda provides a unified environment. For those who are simply looking for assistance in only a subset of what Barracuda provides, they can simply choose to use, for example, the localization portion of the Barracuda framework.

The basic personality of Barracuda is based on a strongly-typed component view of presentation elements. More specifically, it takes a component view of the data that is stored in a DOM template, lifting the definitions of those components from well-known GUI building technologies such as Swing or Motif. Barracuda then wraps this component view with vital services represented as a set of classes that do everything from automatically detecting the device type of the client, to validating input data and then generating a response that is localized to the client's native language with the flip of a switch.

In selecting a component model for implementing presentations, Barracuda not only abstracts away much of the cumbersome and intimidating nature of DOM programming, but it also benefits the developer by relying on concepts that are well-known in the presentation industry.

Barracuda and MVC

All discussions about presentation frameworks must at some point describe their particular implementation of the Model-View-Controller design pattern, introduced earlier in Chapter 3, "Presentation Technologies." Quickly reviewing its division of presentation-building labor, the MVC architecture describes:

- A Model that represents application data or state,
- The View that processes, formats and renders the display of the Model, and
- The Controller that is responsible for taking user/client input and updating the Model.

A number of presentation frameworks build on top of presentation technologies according to MVC2, or Model 2. This includes Apache's Struts, built on top of JSP. Model 2 is a variant of MVC that describes how an HTTP request is processed by a Controller. The Controller updates the server state representing the Model, then forwards control to something else that extracts data from the Model and generates an HTTP response as a View in the form of updated markup. Describing MVC this way is so generic that you can apply just about any presentation technology and say that it follows the MVC model.

Flow Versus Components

If you've spent some time applying the MVC model to different presentation technologies and frameworks, you've probably realized that you can interpret just about any presentation technology as following the MVC architecture. In fact, you may have observed in Chapter 3, "Presentation Technologies," that I chose not to try to cast XMLC in the MVC model. Shoehorning any technology into a model adds little value to the reader.

The Model 2 interpretation of MVC focuses on application flow, and the roles and interaction of MVC components. As a result, it's relatively easy to describe a flow that incorporates processing and decision making (Controller), data (Model), and presentation (View).

Barracuda builds on a different interpretation of MVC, following the Java Foundation Classes, or Swing, more closely. Barracuda and Swing both address the components that represent well-defined Model and View interfaces. Swing and Barracuda do differ in the "accent" they place on MVC components, as you might expect from the client-thin browser environment as compared with a client-side Java, thick-client environment.

Applying a GUI Abstraction

To those of us from the world of Motif, Windows, and other GUI libraries, Web presentations come as a bit of a shock. As we discussed earlier, user interfaces dominated by 3270-style terminal forms are not the sexiest things in the world.

Barracuda is the mapping of many of the approaches to GUI building popularized by Motif and the Java Foundation Class' Swing. These and other GUI libraries take advantage of a component view of GUI elements. In true object-oriented fashion, a component, such as a button, is responsible for painting or rendering itself. Its behavior or appearance is modified by the adjustment of a published attribute, and it uses *callbacks* to activate areas of logic that were registered during development. A callback can be linked with the push of a button, or the release of that same button.

A Component View of the DOM Template

Let's address how these visual components map to the Barracuda and DOM world. Simply put, Barracuda puts a component face on top of the DOM. Individual components map, or *bind*, to different areas of the DOM. And the developer interacts with the DOM only by going through the components.

Rendering a page in an HTTP world takes on an expanded meaning. When a Barracuda component is instructed to render itself in a View, it extracts data from the Model and places it into the portion of the DOM tree for which it is responsible. The component is smart about the care and feeding of the entity and data that it represents, such as an ordered list, or a table. For example, if it's a list component, it will clear out any dummy data that remains in the DOM template.

As we'll discuss later, Barracuda introduces the notion of *directives*. These are keys, represented as class attribute values, embedded in nodes of the DOM template that are put there to influence the component's behavior in fetching data from the Model.

Layout by DOM

A view is what a component renders itself in, such as an HTML document. `render()` is analogous to the `paint()` method in standard GUI programming. A component knows everything there is to know about how it represents the data as a list, option menu, and so on.

Components give us a view of the DOM, but it's the DOM template that actually represents the layout of the document that will eventually be returned to the client.

The component is responsible for taking data from the model and inserting into the DOM. This process makes it a lot easier to deal with complex DOM structures and the operations that populate them with live data.

A Collection of Capabilities

Barracuda is more than a component view of creating Web presentations. One of its more intriguing aspects is the modular nature of the packaging of the complete Barracuda solution.

Barracuda was designed to fulfill a set of commonly needed runtime capabilities that reduce the need for low-level architecture definition and development. Figure 13.1 generalizes the places where Barracuda offers support during the round trip of an HTTP request and subsequent response.

Generally speaking, Barracuda handles both sides of the HTTP equation where common tasks are to be found, including figuring out the client type, generating events in response to decomposing the request, and validating the data that arrives from the client. Assisting the developer with gathering data from the model representing application state or data from a database, Barracuda leverages XMLC-generated DOM templates that are shrouded by a set of visual (and non-visual) components, such as buttons and lists.

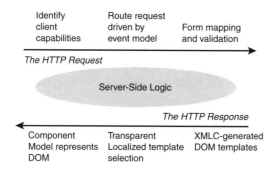

FIGURE 13.1

Functional roles of Barracuda development at runtime.

The value is that Barracuda defines a framework and a set of classes for accomplishing the following common issues:

- Client capability—Automatically detects the distinguishing characteristics of the request-originating client. Client traits include browser type, device type, and the preferred language.

- Event model—Maps client-side events to event objects on the server, which in turn update any interested listeners that have been registered.

- Form mapping and validation—Automatically maps form elements into Java objects that are delivered to a validation mechanism.

- Localization—Automatically generates DOM templates for supported locales, a process that is made transparent to the developer. Loading of the desired locale DOM is automatic.

- Component model—All updates to the manipulated DOM are done through a component view.

- XMLC—Barracuda is built on top of XMLC. XMLC's natural features and development philosophy of separating cleaning markup from markup-building logic are inherited by Barracuda.

There are features of Barracuda that go beyond the traditional component models. For example, Barracuda components differ from Swing components in that they are modeled after data, rather than the UI functionality associated with data. This means that you need only one Barracuda `textarea` component representing multiple areas of text in a DOM template. This is similar to the approach we took in the VendQuest questionnaire template.

> ### The Tackle Box Analogy
>
> Christian refers to Barracuda's "tackle box" approach to supporting a presentation framework. Rather than representing an all-or-nothing toolset, Barracuda's features are built with little to no interdependencies. This makes it easy for a developer to choose, for instance, to only use the localization portion of the framework for their needs. The tackle box analogy symbolizes the developer's ability to pick those services (or hooks/lures) that she needs.

Because most of the knowledge of the layout of the markup presentation is contained in the DOM's structure (as a template), Barracuda components are very lightweight, because they don't have to worry about placement issues.

Other differences include

- Pluggable renderers—Used by the developer to tell components how to render themselves in new user interface types, such as an i-mode phone or a kitchen device supported by a new XML language.
- BTemplate—A new style of component that gives the developer the ability to bind a template engine to a particular area of a DOM tree.
- Component framework—A linkage of components and the Barracuda event model that insulates the developer from having to deal with the facts of event client-side events that are linked with server-side listeners.

Barracuda Candy

Christian coined the term *Barracuda candy* to highlight the kind of features in Barracuda that earn a "wow" response from those evaluating Barracuda for the first time.

One of these features is the ability to detect whether JavaScript is actually enabled in the client without relying on cookies or session information. Another is the ability to disable the back button. Using a dynamic HTML in-page submit, this prevents a user from going backwards from a form when you don't want them to. Yet another is the scripting framework. There are not yet a lot of pre-canned scripts, but all the wiring is in place to be able to easily add scripts to the client markup programmatically.

Component Model

In traditional component models, the information required to structure and present the data to the user is kept in a single component hierarchy. The component hierarchy is represented by *geometry widgets* that organize the placement of the components that they contain. The contained components, such as a list widget, contain the items they will display to the user.

In a server-side component model like Barracuda, things are a little different. First, it's the DOM template that represents the structure and general layout of the presentation. That shouldn't be a great surprise if you've already read the first 12 chapters of this book. The roles of the components in the Barracuda model are to

1. Represent, through binding, the sub-templates within the DOM

2. Be responsible for the collection of data from the Model to be stored in the bound areas of the DOM

The relationship of the DOM's role and the component's role requires what Barracuda refers to as a *two phase rendering process*. There is no X-Windows or Windows Library on the client. There is only self-describing markup, and that markup's structure is organized by the DOM. And it's up to the components to present an easy-to-use abstraction of how data is managed within sections of that DOM.

Basic Barracuda Components

A presentation consists of a hierarchy of components. Each component is bound to portions of the DOM template. The components take care of rendering their associated data into the DOM template. Figure 13.2 represents the complete set of Barracuda components, how they're sub-classed from BComponent, and how some of them relate to one another.

BComponent defines a standard signature that is inherited by each child component. Most noteworthy, each component inherits its render() method from BComponent. The capability for components to be represented as a hierarchy is inherited from the BContainer interface.

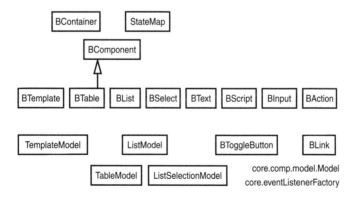

FIGURE 13.2

The complete set of Barracuda components, how they're subclassed from BComponent, *and how some of them relate to one another.*

Components have the following characteristics:

- They may be visual or non-visual.
- They do not adhere to a strict lifecycle. Developers may create and destroy them, or cache them away on a per-session basis.
- Some components offer event model integration. By adding an event handler, the server is automatically notified when a client event occurs.

Binding Components to a DOM

We've talked about binding, but what does it actually mean? Figure 13.3 illustrates the relationship of some HTML markup to the resulting tree of Barracuda components.

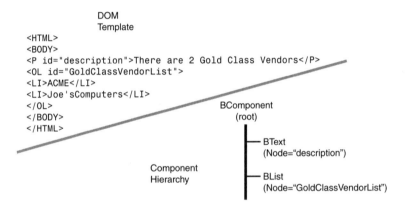

FIGURE 13.3

How an HTML template maps to hierarchical Barracuda components.

The upper left portion of Figure 13.3 represents a typical HTML page containing a paragraph followed by an ordered list. The following sequence of events take us from the loading of a DOM template to its delivery to the client:

1. The DOM template is loaded by the application.
2. The component hierarchy is created. Each component, with the exception of the parent component, is bound to a specific area (that is, node) of the DOM.
3. The parent component is asked to render itself. The parent, with no view of its own, cascades the render request to its child components.
4. The first component with a view, a Text component of type BText, simply updates the first text child it contains, that is, the content of the paragraph, with text information from the Model.

5. The next component, BList, bound to the ordered list, responds to the render request by first removing all the elements it contains (that is, li). It then queries the Model for a fresh set of data representing the gold class sponsor vendors, with which it then updates the sub-template to which it is bound.

6. The final rendering is to turn the DOM template into a client view, sent back to the client as HTML.

Table 13.1 introduces the collection of components as supported by Barracuda. Keep in mind that Barracuda can easily be extended to support custom components as well.

TABLE 13.1 Barracuda Component Descriptions

Component	Role
BInput	Manipulates HTML input element within the DOM.
BToggleButton	Manipulates HTML radio/check box input elements within the DOM.
BAction	Binds server-side event handlers to DOM elements. These elements generate events when rendered on the client (for example, buttons, links, and input elements).
BLink	Extends BAction in order to set text in the DOM, such as the name of a link.
BText	Binds text string into a DOM node.
BTable	Generates a table structure within the DOM.
BList	Generates a list structure in the DOM.
BSelect	Manipulates a select element in the DOM.
BTemplate	Treats the DOM as a template engine. Queries the model based on key values found in the template.

Example: VendorSpotlight

We're going to use Barracuda to implement a presentation that generates a simple Vendor Spotlight page that features a particular vendor and some information about them.

In this example, we'll focus on the use of

- The View
- The Model
- Barracuda directives

There's not a lot of presentation wizardry involved, other than importing a portion of one HTML template, as a header navigational bar, into the main template. The data will come from accessing a Model representing the data source (of hard-coded strings). After we discuss how to get the application up and running, we'll review the details regarding how Barracuda does its stuff.

Configuration

You take the following steps to use Enhydra AppWizard to establish a standard servlet Web application to build from. After typing `appwizard`, select Web Application as the application type, and have the source tree implement the familiar Welcome stub application. Then take the following steps:

1. Rename `WelcomeServlet.java` to `VendorSpotlightServlet.java` in `/presentation`.
2. Rename `Welcome.html` to `VendorSpotlight.html` in `/resources`.
3. Change all references of `Welcome` to `VendorSpotlight` in the `make` file in `/presentation`.

So far, all you've done is deal with filenames and references to them from the `make` files. Now you need to introduce the Barracuda 1.0 environment into the equation. The two jar files you'll need are seen here:

- `barracuda-core.jar`
- `log4j.jar`

These two jar files contain all the components you need to take advantage of the Barracuda features discussed in this chapter.

HTML and Directives

The target HTML template is displayed in Listing 13.1. Prepare to take yourself out of the XMLC mindset, and take a look at a new use for `id` and `class` attributes.

First of all, the familiar looking use of an `id` attribute, `id="VendorSpotlight"`, indicates the top of the HTML document. This will be used by Barracuda to eventually bind the document to its DOM template representation.

LISTING 13.1   `VendorSpotlight.html`

```
<html id="VendorSpotlight">
<head><title class="Dir::Get_Data.VendorSpotlight.Title">Mock Title</title>
➥</head>
<body style="font-family: Georgia, Arial, Times New Roman" bgcolor="#FFFFFF">

<h2 class="Dir::Get_Data.VendorSpotlight.Vendor">Mock Vendor Name</h2>
 <ul>
<li class="Dir::Get_Data.VendorSpotlight.Descr">Mock Short Description</li>
<li class="Dir::Get_Data.VendorSpotlight.Country">Mock Country</li></ul>
```

LISTING 13.1   Continued

```
</body>
</html>
```

In the areas where dynamic content is identified, you use a `class` attribute to indicate a Barracuda directive that will be used by the application to find the Model that will populate it with content. The process is very similar to the use of XMLC's `id` attributes, only instead of generating convenient accessor methods, you're going to work with a keyword table. More in the next section.

The Presentation Logic (Using `BTemplate`)

It takes awhile to figure out how `VendorSpotlightServlet` is different than the typical `doGet()` servlet. Listing 13.1 is the complete presentation logic that implements `VendorSpotlight`. Rather than use element-specific components, such as `BList` or `BTable`, we will use the generic `BTemplate` component.

As with all the other "B" components, `BTemplate` is derived from the `BComponent` class. It therefore inherits the `render()` method, which will stimulate it to gather data from the Model. As a kind of generic component, `BTemplate` appears to be very handy when generating pages such as reports. Rather than having specific knowledge about how to do the housekeeping of a particular element, such as a table, as `BTable` does, `BTemplate` focuses on the use of directives that are used to tell the component where to fetch data from the model. The generic nature of this component makes it a natural for introducing Barracuda programming.

Listing 13.2 fully implements the `VendorSpotlight` application. Its resulting presentation is shown in Figure 13.4.

FIGURE 13.4
Presentation of the VendorSpotlight application.

LISTING 13.2 VendorSpotlightServlet.java

```java
package example.presentation;

import java.util.*;
import javax.servlet.*;
import javax.servlet.http.*;

import org.w3c.dom.*;
import org.enhydra.xml.xmlc.*;

import org.enhydra.barracuda.core.comp.*;
import org.enhydra.barracuda.core.comp.helper.*;

public class VendorSpotlightServlet extends ComponentGateway {

  // xmlc factory (ok as static because its threadsafe)
  private static XMLCFactory xmlcFactory = null;

  // Handle the default HttpRequest.
  public Document handleDefault (BComponent root,
   ViewContext vc, HttpServletRequest req,
   HttpServletResponse resp) {

   // Load the DOM template object.
   if (xmlcFactory==null) {
    xmlcFactory = new XMLCStdFactory(this.getClass().getClassLoader(),
      new StreamXMLCLogger());
   }
   XMLObject page = xmlcFactory.create(VendorSpotlightHTML.class);

   //Find the topmost node in the parent document.
   Node node = page.getDocument().getElementById("VendorSpotlight");

   // Create a view on that node.
   TemplateView tv = new DefaultTemplateView(node);

   // Create the component and bind it to the view and the model
   BTemplate templateComp = new BTemplate(tv);

   templateComp.addModel(new VendorSpotNavBarModel());
   templateComp.addModel(new VendorSpotlightModel());

   //add the component to the root
   root.addChild(templateComp);

   //return the page
   return page;
```

LISTING 13.2   Continued

```
}


// VendorSpotlightModel
//Here is where we fetch data from the Model, using the
//directives to indicate which data goes where.
class VendorSpotlightModel extends AbstractTemplateModel {

  public String getName() {
   return "VendorSpotlight";
  }

  // Provide items by key.
  // We're obviously hardcoding the results we could fetch
  // from an EJB, data (JDBC) object.
  public Object getItem(String key) {
   ViewContext vc = getViewContext();
   if (key.equals("Vendor")) return "ACME Corporation";
   else if (key.equals("Title")) return "Vendor Spotlight";
   else if (key.equals("Descr")) return "Just two guys in a garage.";
   else if (key.equals("Country")) return "United States";
   else if (key.equals("NavBar")) {
     // Grab the other HTML DOM template.
     XMLObject navbar = xmlcFactory.create(NavBarHTML.class);
     // Get to the element containing the table.
     Node navbarNode = navbar.getElementById("NavBar");
     Document doc = vc.getElementFactory().getDocument();
     return doc.importNode(navbarNode, true);
     } else return "Error";
  }
}

class VendorSpotNavBarModel extends AbstractTemplateModel {

  public String getName() {
   return "VendorSpotNavBar";
  }

  public Object getItem(String key) {
   ViewContext vc = getViewContext();
   if (key.equals("PrevVendorLink")) return "previous vendor";
   else if (key.equals("NextVendorLink")) return "next vendor";
   else return "Error";
  }
 }
}
```

Walking through Listing 13.2, the first noteworthy item is that `VendorSpotlightServlet` is defined as a subclass of Barracuda's `ComponentGateway`. Barracuda declares `ComponentGateway` as follows:

```
public abstract class ComponentGateway
  extends javax.servlet.http.HttpServlet
```

As an extension of `HttpServlet`, `ComponentGateway` is the handshake between Barracuda and the servlet environment. `HandleDefault()` is the entry point into the servlet. `ComponentGateway` overrides the standard `doGet()`, mapping the GET request to `HandleDefault()`.

With the DOM template, `VendorSpotlightHTML.class`, generated earlier from the HTML source in Listing 13.1 by XMLC, the application locates the top of the template from which all binding (of components to the DOM) will occur.

The DOM is decomposed by `DefaultTemplateView()` into Barracuda classes in preparation for accessing the directives, extracted from the DOM tree, and the tree as a whole. Directives are parsed and stored in a Barracuda package `StateMap` class as representing key-value pairs.

Accessing the Model Using Directives

Now that the template View has been prepped, you're now ready to access the Model. This is where we see the role the component takes to control (and therefore simplify) how data is extracted from the model and inserted into the DOM.

Note that we're actually working with two Models. The first is the Model that addresses the `VendorSpotlight.html` page. This will be the focus of our discussion for now. We'll get to the other Model, represented by the `SpotlightNavBar.html`, later in this chapter.

The Model is always represented within a component in the form of an inner class. In the case of a `BTemplate` component, the inner class is a subclass of `AbstractTemplateModel`. `VendorSpotlightModel()` is our example's inner class, representing the close binding of the model to the overall component.

Later on, we'll review the topic of Barracuda directives in greater detail. For now, let's touch on the topic of directives in order to briefly review the role of `VendorSpotlightModel()`. The Model is referenced from previously extracted keys that were introduced as class attributes in the HTML.

In `getItem()`, for each match encountered, data is returned from the Model of hard-coded strings. Looking at the HTML in Listing 13.1, you can see how directives are being used to populate specific elements with data from the model. For instance, the HTML fragment

```
<title class="Dir::Get_Data.VendorSpotlight.Title">Mock Title</title>
```

is telling `VendorSpotlightModel()` the name of the data, `Title` to replace its content, `Mock Title`. Not exactly an embedded programming language, but we'll get to that later.

Rendering the Model

At first glance, the logic of getItem() looks a little confusing. You might expect that it would be in a looping statement in order to establish a match with each directive. This can be explained by the tight relationship created by Barracuda of the act of rendering to accessing the model.

If you were to put a call to System.out.println() in front of each significant method call in VendorSpotlightServlet, then another call inside of getItem(), you might see the following:

```
vendorspotlight: inside vendorspotlight
vendorspotlight: picked up the dom template
vendorspotlight: creating a view with defaultTemplateView()
vendorspotlight: creating a model with VendorSpotlightModel()
vendorspotlight: creating a binding with BTemplate()
vendorspotlightmodel: key: Title
vendorspotlightmodel: key: Vendor
vendorspotlightmodel: key: Descr
vendorspotlightmodel: key: Country
vendorspotlightmodel: key: Vendor
```

We stated earlier that any component child of BComponent will be instructed to render itself when BComponent is rendered. Components inherit the render() method from the interface BContainer. The effect on our BTemplate component, representing the entire view of the document, is the invocation of getItem() five times, reflecting each of the directive-specified data bindings.

The notion of the role of render() reflects how Barracuda differs from its own modeling of the Swing component strategy. Although Swing rendering deals more with the actual creation and placement of UI components, Barracuda focuses more on the model extraction and its insertion into visual elements. Again, issues of placement are already addressed by virtue of the role of the DOM template.

More Than Strings

Extracting data from the model can be more than about returning strings. In fact, the Model can return any of the following three objects:

- Nodes
- BComponents
- Strings

In the case of the NavBar directive in Listing 13.2, our intent in VendorSpotlightModel() is to import a portion of another document, shown in Listing 13.3, that will serve as the navigational bar embedded in the top row of the table.

LISTING 13.3 NavBar.html

```
<html id="VendorSpotlight">
<link rel="stylesheet" href="media/sfa.css" type="text/css">

<body bgcolor="#FFFFFF" text="#000000">
<table id="NavBar" width="100" border="0" cellspacing="0" cellpadding="10">
 <tr>
  <td class="navDirs" align="left"> <a href="prevVendor.html"
➥class="Dir::Get_Data.VendorSpotNavBar.PrevVendorLink">Previous</a> </td>
  <td class="sfaTitle" align="center">
SFA
  </td>
  <td class="navDirs" align="right"> <a href="nextVendor.html"
➥class="Dir::Get_Data.VendorSpotNavBar.NextVendorLink">Next</a></td>
 </tr>
</table>
</body>
</html>
```

Having loaded the DOM template for this second document, `importNode()` is called to insert the extracted template into its new home:

```
XMLObject navbar = xmlcFactory.create(NavBarHTML.class);
Node navbarNode = navbar.getElementById("NavBar");
Document doc = vc.getElementFactory().getDocument();
return doc.importNode(navbarNode, true);
```

What we now have is a composite view consisting of the processed (or ready for processing) main template with inserted navigation bar, and a navigation bar that has been incorporated into the parent view, but whose directives have yet to be processed. It's now time to talk about our other Model processing method in Listing 13.2, `VendorSpotNavBarModel()`.

The `getItem()` call in `VendorSpotNavBarModel()` can now be invoked to get the directive keys `PrevVendorLink` and `NextVendorLink` that will update the `Prev` and `Next` hyperlinks. The following HTML fragment extracted from Listing 13.3 shows how the directive-naming convention uniquely identifies the `NavBar` markup using `VendorSpotNavBar` in the directive name:

```
<a href="prevVendor.html"
➥class="Dir::Get_Data.VendorSpotNavBar.PrevVendorLink">Previous</a>
```

For now, we're replacing the links with meaningless strings. You can take this example and extend it with real hyperlinks as well.

Summarizing

Summarizing what you just witnessed in our example is the construction of a composite view using the BTemplate component:

- A View is classified as something that has a one-to-one relationship with a DOM node. A view is bound to that node.
- Our example takes a special kind of view called a TemplateView, because we are accessing the DOM through the BTemplate class.
- Inner classes extending AbstractTemplateModel are defined to enable the component to bind View(s) to a Model.
- Directives can be used to extract strings or other markup from the model.

Directives

A typical challenge regarding how presentation strategies avoid creating yet another embedded language is "How do you minimize the Java code's pre-knowledge about the markup template that it's manipulating?" This is particularly important if your presentation code is setting out to support a range of devices.

One solution is to embed logic in the markup itself, playing a role in the generation of content dynamically. But then we're back to square one, putting a layer of JSP-isms on top of XMLC.

Barracuda directives are an attempt at being realistic and seeking a middle ground. Yes, as we've just seen, Barracuda directives influence the behavior of the code, but they do not represent code themselves. Instead, they're *smart classes* that are used to

- Identify markup with informative, structured keys for extracting values from the Model.
- Indicate markup that is to be replicated.

We have yet to address this second role of directives. Before we do so, let's more formally review directives. Directives take the form

```
Dir::<Directive Command`>.<Model>.<Keyword>
```

For example:

```
<option class="Dir::Get_Data:VendorSpotlight.Vendor">ACME</option>
```

This naming convention does a pretty good job of preventing name space collision within the same application. The use of the getName() method, as required by the AbstractTemplateModel class, is used by Barracuda to find the directives that match the Model representation. In the NavBar case, it was VendorSpotNavBar.

The directives supported by Barracuda, as defined in the `TemplateDirective` class, are

- `Get_Data::.<model>.<key>`
- `Set_Attr::.<model>.<key>.<attr>`

`Get_Data` is for specifying a model based on a key and placing it into the content of the document. `Set_Attr` is used when it's an attribute that is to be updated from the Model, such as an `alt` attribute.

The directives for iteration are

- `Iterate_Start.<model>`
- `Iterate_Next.<model>`
- `Iterate_End.<model>`

`Iterate_Next` asks the model for the next record if it exists.

And then there is

- `Discard`

for discarding the element altogether.

The Barracuda folks maintain that this is as far as directives will ever go, avoiding the path taken by embedded languages. Read their lips: No conditional tests—although the door is left wide open for those interested in creating custom directives:

`(Dir::<command>.<model>.<key>.<attr>)`.

Building Directive Iterations

Iteratives are used to fetch batches of data to build up a portion of the DOM template, such as a list or a table or rows. How you implement the Model's support for iteratives is up to the details of your Model, but Barracuda provides the interface definition that you must implement. `IterativeModel` is described here:

```
public interface IterativeModel {
  public void preIterate();
  public void postIterate();
  public boolean hasNext();
  public void loadNext();
}
```

This interface defines four key methods that enable the component to iterate through the model's data:

- `preIterate()`—The model uses this method to prepare the scene for iteration. It is called when the component begins to process a data series. Typically used to set a counter variable.
- `hasNext()`—The component tests the Model to see whether new data remains. This typically tests a counter.
- `loadNext()`—The component calls this method to grab the next data item. It could be a counter increment for extracting data from an array of data.
- `postIterate()`—This method is called when the iteration is complete and needs to perform cleanup.

Suppose we have a Model called `VendorListModel`, representing a list of vendors. By implementing these methods, the `BTemplate` component can iterate through the data in the `VendorListModel`. Every time it requests a specific key, the model just returns the value from the current row of data. In our example, only one key is used, `VendorName`:

```
<ol id="VendorList">
<li class="Dir::Iterate_Start.VendorList Dir::Iterate_Next.VendorList"><span
➥class="Dir::Get_Data.VendorList.VendorName">ACME</span> </li>
<li class="Dir::Iterate_End.VendorList Dir::Discard">IBM</li>
<li class="Dir::Discard">Apple</li>
</ol>
```

As you can see, `Discard` directives can be used to mimic one of the key attributes of XMLC, which is to remove mocked-up content. And, like XMLC, the use of attributes removes the need to rely on introducing new `element` tags.

That wraps up our discussion of how you can use the `BTemplate` component to take advantage of one of Barracuda's more interesting features, directives.

Localization

Localization is getting hot. The world is shrinking, thanks in large part to the pervasive nature of the Internet. Once delegated to the second- or third-tier application requirements, along with security features, localization is now a first-tier consideration because of the direct influence of the international worldwide open source community.

Those who created the first two or three versions of their product are now ready to move to other countries with their next generation product. Barracuda greatly simplifies the task of localization by defining both an application configuration architecture and reasonably high-level API abstractions.

Some Localization Strategies

As we briefly discussed in Chapter 9, "Presentation Strategies," there are some straightforward options for achieving localized versions of each Web page. One is to put `id` attributes in every place where text occurs and replace them with their localized interpretations at runtime. This is a costly strategy in both developer effort and simple runtime processing.

Another option is to localize the textual portions of the template, and then, based on the locale of the target, load the appropriate template. Although this has a number of advantages, including minimizing the impact on the locale-aware Java logic that must be generated, it shifts the burden to maintain legions of markup pages. If you need to rework the basic template, you must rework them all. This is fine, if you like to hire lots of part-time high school students.

From pragmatic experience, particularly for those companies focusing on, for example, the European market, none of these options are very satisfactory.

To address the issue of localization in an architecturally satisfying way, Barracuda leverages the best of

- Ant
- Java resource bundles
- The XMLC template compilation

Java Resource Bundles

Part of the answer that Barracuda has designed lies in the native J2SE support for the mechanism of *resource bundles*. Resource bundles simplify the task of keeping locale-specific information and content separate from Java logic.

The naming convention of the properties file used by Barracuda for localized strings mimics the file naming convention used by standard Java resource bundling

```
baseclass + "_" + language + "_" + country + "_" + variant + ".properties"
```

where the `baseclass` is the "family name" and `language` is the locale. Each record in the properties file is considered a class:

```
VendorSpotlight_Canadian_French_Canadian.properties
```

XMLC Localization taskdef

Another component to how Barracuda addresses localization takes advantage of the Ant taskdef feature. Ant taskdefs are custom chores assigned to the Ant build process. Barracuda uses an XMLC taskdef to generate DOM templates using XMLC. For localization, Barracuda's XMLC taskdef is extended to set the stage for easing the chore of localization.

At this point, let's use `VendorSpotNavBar.html` to step through the details of how you move an application through the localization process. For the purpose of this illustration, we'll confine the localization to the navigation bar links, Previous and Next:

1. Create `VendorSpotNavBar.html`.

2. Create `VendorSpotNavBar.properties`, a standard Java properties file. This file isolates all the static text in `VendorSpotNavBar.html`. In our case, it's pretty darn simple because the only static strings are `"Previous"` and `"Next"`. Both keys must be unique:

   ```
   VendorSpotNavBar.Prev = "Previous"
   VendorSpotNavBar.Next = "Next"
   ```

3. Now for the localization step. Create properties files for each localization. The French flavor would reside in `VendorSpotNavBar_fr.properties`:

   ```
   VendorSpotNavBar.Prev = "Précédent"
   VendorSpotNavBar.Next = "Suvant"
   ```

   The `id` attributes are identical to the original properties file. The file is named according to the standard resource bundle naming conventions of: `_[language]_[country]_[variant]`. This convention applies to Java locales, so a properties file created for the dialect of French used in Canada would appear as: `VendorSpotNavBar_fr_ca.properties`

4. Finally, the Ant taskdef `xmlc_localization` detects the presence of the properties file. It then invokes the `xmlc` command to generate a DOM that is unique to the contents of the properties files. In this case, we now have a DOM with French content.

The result of our example is that we now have

- A new HTML file: `VendorSpotNavBar_fr.html`
- A new Java file: `VendorSpotNavBarHTML_fr.java`
- A new template file: `VendorSpotNavBarHTML_fr.class`

Matching Strings

One of the curious ways that Barracuda addresses the issue of associating each localized string with its proper place in the HTML markup is to rely on a perfect match of the string in the master properties file, `VendorSpotNavBar.properties`, with the target HTML file.

When a match is found, the properties object, such as `VendorSpotNavBar.Prev`, is assigned as an `id` attribute to the target HTML file. The taskdef then uses these `ids` to grab the values in the localized properties files in order to plug in the proper string value.

Loading Templates by Locale Using `ViewContext`

How does our logic now take advantage of all these localized DOM template classes? Barracuda takes care of that by providing the class `DefaultDOMLoader.java`. This class provides a mechanism to load a DOM object based on class name and locale in much the same manner that a Java resource bundle works.

The steps our code must take are as follows:

1. Determine the locale.

   This is accomplished with a method call to `getClientLocale()`, one of the many methods of the `ViewCapabilities` class for detecting the traits of the client. `ViewCapabilities` extracts the information it needs from `HTTPRequest`:

   ```
   ViewContext vc = getViewContext();
   Locale locale = vc.getViewCapabilities().getClientLocale();
   ```

   `ViewCapabilities` identifies the language, country, and variant codes passed through the `HttpRequest` object. If these values are missing, it will see whether the locale information has been cached in the session. If all else fails, it will default to the locale of the application's hosting server environment.

   Other methods of `ViewCapabilities` are listed in Table 13.2.

2. Now that we've got our target locale, we need to get our DOM object. We can usually do this with one line of code:

   ```
   XMLObject page = (XMLObject) DefaultDOMLoader.getGlobalInstance().
   ➡getDOM(VendorSpotNavBarHTML.class, locale);
   ```

   Using the `locale` value, `DefaultDOMLoader` will seek out a DOM template class with, for example, `_fr` appended to `VendorSpotNavBarHTML`, as in `VendorSpotNavBarHTML_fr.class`.

3. At this point, we're all set to use our `BTemplate` representing the DOM template. Clearly, other data requires localization, such as "two guys in a garage." One option is to populate the same properties files with these values, fetching them using the resource bundle `getBundle()` call to populate the Model.

In keeping with the Barracuda philosophy, this entire localization mechanism can be used independently of the other Barracuda features by XMLC developers.

TABLE 13.2 Other `ViewCapabilities` Methods

Method	Returned data
`getClientType()`	HTML_3x, HTML_4x, WML_1_2
`getFormatType()`	HTML, WML, XMLC
`getScriptingType()`	JavaScript, VBScript, WMLScript

Summary

We have covered but a small portion of Barracuda's overall set of capabilities to simplify the task of presentation development on top of XMLC.

Barracuda is a very interesting approach to a presentation framework, because it attempts to import the concepts of traditional client/server development to the Web application development space. In the process of doing this, it greatly simplifies what can be rather tedious tasks when implemented under XMLC. In the process of simplifying many tasks, Barracuda introduces a standard approach that greatly reduces the overall time required for presentation design and development.

Just as noteworthy is the architectural effort behind Barracuda to implement all its functional capabilities as tools that can be chosen from a menu. This eliminates the heavy-handed criticism from which other frameworks suffer. The bottom line is that Barracuda offers great value without throwing away the original value proposition of XMLC.

XMLC Command Line Options

IN THIS APPENDIX

This appendix lists all of the supported command line options for the xmlc command. For detailed examples of selected command options, refer to Chapter 7, "The xmlc Command."

From the command line, the xmlc command supports the following syntax:

```
xmlc [options] [options.xmlc ...] markup_file
```

xmlc Command Options

- -class <class>—Sets the fully qualified class name for the generated class or interface.

- -classpath <path>—javac pass-through option.

- -d <dir>—Specifies the destination directory for the class file. This option is passed on to javac.

- -delete-class <classname>—Deletes all HTML or XML elements that have a CLASS attribute with value <classname>. This is useful for removing mockup data. Note: This class name has nothing to do with a Java class. You can include multiple instances of this option.

- -docout <outfile>—Writes a static document to <outfile> instead of generating and compiling Java code. You can use this option for pages that have URLs that need mapping, but no dynamic content. It is also an excellent debugging option.

- -dom <DOMname>—Specifies the type of DOM to generate. The default behavior is the LazyDOM. Valid values are xerces and lazydom.

- -domfactory <classname>—Specifies the Java class for creating DTD-specific documents. This option is not supported for HTML input documents. The DOM factory must have a constructor that does not take any arguments. This class must implement the interface org.enhydra.xml.xmlc.dom.XMLCDomFactory and be on the CLASSPATH.

- -dump—Displays the contents of the DOM tree generated from the input markup document.

- -extends <classname>—Specifies the class that the generated document extends. This class must extend XMLObjectImpl for XML documents, extend HTMLObjectImpl for HTML documents, and be available on the CLASSPATH. The class is normally an abstract class.

- -for-recomp—Generates support for automatic class recompilation. The information is stored in a file with an .xmlc suffix appended to the class name, as specified with the -class option. Implies the -generate both option.

  The three files generated by -for-recomp are as follows:

  - <classname>.class—The interface definition;

  - <classname>Impl.class—The implementation of the interface; and

- `<classname>.xmlc`—The file of generated XMLC metadata for instructing subsequent recompilations of markup files during application execution.

The contents of `<classname>.xmlc` appear as follows, where the example input markup page was named `test.html`:

```
<?xml version="1.0" encoding="UTF-8" standalone="yes"?>
<xmlc xmlns:xsi="http://www.w3.org/1999/XMLSchema-instance"
xsi:noNamespaceSchemaLocation="file:/org/enhydra/xml/xmlc/metadata/
➡xmlc-1.0.1.xsd">
<compileOptions keepGeneratedSource="true"/>
<documentClass delegateSupport="true" generate="both"
recompilation="true"/>
<inputDocument url="test.html"/>
<javaCompiler javac="C:/jdk1.3//bin/javac"/>
<parser/>
<html/>
<domEdits/>
</xmlc>
```

More information about XMLC metadata can be found in Appendix B, "XMLC Metadata."

- `-g`—javac pass-through option.
- `-generate <type>`—Specifies what XMLC generates:
  - `class`—XMLC generates a class that does not depend on an interface (default).
  - `interface`—XMLC generates only an interface.
  - `both`—XMLC generates both an interface and an implementation class. The implementation has the suffix `Impl` appended to the class name, and uses the class name specified with the `-class` option.
  - `implementation`—XMLC generates the class that implements the interface, but not the interface.
- `-html:addattr <attr>`—Adds the specified attribute `<attr>` to the list of valid HTML attributes. The parser then allows the attribute for all tags. This is used by the HTML Tidy parser only.
- `-html:addtag <tag> <flags>`—Adds the specified `<tag>` to the list of valid HTML tags. The parser then allows the tag. The tag name is case-insensitive. `<flags>` is a comma-separated list that contains the content model and other options that describe the tag. You can specify the following values:
  - `inline`—Tag applies to character-level elements.
  - `block`—Tag applies to block-like elements such as paragraphs and lists.

- empty—Tag does not have a closing tag.
- opt—Closing tag is optional for this tag. You must specify at least one of the following flags: inline, block, or empty. This is used by the HTML Tidy parser only.

- -html:addtagset <tagsetname>—Adds a predefined set of tags to the list of valid HTML tags. You can specify:
  - cyberstudio—Tags added by Adobe Cyberstudio, which are ignored by most browsers. Used only by the HTML Tidy parser.
- -html:frameset—Deprecated and is ignored.
- -html:old-class-constants—Generates old-style, all uppercase class names. Available for compatibility with applications generated by older versions of XMLC.
- -implements <interface>—Specifies the interface that the generated class will implement. You can include multiple instances of this option.
- -info—Prints information about the document object, including ids and URLs.
- -javac <prog>—Specifies the name of the Java compiler to use.
- -javacflag <flag>—Passes the specified flag to the javac program, including any leading hyphen (-) or plus (+) characters. You can include multiple instances of this option. Use the -javacopt option for compiler options that require values.
- -javacopt <opt> <value>—Passes the specified option and value to pass to javac, including any leading hyphen (-) or plus (+) characters.
- -keep—Saves the generated Java source file. An excellent option for studying how xmlc generates DOM templates and accessor methods.
- -methods—Prints the signature of each generated access method. Lists any methods or access constants that were not generated because they were not valid Java identifiers.
- -nocompile—Does not compile the generated Java source file.
- -O—javac pass-through option.
- -parseinfo—Prints detailed information about the parsing of the page.
- -parser <parser>—Specifies the parser that XMLC uses:
  - tidy—Enables the HTML Tidy parser. This is the default HTML parser and always performs validation.
  - swing—Enables the Swing parser for HTML. This parser always performs validation.
  - xerces—Enables the Xerces parser for XML. This is the default XML parser and performs XML validation by default.

- `-sourceout <sourceout>`—Specifies the root directory for source files generated by XMLC. If you specify the `-keep` option, the generated source files are stored in this directory.

- `-ssi`—Enables processing of server-side includes in the input document. As explained in Chapter 7, "The xmlc Command," this feature does not support true server-side include behavior. Instead, it simply enables the compile-time inclusion of markup files referenced from the target markup file.

- `-urlmapping <origURL> <newURL>`—Maps all occurrences of `<origURL>` to `<newURL>`. You can include multiple instances of this option.

- `-urlregexpmapping <regexp> <replace>`—Maps all occurrences of the URL that matches regular expression `<regexp>` to the the URL specified by `<replace>`. You can include multiple instances of this option. This option uses the `gnu.regexp` package and recognizes regular expressions with POSIX extensions.

- `-urlsetting <id> <newURL>`—Changes the URL for the specified `<id>` to the specified `<newURL>`. You can include multiple instances of this option.

- `-validate yes|no`—Changes the default document validation mode of the parser. If you specify an option value that the parser does not support, XMLC generates an error. The default behavior is `yes`.

- `-verbose`—Generates useful output about the compilation process.

- `-version`—Prints the version number of the `xmlc` command used. If you do not specify any other options, XMLC quits after printing the version number. You do not need to specify a `<docfile>` with this option. For this book, `xmlc -version` returns:
  ```
  Enhydra XMLC version 2.0.1
  See http://xmlc.enhydra.org for latest distribution
  ```

- `-xcatalog <catalog>`—Specifies the catalog file to use for resolving external entities. You can use this option to specify local DTDs.

A

**XMLC
COMMAND LINE
OPTIONS**

XMLC Metadata

IN THIS APPENDIX

Command options for the xmlc command can be passed to XMLC in the form of an XML language called *Enhydra XMLC metadata*. Governed by XML rules and an XML schema, XMLC metadata gives you greater control and flexibility to affect the behavior of the xmlc command.

Many of the directives and their sub-element options map directly to the effects of command line options.

<compileOptions/> Elements

Specifies options for the document compiler.

Attributes:

printVersion	Prints the XMLC version number (Boolean value).
keepGeneratedSource	Keeps the generate Java source, does not delete it (Boolean value).
printDocumentInfo	Prints useful information about the contents of the document, such as ids and URLs (Boolean value).
printParseInfo	Prints detailed information about the page parsing (Boolean value).
printDOM	Prints out the DOM tree for the page (Boolean value).
printAccessorInfo	Prints the signature of each generated access method and constant (Boolean value). This also lists the methods and access constants that were not generated as a result of invalid Java identifiers.
compileSource	If true, the generated source is compiled; if false, doesn't compile the source. Default is true (Boolean value).
inputDocument	URL of the document to compile.
processSSI	If true, processes server-side include directives. If false, passes them through as comments. Default is false.
sourceOutputRoot	Specifies the root directory for the generate source files. A full package hierarchy is created under this directory. If not specified, the file is created in the current directory. If -keep is specified, the generated source files will be saved under this directory.
classOutputRoot	Specifies the root directory for the compiled class files. A full package hierarchy is created under this directory. If not specified, the file is created in the current directory. The metadata file for recompilation is also created in this directory.

compileSource	If false, the source code will not be generated or compiled. This is useful with the documentOutput option, for validating documents, and for printing information about the documents. Default is true (Boolean value).
documentOutput	Writes the document, after DOM editing, to the file. This is useful for pages where the URLs must be mapped to reference dynamic pages, but there is no other dynamic content. Normally used with createCode="false".
warnings	Enables or disables the printing warnings. This is a Boolean value, default is to enable warnings.

Context: <xmlc>

<inputDocument> Elements

<inputDocument>   Specifies the document to compile.

Attributes:

url	URL of the document to compile.
processSSI	If true, processes server-side include directives. If false, passes them through as comments. Default is false.
documentFormat	The format of the document. Value is one of xml, html, or unspecified. If unspecified, then the first line of the file is checked for an XML header. If an XML header is found, xml is assumed; otherwise html is assumed. The default is unspecified. This attribute is only required for parsing XML files that don't have a XML header as the first line.

Context: <xmlc>

Content: <include>

Indicates that a file is included by the source document. This is normally only specified by the metadata files that XMLC creates to support automatic recompilation. They will be created when server-side includes are used. This tag may be nested to indicate nested includes.

Attributes:

url	Filename or URL of the included file. Relative names are interpreted as being relative to the including file.
recompileSource	Specifies the classpath-relative path of the source file that the recompilation factory will use. This is compiled into the class as

B

XMLC METADATA

the value of the XMLC_SOURCE_FILE field. If not specified, the file path is generated by converting the package name into a file path and merging with the base name of the source file.

Context: <inputDocument>

Content: <include>

<parser> Elements

<parser>   Specifies the parser and parsing options.

Attributes:

name	Name of the parser. The valid values are as follows:
	tidy—Use the Tidy parser for parsing HTML. This is the default for HTML. Validation is always done by this parser.
	swing—Use the Swing parser for parsing HTML. Limited validation is always done by this parser.
	xerces—Use the Xerces parser for parsing XML. This is the only XML parser and is the default. Validation is optional with this parser. The default is to validate.
validate	Changes the default document validation mode of the parser. An error is generated if the value isn't supported by the parser. This is a Boolean value, and if unspecified, the default parse validation is used.
warnings	Enables or disables the printing warnings. This is a Boolean value, and the default is to enable warnings.

Context: <xmlc>

Content:

Specifies an XCatalog file to use in resolving external entities when parsing XML files. This element may be specified multiple times. The catalogs will be searched in the order specified.

Attribute:

url	The URL of the XML catalog file.

Context: <parser>

<html> Elements

<html>   Section containing HTML-specific options.

Attribute:

encoding   Specifies the encoding to use when reading a HTML document. This is an HTML encoding name, not a Java encoding name.

Context: `<xmlc>`

Content: `<htmlTagSet>, <htmlTag>, <htmlAttr>, <compatibility>`

`<htmlTagSet/>`   Adds a predefined set of proprietary HTML tag and attributes to the list of valid HTML tags. This option is only used by the Tidy parser.

Attributes:

tagSet   The name of the tag set. The following tag set is defined:

                              `cyberstudio`—Tags added by Adobe CyberStudio. These tags are for CyberStudio's own use, and are assumed to be ignored by browsers.

Content: `<html>`

`<htmlTag/>`   Adds a proprietary tag to a set of valid HTML tags.

Attributes:

name   The name of the tag.

inline   This tag is a character-level element.

block   This tag is for block-like elements; for example, paragraphs and lists.

empty   The tag does not have a closing tag.

optclose   The closing tag is optional.

Context: `<html>`

`<htmlAttr/>`   Adds a proprietary attribute to the list of valid HTML attributes. The attribute will be allowed on all tags. This option is only used by the Tidy parser.

Attribute:

name   The name of the attribute. It will be allowed for all HTML tags.

Context: `<html>`

`<compatibility>`   Enables compatibility with the way older versions of XMLC handled HTML.

Attributes:

oldClassConstants   Older versions of XMLC generated HTML class attribute constants as all upper-case (for example, `CLASS_DELETEROW`), with values being case-preserved. If a true value, this option will reproduce the old behavior. This option is intended to aid in the porting of existing applications; it might not be supported in future releases.

oldNameConstants   Older versions of XMLC generated HTML name attribute constants as all upper-case (for example, NAME_INPUT), with values being case-preserved. If a true value, this option will reproduce the old behavior. This option is intended to aid in the porting of existing applications; it might not be supported in future releases.

Context: <html>

DOM Editing Elements

<domEdits>   This is a section containing DOM editing specifications. These are modifications done to elements in the DOM during the compilation of a document.

Context: <xmlc>

Content: <urlEdit>, <urlMapping>, <urlRegExpMapping>, <deleteElement>

<elementEdit>   This is an abstract type used as a base for all element editing definitions. This provides for the definition of which attributes and elements are to be operated on by the derived edit definitions.

Attributes:

elementIds   Restricts replacement to the elements matching any of the ids in the space-separate list.

elementClasses   Restricts replacement to the elements matching any of the class names in the space-separate list. These are class attribute values as specified by the HTML CLASS attribute, not Java class names.

elementTags   Restricts replacement to the elements matching any of the tag names in the space-separate list. Case is ignored for HTML.

<urlEdit>   This is an abstract type used as a base for all URL editing definitions.

Base Type: <elementEdit>

Attribute:

editAttrs   List of attributes that are to be edited. If not specified, defaults to the attributes that the XMLCDomFactory object for the document defines as containing URLs.

Context: <domEdits>

<urlMapping/>   Specifies the literal replacement of URLs in element attributes. When used in

the `<domEdits>` section, it applies globally to elements. When used in an element or sub-document, it applies only to that context.

Base Type: `<urlEdit>`

Attributes:

url	The existing URL. If not specified, all URLs for the matching elements will be replaced.
newUrl	This is the replacement URL.

Context: `<domEdits>`

`<urlRegExpMapping/>` Specifies the regular expression replacement of URLs in element attributes. If the regular expression matches, it is edited using a substituted replacement pattern. POSIX-extended regular expressions are used, implemented by the `gnu.regexp` package. See the documentation on this package for details of the regular expression and substitution syntax. When used in the `<domEdits>` section, it applies globally to elements. When used in an element or sub-document, it applies only to that context.

Base Type: `<urlEdit>`

Attributes:

regexp	The POSIX regular expression to match against URL tag attributes.
subst	The substitution expression to use to generate the replacement URL.

Context: `<domEdits>`

`<deleteElement>` Deletes all matching elements. This is often used to specify the element class of mockup data that is to be deleted from the document.

Base Type: `<elementEdit>`

Context: `<domEdits>`

`<documentClass>` Elements

`<documentClass>` Specifies the properties of the XMLC document class to generate.

Attributes:

name	The fully-qualified name of the class to generate. If the generate attribute specifies class, then this is the name of the class. Otherwise, this is the name of the interface to generate, and the generated implementation will have `Impl` appended to this name.

`generate`	Specifies what kind of classes should be generated. Normally, either `class` or `both` are used: `class`—Generates a simple class (default). `interface`—Generates just an interface, not the implementation. `implementation`—Generates an implementation of the interface (named in the form `nameImpl`) but not the interface. `both`—Generates both an interface and an implementation.
`delegateSupport`	Generates code for delegate support used by the XMLC document class for reloading. This is a Boolean value, and the default is false.
`createMetaData`	Creates a XMLC metadata XML file in the same directory as the class file. This is used by the XMLC recompilation factory. It is a Boolean value, and the default is false.

`recompilation`	Sets all options required for XMLC recompilation. It's a Boolean value, and the default is false. Setting this to true results in one of the following:
	
	`generate="both"`
	
	`delegateSupport="true"`
	
	`createMetaData="true"`

`extends`	Specifies the class that the generated class will extend. This class must extend `org.enhydra.xml.xmlc.XMLObjectImpl` for XML documents, or `org.enhydra.xml.xmlc.html.HTMLObjectImpl` for HTML documents.
`domfactory`	Specifies the Java class for creating DOM documents. This class must implement `org.enhydra.xml.xmlc.dom.XMLCDomFactory`. This option is not supported for HTML documents. The DOM factory must have a constructor that takes no arguments. This class serves as a factory for `Document` objects, giving a mechanism for creating DTD-specific DOMs. The specified class must be available on the CLASSPATH.

dom	Specifies one of a predefined set of DOM factories. This is a shortcut for the domfactory attribute. The following are the valid values, along with the XMLCDomFactory they map to:
	lazydom—The LazyDOM, derived from the Xerces DOM. XML: org.enhydra.xml.xmlc. dom.lazydom.LazyDomFactory. HTML: org.enhydra.xml.xmlc.dom.lazydom. LazyHTMLDomFactory.
	xerces—The Xerces DOM. XML: org. enhydra.xml.xmlc.dom.xerces. XercesDomFactory. HTML: org.enhydra.xml.xmlc.dom.xerces. XercesHTMLDomFactory.
	The default value, if neither the DomFactory or DOM attributes are specified, is LazyDOM.
createGetTagMethods true|false	Specifies that getTagXXX() methods should be generated. These methods have a more generic return type than getElementXXX() methods. By default, they return org.w3c.dom.Element. This is useful when the developer is constructing interfaces that are implemented by multiple XMLC document classes. By having the interface contain both the getTagXXX() and setTextXXX() methods, common code can be written to operate on the interfaces.
getTagMethodReturnType	Specifies the return type generated for getTagXXX() methods. One of the following values may be used instead of a class or interface name:
	Element—A shortcut for org.w3c.Element. This is the default.
	HTMLElement—A shortcut for org.w3c.html.HTMLElement.
	class—The actual class name of the element.
	interface—The value obtained from the nodeClassToInterface method in the XMLCDomFactory object being used to compile the document.

Context: `<xmlc>`

Content: `<implements/>`

`<implements/>` Specifies the name of an interface the document class will implement.

Attribute:

name	The fully qualified class name of the interface that the generated class will implement.

Context: `<documentClass>`

`<javaCompiler>` Elements

`<javaCompiler>` Specifies information about the Java compiler.

Attribute:

javac	Specifies the command name of the Java compiler to use.

Context: `<xmlc>`

Content: `<javacOption>`

`<javacOption/>` Specifies an option to pass to the Java compiler.

Attributes:

name	The name of an option understood by the specified Java compiler. The flag argument should contain the leading - or + characters.
value	The value to associate with the option. Omitted if the option doesn't take a value.

Context: `<javaCompiler>`

The `XMLObjectImpl` Class

IN THIS APPENDIX

XMLObjectImpl is the base class for all XML objects as viewed through the eyes of Enhydra XMLC. It is heavily used by the XMLC compiler to generate the Java logic that constructs the DOM template when loaded by the presentation object. To see how they are used in the generation of a DOM template, use the xmlc command -keep option to preserve the XMLC-generated intermediate Java source file.

The HTML-specific class extension of XMLObjectImpl is HTMLObjectImpl. It extends XMLObjectImpl with HTML-specific methods: cloneNode(), close(), getAnchors(), getApplets(), getBody(), getCookie(), getDomain(), getElementById(), getElementsByName(), getForms(), getImages(), getLinks(), getReferrer(), getTitle(), getURL(), open(), setBody(), setCookie(), setTitle(), toDocument(), write(), writeln().

Methods

setDocument

This method sets the DOM document associated with this object and optional encoding. setDocument() is used by buildDocument() to set the new document. It is done separately from the constructor to allow buildDocument() to not be called immediately.

> Returns: protected void

getDomFactory()

This method gets the XMLC DOM Factory associated with this document type and DOM implementation.

> Returns: protected abstract XMLCDomFactory

getDocument()

This method gets the actual document object. You should normally use the XMLObject methods to access the document functionality; this method is for the initialization of derived objects.

> Description copied from interface: XMLObjectgetDocument()
> Specified by: getDocument in interface XMLObject
> See also: XMLObject.getDocument()
> Returns: Document

getMIMEType()

This method gets the MIME type associated with the document; or null if none was associated.

> Description copied from interface: XMLObject
> Specified by: getMIMEType in interface XMLObject
> See also: XMLObject.getMIMEType()
> Returns: java.lang.String

`getEncoding()`

Gets the encoding specified in the document. Note that this is the symbolic name of the XML encoding, which is not the same as the Java encoding names.

> Description copied from interface: `XMLObject`
>
> Specified by: `getEncoding` in interface `XMLObject`
>
> See also: `XMLObject.getEncoding()`
>
> Returns: `java.lang.String`

`setDelegate(XMLObject delegate)`

Sets the delegate object. Delegation is used to support automatic recompilation of documents into XMLC objects. If the delegate is not null, the methods of the delegate are called to handle most of the methods of this object.

> Description copied from interface: `XMLObject`
>
> Specified by: `setDelegate` in interface `XMLObject`
>
> See also: `XMLObject.setDelegate(org.enhydra.xml.xmlc.XMLObject)`
>
> Returns: `void`

`getDelegate()`

Gets the delegate, a key aspect of DOM auto-recompilation.

> Specified by: `getDelegate` in interface `XMLObject`
>
> See also: `XMLObject.getDelegate()`
>
> Returns: `XMLObject`

`cloneDeepCheck(boolean deep)`

Checks that `cloneNode` on an entire document is done with the `deep` value set to true.

> Returns: `void`

`cloneNode(boolean deep)`

Clones the entire document. Derived objects should override this to get the correct derived type. Cloning with `deep` being false is not allowed.

> See also: `Node.cloneNode(boolean)`
>
> Returns: `abstract Node`

`getDoctype()`

The document type declaration (see `DocumentType`) associated with this document. For HTML documents, as well as XML documents without a document type declaration, this returns null.

The DOM Level 2 does not support editing the document type declaration, therefore `docType` cannot be altered in any way, including through the use of methods, such as `insertNode` or `removeNode`, inherited from `Node`.

>Description copied from interface: `Document`
>
>Specified by: `getDoctype` in interface `Document`
>
>See also: `Document.getDoctype()`
>
>Returns: `DocumentType`

`getImplementation()`

The `DOMImplementation` object that handles this document. A DOM application may use objects from multiple implementations.

>Description copied from interface: `Document`
>
>Specified by: `getImplementation` in interface `Document`
>
>See also: `Document.getImplementation()`
>
>Returns: `DOMImplementation`

`getDocumentElement()`

This is a convenience attribute that allows direct access to the child node that is the root element of the document. For HTML documents, this is the element with the tagName `HTML`.

>Description copied from interface: `Document`
>
>Specified by: `getDocumentElement` in interface `Document`
>
>See also: `Document.getDocumentElement()`
>
>Returns: `Element`

`importNode(Node importedNode, boolean deep) throws DOMException`

Imports a node from another document to this document. The returned node has no parent; (parent `Node` is null). The source node is not altered or removed from the original document; this method creates a new copy of the source node. For all nodes, importing a node creates a node object owned by the importing document, with attribute values identical to the source node's `nodeName` and `nodeType`, plus the attributes related to namespaces (`prefix`, `localName`, and `namespaceURI`). As in the `cloneNode` operation on a `Node`, the source node is not altered. Additional information is copied as appropriate to the `nodeType`, attempting to mirror the behavior expected if a fragment of XML or HTML source was copied from one document to another, and recognizing that the two documents may have different DTDs in the XML case. The following list describes the specifics for every type of node.

ELEMENT_NODE—Specified attribute nodes of the source element are imported, and the generated Attr nodes are attached to the generated Element. Default attributes are not copied, though if the document being imported into defines default attributes for this element name, those are assigned. If the importNode deep parameter was set to true, the descendants of the source element will be recursively imported and the resulting nodes reassembled to form the corresponding subtree.

ATTRIBUTE_NODE—The specified flag is set to true on the generated Attr. The descendants of the source Attr are recursively imported and the resulting nodes reassembled to form the corresponding subtree. Note that the deep parameter does not apply to Attr nodes; they always carry their children with them when imported.

TEXT_NODE, CDATA_SECTION_NODE, COMMENT_NODE—These three types of nodes inheriting from CharacterData copy their data and length attributes from those of the source node.

ENTITY_REFERENCE_NODE—Only the EntityReference itself is copied, even if a deep import is requested, since the source and destination documents might have defined the entity differently. If the document being imported into provides a definition for this entity name, its value is assigned.

ENTITY_NODE—Entity nodes can be imported; however, in the current release of the DOM, the DocumentType is readonly. Ability to add these imported nodes to a DocumentType will be considered for addition to a future release of the DOM. On import, the publicId, systemId, and notationName attributes are copied. If a deep import is requested, the descendants of the source Entity is recursively imported and the resulting nodes reassembled to form the corresponding subtree.

PROCESSING_INSTRUCTION_NODE—The imported node copies its target and data values from those of the source node.

DOCUMENT_NODE—Document nodes cannot be imported.

DOCUMENT_TYPE_NODE—DocumentType nodes cannot be imported.

DOCUMENT_FRAGMENT_NODE—If the deep option was set true, the descendants of the source element will be recursively imported and the resulting nodes reassembled to form the corresponding subtree. Otherwise, this simply generates an empty DocumentFragment.

NOTATION_NODE—Notation nodes can be imported; however, in the current release of the DOM, the DocumentType is readonly. Ability to add these imported nodes to a DocumentType will be considered for addition to a future release of the DOM. On import, the publicId and systemId attributes are copied. Note that the deep parameter does not apply to Notation nodes, because they never have any children.

Description copied from interface: Document

Specified by: importNode in interface Document

See also: Document.importNode(org.w3c.dom.Node, boolean)

Returns: Node

`createElement(java.lang.String tagName)`

Creates an element of the type specified. The instance returned implements the `Element` interface, so attributes can be specified directly on the returned object. In addition, if there are known attributes with default values, `Attr` nodes representing them are automatically created and attached to the element. To create an element with a qualified name and namespace URI, use the `createElementNS` method.

> Description copied from interface: `Document`
>
> Specified by: `createElement` in interface `Document`
>
> See also: `Document.createElement(java.lang.String)`
>
> Throws: `DOMException`
>
> Returns: `Element`

`createElementNS(java.lang.String namespaceURI, java.lang.String qualifiedName)`

Creates an element of the given qualified name and namespace URI. HTML-only DOM implementations do not need to implement this method.

> Description copied from interface: `Document`
>
> Specified by: `createElementNS` in interface `Document`
>
> See also: `Document.createElementNS(java.lang.String, java.lang.String)`
>
> Throws: `DOMException`
>
> Returns: `Element`

`createDocumentFragment()`

Creates an empty `DocumentFragment` object.

> Description copied from interface: `Document`
>
> Specified by: `createDocumentFragment` in interface `Document`
>
> See also: `Document.createDocumentFragment()`
>
> Returns: `DocumentFragment`

`createTextNode(java.lang.String data)`

Creates a `Text` node given the specified string.

> Description copied from interface: `Document`
>
> Specified by: `createTextNode` in interface `Document`
>
> See also: `Document.createTextNode(java.lang.String)`
>
> Returns: `Text`

The XMLObjectImpl Class

APPENDIX C

421

C

THE
XMLObjectImpl
CLASS

createComment(java.lang.String data)

Creates a Comment node given the specified string.

Description copied from interface: Document

Specified by: createComment in interface Document

See also: Document.createComment(java.lang.String)

Returns: Comment

createCDATASection(java.lang.String data)

Creates a CDATASection node whose value is the specified string.

Description copied from interface: Document

Specified by: createCDATASection in interface Document

See also: Document.createCDATASection(java.lang.String)

Throws: DOMException

Returns: CDATASection

createProcessingInstruction(java.lang.String target, java.lang.String data)

Creates a ProcessingInstruction node given the specified name and data strings.

Description copied from interface: Document

Specified by: createProcessingInstruction in interface Document

See also: Document.createProcessingInstruction()

Throws: DOMException

Returns: ProcessingInstruction

createAttribute(java.lang.String qualifiedName)

Creates an Attr of the given name. Note that the Attr instance can then be set on an Element using the setAttribute method. To create an attribute with a qualified name and namespace URI, use the createAttributeNS method.

Description copied from interface: Document

Specified by: createAttribute in interface Document

See also: Document.createAttribute(java.lang.String)

Throws: DOMException

Returns: Attr

```
createAttributeNS(java.lang.String namespaceURI, java.lang.
String qualifiedName)
```

Creates an attribute of the given qualified name and namespace URI. HTML-only DOM implementations do not need to implement this method.

> Description copied from interface: `Document`
>
> Specified by: `createAttributeNS` in interface `Document`
>
> See also: `Document.createAttributeNS(java.lang.String, java.lang.String)`
>
> Throws: `DOMException`
>
> Returns: `Attr`

```
createEntityReference(java.lang.String name)
```

Creates an `EntityReference` object. In addition, if the referenced entity is known, the child list of the `EntityReference` node is made the same as that of the corresponding `Entity` node. If any descendant of the `Entity` node has an unbound namespace prefix, the corresponding descendant of the created `EntityReference` node is also unbound (its namespace URI is `null`). The DOM Level 2 does not support any mechanism to resolve namespace prefixes.

> Description copied from interface: `Document`
>
> Specified by: `createEntityReference` in interface `Document`
>
> See also: `Document.createEntityReference(java.lang.String)`
>
> Throws: `DOMException`
>
> Returns: `EntityReference`

```
getElementsByTagName(java.lang.String tagname)
```

Returns a `NodeList` of all the `Elements` with a given tag name in the order in which they would be encountered in a pre-order traversal of the Document tree.

> Description copied from interface: `Document`
>
> Specified by: `getElementsByTagName` in interface `Document`
>
> See also: `Document.getElementsByTagName(java.lang.String)`
>
> Returns: `NodeList`

```
getElementsByTagNameNS(java.lang.String namespaceURI, java.lang.String
localName)
```

Returns a `NodeList` of all the `Elements` with a given local name and namespace URI in the order in which they would be encountered in a pre-order traversal of the `Document` tree.

> Specified by: `getElementsByTagNameNS` in interface `Document`
>
> Description copied from interface: `Document`

The XMLObjectImpl Class

APPENDIX C

423

C

THE
XMLObjectImpl
CLASS

See also: `Document.getElementsByTagNameNS(java.lang.String, java.lang.String)`

Returns: `NodeList`

`getElementById(java.lang.String elementId)`

Returns the `Element` whose `id` is given by `elementId`. If no such element exists, returns `null`. Behavior is not defined if more than one element has this `id`. The DOM implementation must have information that says which attributes are of type `id`. Attributes with the name `id` are not of type `id` unless so defined. Implementations that do not know whether attributes are of type `id` or not are expected to return null.

Specified by: `getElementById` in interface `Document`

Description copied from interface: `Document`

See also: `Document.getElementById(java.lang.String)`

Returns: `Element`

`getNodeName()`

The name of this node, depending on its type; see the earlier list.

Description copied from interface: `Node`

See also: `Node.getNodeName()`

Throws: `DOMException`

Returns: `java.lang.String`

`getNodeValue()`

The value of this node, depending on its type; see the earlier list. When it is defined to be null, setting it has no effect.

Description copied from interface: `Node`

See also: `Node.getNodeValue()`

Throws: `DOMException`

Returns: `java.lang.String`

`setNodeValue(java.lang.String nodeValue)`

See also: `Node.setNodeValue(java.lang.String)`

Throws: `DOMException`

Returns: `void`

getNodeType()

A code representing the type of the underlying object, as defined earlier.

> Description copied from interface: Node
>
> See also: Node.getNodeType()
>
> Returns: short

getParentNode()

The parent of this node. All nodes, except Attr, Document, DocumentFragment, Entity, and Notation may have a parent. However, if a node has just been created and not yet added to the tree, or if it has been removed from the tree, this is null.

> Description copied from interface: Node
>
> See also: Node.getParentNode()
>
> Returns: Node

getChildNodes()

A NodeList that contains all children of this node. If there are no children, this is a NodeList containing no nodes. The content of the returned NodeList is "live" in the sense that, for instance, changes to the children of the node object that it was created from are immediately reflected in the nodes returned by the NodeList accessors; it is not a static snapshot of the content of the node. This is true for every NodeList, including the ones returned by the getElementsByTagName method.

> Description copied from interface: Node
>
> See also: Node.getChildNodes()
>
> Returns: NodeList

getFirstChild()

The first child of this node. If there is no such node, this returns null.

> Description copied from interface: Node
>
> See also: Node.getFirstChild()
>
> Returns: Node

getLastChild()

The last child of this node. If there is no such node, this returns null.

> Description copied from interface: Node
>
> See also: Node.getLastChild()
>
> Returns: Node

The XMLObjectImpl Class

425

APPENDIX C

C

THE
XMLObjectImpl
CLASS

getPreviousSibling()

The node immediately preceding this node. If there is no such node, this returns null.

> Description copied from interface: Node
>
> See also: Node.getPreviousSibling()
>
> Returns: Node

getNextSibling()

The node immediately following this node. If there is no such node, this returns null.

> Description copied from interface: Node
>
> See also: Node.getNextSibling()
>
> Returns: Node

getAttributes()

A NamedNodeMap containing the attributes of this node (if it is an Element) or otherwise null.

> Description copied from interface: Node
>
> See also: Node.getAttributes()
>
> Returns: NamedNodeMap

getOwnerDocument()

The Document object associated with this node. This is also the Document object used to create new nodes. When this node is a Document or a DocumentType which is not used with any Document yet, it is null.

> Description copied from interface: Node
>
> See also: Node.getOwnerDocument()
>
> Returns: Document

insertBefore(Node newChild, Node refChild) throws DOMException

Inserts the node newChild before the existing child node refChild. If refChild is null, insert newChild at the end of the list of children. If newChild is a DocumentFragment object, all of its children are inserted, in the same order, before refChild. If newChild is already in the tree, it is first removed.

> Description copied from interface: Node
>
> See also: Node.insertBefore(org.w3c.dom.Node, org.w3c.dom.Node)
>
> Throws: DOMException
>
> Returns: Node

`replaceChild(Node newChild, Node oldChild) throws DOMException`

Replaces the child node `oldChild` with `newChild` in the list of children, and returns the `oldChild` node. If `newChild` is a `DocumentFragment` object, `oldChild` is replaced by all of the `DocumentFragment` children, which are inserted in the same order. If `newChild` is already in the tree, it is first removed.

> Description copied from interface: `Node`
>
> See also: `Node.replaceChild(org.w3c.dom.Node, org.w3c.dom.Node)`
>
> Throws: `DOMException`
>
> Returns: `Node`

`removeChild(Node oldChild) throws DOMException`

Removes the child node indicated by `oldChild` from the list of children and returns it.

> Description copied from interface: `Node`
>
> See also: `Node.removeChild(org.w3c.dom.Node)`
>
> Throws: `DOMException`
>
> Returns: `Node`

`appendChild(Node newChild)`

> Description copied from interface: `Node`
>
> Throws: `DOMException`
>
> Returns: `Node`

`normalize()`

Puts all `Text` nodes in the full depth of the sub-tree underneath this `Node`, including attribute nodes, into a "normal" form where only markup (for example, tags, comments, processing instructions, `CDATA` sections, and entity references) separates `Text` nodes; that is, there are neither adjacent `Text` nodes nor empty `Text` nodes. This can be used to ensure that the DOM view of a document is the same as if it were saved and re-loaded, and is useful when operations (such as XPointer lookups) that depend on a particular document tree structure are to be used. In cases where the document contains `CDATASection`, the normalize operation alone may not be sufficient, since XPointers do not differentiate between `Text` nodes and `CDATASection` nodes.

> See also: `Node.normalize()`
>
> Description copied from interface: `Node`
>
> Returns: `void`

The XMLObjectImpl Class

APPENDIX C

427

C

THE
XMLObjectImpl
CLASS

supports(java.lang.String feature, java.lang.String version)

Tests whether the DOM implementation implements a specific feature and that that feature is supported by this node.

> Description copied from interface: `Node`
>
> See also: `Node.supports(String, String)`
>
> Returns: `boolean`

getNamespaceURI()

The namespace URI of this node, or null if it is unspecified. This is not a computed value that is the result of a namespace lookup based on an examination of the namespace declarations in scope. It is merely the namespace URI given at creation time. For nodes of any type other than `ELEMENT_NODE` and `ATTRIBUTE_NODE`, and nodes created with a DOM Level 1 method, such as `createElement` from the `Document` interface, this is always null. Per the Namespaces section in the XML Specification, an attribute does not inherit its namespace from the element it is attached to. If an attribute is not explicitly given a namespace, it simply has no namespace.

> See also: `Node.getNamespaceURI()`
>
> Description copied from interface: `Node`
>
> Returns: `java.lang.String`

getPrefix()

The namespace prefix of this node, or null if it is unspecified. Setting this attribute, when permitted, changes the `nodeName` attribute, which holds the qualified name, as well as the `tagName` and name attributes of the `Element` and `Attr` interfaces, when applicable. Changing the prefix of an attribute that is known to have a default value, does not make a new attribute with the default value and the original prefix appear, since the `namespaceURI` and `localName` do not change.

> Description copied from interface: `Node`
>
> See also: `Node.getPrefix()`
>
> Returns: `java.lang.String`

setPrefix(java.lang.String prefix)

> See also: `Node.setPrefix(java.lang.String)`
>
> Returns: `void`

`getLocalName()`

Returns the local part of the qualified name of this node. For nodes created with a DOM Level 1 method, such as `createElement` from the `Document` interface, it is null.

Description copied from interface: `Node`

See also: `Node.getLocalName()`

Returns: `java.lang.String`

`hasChildNodes()`

This is a convenience method to allow easy determination of whether a node has any children.

Description copied from interface: `Node`

See also: `Node.hasChildNodes()`

Returns: `boolean`

`hasAttributes()`

Returns whether this node (if it is an element) has any attributes.

Description copied from interface: `Node`

See also: `Node.hasAttributes()`

Returns: `boolean`

`toDocument()`

Converts the document to a string representation of the document, that is, a string containing XML. The results can be parsed into the same DOM hierarchy. The formatting provided by this method does not begin to cover all of the issues involved with publishing a XML document, such as character encoding. Use the `org.enhydra.xml.io.DOMFormatter` class if more options are required.

Description copied from interface: `XMLObject`

See also: `XMLObject.toDocument()`

Returns: `java.lang.String`

`syncWithDocument(Node node)`

Generated function to synchronize the fields used by the access methods. This synchronizes just the node and is not recursive.

Returns: `protected abstract void`

syncAccessMethods()

Initializes the fields used by the generated access methods from the current state of the document. Missing DOM element ids will result in their access method returning null.

> Specified by: syncAccessMethods in interface XMLObject
>
> See also: XMLObject.syncAccessMethods()
>
> Description copied from interface: XMLObject
>
> Returns: void

isURLAttribute(Element element, java.lang.String attrName)

> Specified by: isURLAttribute in interface DocumentInfo
>
> See also: DocumentInfo.isURLAttribute(org.w3c.dom.Element, java.lang.String)
>
> Returns: boolean

doSetText(Element element, java.lang.String text)

Used internally to implement a setText<attributeValue>() method. Adds check for null value and helps to minimize the amount of generated code.

> Returns: protected final void

The Base Presentation Object

IN THIS APPENDIX

The Base Presentation Object

The Base Presentation Object is a possible strategy for enforcing a consistent, controller-like methodology for handling "events" generated by Web page interactions with the client. It is not inherent to XMLC development, instead serving as a possible strategy that an architect might propose. It is the strategy that was selected to implement the ShowFloor application.

As an abstract class, BasePO methods are inherited by the child presentation objects, or POs. These presentation objects are invoked from Web pages with a parameter named event and a value such as browse, edit, login, register, or whatever value expected by the developer. When no event parameter is passed, a default handler is provided.

Listing D.1 contains the complete code for BasePO.java. Please refer to Chapter 9, "Presentation Strategies," for an expanded discussion of the Base Presentation Object and each of its methods.

LISTING D.1   BasePO.java

```java
package com.otterpod.sfa.presentation;

import com.otterpod.sfa.business.vendor.*;
import com.otterpod.sfa.business.visitor.*;
import com.otterpod.sfa.business.booth.*;
import com.otterpod.sfa.*;

import com.lutris.appserver.server.StandardAppUtil;
import org.enhydra.xml.xmlc.XMLObject;
import com.lutris.appserver.server.httpPresentation.*;
import com.lutris.appserver.server.session.*;
import com.lutris.appserver.server.Enhydra;
import com.lutris.xml.xmlc.*;
import com.lutris.xml.xmlc.html.*;
import com.lutris.logging.*;
import com.lutris.util.KeywordValueException;
import com.lutris.appserver.server.user.User;
import org.w3c.dom.*;
import org.w3c.dom.html.HTMLElement;
import java.lang.reflect.*;
import java.util.*;

/*
 * This is the parent Presentation object.
 * All presentation objects extend this class.
 *
 * The run() method looks for an event parameter and then calls
```

LISTING D.1   Continued

```
 * handle<EventName>.  If the "event" parameter is not defined
 * then the handleDefault() method is called in your child class.
 *
 */
public abstract class BasePO implements HttpPresentation {
    private static String EVENT = "event";
    private static String STANDARD_METHOD_PREFIX = "handle";

    /*
     * This is the procedure that is called if there is no "event"
     * HTTP parameter found. It must be overridden by the subclass to
     * do default processing or error checking/handling.
     *
     * Returns the String representation of the HTML or other format
     * of the document to be displayed. This method would need to be changed
     * if you wanted to return binary data as well.
     */
    public abstract XMLObject handleDefault()
        throws HttpPresentationException;

    /*
     * This method should be implemented in the subclass so that it returns
     * the authorization level necessary to access the PO.
     */
    abstract protected int getRequiredAuthLevel();

    /*
     * Saved input and output context, and session data
     */
    protected HttpPresentationComms myComms = null;
    protected ShowFloorSessionData mySessionData = null;

    /*
     * Gets HttpPresentation object
     *
     * Returns: The saved comms objects
     * to whichever subclass needs it
     */
    public HttpPresentationComms getComms() {
        return this.myComms;
    }

    /*
     * Gets the session data
     *
```

LISTING D.1   Continued

```java
 * Returns: session data
 */
public ShowFloorSessionData getSessionData() {
    return this.mySessionData;
}


/*
 * This implements the run method in HttpPresentation.
 *
 * @param HttpPresentationComms
 * @exception Exception
 */
public void run(HttpPresentationComms comms) throws Exception {
    // Reroute based on content.
    rerouteForContent(comms);

    // Initialize new or get the existing session data
    initSessionData(comms);

    // Check if the user can access the given page.
    checkAuthLevel();

    try {
        // Handle the incoming event request
        handleEvent(comms);
    } catch (Exception e) {
        throw new Exception("Exception in run " + e);
    }
}


/*
 * Method that determines which content to output based on
 * the accept type.
 */
protected void rerouteForContent(HttpPresentationComms comms)
    throws ShowFloorPresentationException {
    DeviceUtils.rerouteForContent(comms);
}


/*
 * Method to get or create the ShowFloorSessionData object
 * from the user session. This object is saved in the
 * ShowFloorPresentation object
 */
protected void initSessionData(HttpPresentationComms comms)
```

LISTING D.1   Continued

```
        throws ShowFloorPresentationException {

        this.myComms = comms;
        try {
          Object obj = comms.sessionData.get(ShowFloorSessionData.SESSION_KEY);
          // If we found the session data, save it in a private data member
          if (obj != null) {
              this.mySessionData = (ShowFloorSessionData) obj;
          } else {
              // If no session data was found,
              // create a new session data instance
              this.mySessionData = new ShowFloorSessionData();
              comms.sessionData.set(ShowFloorSessionData.SESSION_KEY,
➥this.mySessionData);
          }
        } catch (KeywordValueException ex) {
            throw new ShowFloorPresentationException("Trouble initializing
➥user", ex);
        }
    }

    /*
     * Return the current authorization level (set during login)
     * Returns: an int equal to the current authorization level.
     */
    protected int getCurrentAuthLevel()
        throws ClientPageRedirectException, ShowFloorPresentationException {
➥int accessLevel = 0;

        try {
            accessLevel = getSessionData().getUserAuth();
        } catch (Exception ex) {
            throw new ShowFloorPresentationException("Trouble getting
➥current authorization level", ex);
        }
        return accessLevel;
    }

    /*
     * Checks the session data to see if the user has the authorization to
     * access the given page.  Authorization levels include:
     * UNAUTH_USER (0)  —   login not required.
     * MYSFA_USER  (1)  —   login as mySFA user required.
     * ADMIN_USER  (2)  —   login as administrator required.
     *
```

LISTING D.1   Continued

```
      * Redirects to login page if user not authorized to access page.
      */
     protected void checkAuthLevel()
         throws ClientPageRedirectException, ShowFloorPresentationException {
         int currentAuth = getCurrentAuthLevel();

         try {
             if (currentAuth < getRequiredAuthLevel()) {
                 if (currentAuth > ShowFloorConstants.MYSFA_USER) {
                     throw new ClientPageRedirectException(
➥ShowFloorConstants.ADMIN_LOGIN_PAGE);
                 }

                 throw new ClientPageRedirectException("/" +
➥ShowFloorConstants.HTML_PAGE);
             }
         } catch (Exception ex) {
             throw new ShowFloorPresentationException("Trouble
➥checking for user login status", ex);
         }
     }

     /*
      * Method to call the proper method for the incoming event
      *
      * @param HttpPresentationComms
      * @exception Exception
      */
     public void handleEvent(HttpPresentationComms comms) throws Exception {
         String    event = comms.request.getParameter(EVENT);
         XMLObject returnDoc = null;
         try {
             if (event == null || event.length() == 0) {
                 returnDoc = handleDefault();
             } else {
                 returnDoc = getPage(event);
             }
             comms.response.writeDOM(returnDoc);
         } catch (Exception e) {
             throw new Exception("Exception writing dom:" +  e);
         }
     }

     /*
      * Logs user out from the session by setting the usr to null
```

LISTING D.1 Continued

```
   * in the session data.
   */
  public XMLObject handleLogout() throws ShowFloorPresentationException {
      try {
          mySessionData = null;
          SessionManager sessionManager = myComms.session.getSessionManager();
          sessionManager.deleteSession(myComms.session);
          throw new ClientPageRedirectException(ShowFloorConstants.HTML_PAGE);

      } catch (Exception e) {
          throw new ShowFloorPresentationException("Trouble
➥logging out user", e);
      }
  }

  /*
   * If an event parameter is defined then this builds and invokes
   * the method that handles that event.
   */
  public XMLObject getPage(String event) throws Exception {
      try {
          Method method = this.getClass().getMethod(toMethodName(event),null);
          XMLObject thePage = (XMLObject) method.invoke(this, null);
          return thePage;

      } catch (InvocationTargetException ex) {

          // Rethrow the originating exception if as it
          // should be propagated as is.
          // It could be a page redirect exception, etc.
          if (ex.getTargetException() instanceof Exception) {
              throw (Exception) ex.getTargetException();
          } else if (ex.getTargetException() instanceof Error) {
              throw (Error) ex.getTargetException();
          } else {
              throw ex;
          }
      } catch (NoSuchMethodException ex) {

          // The method to handle the event does not exist.
          throw new ShowFloorPresentationException("NO EVENT HANDLER
➥FOUND FOR EVENT: " + event, ex);
      } catch (IllegalAccessException ex) {
```

Listing D.1 Continued

```
            // The method to handle the event does not exist.
            throw new ShowFloorPresentationException("ILLEGAL ACCESS TO
➥EVENT HANDLER (is it public?): " + event, ex);
        }
    }

    /*
     * This sets the first letter of the event parameter value in order
     * to adhere to Java method naming conventions.
     *
     * @param String event the incoming name of the event
     * Returns: String the properly capitalized name
     */
    private String toMethodName(String event) {

        //STANDARD_METHOD_PREFIX is the string "handle"
        StringBuffer methodName = new StringBuffer(STANDARD_METHOD_PREFIX);

        methodName.append(Character.toUpperCase(event.charAt(0)));

        if (event.length() > 1) {
            methodName.append(event.substring(1));
        }

        return methodName.toString();
    }

    /*
     * Returns the application object associated with the
     * current request.
     *
     * Returns: the application object.
     */
    public ShowFloor getApplication() {
        return (ShowFloor) Enhydra.getApplication();
    }

    /*
     * Method to write a debugging message to the debug log
     * channel when the DEBUG flag is turned on
     */
    public static void writeDebugMsg(String msg) {
        Enhydra.getLogChannel().write(Logger.DEBUG, msg);
    }
```

LISTING D.1 Continued

```java
/*
 * Returns true if the given string is null, empty, or contains
 * only white space.
 */
protected static boolean isNullField(String field) {
    if (field == null) {
        return true;
    }

    if (field.trim().equals("")) {
        return true;
    }
    return false;
}

/*
 * Returns true if the given string is null, empty, or contains
 * only white space.
 */
protected static boolean checkField(String field, int size) {
    if (field == null || field.equals("")) {
        return false;
    }
    if (field.length() <= size) {
        return true;
    }
    return false;
}

}
```

References

IN THIS APPENDIX

- **References 442**

Arrington, C. T. *Enterprise Java with UML*. John Wiley & Sons, 2001.

Beasley, Rick, Kenneth Michael Farley, John O'Reilly, and Leon Squire. *Voice Application Development with VoiceXML*. Sams Publishing, 2001.

Bradley, Neil. *The XML Companion*. Addison-Wesley, 1998.

Daconta, Michael C., and Al Saganich. *XML Development with Java 2*. Sams Publishing, 2000.

Feng, Yu, and Jun Zhu. *Wireless Java Programming with J2ME*. Sams Publishing, 2001.

Forta, Ben, with Edwin Smith, Scott M. Stirling, Larry Kim, Roger Kerr, David Aden, and Andre Lei. *JavaServer Pages Application Development*. Sams Publishing, 2001.

Fowler, Martin, with Kendall Scott. *UML Distilled: A Brief Guide to the Standard Object Modeling Language*. 2nd ed. Addison-Wesley, 1999.

Hunter, Jason, with William Crawford. *Java Servlet Programming*. 2nd ed. O'Reilly, 2001.

Maruyama, Hiroshi, Kent Tamura, and Naohiko Uramoto. *XML and Java: Developing Web Applications*. Addison-Wesley, 1999.

McLaughlin, Brett. *Java & XML*. 2nd ed. O'Reilly, 2001.

Ray, Erik T. *Learning XML*. O'Reilly, 2001.

Richter, Charles. *Designing Flexible Object-Oriented Systems with UML*. New Riders Publishing, 1999.

Watt, Andrew H. *Designing SVG Web Graphics*. New Riders Publishing, 2002.

INDEX

A

I

J

O

Y-Z